Sportsmanship

Sportsmanship

Multidisciplinary Perspectives

Edited by Tim Delaney

McFarland & Company, Inc., Publishers
Jefferson, North Carolina

Also of Interest

The Sociology of Sports: An Introduction, 2d ed., Tim Delaney and Tim Madigan (McFarland, 2015)

Beyond Sustainability: A Thriving Environment, Tim Delaney and Tim Madigan (McFarland, 2014)

Acknowledgments: I would like to thank all of the contributing authors for their hard work on their essays. I would also like to give special thanks to Christina.

Library of Congress Cataloguing-in-Publication Data

Names: Delaney, Tim, editor.
Title: Sportsmanship : multidisciplinary perspectives / edited by Tim Delaney.
Description: Jefferson, North Carolina : McFarland & Company, Inc., Publishers, 2016. | Includes bibliographical references and index.
Identifiers: LCCN 2016003943 | ISBN 9780786498031 (softcover : acid free paper) ♾
Subjects: LCSH: Sportsmanship. | Sports—Moral and ethical aspects.
Classification: LCC GV706.3 .S74 2016 | DDC 175—dc23
LC record available at http://lccn.loc.gov/2016003943

British Library cataloguing data are available

ISBN (print) 978-0-7864-9803-1
ISBN (ebook) 978-1-4766-2380-1

Printed in the United States of America

McFarland & Company, Inc., Publishers
Box 611, Jefferson, North Carolina 28640
www.mcfarlandpub.com

To my first formal sports coach, Paul Hahn.
Coach Hahn inspired many youth in our neighborhood
to be good sports, play to have fun, and play to win.
To this day, most of us who played ball together
under Coach Hahn remain best friends.
This is in no small part due to the spirit of sportsmanship
instilled in us all by Coach Hahn.

Table of Contents

Introduction

Like many youth, I started playing sports at a very young age and by the time I was eight years old I was participating in the first of many formal sports programs. Born and raised in the United States, I played most of the popular American sports as a youth, teenager and young adult, including football, baseball, basketball, track and field and cross country. I also enjoyed many sports in an informal setting such as bowling, kickball, dodge ball, swimming and so on. And although I was not an elite athlete in most sports, I enjoyed playing them all.

Forging new friendships and strengthening existing ones were among my primary motivations for sport involvement. Being physically active and competing against others quickly became other motivators. And, of course, like most youth, I dreamed of becoming a star athlete and playing for my favorite professional team. I always wanted to be the next Jim Brown, the star running back for the Cleveland Browns. As you might guess, that never happened!

I was lucky as a youth athlete because all of my coaches, starting with Coach Paul Hahn, stressed that having fun was as important as winning. My coaches also taught me that there was honor in being a good sport and dishonor in cheating as a means to achieve victory. My parents had also raised me to be a "good" person so I think the idea of being a good sport has been with me since the beginning. I noticed, however, that my high school and college coaches began to stress winning as the most important thing and that meant winning at any cost. I have known coaches over the years that have taught players how to cheat without getting caught and I have known many athletes that believe that "the end—winning—justifies the means"—even if that means cheating in order to attain those goals.

My years as a competitive athlete are long behind me. But I have remained a huge fan of sports and follow many of my favorite sports teams very passionately. I have noticed in myself that as I cheer for my favorite teams and athletes to win that, while I desire acts of sportsmanship, I am often most happy when my favorite teams and athletes attain victory, especially championships, even if certain sporting behaviors along the way were less than proper sportsmanship. Thus, I understand as well as anyone the grey areas of sports and sportsmanship.

At age seventeen, I started college and majored in business and sociology. I played sports as an undergraduate but was certainly long aware of my own sporting limitations. I never really saw myself as a coach either. So I knew my passion for sports would center on that of a spectator and fan. About a decade after earning my bachelor's degree I decided to attend graduate school. I was almost shocked to learn that I could declare sport sociology as my primary area of study. Imagine, a personal passion within the academic framework. After earning my M.A. at California State University Dominquez Hills in Los Angeles, where I studied under one of the pioneers of sport sociology, Hal Charnofsky, I attended the University of Nevada Las Vegas and once again declared sport sociology as my primary area of sociological study. At UNLV, I studied under a true early giant of sport sociology, James H. Frey. Jim introduced me to many of the other leading figures in sport sociology and for that I am deeply indebted. Studying sport academically made me think of it from many different perspectives, beginning with the realization that sport is a major social institution. And as a major social institution it had value as an area of academic study. It is often said that sport is a microcosm of society and I believe that to be true. Thus, we study sport because it tells us, among other things, a great deal about cultural norms and values of particular societies.

Having earned an M.A. and Ph.D. in sport sociology, I consider myself a sport sociologist. I have regularly taught sport sociology courses for many years now. I have also published in the field of sport sociology. I find myself teaching students that sport is much more than the games we play and the players and teams that we cheer for; sport reflects the values and norms of our society. Because of this, we need to be mindful of the lessons our youth are learning as they play and consume sport. I like to encourage the idea that winning fairly is the most honorable form of victory. And thus, the ideals of sportsmanship should be ranked above most other aspects of sports. If only there was a special day set aside each year to acknowledge sportsmanship. Well, to the surprise of most, there is! Did you know there is a National Sportsmanship Day?

When I teach sport sociology courses, or talk with many of my fellow sports fans, I am a bit dismayed by how few people, especially coaches and student-athletes, are aware of National Sportsmanship Day. I cannot really blame the students in general, or athletes in particular, that they are unaware of National Sportsmanship Day because it does not seem to be publicized enough in the American or international media. This is quite interesting as nearly everyone involved in sports, including the sports media (i.e., ESPN), promotes the idea of "good sportsmanship." One might think that ESPN, as the "leader in sports coverage" (as they like to self-promote), with its 24-hour sports programming and with its numerous affiliates such as ESPN2, ESPN3 (online), ESPNU, ESPN News, ESPN Deportes, and so forth, does nothing special to promote this day dedicated to sportsmanship. Surely, one of the ESPN channels could spend a day highlighting the value of sportsmanship in special segments, but they ignore the opportunity to promote sportsmanship in a more meaningful manner. ESPN is not to be blamed, however, for the failure of all the other media outlets who do not promote National Sportsmanship Day.

So what is National Sportsmanship Day? National Sportsmanship Day was founded by the Institute for International Sport in 1991 with a primary goal of providing thoughtful discussions and activities designed to enable sports to reach its full potential as a positive force in society (Institute for International Sport 2015). There are four key objectives of National Sportsmanship Day:

1. To promote ethics, honesty, and fair play in athletics and society through education and sport.
2. To designate a day each year during which student-athletes, coaches, administrators and parents engage in thoughtful and reasoned discussion about the role of sportsmanship.

3. To provide participating schools, clubs, and athletic organizations a template to successfully celebrate the day with sportsmanship themed activities, discussion topics, etc.

4. To make participation in National Sportsmanship Day an anchor event that fosters good sportsmanship on a year-round basis [Institute for International Sport; available: http://www.internationalsport.org/nsd/overview.cfm].

Interestingly, the Institute for International Sport has not established a specific date for its annual acknowledgement of sportsmanship but it does always occur during the first week of March. Perhaps, then, the Institute should do a better job of promoting National Sportsmanship Day to the media and establishing a specific annual day would help.

I created the annual "Sportsmanship Day Symposium" at my college—the State University of New York at Oswego—to draw attention to the annual National Sportsmanship Day and to provide a multi-disciplinary forum that examines the role of sportsmanship on my own campus as well as nationally and internationally.

The Sportsmanship Day Symposium is designed to promote the objectives of the National Sportsmanship Day; that is, we (1) promote ethics, honesty and fair play in athletics and society through education and sport; (2) have designated a specific day (the first Thursday of March) to provide thoughtful and reasoned discussion about the role of sportsmanship; (3) provide a template for celebrating sportsmanship; and (4) hope that this event will help to foster good sportsmanship on a year-round basis.

On March 5, 2015, we held our seventh annual Sportsmanship Day Symposium and over the years we have had students and professors from multiple disciplines present their ideas on what sportsmanship means to them. In 2013, the Symposium had grown to include NCAA Division III sponsorship (via the State University of New York Oswego Athletic Department). I am especially excited about the future of the annual Sportsmanship Day Symposium as, beginning in 2016, it also serves as the cornerstone of SUNY Oswego's newly developed sport studies program.

My colleague and good friend, as well as a contributor to this book, Chris Mack, and I had an informal discussion about starting a sport studies program at our university while carpooling to campus one morning. Chris casually mentioned that we should start a sport studies program and the next thing we knew we decided that there should be a corresponding academic minor. We then discussed core courses and electives, and before long we drew up a formal proposal to administrators. In brief, the sports studies program is designed to expand the student's knowledge of sport by presenting empirical data, theoretical inquiry and a multi-disciplinary analysis to what is known about the social arrangements within and around the sports world. The program examines sport in the contexts of historical and contemporary culture and it examines sport's cultural relationship with education, the economy, families, the media, psychology and politics, and it considers race, class and gender differences in the sport experience.

This interdisciplinary program examines sport in a global context, fosters a spirit of inquiry and calls on students to broaden their perspectives. It emphasizes skills in multi-cultural analysis and critical thinking and offers a focus on the experiences of marginalized groups, such as racial and ethnic minorities, people with disabilities and women in athletics. The sport studies program provides an excellent foundation for pursuing careers in sports management, sports journalism and sports information, and for those who want to pursue a graduate degree or to combine their sport studies interest with their major. Students who minor in sport studies will fulfill the core requirements (nine hours) and select elective courses (nine hours) based on their interests and the recommendations and advisement of the sport studies program director or any of the sport studies advisors. All sport studies minors are obligated to provide a professional presentation of their research at the annual Sportsmanship Day Symposium. In this manner, we can assure that the sport studies students at SUNY Oswego are being exposed to the importance of sportsmanship.

At the start of each year's Sportsmanship Day Symposium, I give an introductory talk that, of course, centers on the ideals of sportsmanship. I begin by providing a definition of sportsmanship—after all, we need some sort of parameters established if we are going to talk about such a specific topic—and then I give recent examples of good sportsmanship and bad sportsmanship. (I will provide my definition of sportsmanship in "Sportsmanship: A Sociological Perspective.") Over the years, as students and faculty gave their presentations, it became quite clear to me that not everyone has the same definition or perspective of sportsmanship as I do. Students tend to say things such as "I don't really know how to define sportsmanship, but I know a good sport or a poor sport when I see one" and "I'm not sure anyone can really define sportsmanship as it means different things to different people." Initially, this kind of bothered me; after all, I had started the day's events by giving a definition of sportsmanship and then a number of speakers would question whether or not "sportsmanship" can be defined. As an academic I would insist that all concepts can, and must be, defined or else how is it possible to speak about a topic and talk about examples of behaviors that fall within or outside those pre-established parameters? However, my attitude began to change after a few years of the Sportsmanship Day Symposium as I realized that people from different academic backgrounds have different ideas about "sportsmanship." It would also stand to reason then that people from different cultures would also have different ideas on sportsmanship. And thus, the idea to put together an interdisciplinary and cross-cultural book on sportsmanship arose.

In *Sportsmanship: Multidisciplinary Perspectives*, we have compiled the most comprehensive collection of essays on the meaning of sportsmanship in existence. The twenty-six total contributing scholars represent dozens of unique academic disciplines and reside from five different countries. They have covered a wide range of topics related to sportsmanship, including good sportsmanship and poor sportsmanship; cheating; ethics; sports, leisure and recreation in prison; youth sports; physical education; cognitive psychology; applied sportsmanship; ideals of sportsmanship throughout history; the Irish in sport; sportsmanship from the perspective of coaches, athletes and referees; gender; economics; race and ethnicity; the media, including film and sports journalism; and the impact of professionalism and commercialization. The collection concludes with a look at the role of sportsmanship in the future.

The contributing authors and I hope that you will enjoy this comprehensive and multi-disciplinary look at sportsmanship. We also hope that you will be inspired to become "ambassadors of sportsmanship" so that sportsmanship is much more than a concept, so that it becomes a way of life—both in sport and in other spheres of life.

Part A

Good Sportsmanship and Poor Sportsmanship

Everyone has heard of "sportsmanship" and most people think they know what the word means. But can you define "sportsmanship"? Answering this question is harder than one might think. To begin with, parameters have to be established as to what constitutes sportsmanship, and trait characteristics must also be detailed. We would assume sportsmanship involves behavior and these behaviors can be considered "good," as in good sportsmanship, or they could be labeled as "poor," as in poor sportsmanship. Generally speaking, good sportsmanship involves participants engaging in proper, or ideal, behavior while playing sports; whereas poor sportsmanship involves sport participants who engage in unacceptable behaviors. It is worth noting that some people may use the term "bad" sportsmanship instead of "poor" sportsmanship; either is generally fine as most people seem to think of bad sportsmanship as the same as poor sportsmanship.

In this part of the book we will learn about the sociological perspective on sportsmanship, including examples of "good" sportsmanship and "poor" sportsmanship; we will learn about what it means to be a "good sport" and "poor sport"; explanations as to why cheating (e.g., doping) is an example of poor sportsmanship; sports and leisure in prison; and the role of ethics and the civilizing process in sports.

Sportsmanship
A Sociological Perspective

Tim Delaney

Sport is a major social institution in the United States and in most societies around the world. The passion and devotion of billions of global sports fans directed toward their favorite athletes and sports teams places the institution of sport at the same level of importance as such other major social institutions as the family, religion, education, economics and politics. Sport is so pervasive that it extends into a plethora of social arenas including the social and traditional media, the arts, popular culture, a community's way of life, and national identity. Sport reflects the norms, values and customs of the general culture of a society. Societies that place a high value on winning and success are likely to create sports environments where the "win-at-all-costs" mentality fosters. This type of philosophy often contributes to a number of questionable behaviors on the part of sport participants (e.g., athletes, coaches, trainers, management, owners, fans and spectators) including elitism, sexism, racism, ageism, nationalism, extreme competitiveness, abuse of drugs (including athletes who take performance-enhancing drugs), gambling, and players engaging in a number of deviant behaviors (e.g., cheating, taking a dive, illegal contact with the ball, late hits against opponents, taunting, and harassment). On the other hand, a number of very positive attributes are associated with sports including the notions of cooperation and team work, a sense of fair play, hard work and dedication, striving for personal excellence, obedience to rules, commitment and loyalty, and sportsmanship.

While adults are well aware of the fact that the institution of sport is far from perfect, generation after generation of parents have encouraged their children to play sports because of the positive attributes associated with sports.

Developing Positive Character Attributes via Sport Participation

It has long been assumed that sport participation, at the very least, helps to develop motor skills and promotes physical fitness, especially for youths. Before the child is even old enough to walk parents will engage in such activities as rolling a ball to their baby to teach hand and eye coordination. The infant child is given blocks to build and basic developmental challenges such as placing shaped objects into specific shaped openings. Parents generally teach their children how to throw and catch a ball to further develop balance and coordination. Before long, the toddler is playing with toy baseball bats, throwing a Nerf-type football, and throwing a basketball through a toy hoop. Parents also realize that most young children have a great deal of energy and that it is important to let them burn it off through such basic activities as running and jumping. If children do not have access to a yard to play in, parents are likely to take their kids to a playground where they can use such playground equipment as play systems (like obstacle courses), balance beams (to walk across), upper body/overhead (muscle bars), swings, slides, and motion equipment (e.g., mini spring pod platforms). As the children get to be a little older, they are often taught such basic sports as swimming, kickball, and stick ball. All of these play and sporting activities are healthy behaviors that should be encouraged.

Benefits of Sport Participation

Medical professionals argue that youth need to exercise to fight off the increasing likelihood of becoming obese, to lower the risk of heart disease and to help stimulate brain development and learning (*CBS This Morning* 2014). The *Palo Alto Medical Foundation* (2015) indicates that playing sports encourages participants to eat healthy and to become aware of proper nutrition. Research has shown that there are "many different psychological and social health benefits" commonly associated with physical activity "with the most common being improved self-esteem, social interaction followed by fewer depressive symptoms" (Eime, Young, Harvey, Charity and Payne 2013). Eime and associates (2013) indicate that sport participation may be associated with improved psychosocial health above and beyond simple physical activity and state, "Specifically, team sport seems to be associated with improved health outcomes compared to individual activities, due to the social nature of the participation." Eime et al. (2013) conclude, "It is recommended that community sport participation is advocated as a form of leisure time PA [physical activity] for children and adolescents, in an effort to not only improve physical health in relation to such matters as the obesity crisis, but also to enhance psychological and social health outcomes." *The British Heart Foundation National Centre for Physical Activity* (2013) supports the use of physical activity to "prevent ill health and reduce the number of people dying prematurely; enhance mental health, quality of life and self-reported well-being; delay the need for care in older adults (ages 65+); and reduce health inequalities and improve wider factors influencing health and well-being." *Sport England* (2015) reports that "whatever our age, there is good scientific evidence that being physically active can help us lead healthier lives [and that] regular physical activity can reduce the risk of many chronic conditions, including coronary heart disease, stroke, Type 2 diabetes, cancer, obesity, mental health problems and musculoskeletal conditions."

The examples cited above represent a mere sampling of the literature available to support the positive health benefits of physical activity in general, and in sport in particular. However, we need to go beyond the physical benefits of sport participation in order to explore the role of sportsmanship. Proponents of youth sport participation also cite its character development aspect. In the United States, the idea that "sport builds character" can be traced back to the post–Civil War era. It is worth noting, however, that this idea of sport building proper character was originally only applied to boys as girls were discouraged from sports (especially until the passage of the 1972 Title IX legislation). As Radar (2004) explains, a number of social leaders were concerned that modern life had become too soft and effeminate:

> Frontiers and battlefields no longer existed to test manly courage and perseverance. Henry W. Williams observed that the "struggle for existence, though becoming harder and harder, is less and less a physical struggle, more and more a battle of minds." Apart from sports, men no longer had arenas for testing their manliness. Theodore Roosevelt worried lest prolonged periods of peace would encourage "effeminate tendencies in young men." Only aggressive sports, Roosevelt argued, could create the "brawn, the spirit, the self confidence, and quickness of men" that was essential for the existence of a strong nation [p. 105; for the Williams quote see Williams 1895; for Roosevelt, see Dubbert 1979].

As the quote above makes clear, the post–Civil War period was looked upon as a point in American history where traditional expression of manliness took on new meanings. Throughout the 20th century rapid industrial and technological advancements made life increasingly "easier" for many folks because they did not have to make a living via physical (manual) labor but rather through office work (professional or white collar labor). Sports, especially aggressive ones, were viewed as a way for males to express their manliness.

If military fitness preparedness is a measure of "manliness" and proper character, we seem to have fallen victim of the "going soft" warning of Williams and Roosevelt. Most young Americans (like young adults in other nations) have grown up with war and yet many of them are not physically (and otherwise) eligible for military service. According to *Mission: Readiness* (2015), a "nonpartisan national security organization of over 500 retired admirals, generals, and other retired senior military leaders," more than 70 percent of 17- to 24-year-olds in the U.S. cannot serve in the military, primarily because they are too poorly educated, too overweight, or have a serious criminal record. This 70 percent figure is slightly better than the 75 percent figure *Mission: Readiness* cited in 2009. In 2009, nearly 25 percent of young Americans lacked a high school diploma, a requirement for admittance to the U.S. military (some students may receive a waiver if they have received a general equivalency degree or if they score well enough on the military's entrance exam); 10 percent of young adults had at least one felony or serious misdemeanor conviction (an automatic disqualification); 27 percent were too overweight for the military; and nearly a third (32 percent) of all young people had health problems other than their weight that would keep them from serving (*Mission: Readiness* 2009). The growing rate of obesity in the United States (and other parts of the world), which is connected to the increasing sedentary lifestyle of so many youth and young adults is a leading cause for health problems in general and a lack of qualification for military service. Perhaps, as a nation, we are too soft? To combat the problems cited by organization, *Mission Readiness* (2015) is trying to ensure a strong nation (United States) and a secure future via a number of strategic program ideas including: expanding high-quality early childhood education programs; increasing access to healthier food at school; and improving the quality and quantity of physical education.

This bit of militaristic-historical information helps to provide a framework for when advocates first touted sport as a means of building character, but it does not inform us as to what good character is—other than the idea that boys were supposed to be aggressive and physical—and whether or not sport can provide it.

Positive Character Traits

Having good "character" has different meanings for people. Typically, "good" character is displayed when someone abides by the rules and acts according to social expectations (Delaney and Madigan 2015). For many, good character's connection to abiding by the rules and engaging in proper behavior is also linked to morality and this tie to morality can be traced back, at the very least, to the time of Aristotle and the Ancient Greeks. "Aristotle said that character is the composite of good moral qualities, whereby one shows firmness of belief, resolution, and practice about such moral values as honesty, justice, and respect. He also said that character is right conduct in relation to other persons and to self. Our humanness, he continues, resides in our ability and capacity to reason, and virtue results when we use our reasoning ability to control and moderate our self" (Stoll and Beller 2000:18). From this quote we may derive a number of further instances including the ideas that good character is connected to sound reasoning and the ability to do the "right" thing even when others around you are not. Stoll and Beller (2000) explain, "To say, 'Cheating is wrong,' is inadequate. One must know why it is wrong and put into action what one values, knows, and reasons is right. It is easy to say that one does not cheat but another thing not to cheat when surrounded by others who are cheating" (p. 19). Thus, when some athletes try to justify their taking performance-enhancing drugs because "everyone else is doing it" this is not a sign of good character; if you know taking banned substances like anabolic steroids is a form a cheating, you must apply moral reasoning and not take the illegal substances. The many athletes who do not take illegal drugs, even when surrounded by those who do, are the ones showing good character.

Character has a number personal qualities associated with it. "They include responsibility, persistence, courage, self-discipline, honesty and integrity, the willingness to work hard, compassion for others, generosity, independence, and tolerance" (Griffin 1998:27). The Josephson Institute Center for Youth Ethics describes "six pillars" of character: trustworthiness (which includes being honest, not deceiving others, cheating or stealing, loyalty and being reliable); respect (treating others with respect, using good manners, considerate and dealing with anger, insults and disagreements in a peaceful manner); responsibility (doing what you are supposed to do, planning ahead, perseverance, accountability and setting a good example for others); fairness (playing by the rules, taking turns and sharing, being open-minded, don't take advantage of others and treating all people equally and fairly); caring (kindness, compassion, showing gratitude) and citizenship (cooperate with others, be a good neighbor, obey the rules and laws, protect the environment and volunteer to help others) (Josephson Institute 2014). In addition to all these well-stated quality traits are at least two other considerations that are directly associated with sports: friendship (the ability to develop friendships while playing sports seemingly implies that a person has good character) and leadership (sports provide people with an opportunity to strive and achieve goals while demonstrating to others the proper way to get things done) (Palo Alto Medical Foundation 2015). Character, then, refers to individual personality and behavioral traits, both good and bad, which define who a person is. Those who abide by the rules and societal expectations while possessing the positive traits described above are said to have "good" character; whereas those who do are said to have "poor" character.

A great deal of emphasis is placed on childhood and adolescence as a critical time in character building formation and development. "Social development comprises such things as friendship, social ranking, status, power, rejection and acceptance, inclusion and exclusion, dominance and submission, leadership, connection to the group, cooperativeness, aggression and passivity and withdrawal, and conflict" (Griffin 1998: 27). As Delaney and Madigan (2015) explain, "The ability to get along cooperatively with others and a willingness to accept society's rules are signs of good character and proper social development. Sports provide a good mechanism to develop character, and it does so under the watchful public eye. Because of this, youth receive immediate feedback regarding their behavior. At the same time, they become increasingly aware of their sense of self and role in the community" (p. 120).

Stoll and Beller believe that sports can build positive character traits in participants if the athletic programs (which includes the role of the coaches, administrators and parents of youth sport participants) themselves are designed to contribute positively to the ethical and moral development of athletes. "While teaching the will to win does not have to be eliminated, coaches, athletic administrators, and others in sport leadership positions must re-evaluate their philosophy regarding the importance of winning as it relates to character development, particularly when the participants are children and young adults. Without this fundamental shift in philosophy, sport will never fulfill its potential as a tool to educate and build positive character traits in our nation's youth" (Stoll and Beller 2000:27).

Schreiber (1990) points out that while it is likely sport participation helps to develop good character, what is clearer is that sport participation reveals the character *of* participants. "Perhaps more important, sports *reveals* character—in kids and adults. Just watch a group of kids play basketball, and see if you can't immediately discern who looks to pass, who looks to shoot, who hollers at teammates when they make a mistake, who berates herself for the slightest error, who's the leader, who's eager to take the ball during crunch time, and so on.... Sports is an uncanny truth-detector" (Schreiber 1990:9). Schreiber makes a good point about sport revealing character. It is quite enlightening watching children play, as many of their character traits are revealed. However, it is important to note that some people transform themselves when playing sport in order to perform at a maximum level. Thus, a youth who plays football very aggressively is not necessarily an aggressive person off the field. In short, it is difficult to make general statements regarding sport participation and the building of character.

Griffin (1998) concludes, "No matter how one wants to define character, athletes very likely have no more of it than members of any other group" (p. 67). Some sport participants display positive character traits, which in turn, contribute to good sportsmanship; while others, display poor character traits which contribute to bad, or poor, sportsmanship.

Sportsmanship

A prized principle of sport participation is the development of positive character traits (described above) that collectively can be referred to as "sportsmanship." Sportsmanship involves fair play, courage, tolerance, caring, decency, and respect—for oneself, the competitor, and for the sport itself. Ideals of sportsmanship, such as competitiveness, persistence, self-discipline, trustworthiness, hard work, fair play, obedience to authority, and dedication, are tied to a society's cultural morality. Sportsmanship is tied to morality because it represents an idyllic form of behavior—to be a good sport and play fairly. As an expression of morality, sportsmanship provides a code of acceptable behavior for athletes (primarily) and sport participants (in general) to abide by in the pursuit of fair play on the field as well as respect for others in the stands.

Good sportsmanship involves conduct and attitudes considered befitting participants, especially in regard to a sense of fair play, courtesy toward teammates and opponents, game officials, and others involved in sporting contests, and grace in losing (Delaney and Madigan 2015). It should be noted that because sportsmanship is tied to cultural standards of morality, norms, and values, ideal types of proper and befitting behavior may vary from one society to the next. With these variables in mind, sportsmanship can be defined as "conduct and attitudes considered as benefiting participants, especially in regards to a sense of fair play, courtesy toward teammates and opponents, game officials, and others involved in sporting contests, as well as grace in losing" (Delaney and Madigan 2015:137).

Beginning at a very young age, playing games and participating in sporting activities are all about having fun. Most likely, parents rolled a ball to their infant children and encouraged them to roll it back. Parents and caregivers then encouraged their children to run, jump and throw or kick a ball. And, all of these informal sporting/physical activities were designed to be fun. As sports become formalized good-natured fun seems to lose its primacy; instead, there is a growing emphasis on winning. Former NBA player and current NBA broadcaster Bill Walton, for one, believes that too many people involved in sports place an excessive emphasis on winning instead of sportsmanship, character development, and plain old fun. Walton (2005) believes that it is especially vital to emphasize sportsmanship, teamwork, attitude and respect, and playing sports for the fun of participation at the youth level. Walton argues that children have enough peer pressure and competition to contend with in their daily lives without having a win-at-all-cost mentality thrust upon them in the sports domain.

Walton is a member of the "Jr. NBA and Junior WNBA," a program that conveys, on a global scale, six keys to success: commitment, teamwork, attitude, practice, health and fitness, and sportsmanship (NBA.com 2015). Walton is especially concerned that young people should be taught the fundamentals of the game, safety tips, and the importance of qualities such as confidence, hustle, and dedication. "They also need to learn how to win and lose with class and dignity, plus how to compete like true sportsmen at every level of competition" (Walton 2005:13A). Walton seems to be on to something here. Youth should be primarily concerned with learning the fundamentals of the game and they should be taught the value of sportsmanship and respect for the game and other participants. Ideally, having fun is a part of the youth sport experience.

By the time youth reach high school the prominent aspects of sports begin to shift from learning fundamentals and having fun toward winning. Around this time, some parents, coaches, and young athletes begin to lose sight of notions of fair play and a respect for the rules and ideals of the game. As Reeds (2004) points out, "The games we play and the rules we play them by have been established as meaningful boundaries defining fair play and should not be recognized as a set of trivial pursuits merely getting in the way of victory.... Social learning theory tells us that we learn through reinforcements for behaviors that bring us success. Winning as the desired outcome is a learned behavior and may require a subset of undesired behaviors. Rule violations have been institutionalized into our way of thinking. Sports are played and followed by folks who expect and accept the systematic breaking of rules" (p. 88).

Personal achievement is another aspect that gains prominence at the high school level of sport participation and it is at this point when a distinction between highly talented and less talented athletes becomes clear. In comparison to others, most teen athletes begin to realize their potential and their limitations. While it is important to encourage the continued play of those less talented, the winning priority dictates that their playing time and status will be reduced. Star athletes are encouraged to develop their talents so that they might play at the next level (e.g., college or professional sports, Olympic training). When athletes put forth extraordinary performances, especially against relatively equal opposition, they are praised. However, questions centered on sportsmanship and fair play comes to the forefront when a star athlete puts forth a dominating effort against a clearly out-matched opposition. In some sports, such as girls' high school basketball, there is great disparity between the quality of play from team to team (Feinberg 2006). Consequently, final scores often reflect this disparity of talent. There are occasions when the more talented players and teams may run up the score in order to enhance their statistics (statistics are a means by which personal achievement can be quantified). Those on the other side of the lop-sided game may accuse the opposition of "running up" the score—a violation of fair play and sportsmanship. The ethical debate over whether a team, or individual player, should play to their full potential, even if it means running up the score, or show "mercy" against an out-matched opponent is centered on the premise of sportsmanship and fair play.

Sport competition at the collegiate level represents a peculiar attempt to blend the ideals of sportsmanship with the need to win mentality. The less-talented players from high school years are no longer playing competitively in a formal college setting as the elite athletes have taken over. But in college, the pecking order of playing time being awarded to the most talented players is only enhanced. Elite American collegiate sports are more about making money than they are about the ideals of sportsmanship and fair play for all. Sure, the elite collegiate sports have to publicly demonstrate, or at the very least give "lip service" to the ideals of sportsmanship, but winning is the true measure of success. Because of this, many people, athletes and fans alike, prefer the competition of Division II or III (NCAA or NAIA) athletics. Division III athletes are nonscholarship, which means they play for the love of their sport. They realize that a professional career as an athlete is highly unlikely, and yet they continue to play sports. Ideals of sportsmanship are emphasized more directly in Division III sports than in Division I. For example, the State University of New York Athletic Conference (SUNYAC) makes this announcement before all men's and women's basketball games:

> The student-athletes of the State University of New York Athletic Conference ask our fans to support our goal of promoting positive sportsmanship and developing an enjoyable sporting atmosphere. Just as we compete with respect for our opponents, we expect our fans, both local and visiting, to be courteous to our student athletes, our referees, our coaches, our administrators, and one another. For a positive student experience, profanity, racial or sexist comments, taunting, and other intimidating actions cross the line into poor sportsmanship and are grounds for removal from the site of competition. Let's cheer for our teams, have fun, and support the goals of Division III athletics [copy of the statement used at SUNY Oswego basketball games attained by Delaney].

The importance placed on sportsmanship at the Division III level applies to athletes, coaches, referees, administrators, and fans. This practice should be applied to all levels of collegiate and professional athletics. As Reeds (2004) explains, "Winning fair and square, without seeking an unfair advantage through the breach of rules or through intimidation has a smell all of its own. It smells clean like a load of fresh air-dried laundry. Victories secured through rules violations or perverse posturing or taunting also have a smell all of their own, they stink. They smell like a decaying cesspool. When you hang up your championship banner may it exude the sweet smell of an honest effort and not the exhumed odor of a tainted death" (pp. 89–90).

A sports participant that displays culturally acceptable sports-related behavior is said to be a "good sport" while someone who does not is said to be a "poor sport." A good sport may even be described as honorable. Honor is such an important aspect of sportsmanship at the NCAA Division III level that its annual *Handbook* has long incorporated the concept as part of its "Honesty and Sportsmanship" policy:

> Individuals employed by (or associated with) a member institution to administer, conduct or coach intercollegiate athletics and all participating student-athletes shall act with honesty and sportsmanship at all times so that intercollegiate athletics as a whole, their institutions and they, as individuals, shall represent the honor and dignity of fair play and the generally recognized high standards associated with the wholesome competitive sports [*NCAA Division III Manual* 2014:45].

Despite the fact that honor is an important aspect of sports and sportsmanship, rarely do we hear about "honor calls" in sports; and the higher the level of competitiveness, the less likely such admissions will be forthcoming. Think about it. Can you imagine if during a National Football League playoff game an offensive linemen informs the referee that he lined up off-sides on the play that his team just scored the winning touchdown and requests that the referee throw a penalty flag disallowing the score? The offensive linemen may feel better about his integrity but his teammates, coaches, owner and fans would likely angrily express their displeasure for such an act of ill-timed honesty. Imagine too if Diego Maradona, a former famous soccer player for Argentina's national team, had admitted during the 1986 World Cup quarterfinal match between Argentina and England, that he had illegally punched the ball into the goal leading his team to victory. At the time, Maradona insisted that his hand never touched the ball and that God willed it into the net (Delaney and Madigan 2015). This explains why Maradona's famous goal is known as the "Hand of God" goal. Nearly twenty years later, Maradona admitted that he did indeed punch the ball with his hand (Bechtel 2005). But there is little, if any, honor in this late admission. Furthermore, nearly the entire Argentina fan base would have cried foul if Maradona had corrected the referee during the match.

There are no extra points awarded to athletes during a sporting event to warrant their admission to admit to a foul or infraction that has not been called by an official, so there is little wonder that it seems as though poor sportsmanship and incivility are running rampant in the sports world. We hear about athletes taking performance-enhancing drugs in an attempt to gain an edge over the competition; committing illegal hits and occasional assaults on the field; players taunting opponents; fans throwing objects onto the field/court—endangering athletes, officials and coaches; spectators taunting athletes and rival fans; and so on.

One final point about collegiate sports and sportsmanship. In February 2009, the NCAA Football Rules Committee adopted a "Statement on Sportsmanship" that is now incorporated in its annual *Manual*. The statement, in part, reads:

> The rules committee reminds head coaches of their responsibility for the behavior of their players before and after, as well as during, the game. Players must be cautioned against pre-game

unsportsmanlike conduct on the field that can lead to confrontation between teams. Such action can lead to penalties enforced on the opening kickoff, possibly including disqualification of players [NCAA 2011].

It is interesting to note that the Division III policy on sportsmanship is more about behaviors that are consider proper and honorable while the Division I policy is more about warning against improper behavior and the consequences of misbehaving. It's almost as if poor sportsmanship is expected to happen at the Division I level while good sportsmanship is expected to occur at the Division III level.

Although it would be difficult to try and cover every example of a sportsmanship award offered by a professional sports league to one of its athletes, one example will be shared here. In 2014, the National Football League (NFL) "created a Sportsmanship Award that will be voted on by the players and presented to the winner on the eve of the Super Bowl" (*Associated Press* 2014). The sportsmanship award will be presented along with the MVP and Coach of the Year awards at the annual "NFL Honors" show. The sportsman of the year award will go to the player "who best demonstrates the qualities of on-field sportsmanship, including fair play, respect for the game and opponents, and integrity in competition" (*Associated Press* 2014). It is nice to see the NFL incorporate many of the same ideas discussed here.

With a working definition of sportsmanship in place and a number of clear characteristics of sportsmanship identified we shift our attention to some recent examples of good sportsmanship and poor sportsmanship.

Good Sportsmanship and Poor Sportsmanship

The sports world mirrors society in ways including the reality that there are those who display good sportsmanship, fair play deeds that benefit others; and there are people who display poor sportsmanship, deeds that harm others. Anyone who is involved in sport, whether as an athlete, parent, coach, or fan is likely to conjure images of both types of sportsmanship. And, it is likely, that in some instances, what one person might consider as poor sportsmanship, another person might consider "part of the game." Let's first take a look at a few examples of poor sportsmanship.

Poor Sportsmanship

There are all sorts of examples of poor sportsmanship in sports including athletes who argue with game officials about calls made on the field/court; soccer players who illegally touch the ball (e.g., the Maradona case previously described); basketball and soccer players who take a dive when contact with an opposing player was minimal or non-existent; athletes who trash talk and taunt opponents; athletes and coaches that throw temper tantrums during or after the game; players who refuse to shake the hands of competitors; and running up the score during competition. Discussion here will be limited to the post-game handshake.

The post-game handshake in sports has long been perceived as the ultimate sign of good sportsmanship. The gesture is common at every level of sports and especially in high school, college, professional and international sports competition. (In international soccer it is also common for opposing players to seek out one another and exchange jerseys.) Such a simple gesture of respect for the opponent, the game and competition and the ritualistic behavior is often marred by controversy and poor sportsmanship. In 1994, the high school principals of the eight Ventura County (CA) schools in the Marmonte League imposed a ban on post-game handshakes, citing too many incidents of poor sportsmanship. George Ragsdale, then-Simi Valley High School athletic director, said there were a number of volatile situations, adding that "some players spit on their hands before the handshake. Some mutter insults. Increasingly, some throw punches" (Mydans 1994). Kurt Rambis, a member of the Los Angeles Lakers at the time of the high school handshake ban in the Marmonte League, took on the role of amateur sociologist and, infusing the sport as a microcosm of society approach, stated, "If we're fighting after sporting events, then that's a reflection of our society. There's a tension in our society, a win-at-all-costs type of thing. I see people in the crowd wanting to fight each other. It's ludicrous" (Mydans 1994). Moss Benmosche, then-athletic director at Crenshaw High School in Los Angeles (not a member of the Marmonte League) echoed the concerns of sociologists, "By saying we are not going to have handshakes because we are afraid you are going to fight, we are sending a message. We're saying that we cannot control you, are not sure we can teach you and are going to take the easy way out" (Mydans 1994).

Other school districts have followed the lead of the Marmonte League. In 2013, the Kentucky High School Athletic Association sent out a "Commissioner's Directive" warning schools about participating in organized post-game handshakes because of an increasing number of fights during the ceremonial gesture of good will. Kentucky did not outright ban handshakes, but instead, the organizational component of the ritual. Players were still allowed to shake hands voluntarily (Sondheimer 2013).

In college football, it is common for representative players (usually the team captains) from each team to meet in the center of the field with the referee who reviews a few key points and tosses the coin in the air to determine who will receive the opening kickoff. At this point, it is also customary for these same players to shake hands with one another, and considering that tempers should be under control because the game has yet to be played, few incidents of poor sportsmanship occur during this ritual. However, on November 1, 2014, the University of Maryland's three team captains refused to shake hands with Penn State's captains. Blame the incident on the emotions of players (there was a pregame fracas prior to the coin toss), the declining civility in society in general, or the fact that Maryland has long been a doormat to Penn State—the Nittany Lions held the all-time series lead 35–1–1 heading into the 2014 game—but however you look at it, the incident was an example of poor sportsmanship. Maryland coach Randy Edsall apologized for his players' behavior, saying, "That is not who we are. Our emotions got the best of us, and we've got to be above that. So, I just want to say.... I apologize for that. Feel bad for that" (Moyer 2014a). Maryland Athletic Director Kevin Anderson also issued an apology following the Terrapins 20–19 win over Penn State. Maryland was accessed a 15-yard penalty for unsportsmanlike conduct for the pregame antics and was also fined $10,000 for violating the Big Ten Conference's Sportsmanship Policy (Stubbs 2014; Moyer 2014b).

It seems as though many sports are having a problem with such a basic concept as look your opponent in the eye and offer a sincere, "Good game"-type of exchange while shaking hands. In the Women's Tennis Association (WTA), for example, it has become increasing common for competitors to do a "drive-by" handshake wherein each player lays only a little skin on each other's hands and in some cases the players simply wave to each other (Myles 2014). In one trending video, Barbora Zahlavova, a 28-year-old Czech Republic tennis player, is shown refusing to take part in a "drive-by" handshake and firmly shakes the hand of opponent 20-year-old Elina Svitolina of Ukraine, stopping her in her tracks as Svitolina seems almost shocked by a "real" handshake (Myles 2014).

Zahlavova seems to be trying to give people an etiquette lesson on how to shake hands at the net following a tennis match. She is upset that the "handshake" has seemingly become an empty gesture. There are many times when athlete may not want to shake the hand of an opponent following competition but will do so because it's the "sporting" thing to do. In hockey, there have been many occasions when opponents have not wanted to shake hands with one another but they generally do so regardless. One famous example sticks out above most others—the Dino Ciccarelli (Detroit Red Wings) and Claude Lemieux (Colorado Avalanche) handshake following the 1996 Stanley Cup series concluding game. In the series, Lemieux, known as a dirty player, infamously blindsided Red Wings player Kris Draper, sidelining him for months of rehabilitation. After shaking Lemieux's hand, Ciccarelli told the press, "I can't believe I shook this guy's friggin' hand after the game. That pisses me right off." Many of us may have contemplated at one point or another, "Why did I shake that guy's hand?" In sports, it's a sign of poor sportsmanship to refuse to shake hands with an opponent.

Good Sportsmanship

While shaking hands with an opponent may sometimes be surrounded by instances of poor sportsmanship that is the exception and not the rule. Generally, athletes and coaches, among others in the sports world, can successfully acknowledge the spirit of competition and respect the opponent enough to shake their hand. And, thankfully, shaking hands is just one of potentially countless examples of good sportsmanship found in the sports world. Off-the-field/court, many athletes are dedicated to community service and charitable organizations. They give freely of their time and in some cases their money.

There are many examples of on-the-field/court good sportsmanship behaviors as well, including helping an opponent up from the ground after they have been knocked down, showing respect for a teammate or opponent when they are injured, acknowledging fellow athletes when the reach some sort of sports milestone, congratulating a sportsperson on-the-field who has achieved a personal milestone off-the-field (e.g., the birth of a child or a wedding), and insisting on playing by the rules. It is in individual sports (e.g., tennis and golf) that an athlete is most likely to draw the attention of an official for an infraction he or she caused. Keegan Bradley, for example, withdrew from the BMW Championship in September 2014 because he had lingering doubts about whether he took a legal drop at the end of his opening round. Such a violation would be a rules infraction. Although no one called him on the potential breach, Keegan said, "I just feel withdrawing is the right thing.... I know the official approved the drop, but I just can't be absolutely sure it was the right spot" (Schupak 2014). In another show of sportsmanship, Novak Djokovic gave his opponent, Radek Stepanek, a crucial point during their 2014 Wimbledon match. Stepanek and Djokovic were tied 5–5 in the fourth set with Djokovic leading 2–1 in sets when Stepanek hit a deep ball that was ruled out (of bounds). The replay showed that the ball was in but the Umpire called for the point to be replayed. That's when Djokovic informed the umpire and conceded the point. The umpire accepted Djovovic's admission and awarded the point to Stepanek (Gaines 2014). Djokovic, by the way, went on to win the game, the set, and the match. Stepanek hugged his good sport opponent after the match in another sign of good sportsmanship.

The last story of good sportsmanship to be shared here concerns Lauren Hill, a 19-year-old basketball player who "was diagnosed with a rare brain cancer in November 2013, shortly after committing to Division III Mount St. Joseph in Cincinnati" (*Sports Illustrated* 2014:16). In September 2014, Hill found out that she had only months to live and she feared that she would not make it to her team's season opener, scheduled for late November, against Hiram College (Ohio). Many people with inoperable brain cancer are likely to drown in a sea of negative emotions such as anger, despair, angst, and grief, but not Hill. She wanted to play at least one game of college basketball.

Mount St. Joseph received permission from the NCAA to move up the game so that Hill would be able to play. Mount generally attracts about 100 spectators for women's home basketball games but the demand was so high to see Hill play that Xavier University (Cincinnati) donated its 10,000-seat arena for the high-demand game that ended up being standing-room only. Hill started the game, "took a pass in the post and hit a left-handed lay-up just 17 seconds into [the] game" (Roenigk 2014). The noise from the cheering crowd was near-deafening. The Hiram College players showed great sportsmanship by, essentially, allowing an uncontested shot. Hill exited the game and retreated to the bench so that she could put on her sunglasses and headphones to try and block out her painful migraine headache and nausea. She had joint pain, dizziness and dilapidating heaviness on her right side (MacMullan 2014). Hill would reenter the game with seconds remaining and score another basket, and the crowd again went wild.

Hill was driven to play at least one game of college basketball not just for her own sense of self-fulfillment but because she wanted to raise money for her cancer research charity "The Cure Starts Now." She set a goal of $1 million by December 31, 2014. Following a final push from Hill, an anonymous donor contributed $116,000 pushing the total to over $1.1 million (ESPN.com 2014). Her inspirational story drew praise from athletes, coaches and millions of fans. She is also my nominee for "Sportsperson of the Year."

On April 10, 2015, at age 19, Hill's battle with an inoperable brain tumor came to an end. Her legacy, however, will live on.

Conclusion

Sport mirrors society in a number of ways; it is not bigger than life or separate from life, it is a big part of the lives of billions of people across the globe. As with every social institution, there are positive aspects of sports and there are negative aspects. Promoting good sportsmanship will take away many of the negative aspects of sports (e.g., deviance, violence and inequality). Despite the seemingly increasing number of examples of poor sportsmanship, there are far more instances where good sportsmanship is the rule and not the exception as most people involved in sports have good intentions and believe that it is possible to win fairly and with honor. Furthermore, sportsmanship is not dead. It may often take a back seat to other sport priorities, especially winning and making a profit, but there are many examples of sports participants who do the "right" thing, the "honorable" thing. Promoting sportsmanship, while at times appearing to be one of those concepts related to *political correctness*, is really a matter of basic correctness. It is possible to enjoy sports, both as active participants and as fans, while still maintaining the ethos of good sportsmanship.

Bibliography

Associated Press. 2014. "League Creates New Award for Sportsmanship." *The Citizen*, October 22:B2.

Bechtel, Mark. 2005. "The Right Way to Cheat: Pulling a Fast One Is Sometimes Part of the Game." *Sports Illustrated*, August 24 (http://sportsillustrated.cnn.com).

British Heart Foundation National Centre for Physical Activity. 2013. "Making the Case for Physical Activity." Retrieved May 20, 2015 (http://www.bhfactive.org.uk).

CBS This Morning. 2014. "Doctors Sound Alarm on Concussion Crisis." October 1. Retrieved May 19, 2015 (http://www.cbsnews).

Delaney, Tim, and Tim Madigan. 2015. *The Sociology of Sports: An Introduction*, 2d ed. Jefferson, NC: McFarland.

Dubbert, J.L. 1979. *A Man's Place*. Englewood Cliffs, NJ: Prentice Hall.

Eime, Rochelle M., Janet A. Young, Jack T. Harvey, Melanie J. Charity, and Warren R. Payne. 2013. "A Systematic Review of the Psychological and Social Benefits of Participation in Sport for Children and Adolescents: Informing Development of a Conceptual Model of Health Through Sport." *International Journal of Behavioral Nutrition and Physical Activity*, 10:98. Retrieved May 22, 2015 (http://www.ijbnpa.org).

ESPN.com. 2014. "Hill's Charity Hits $1M in Donations." December 30. Retrieved April 20, 2015 (http://espn.go.com).

Feinberg, Doug. 2006. "Poor Sportsmanship or Good Shooting: Should Epiphanny Prince Have Stayed in to Score 113 Points Against a Helpless Team?" *The Post-Standard*, February 3:C-9.

Gaines, Cork. 2014. "In an Amazing Display of Sportsmanship, Novak Djokovic Gave His Opponent a Crucial Point." *Business Insider*, June 25. Retrieved May 17, 2015 (http://www.businessinsider.com).

Griffin, Pat. 1998. *Strong Women, Deep Closets: Lesbians and Homophobia in Sport*. Champaign, IL: Human Kinetics.

Josephson Institute. 2014. "The Six Pillars of Character." Retrieved April 22, 2015 (http://character counts.org).

MacMullan, Jackie. 2014. "Sports Reporters: Parting Shots." *ESPN*, December 28.

Mission: Readiness. 2009. "Ready, Willing, and Unable to Serve." Retrieved April 27, 2015 (http://cdn.missionreadiness.org).

_____. 2015. "About Us." Retrieved April 27, 2015 (http://www.missionreadiness.org).

Moyer, Josh. 2014a. "Randy Edsall: 'Not Who We Are.'" ESPN.com, November 1. Retrieved April 28, 2015 (http://espn.go.com).

_____. 2014b. "Big Ten Reprimands Diggs, Edsall." ESPN.com, November 3. Retrieved April 28, 2015 (http://espn.go.com).

Mydans, Seth. 1994. "Nice Guys Finish Last in Ban on Handshakes." *New York Times*, April 9. Retrieved April 23, 2015 (http://www.nytimes.com).

Myles, Stephanie. 2014. "How to Shake Hands at the Net, by Barbora Zahlavova Strycova (and Other Less-Awesome Tennis Handshakes)." *Yahoo Sports*, September 16. Retrieved May 2, 2015 (http://sports.yahoo.com).

NBA.com. 2015. "Jr. NBA Jr. WNBA Keys to Success." Retrieved April 21, 2015 (http://www.nba.com).

NCAA. 2011. "Football: 2011 and 2012 Rules and Interpretations: Statement on Sportsmanship." Retrieved April 15, 2015 (http://www.naia.org).

NCAA Division III Manual. 2014. "Bylaw, Article 10, Ethical Conduct: 10.01.1 Honesty and Sportsmanship." August. Retrieved April 3, 2015 (http://www.summit.k12.nj.us).

Palo Alto Medical Foundation. 2015. "The Benefits of Participating in Sports." Retrieved April 4, 2015 (http://www.pamf.org/teen/health/sports).

Radar, Benjamin. 2004. *American Sports: From the Age of Folk Games to the Age of Televised Sports*, 5th ed. Upper Saddle River, NJ: Prentice Hall.

Reeds, Greg. 2004. "Winning and Losing: A Case Study for Fair Play," pp. 87–90 in *Social Diseases: Mafia, Terrorism, Totalitarianism*, edited by Tim Delaney, Valeri Kuvakin, and Tim Madigan. Moscow: Russian Humanist Society.

Roenigk, Alyssa. 2014. "Hill Fulfills Dream, Nets 4 Points." ESPN.com, November 2. Retrieved April 4, 2015 (http://espn.go.com).

Schreiber, Lee. 1990. *The Parent's Guide to Kids' Sports.* Boston: Little, Brown.
Schupak, Adam. 2014. "Bradley WDs from BMW Championship." *Golf Week*, September 6. Retrieved April 16, 2015 (http://golfweek.com).
Sondheimer, Eric. 2013. "Post-Game Handshake Controversy in Kentucky." *Los Angeles Times*, October 9. Retrieved April 15, 2015 (http://articles.latimes.com).
Sport England. 2015. "Sport and Health." Retrieved April 14, 2015 (https://www.sportengland.org).
Sports Illustrated. 2014. "Last Wish Fulfilled." November 10:16.
Stoll, Sharon, and Jennifer Beller. 2000. "Do Sports Build Character?" pp. 18–30 in *Sports in School: The Future of an Institution*, edited by John Gerdy. New York: Teachers College Press.
Stubbs, Roman. 2014. "Maryland-Penn State Postgame: Kevin Anderson Issues Apology, Maryland Defense Steps Up." *Washington Post*, November 1. Retrieved April 23, 2015 (http://www.washingtonpost.com).
Walton, Bill. 2005. "Good Sportsmanship Is Losing Out to Winning." *USA Today*, December 21:13A.
Williams, Henry. 1895. "The Educational and Health Giving Value of Athletics." *Harper's Weekly*, February 16:166.

Being a Poor Sport

VERNER MØLLER

The concept of "sportsmanship" is usually used to designate sporting behavior that is deemed laudable from a moral perspective. If a soccer player goes to ground in apparent pain after a tackle it is up to the referee to decide if play should be stopped to let the player be attended to by his team's medical staff. According to the rulebook play is stopped if, in the opinion of the referee, a player is seriously injured. The referee may assess that the player is not seriously injured and decide to let the play continue. However, players do not always accept the referee's role but take the decision in their own hands. If the ball is in the opposing team's possession, we often see that a player of this team decides to kick the ball out of play and thus annuls the numerical advantage his or her team has in the situation. This is applauded as a sign of sportsmanship. Contrariwise, if the opposing team plays to the whistle in an attempt to exploit the situation it is by the same token assessed as unsporting behavior.

The win-at-all-costs-mentality is something which is opposed by sports educators in favor of the ethos famously expressed by Bishop Ethelbert Talbot during his sermon at St. Paul's Cathedral in celebration of the 1908 London Olympics: "In these Olympiads the important thing is not winning, but taking part" (Coubertin 2000:587). The founder of the modern Olympic Games Pierre de Coubertin who witnessed the Bishop's sermon recognized that this expression was a brilliant maxim to promote the educational dimension of the Games so he made them his own, adding that "the most important thing in life is not victory but struggle: the essential is not to conquer but to fight well" (Coubertin 2000:587). However, this idealistic presentation of the meaning and value of the Olympics seems contradicted by the choreography surrounding sporting events. At the end of each Olympic competition the winner is celebrated, whereas not much attention is paid to the "also-rans" who struggled and fought as well as they could. It is the victor who runs the lap of honor while the losers disappear out of the limelight into the locker room. The winner's ceremony shows the same as it is only the three best-placed athletes or teams that are invited on the podium and once again the winner is the center of attention. The winner is placed visibly highest on the podium and is handed the medal of the most precious metal. It is also the winner's national anthem that is played to conclude the ceremony. After the event the winner gets the most lucrative invitations and contract offers. So there are lots of indications that Talbot's perception of what is most important in the Olympics is out of touch with reality. And there is reason to believe that Coubertin was not a true believer in Talbot's famous maxim. At least he appears somewhat ambiguous when in another essay he writes: "To try to make athletics conform to a system of mandatory moderation is to chase after an illusion. Athletes need the "freedom of excess." That is why their motto is *Citius, altius, fortius*: faster, higher, stronger, the motto for anyone who dares to beat a record" (Coubertin 2000:581).

In actual sporting events we find numerous examples of excessive behaviors that seem in line with Coubertin's observation that mandatory moderation in sports is illusory. Diego Maradona's scoring with his hand against England at the FIFA World Cup in 1986 has become the example par excellence of unsporting behavior or the win-at-all-cost-mentality. But legions of footballers before and after Maradona's successful misdeed have taken advantage of handling the ball. In 2009 it was Thierry Henry who was vilified as being a poor sport after having controlled the ball with his hand in injury time at the World Cup play-off. His hand touch allowed him to pass the ball to his teammate William Gallas, who scored the goal that qualified France for the World Cup tournament at the expense of Ireland. When the press afterwards confronted Henry, he openly admitted: "I will be honest, it was a handball. But I am not the ref. I played it, the ref allowed it. That's a question you should ask him" (Ogden 2009). There is little regret in Henry's statement. Instead he is level-headedly explaining to us the purpose of referees on the pitch. Referees' function is to make sure that games are played by the rules because one cannot rely on sportsmanship and fair play, which is a prerequisite for self-regulation in sport.

This was further confirmed when the 2010 World Cup took place. In the quarterfinals Uruguay played Ghana. In the dying minutes of the game Ghana player Dominic Adiyiah had a goal-bound header saved on the goal line. Uruguay's out field player Luis Suarez used his hand to stop the ball. Suarez was rightly sent off and Ghana awarded a penalty, which they unfortunately failed to convert, allowing Uruguay to progress after the penalty shoot-out. Afterwards Suarez was hailed by his teammate for his match-winning misdeed. One of his teammates even went so far as to carry him on his shoulders to be celebrated by the Uruguayan fans on the stands. As was the case with Henry, international media accused Suarez of being a poor sport. Nobody put the situation into perspective by mention of the fact that the free kick that led to Adiyiah golden opportunity was awarded after a Ghana-player had dived to win it. A probable explanation for this is of course that in modern-day soccer it is so common to dive to win a free kick when a player is about to lose possession or gets into areas where a set piece represent a goal-scoring opportunity that it is only when diving leads to penalties, which are converted more often than not, that diving is viewed as unsporting. But acceptance of this explanation implies acceptance of cheating to some extent whereby sportsmanship as an absolute ideal begins to erode.

There are more serious examples of the problematic win-at-all-cost-mentality. In recent decades athletes' use of doping has become emblematic of a poor sport. In 1988 we saw Ben Johnson exposed and singled out as the unsporting cheat. Later we learned that Carl Lewis, who got the gold medal after the disqualification of Johnson, tested positive for three banned substances prior to the United States Olympic Trials in 1988 at which he qualified for the Olympics (Denham 2004).

During the 2012 London Olympics we witnessed the bizarre situation where eight female badminton players were disqualified for trying to throw matches by serving into the net or hit the shuttlecock wide. This happened because the tournament was organized so the players knew that they would get an easier draw if they lost than if they won. In other words they wanted to lose the game in order to increase their chances of winning the tournament. Afterwards they were punished by their respective national organizations for discrediting the game. However, in order to properly assess if tactically losing badminton players, doping athletes, and handballing soccer players are indeed acting as poor sports we must first determine what we are talking about when we talk about sport. This is not as straightforward as people unfamiliar with the academic sports debate may believe.

Definition Is Key

Many academics find it naïve to attempt to define sport and prefer an anti-essentialist position. One of the most uncompromising anti-essentialists in the field of sport studies, Henning Eichberg, holds that it may even be counterproductive:

> The discourse of *Wesen*, the construction of a universally human "essence"—as well as its *ersatz* concept called "function"—may even hinder an understanding of sport, just as essentialism in general rather hinders the understanding of other cultural phenomena [Eichberg 2005:51].

It is true that one should be cautious about essentialist claims because such claims often tend to promote an overly simplistic and static understanding of human practices and overlook the changing effects of human culture, and also because essentialism is powerful and can be abused as a political weapon. As a potent example one only needs to think of anti–Semitic "essentialization" of Jews in the German propaganda film *The Eternal Jew* (1940). Such abuse makes it tempting to sympathize with the anti-essentialist position. Nevertheless, denying essentialism because of political misuse is unwise because it relativizes everything and makes analyses of cultural phenomena futile. Essentialism is a two-sided sword. To stick with the example, how would an anti-essentialist answer the question: What happened to the Jews in Germany in the 1930s and 1940s and was that essentially a bad thing? Were the person anti-essentialist in all respects he would inevitably have to answer no. The strongest possible response he or she could give to express disapproval would be: "In my opinion it was wrong." But the person would have no alternative to accept that others may have differing but equally valid opinions. In the last analysis it would be a matter of taste. Anti-essentialism is thus an impotent position in moral and scientific matters. It is also self-defeating as Eichberg's article demonstrates.

After having determined that essentialism is a cul-de-sac Eichberg goes on to say that "to avoid the trap of a reified *Wesen* we can ask questions from the other direction—by looking at what is *not* sport." A prerequisite for answering this question in any meaningful way is that one has an accurate—if even tacit—understanding of what sport essentially is. The question "what is not sport" is obviously parasitic on an essentialist understanding of sport.

Another academic who shares Eichberg's anti-essentialist position is sport philosopher Mike McNamee, who nevertheless offers his view on the nature of sport. In the opening chapter of his book *Sports Virtues and Vices: Morality Plays* (2008) he claims that there is an "ethical core of sport" (McNamee 2008:2). How should we understand this if "core" does not refer to something essential about the nature of sport? McNamee would undoubtedly object to this interpretation because in the same chapter he offers "a critique of those essentialists who seek to find some kind of closure to the analysis of the concept of sport simply by defining it in terms of necessary and sufficient conditions"

(McNamee 2008:2). In light of this it is surprising to read McNamee's subsequent claim that sports "are best understood ritually as rule-governed contests with a gratuitous logic and which necessarily embody an ethical dimension" (McNamee 2008:9). Because what does "best understood" and "necessarily embody" mean if there is nothing essential about sport? And why highlight "rule-governed contests" and not "human pastime" if rules are not—contrary to pastime—essential to what we call sport?

McNamee's anti-essentialism is inspired by Ludwig Wittgenstein's work *Philosophical Investigations* in which Wittgenstein uses the example of games to prove his anti-essentialist point. The word "game," he observes, is used to describe a variety of games. But instead of thinking about what all these games have in common in hope of getting to the essence of "game" he suggests we should instead look at various games. "For if you look at them you will not see something that is common to all, but similarities, relationship, and a whole series of them at that.... I can think of no better expression to characterize these similarities than 'family resemblances'" (Wittgenstein 1996:§66–67). This observation is lauded by McNamee as a "more subtle and complex appreciation of the complexity of the relationship between language, thought and the world" (McNamee 2008:11). McNamee offers a clear example of the meaning of family resemblance. The numbers in the following list represents a game and the letters the games' disparate features: (1) abcde; (2) bcdef; (3) cdefg; (4) defgh; (5) efghi; and (6) fghij.

It is clear that 1 and 2 have plenty of features in common so had these two been the only representations of games we might have thought that feature b c d e was essential to both games but not a and f. But when we compare all six games we immediately realize that, despite the "family resemblance" between the games, games 1 and 6 have no feature in common. Thus it seems proven that there is no essence of games. As obvious as it appears, this is too hasty a conclusion. What we tend to overlook when we view the formal representation of games is that both 1 and 6—like the rest of the games—are represented by letters. Once again we find anti-essentialism parasitic on essentialism because the reason why the example appears convincing is because the six representations are essentially the same, namely letters. This is not coincidental. It is rather a prerequisite for any comprehensible claim, so it should come as no surprise that even Wittgenstein's original example has the same inbuilt self-contradiction.

Note that Wittgenstein is not merely talking about "resemblances" but applies the concept "family resemblances" to describe what we observe among the phenomena we call games. Again this is no coincidence. The term "resemblance" would have been too vague because we find resemblances between all sorts of things. A snake and a stick are both long and round; a stick and a stool are both made of wood; a stool and a lipstick that are both red, etc. In this way all phenomena in the world could be found to have resemblances. The term "family" indicates that there are some phenomena, which belong to the category and some which do not, as is the case with the separate categories "family" and "friends." It is unhelpful to maintain that categories are formed by convention, because this fails to explain what has formed these categorical conventions.

The only two possible explanations are: there is something essential that ties them together; or they are accidental. If the latter were the case that would imply that the snake, the stick, the stool and the lipstick by a similar accident could have formed a specific category and been equally comprehensible by convention. This is clearly unimaginable because if all things in the universe could be tied together by fortuitous similarities (as the "etc." at the end of the list indicates) that would dissolve the meaning of categorization all together. So there seems to be no alternative to accepting essential underpinnings of meaningful categories.

Now, if we take a picture of a group of family and friends, there will be taller frames and shorter frames, lighter skin and darker skin, bigger ears and smaller ears, longer noses and smaller noses, etc. Some of the persons would have more features in common than others and we would guess that those who look most the same would be family and the rest would be friends. A proselyte of Wittgenstein might of course claim that he or she found "family resemblance" between everybody because every person in the picture might share certain characteristics with some others across the group. But this would be wrong by definition in so far as the proselyte was informed that the group consisted of both family and friends. Another possibility is that the proselyte—following Wittgenstein's recommendation—would look and after close inspection claim that a particularly small person who also happened to be the only one who was bald and had an up-turned nose was definitely not family but belong to the "friends" category.

At the time of Wittgenstein there was no safe way to establish whether this claim would be right or not. Today, however, science has developed DNA analyses, which can determine whether or not a person belongs to a certain family. For the scientific method to be authoritative it is of course necessary to define the term "family." Some might suggest that adopted children are family and if we include adopted children in the definition of family obviously DNA analysis is useless as a validation tool. Others might even claim their pets to be part of the family, which means that they use the term "family" in the broader meaning of household. But if "family" is defined narrowly as blood relatives DNA analysis is valid because blood relatives share essential characteristics. It was this intuition Wittgenstein exploited in his attempt to make his anti-essentialism point by using the concept "family resemblance."

Even though we can make sense of various everyday usages of terms such as "family" we have to define the phenomenon subject to our analysis properly if we want to produce an authoritative analysis of a given phenomenon. That is, we must present the essential characteristics of the phenomenon in question.

What Are We Talking About When We Talk About Sport?

One of the reasons why sport is difficult to discuss in a meaningful way is that the term "sport" has been used as a common denominator for a variety of disparate activities. Another reason is that the usage of the term has changed over time, originally referring to activities enjoyed by the leisure class but today designating both amateur and professional play, games and contests of all sorts and in growing numbers.

It is truly difficult, if not impossible, to find a common essence in activities such as fox hunting, jogging, angling, football and gardening. Each of these activities, however, can be defined separately. Consequently, we understand that sport is not analytically comprehensible as merely a class of activities despite the fact that the term is used this way in everyday language. It is important to understand that there is not identity between things and phenomena in the world and the concepts or languages in which they are communicated. As efficient and impressive as language is in regards to communicating facts, thoughts and feelings it is still a symbolic representation of reality, and as reality changes we find, unsurprisingly, changes in concepts and languages as well.

As historian Eric Hobsbawm (1987) explains:

> Young aristocrats might, as in Britain, try their hand at any form of physical prowess, but their special field was exercise connected with riding and killing, or at least attacking, animals and people: hunting, shooting fishing, horse-races, fencing and the like. Indeed in Britain the word "sports" was originally confined to such pursuits, the games and physical contests now called "sports" being classified as "pastimes" [p. 181].

The fact that the meaning of the term "sport" has changed over the course of time does not imply that there is no essence to what we today call sport and which is different to what was in former times identified by the same word. This is true because the essence does not lie in the word. "Sport" like any other word is nothing more than an arbitrary sound or organization of a number of letters by which a certain phenomenon or class of phenomena is conceptualized. Thus, as argued above, the crucial thing is how the phenomena, represented by that particular word, are defined. Accordingly, "sport" must be understood as a label which can be loosely or rigidly defined. But to be useful as an analytical concept "sport" must be rigidly defined as activities with essential qualities and characteristics. So in what follows we exclusively apply the term sport to activities that satisfies the following four criteria which we find essential to sports:

1. The activity is played out as a competition, which is taken seriously even though it serves no external purpose and in that sense can be regarded as unserious.
2. The aim is to win and to move upwards within the activity's hierarchical structure.
3. The activity is organized and functions in an institutionalized framework, in which results are recorded and are ascribed significance.
4. The activity is governed by a written set of rules, which are administered by a judge who ideally is impartial.

These criteria immediately cover all sports on the Olympic program. Still they are sufficiently distinct to exclude a vast number of activities, which in everyday language is indiscriminately referred to as sport but which would make any consistent analysis impossible if included. The recreational run or bike ride—even those performed on a racing bike with high speed—alone or with a group of friends falls outside the sports category. This type of activities is better characterized as recreational pastimes or physical exercise. Unorganized badminton and basketball matches, wrestling on the lawn or a race to see who can get to the garden gate first can be truly competitive but is not sport as proposed here.

An important thing to note is that sport, with its tournaments, championships, divisions and rankings, is hierarchical in nature and implies an aspiration to move upwards in the sporting hierarchy. This is a fundamental sporting principle that explains why teams fight to the bitter end to avoid relegation despite the fact that winning is more fun than losing and relegation to a lower level would make wins easier to come by in a lower division. Despite the prospect of more wins in the following season no sporting team celebrates relegation. The underlying reason for this is that, even though winning is an essential catalyst for the sporting activity, sport entails more than the satisfaction of winning. Sport also implies an aspiration towards excellence. That is the reason why athletes do not look for opponents they can easily beat but rather those who represent challenging opposition. Ultimately any sport's driving force is ambition to overcome the strongest opposition possible. This is reflected in the governing institution's organization of competitions so opponents are matched evenly on the basis of previous results. And also by the involvement of an (ideally) impartial referee whose presence allows the competing athletes to focus entirely on their performances without distracting concerns whether actions in the contest, a tackle for instance, are in accordance with or a violation of the rules.

It is true that the game called ultimate, which originated from the American counterculture of the 1960s, represents an exception in so far as the rules in this sport are overlooked by the players themselves. This approach demonstrates a critique of the traditional organized sports system. However, as the game established itself and became more competitive the original spirit of the game came under pressure (Holtzman-Conston 2010). Even though playing without referees is still the norm for league play this modus operandi "has been supplanted in club competition by the use of 'observers' to mediate disputes, and the nascent professional leagues even employ empowered referees" (Storck 2014:1). So rather than falsifying the hypothesis that the above-mentioned criteria are essential to modern-day competitive sports the development of the exceptional game ultimate seems to support it.

However, the example of ultimate teaches us another significant lesson, namely that the same activity can be engaged in both as a sport and as a non-sport. This may at first glance seem to contradict our essentialist perception of sport because we conventionally identify football as a sport regardless of whether football is played by kids in the schoolyard or by professional stars in football leagues. But if schoolyard football played during breaks is assessed by the above-mentioned criteria it is immediately clear that the kids are not engaged in sport in the strict sense proposed here. In order for us to understand sportsmanship and what it means to be a poor sport it is necessary to differentiate between games and contests as playful pastimes and games and contests where competition is taken seriously. It is only the latter we refer to by the term sport.

Being a Good Sport

In his book *Fair and Foul* (2006) D. Stanley Eitzen mentions a number of lauded examples from the world of sport in which fair play trumped the will to win. In 1987 Rockdale County won the state basketball championship only to lose it a few months later when the coach of the team, for whatever reason, realized that in the final game he had unknowingly introduced an ineligible player on the court, and informed the authorities about the rule infraction. "As a result, the school forfeited the only state championship they had ever won" (Eitzen 2006:52). Perhaps even more moving is the example of Jake Porter, a mentally challenged player on the Northwest high school football team in McDermott, Ohio. Jake had not had a single run with the ball for three years so his coach arranged with the opposing team's coach that he could let Jake play one play towards the end of the game, just taking a knee. "But the visiting coach told his players to let Jake run the ball and score a touchdown. Jake went in the game and scored with a forty-nine-yard run." To underline the value of the incident Eitzen ends this example with a description of the emotional impact of this gesture. "Imagine having 21 teammates on the field. In the stands mothers cried and fathers roared. Players on both sidelines held their helmets to the sky and whooped" (Eitzen 2006:53).

Both of these are encouraging examples of the virtues of honesty, empathy and generosity. This, however, does not translate to being a good sport. On the contrary, both are examples of unsportsmanlike conduct because they undermine the meaning and value of the game. In the first instance, the coach may have sat down months after the feat to enjoy the decisive game on video and only then realizing his blunder have felt so embarrassed that the title did not mean anything to him anymore. By reporting the incident, which had had no impact on the outcome of the game, he not only lost the title for himself. He did the same for all his players. The team that was crowned champions at the expense of Rockdale County did not win the tournament but was handed the victory as a desktop decision. So the championship was suddenly of no sporting value. The players of the promoted team could not know for sure if they deserved the title more than Rockdale County because their own coach may have made a similar mistake without ever realizing it, or they might have scored a crucial point in another game because the referee wrongly awarded the team a free throw. The coach who decided to report his unintentional and overlooked rule infraction to the authorities to make them discard his team's title made a name for himself by making the tournament insignificant.

The other example illustrates the dilemma between being a good person and being a good sport. The fact that Jake's coach had kept him on the bench for three years bears witness to his coach's sporting attitude. He could not play Jake because he was not good enough and thus would reduce his team's chance of winning. But he could empathize and pity him. This was by all appearances the reason why he arranged with the opposing team's coach to allow him one play towards the end of the game that would not influence the result. So when Jake was allowed to score a touchdown the game was in effect suspended. The only person on the field at the moment with a sporting attitude was Jake who was fooled into believing that he had experienced a sporting moment of glory. As an example of human empathy the gesture may be praiseworthy but contrary to what Eitzen holds this is not an example of fair play as it was not play at all in a sporting sense.

A third of Eitzen's examples worth mentioning is about the ethics of cyclists in the Tour de France. Eitzen refers to the situation in 2003 when Lance Armstrong's handlebar caught the sash lift of a spectator's bag so he fell off the bike. "The leaders, including Armstrong's main rival Jan Ullrich, slowed down to wait for Armstrong. Two years earlier Armstrong did the same for Ullrich when he crashed. 'It was proper for me to do what I did and proper for Jan to do what he did. I appreciate that'" (Eitzen 2006:53).

This example is different from the other two because the praised conduct, rather than being gestures of fair play, was a necessity for the competition to work. If riders take advantage of a competitor's crash, puncture or mechanical defects the sport would become too much of a lottery and this would devalue the sporting element of cycling. Thus it was a matter of course and not a matter of fair play that both riders waited for their rival in the respective situations. Tellingly, the same year Eitzen published his book Jan Ullrich was suspended right before the beginning of the Tour de France for his involvement in the blood doping scandal known as Operacion Puerto, in which more than fifty riders were found to be banking blood in a clinic in Madrid with a view to take advantage of performance-enhancing transfusions. Later we have learned that Armstrong was using similar means in his preparation for the seven Tour de France victories he won. So while these two athletes were hailed for their fair play attitude as they abstained from taking advantage of their rival's crash they both had done everything possible to prepare for the race unconcerned about fair play and a level playing field. As devoted sportsmen they had suspended all considerations in their pursuit of sporting success.

Conclusion

We may not like it when we face it but the uncompromising attitude is what attracts our attention and makes us interested in sport. If we extrapolate the Jake Porter example and let all who are unable to score a touchdown in proper competition run unopposed the crying mothers and roaring fathers might soon be silent in the stands if they would even bother to turn up at all.

If we similarly extrapolate the example of the coach who found he had made an insignificant rule infraction, the coach of the new champion team might report a comparable rule violation, and if not him, all the players in the various teams could turn up at the office of those responsible for the arrangement of the tournament and confess overlooked offences that deserved retroactive punishment. It goes without saying that under such circumstances it would be impossible to determine who should be declared champions, and the whole idea of sport would be gone. Thus the extrapolation helps to show that if spectacular behavior hailed as true sportsmanship became the rule rather than the exception it would lead to the erosion of sport. In light of this it is impossible to conclude that those sportspeople who make headlines because of exceptional commendable ethical acts on the sports field are also proving themselves to be good sports. By the same token, it is impossible to infer that those who are ambitious and devoted to such an extent that they don't shy away from rule violations if necessary to succeed deserve being labeled poor sports.

If we return to the examples of the handballing soccer players, the doping athletes and the tactically losing badminton players we find three disparate instances of genuine sporting commitment. Thierry Henry and Diego Maradona did their utmost to outsmart their opponents, including the referee. Henry's deed saw him rescue France's progress to the World Cup tournament, and Maradona's scoring by hand set Argentina on course to win the World Cup. Had this kind of rule violations not been tacitly accepted as a possibility in the game, both teams would have been disqualified retrospectively.

The doping athletes are different in that they do not violate the rules in the heat of the moment. They do it deliberately as part of the preparation. Well aware that it is against the rule they take a calculated risk. This makes it much less excusable. Still it is mistaken to label the act as unsporting because it is the obsession with the sport that lures the doping athletes into the malpractice when they have exhausted all other means to enhance their performance including physical, technical, and mental training, dieting, etc. So the practice derogatorily called "a short cut" is in fact a demanding and stressful extra layer in the preparation for competition. So even though we do not condone it, it would be wrong to claim that doping is unsporting behavior.

The third and final example, the badminton players who tried to throw matches, is at first glance the one that comes closest to unsporting behavior in so far as the will to win is essential to sport. But as soon as we consider the context we realize that the players' grotesque attempt to lose games was a consequence of ambition to win the tournament and thus move upwards within the activity's hierarchical structure. This is rational sporting behavior. So the organizers of the tournament that invited speculation in losing matches are the ones to blame. It was poor organizing that made the badminton players look like being poor sports. Truly poor sports are indeed few and far between if we assess the athletes in light of what sport essentially is, rather than what we for moral reasons would like it to be.

Bibliography

Coubertin, Pierre de. 2000. *Olympism: Selected Writings*. Lausanne: International Olympic Committee.

Denham, Bryan E. 2004. "Hero or Hypocrite? United States and International Media Portrayals of Carl Lewis and Revelations of a Positive Test." *International Review for the Sociology of Sport*, 39 (2):167–185.

Eichberg, Henning. 2005. "Three Dimensions of Playing the Game: About Mouth Pull, Tug-of-War and Sportization," pp. 51–80 in *The Essence of Sport*, edited by Verner Møller and John Nauright. Odense: University Press of Southern Denmark.

Eitzen, D. Stanley. 2006. *Fair and Foul: Beyond the Myths and Paradoxes of Sport*. Lanham, MD: Rowman & Littlefield.

Hobsbawm, Eric. 1987. *The Age of Empire 1875–1914*. London: Weidenfeld and Nicholson.

Holtzman-Conston, Jordan. 2010. *Countercultural Sports in America: The History and Meaning of Ultimate Frisbee*. Saarbrücken: LAP Lambert Academic.

McNamee, Mike. 2008. *Sports, Virtues and Vices: Morality Plays*. London: Routledge.

Ogden, Mark. 2009. "Thierry Henry Admits to Handball That Defeated Ireland in World Cup Play-Off." *The Telegraph*, November 19. Retrieved June 1, 2015 (http://www.telegraph.co.uk).

Storck, Angelyn. 2014. *A Beginners Guide to Ultimate (Sport)*, Vol. 1. London: SamEnrico.

Wittgenstein, Ludwig. 1996. *Philosophical Investigations*, 3d ed. Oxford: Basil Blackwell.

Understanding Doping as "Cheating" from the Perspective of History

IAN RITCHIE

On August 16, 1954, *Sports Illustrated* published its first issue. In the magazine's first full-length feature article, author Paul O'Neil recounted the drama of what became known as the "mile of the century" race at the British Empire and Commonwealth Games in Vancouver, Canada. The race featured England's Roger Bannister and Australia's John Landy, who at the time were the top two milers in the world. The status of the race was high because Bannister was the first runner to break the four-minute mile mark, at Oxford's Iffley Road Track in May of that year, only to have Landy break Bannister's record in an event that took place in Finland in June. During the 1950s sports fans were fascinated by running, the drama of the four-minute barrier, and the men who were competing to be the "fastest man in the world" (Bascomb 2004). Top running races were the "Super Bowl" events of the day, and O'Neil's (1954:21) reference in his article to the "mile of the century" as "the most widely heralded and universally contemplated match foot-race of all time" would not have seemed an exaggeration at the time.

Bannister is an important figure in the history of modern sport, in part for his remarkable accomplishments and in particular for his record-breaking run at Oxford in 1954. He will always be remembered as the first to break the "four minute barrier." But Bannister was important for another, much more important reason: he represents a transition to a new paradigm of human performance that was occurring during his competitive years. In the elite English school system in which Bannister honed his athletic skills during the mid–20th century, "proper" sport was amateur sport, in which "true" athletes, who understood the value of sportsmanship, certainly trained hard and were committed to competition, but the values instilled in them from the culture of amateurism meant that training and competition should not be done excessively and true amateurs, it was thought, never competed for the purpose of making money. A cash pay-out for any kind of athletic endeavor was literally cheating and contrary to the true nature or spirit of sport. Furthermore, the amateur traditions and values that had developed in the elite public school system of England in the late 19th century had an immense impact on sport traditions around the world and on the most important event of all—the Olympic Games.

But those traditions and values, including what was considered true "sportsmanlike" conduct, were changing dramatically in Bannister's day. In the midst of Cold War political confrontations and the Olympic Games becoming in the post–World War II era the central grounds upon which sporting—and by association political prowess—was tested, sport was increasingly directed towards winning at all costs, pushing the human body to ever-new limits, and an emphasis on winning medals in both East and West Bloc countries. Bannister (1964) himself lamented these changes, writing in 1964, after his career had ended, that the world was witnessing a "new professionalism not only in the sense of direct and indirect payment for sport, but also in devoting unlimited time and energy to sport, to the total exclusion of any other career" (pp. 71–72).

We will return to the case of Bannister at the end of this essay because his career as a high-performance runner speaks directly to the central purpose of this essay: to consider the ways in which what is considered "cheating" or what is considered "unsportsmanlike" in sport vary historically, and in turn to consider some of the social and political determinants that lead to those historical changes. Specifically, this essay looks at what many today consider the most important example of cheating and unsportsmanlike behavior: the use of performance enhancing substances—"doping." Few would question the assertion that athletes who use performance enhancing substances are conducting themselves in an unethical way and demonstrating a lack of respect for their competitors. It has become a virtually taken-for-granted truism that the act of taking a drug to enhance one's performance in sport is an act of unsportsmanlike conduct. But when the real history of doping practices and the history of the anti-doping movement—the latter referring to how and why rules against performance enhancing substances were created and who created them—are considered, the picture of doping as inherently unsportsmanlike becomes much less clear than what most assume.

There are several ways in which one can approach the topic of sportsmanship and these many approaches are presented in the various chapters in this volume. This essay attempts to add to the other approaches by presenting a sociological and historical consideration of doping in sport and, more generally, of changing values in sport and what that means for conceptions of ethical, values-based, conduct in sport. The discussion begins with a history of doping practices in modern sport and the creation of anti-doping rules. The essay then goes on to discuss the implications of this history, suggesting that the real history of doping and anti-doping make us question the notion that certain practices in sport are inherently "cheating" or "unsportsmanlike." Indeed, the central point this essay makes—one reiterated more fully in the conclusion—is that to carefully consider issues such as doping from the perspective of history has important implications for what we think of as ethical versus unethical behavior in sport. Being alert to the forces of history that influence sport makes us question and potentially re-evaluate what is considered sportsmanlike.

A Brief History of Doping and the Construction of Anti-Doping Rules

This section provides a brief history of doping and anti-doping in modern sport, "modern" defined as sport since the mid-to-late 1800s, when sport became organized under conditions of codified rules such that people from diverse backgrounds and in often distant geographical locations could play the same game. From the late 1800s on sport became both more organized in many nations around the world and during this era international competitions such as the Olympic Games and World Cup emerged. Having this history of doping and anti-doping in hand will enable us to think critically about what "cheating" and "sportsmanlike" behavior mean historically, a topic be taken up in the next section.

Most people today assume that the use of performance enhancing substances in sport has always been considered unethical, or in other words that it has always been considered cheating. However, good historical accounts show us that that is not the case. Waddington (2006) points out that drug use has existed in sport for years, yet it has only been since the 1960s that doping practices have received widespread condemnation. This raises the important question: "[w]hat is it about the structure of specifically modern sport, and of the wider society of which sport is a part, that has been associated with the development of anti-doping policies in sport?" (Waddington 2006:121). To help respond to Waddington's question, there has been a growth in sociological and historical research, especially in the last ten years or so, into the conditions that led to anti-doping rules and procedures, and more widely to general moral condemnations of athletes who were caught doping or who were suspected of doing so. The following calls upon that research to consider the circumstances that led to the first major rules with sanctioning power—the power to test athletes using technological means and subsequently punish them with time-specific bans from competition. The most important rules were created in the 1960s, but to truly understand those rules and to evaluate their legitimacy, it is crucial to understand the history of why those rules were created and who created them.

Historian Paul Dimeo (2007) demonstrates that the period lasting from the late 1800s up to World War II was an interesting one in terms of emerging attitudes regarding the morality of substance use. Some of the substances used then were very different from those that we might think of as performance enhancing today: alcohol, strychnine, kola, tobacco, ultraviolet rays, purified oxygen, and other substances or methods were used in various athletic environments, especially competitions that pushed the body to extremes such as long distance running, pedestrian walking events, and cycling races, all of which were fairly common and would at times last several days and cover extremely long distances (Dimeo 2007). While today we may not think of these substances as useful in enhancing performance, the important point to remember, as historian John Gleaves (2011) points out, is that intent is really the more important factor. In other words, athletes and coaches believed the substances helped them perform in one way or another, and in that sense these substances have to be thought of as performance enhancers in the same way that today we think of, for example, anabolic steroids as such (Gleaves 2011). But both Dimeo and Gleaves make the more important point that during this time there tended to be relatively little concern about athletes using these various substances, as difficult as this might be for us to comprehend today. Athletes, coaches, and sports fans alike maintained an open curiosity with respect to the potential impact various substances might have on athletes' bodies and their performances. While there were some voices of disapproval based primarily on religious temperance, few questioned the morality of the use of these substances (Dimeo 2007).

The original rules against the use of "dope" came in the context of horse racing, not human competition, and interestingly rules were created because unscrupulous owners and trainers impaired horses' performances in order to profit from fixed races for gambling purposes (Gleaves and Llewellyn 2014). In human competition, the condemnation of substance use emerged slowly in the first few decades of the 20th century. A crucial point in understanding the first condemnations of doping that occurred at the highest levels of sport—a point that is central to the discussion in this essay—is that the reproaches made against doping were based primarily on the defense of amateurism. A divide emerged in the 1920s and 1930s between amateur athleticism and true "sportsmanlike" behavior that amateurs represented, on the one hand, and professionalism that was quickly emerging as a force in sport in the first few decades of the 20th century, on the other hand (Gleaves 2011). The amateur versus professional distinction was very much one determined by class positions and the line between "clean" versus "doped" athletes and what was considered allowable or not had its roots in the class positions of athletes and administrators who were condemning them or not. Criticisms of working class athletes were few, but the amateurs, it was thought, represented true "sportsmanship" and participated in "pure" sport beyond the reach of crass commercialism. As Gleaves (2011) says, "Anti-doping rules predicated on amateurism's ideals would simply become another tool for excluding or otherwise marginalizing working-class professionals" (p. 241).

We can see this class divide in the important case of two athletes who competed in the Olympic marathon event. The sport of marathon running was, by the turn of the century, considered a borderline case between professional and amateur because while it played a central role in major events like the Olympic Games, which was amateur based, prize money was regularly awarded in other events and in long distance running more generally. Runners Thomas Hicks and Dorando Pietri won the 1904 and 1908 Olympic marathons respectively, but it was known that both took a combination of strychnine and other substances. Yet interestingly, both escaped any moral condemnation from officials in the International Olympic Committee (IOC) because they "fell outside the moral code of amateur sport" (Gleaves and Llewellyn 2013:6).

The amateur versus professional division ultimately set the stage for the first anti-doping rules in human competition. The first organization to create a statement of principle against doping was the International Amateur Athletic Federation (IAAF). At the IAAF's 1928 Congress in Amsterdam, the central point of the discussions was to curtail the development of professionalism in sport. Sigfrid Edström, who was the IAAF's President and a loyal defender of amateurism, encouraged IAAF members to take a stand against "dopers" and the group unanimously adopted a rule against "stimulants." The IAAF's rule published in its *Handbook* stated that "doping is the use of any stimulant employed to increase the power of action in athletic competition above the average" and infringement of the rule could lead to suspension "from participation in amateur athletics" (cited in Gleaves and Llewellyn 2014:846).

The IOC, which by the 1930s was the most powerful organization in international sport, was motivated as well to condemn doping based on the defense of amateurism. Amateurism was particularly important for the Olympic Games, as the Games were founded on the principle that the event was a social movement—not just a sports event—that had as one of its goals the betterment of humankind. Defending amateurism was paramount in the decades leading up to World War II; the IOC strongly defended amateurism against the perceived rise of professional sporting traditions and tightened its rules in the *Olympic Charter* between 1894, the year of its foundation, and the start of the War (Ritchie 2014).

IAAF President Edström also held a vice-president position in the IOC and he suggested a committee be created to study the issue of doping. The president of the IOC was Henri de Baillet-Latour (1925–1942) who, among other things, was a wealthy horse owner fully aware of the problems in that sport. Baillet-Latour drafted a letter in advance of the formation of the committee, stating that "amateur sport is meant to improve the soul and the body [and] therefore no stone must be left unturned as long as the use of doping has not been stamped out." He also made the claim—a very inflated one as it turns out—that "[d]oping ... very likely implies an early death" to athletes (cited in Gleaves and Llewellyn 2014:847).

The special commission that was created before the IOC held its yearly meeting in Cairo in 1938 included Edström and a young rising star in the IOC's administration, American Avery Brundage. Before the Cairo meeting, Brundage wrote that "[t]he use of drugs or artificial stimulants of any kind cannot be too strongly denounced and anyone receiving or administering dope or artificial stimulants should be excluded from participation in sport of the O.G. [Olympic Games]" (cited in Gleaves and Llewellyn 2014:849). The formal statement against doping from the commission's report repeated Brundage's hand-written note almost word-for-word and it was subsequently published in the IOC's 1938 *Bulletin*. Eventually, the position statement was included in the Olympic Charter under the heading "Resolutions Regarding the Amateur Status" and this statement of principle, that considered the principle of fighting doping as a subset of concerns about amateur values, remained in the Olympic Charter until 1975 (Gleaves and Llewellyn 2014:849; Ritchie 2014:828–829).

Just as was the case during the period before World War II, the period just after the War was one of "mixed messages" in terms of attitudes towards substance use. But it was also a period during which a "new ethics" emerged and the stance against drug use became stronger at the top levels of sport administration (Dimeo 2007:87–104). The two major categories of drug use were amphetamines to create energy, and somewhat later on, anabolic steroids to build muscle. In terms of the former, a "pep pill mania" of sorts existed in several sports—both professional and amateur—during the 1950s and 1960s and it reflected a general public acceptance in which the use of stimulants to create energy or fight fatigue was, in Dimeo's (2007) words, "an acceptable and legitimate public medicine" (p.62). As for anabolic steroids, they had only been synthesized in a laboratory setting in the 1930s. However, by the late 1940s and increasingly in the 1950s there was a rising interest in the drug's potential to strengthen and rejuvenate the body. This was best exemplified in Paul de Kruif's (1945) top-selling publication *The Male Hormone*, which strongly defended the ability of steroids to enhance energy, build strength, combat fatigue, improve quality of life, and even to extend the duration of life.

At the highest levels of competitive sport, both sides of the "Iron Curtain" became committed to the use of anabolic steroids to improve performance and win medals (Dimeo 2007:71–76). After the 1954 World Weightlifting Championships, American coach Bob Hoffman and the team's physician John Ziegler were convinced that Soviet weightlifters were, as Hoffman phrased it, "taking the hormone stuff to increase their strength" (cited in Todd 1987:93). Then, with the aid of the Ciba Pharmaceutical Company, which produced the synthetic steroid methandieone (Dianabol), Ziegler gave the drug to weightlifters at the York Barbell Club in Pennsylvania. By the 1960s the use of anabolic steroids was common in weightlifting circles but also spread to shot putting, hammer throwing, discus, and several other Olympic, strength-related events (Dimeo 2007:76–78).

Avery Brundage became President of the IOC from 1952 to 1972 and he attempted to control what its members perceived—quite correctly as it turned out—to be a rising tide of doping use. Two incidents in the sport of cycling heightened concerns. First, Danish cyclist Knud Enemark Jensen collapsed and died during the road race in the 1960 Rome Summer Games, and subsequently British cyclist Tommy Simpson died during the 1967 Tour de France. Jensen's case was particularly important because he died during the Olympic Games, and while it has recently been discovered by cycling and doping historian Verner Møller (2010) that Jensen's death was due not to amphetamine use but to a series of other factors, including extreme dehydration caused from excessive temperatures in Rome on the day of competition, Jensen's case and the assumption that he died from an amphetamine overdose put anti-doping squarely on the IOC's policy agenda.

For President Brundage, doping was one example of more general challenges to the "purity" of Olympic sport. Brundage, following Olympic founder Pierre de Coubertin, was adamant that the Olympic movement was a social one, the aim of which was the betterment of humankind; the values of amateurism in his mind therefore needed to be upheld at any cost and sport—Olympic sport in particular—had to avoid any vested political or commercial interests. In Brundage's (cited in Guttmann 1984:115–116) words: "[s]port, which still keeps the flag of idealism flying, is perhaps the most saving grace in the world at the moment, with its spirit of rules kept, and regard for the adversary, whether the fight is going for or against." It is in this context that Brundage's actions to fight doping must be considered. Just 15 days after Jensen's death, Brundage and the IOC Executive Board met to voice their concerns, and then in 1962 Brundage organized a doping subcommittee under the direction of the head of the Royal College of Surgeons of England, Sir Arthur Porritt.

The IOC's *Bulletin* in 1963 published the subcommittees stance, defining doping as "an illegal procedure used by certain athletes, in the form of drugs; physical means and exceptional measures which are used by small groups in a sporting community in order to alter positively or negatively the physical or physiological capacity of a living creature, man or animal in competitive sport" (cited in Hunt 2011:15). The statement was problematic because, among other points, many of the doping practices of athletes were not illegal at all, and "exceptional measures" was much too vague in terms of delineating what was cheating or not.

But the IOC continued its fight against doping for the remainder of the 1960s. During the IOC general meetings in Tokyo in 1965, Porritt stated that the IOC should issue a formal and more carefully worded statement, create sanctioning procedures, and include a promissory clause which athletes would have to sign as a condition of participation. During the IOC's meetings in Tehran in May 1967, the IOC formally defined doping, voted to introduce drug testing, and stated that athletes would be required to sign a pledge that they were drug free. The IOC formally defined doping as "the use of substances or techniques in any form or quantity alien or unnatural to the body with the exclusive aim of obtaining an artificial or unfair increase of performance in competition" (cited in Todd and Todd 2001:68). Limited random tests were conducted at the 1968 Mexico City Games, and while a test for anabolic steroids at that time did not exist, those tests were developed in 1973 and testing for steroids was first implemented at the Montreal Summer Games in 1976.

Reconsidering Doping as "Cheating"

The summary just presented is necessarily brief, and certainly there is a lot more to the story of how and why drugs became a systematic problem in modern sport and how and why rules were created to combat the problem (see Beamish and Ritchie 2006). Despite its brevity, there are three important initial points about the history just presented. First, while the anti-doping movement certainly involved a number of powerful sports organizations, any history of anti-doping must emphasize the IOC in particular because that organization has been the world leader in terms of sport policy. The IOC's policies in the last half-century have guided other national and international organizations, including their anti-doping policies (Hunt 2011). Second, while the history ends at what might seem like a strange point in time, because certainly there have been significant events since the late-1960s, the importance of those more recent events pales in comparison to the history of why the original rules against doping were created in the first place. Finally, the history of anti-doping from the late 19th century up to the late 1960s has important implications in terms of how we think about the concept of sportsmanship.

A central point to the history just presented is that at the heart of the drive to prohibit drugs and eventually test and potentially punish athletes was the defense of amateurism. The most important figures in the history of anti-doping—Sigfrid Edström, Henri de Baillet-Latour, Avery Brundage, Arthur Porritt, and others who could not be named here because of space limitations (see Dimeo 2006)—all had a particular world view based on their personal experiences, their cultural impression of what "proper" sport was, and their class positions. All came from or achieved privileged positions in society and the basis of their view of "proper" sport was either directly handed down to them from the nineteenth-century English public school system or that system indirectly influenced them through organizations such as the IOC that built its own version of amateurism into its rules and policies. The English amateur-based school system was one in which "proper" athletes—virtually all of which were men—were sculpted through sport into honorable and disciplined political, economic, and military leaders (Mangan 2012). The tradition of amateurism that Edström, Baillet-Latour, Brundage, and Porritt were defending was what defined "sportsmanship," and inasmuch as the amateur code became the central ethos of the Olympic movement and its guiding philosophy, defending sport's purity was synonymous with defending the Olympic movement itself and its greater social goals.

Leading up to the creation of the first prohibitions in 1967, the IOC was in fact concerned about a number of factors that seemed to be taking sport away from its perceived amateur foundation. Brundage himself was concerned about doping but that problem was merely a subset of greater problems, including an accelerated emphasis on competition and winning medals, and the movement towards full-time training in both the East and the West Bloc countries (Wrynn 2006). Practices such as increased time and effort committed to training and competition, or in some cases athletes receiving money for performance, were becoming increasingly common and, from the perspective of many IOC members, it is understandable why, given the nineteenth-century set of values upon which the movement had been founded, they would perceive the world of sport to be spinning out of control. However, the IOC could do little about many of these issues. Indeed, by the early 1970s, after years of pressure from commercial companies, including ones that wanted to take advantage of the increasingly international visibility of Olympic athletes to sell products or services, and after years of debate within the ranks of the IOC itself, amateur ideals were formally abandoned and the relevant rules and restrictions were removed from the Charter (Beamish and Ritchie 2004; Beamish and Ritchie 2006).

But by the time amateurism was effectively gone, doping control was well on its way to becoming institutionally powerful as an increasing number of administrators, scientists, technicians, and medical experts with high-level positions in the Olympic movement sought to legitimize anti-doping and their positions within an increasingly complex infrastructure created to catch "cheaters" (Henne 2014). Policies, testing protocols, and public opinion as well moved quickly as alarmist positions about the "evils" of doping and its threat to the "purity" of sport grew (Dimeo 2007).

The last point about the "purity" of Olympic sport warrants closer attention. The Olympic movement has always been different from other international sport movements, in that its proponents have always claimed it was a social movement, not just a sports event, the purpose of which is the betterment of humankind. Crucial to the success of the movement has been the image of Olympic sport as "pure" and that the IOC is representing sport's "spirit" in an unadulterated form beyond political, economic, or social affairs (Ritchie 2014). As IOC president Brundage (cited in Guttmann 1984:115–116) said at the end of several speeches: "When, if ever, the spirit of sport ... reigns over international affairs, the cat force, which rules there now, will slink away, and human life emerge for the first time from the jungle." But without amateurism as the basis for "pure" sport, another means was necessary to present Olympic sport as "clean" and "pure." As Dimeo (2006) expresses it, anti-doping became that means as the defenders of drug policies sought to return the movement to its mythical original state: anti-doping was "an exercise of power in which the authorities had to protect sport: that meant disseminating the myth of its purity" (pp. 199–120).

The fact that the defense of amateurism lay at the heart of the anti-doping movement has important implications for, first of all, thinking about anti-doping policies today. True sportsmanship up to the 1970s was defined as athletes who followed the amateur code, did not treat sport as a full- or even part-time occupation, and certainly "true" athletes would never receive financial compensation. But if anti-doping was largely based on these amateur sensibilities, what does this mean for the legitimacy of anti-doping historically? Beamish (2011) states frankly that the original rules were "intimately tied to [Olympic founder] Coubertin's original lofty principles, and indeed, the use of performance-enhancing substances was, within that context, cheating.... [However] [o]nce the Olympic Games' fundamental principles were removed, the IOC's most principled rationale for a banned list vanished" (p. 71).

Secondly, it is important to think carefully about what "sportsmanship" has meant historically and how that notion has changed. Many people before approximately 40–50 years ago would have thought that an athlete taking cash payment for performance was quite literally a "cheater," in the same sense that many people today think of an athlete who takes a performance-enhancing drug a "cheater." This brings to light how extremely different conceptions of "sportsmanship" have been. Will the future bring us to a point in which we no longer think of athletes who take performance-enhancing drugs as cheaters? This of course remains to be seen, and we will return shortly to some alternative ideas to current anti-doping policies. But it is worthwhile to revisit the example of Roger Bannister mentioned in the introduction, to highlight the ever-changing conceptions of "sportsmanship."

As was discussed earlier, Bannister adamantly defended amateur traditions, and during his career he competed as a member of the powerful Amateur Athletic Association in England. Publically, he presented himself as the embodiment of the "pure" sportsman who would never consider remuneration for running and who performed for the sheer love of sport. But behind the scenes Bannister did as much as any other single athlete to push sports towards the new form of professionalism he so condemned. To enhance his performance, Bannister used the most advanced technology, medical and scientific discoveries, and training regimens available in the 1950s. Realizing the four-minute barrier would not fall without the most up-to-date performance advantages, Bannister used the new "fartlek" technique that integrated short bouts of speed into long distance runs; interval training methods; specially made lightweight shoes with spikes and graphite soles; pacemakers to aid him in his runs, including during the race on the Oxford University track where he broke the four-minute mark; and Bannister even applied his working knowledge in human physiology, based in part on oxygen-enriched treadmill experiments he performed on himself and others. With a medical degree and a Masters in physiology, Bannister pushed the boundaries of scientific knowledge of human performance; his approach, as Bascomb (2004) describes, was "decidedly scientific," as "[f]ew had examined the human body's capacity to withstand punishment as Roger Bannister had.... Arterial pCO_2, blood lactate, pulmonary ventilation, carotid chemoreceptors, oxygen mixes, hyperpnea, and gas tensions—this was how Bannister described the effects of training on his body" (p. 90). Bannister, in short, is perhaps more emblematic of the new paradigm of human performance than any other single individual. Many in his day, if they had known about his scientific approach to training and competition, would have thought his actions to be, despite his public image, unsportsmanlike. Bannister, in short, attests not to the idea that sportsmanlike conduct is fixed, but to the fact that it is an ever-shifting social practice.

Conclusion

The central point of this essay has been to encourage sociological and historical thinking about what sportsmanship means and to consider some of the changing patterns in sport that have influenced what we think of as "proper" conduct in sport. By taking on many of the taken-for-granted assumptions about what is considered by many to be the most unsportsmanlike act of all in the world of sport today—the use of a performance enhancing drug to improve performance—it is the hope of this essay to reflect on the wider historical forces that impact the manner in which we think about what is proper or not in sport. In this sense, this essay follows the teaching of American sociologist C. Wright Mills (1959), who in his famous book *The Sociological Imagination* wrote that any sound sociological analysis must examine the intersection of personal biography and the history of social structure to complete its "intellectual journey" (p. 6). We should all think historically, Mills implored, in order to understand our day-to-day lives. This includes attitudes towards dominant values and assumption about what sport "is" and what is "sportsmanlike" or not.

It may appear that an outcome of the history of doping and anti-doping presented here is to condone the use of performance enhancing drugs in sport; however, nothing could be further from the truth. The purpose has been to put the growth of the use of performance enhancing drugs into its proper historical perspective. As Beamish and Ritchie (2006) express, "[t]he use of performance-enhancing substances is part of the internal logic that drives the comprehensive high-performance sport systems that developed over the last half-century and their use will continue unabated as long as the social and political relations of sport remain in their current trajectory" (p. 5). In other words, doping has inevitably flowed from the creation of high-performance sport systems and the logic of winning at all costs that emerged from the Cold War and the pursuit of medals to establish nations' political supremacy. To treat the issue from the perspective of testing and punishing individual athletes does no justice to the more complex set of social and historical factors that led to the systematic use of performance enhancers in the first place.

The second major point of this essay has been to summarize scholarship that questions the legitimacy of anti-doping policy. Several scholars, including Beamish (2011), Kayser and Smith (2008), and Kayser, Mauron and Miah (2005; 2007) have called for a "harm reduction" model to replace current anti-doping policy. This alternate model takes into account the myriad number of risks high-performance athletes put their bodies through in their day-to-day training regimens and calls for policies to recognize those risks and not just ones associated with doping. Interestingly, of the references mentioned, all were in respectable publication forums but one in particular, Kayser, Smith and Miah (2005), was published the journal *Lancet*, one of the most respected medical journals in the world, and the Kayser and Smith (2008) article included signatories from over 30 experts from around the world who agreed in principle that an alternate model to the current anti-doping regimen is warranted. The harm reduction model calls for more careful and open medical supervision, with greater athlete input, into the many practices—drug use included but also many others—that put athletes' bodies at risk. Athletes, the authors claim, would be able to make more informed choices about what risks to take, or not, and would be able to do so with the best medical supervision possible. However, such a model is virtually impossible under the current regime, in which doping is considered unquestionably unacceptable while most other practices—some of which put athletes' bodies at greater risk than many of the substances on prohibited drug lists—are regarded as acceptable and a "natural" part of training and competition.

"Sportsmanship" today is something far removed from what the defenders of amateurism envisioned for the "sportsmanlike" athlete. The point of this essay has been to document the changing conceptions of sportsmanship and how old conceptions of amateurism were the basis for the creation of doping rules. Applying something like the harm reduction model just mentioned to the issue of doping would bring an important sport policy more in line with the reality of what high-performance sportsmen and sportswomen are doing today and the dominant values and practices in international, high-performance sport. Such a model would not take us back to older notions of sportsmanship as they were envisioned by former IOC Presidents Coubertin, Baillet-Latour, or Brundage, but of course those notions are long gone anyway. But it would take into consideration what "sportsmanship" has become in the late-twentieth and early-twenty-first centuries. In other words, it would take in the account that "sportsmanship" is an ever-shifting historical concept.

Bibliography

Bannister, Roger. 1964. "The Meaning of Athletic Performance," pp. 71–72 in *International Research in Sport and Physical Education*, edited by Ernst Jokl and Emanuel Simon. Springfield, IL: Thomas.

Bascomb, Neal. 2004. *The Perfect Mile: Three Athletes, One Goal, and Less Than Four Minutes to Achieve It.* Boston: Houghton Mifflin.
Beamish, Rob. 2011. *Steroids: A New Look at Performance-Enhancing Drugs.* Santa Barbara: Praeger.
Beamish, Rob, and Ian Ritchie. 2004. "From Chivalrous 'Brothers-in-Arms' to the Eligible Athlete: Changed Principles and the IOC's Banned Substance List." *International Review for the Sociology of Sport*, 39 (4):355–371.
_____. 2006. *Fastest, Highest, Strongest: A Critique of High-Performance Sport.* London: Routledge.
de Kruif, Paul. (1945). *The Male Hormone.* New York: Harcourt, Brace.
Dimeo, Paul. 2007. *A History of Drug Use in Sport 1876–1976: Beyond Good and Evil.* London: Routledge.
Gleaves, John. 2011. "Doped Professionals and Clean Amateurs: Amateurism's Influence on the Modern Philosophy of Anti-Doping." *Journal of Sport History*, 38 (2):237–254.
Gleaves, John, and Matthew Llewellyn. 2014. "Sport, Drugs and Amateurism: Tracing the Real Cultural Origins of Anti-Doping Rules in International Sport." *The International Journal of the History of Sport*, 31 (8):839–853.
Guttmann, Allen. 1984. *The Games Must Go On: Avery Brundage and the Olympic Movement.* New York: Columbia University Press.
Henne, Kathryn. 2014. "The Emergence of Moral Technopreneurialism in Sport: Techniques in Anti-Doping Regulation, 1966–1976." *The International Journal of the History of Sport*, 31 (8):884–901.
Hunt, Thomas M. 2011. *Drug Games: The International Olympic Committee and the Politics of Doping, 1960–2008.* Austin: University of Texas Press.
Kayser, Bengt, Alexandre Mauron, and Andy Miah. 2005. "Legalization of Performance-Enhancing Drugs." *Lancet* 366:S21.
_____. 2007. "Current Anti-Doping Policy: A Critical Appraisal." *BMC Medical Ethics*, 8 (2). Retrieved June 25, 2015 (http://www.biomedcentral.com).
Kayser, Bengt, and Aaron Smith. 2008. "Globalization of Anti-Doping: The Reverse Side of the Medal." *British Medical Journal*, 337:85–87.
Mangan, J.A. 2012. *"Manufactured" Masculinity: Making Imperial Manliness, Morality and Militarism.* London: Routledge.
Mills, C. Wright. 1959. *The Sociological Imagination.* New York: Oxford University Press.
Møller, Verner. 2010. *The Ethics of Doping and Anti-Doping: Redeeming the Soul of Sport?* London: Routledge.
O'Neil, Paul. 1954. "Duel of the Four-Minute Men." *Sports Illustrated*, August 16:20–23.
Ritchie, Ian. 2014. "Pierre de Coubertin, Doped 'Amateurs' and the 'Spirit of Sport': The Role of Mythology in Olympic Anti-Doping Policies." *The International Journal of the History of Sport*, 31 (8):820–838.
Todd, Jan, and Terry Todd. 2001. "Significant Events in the History of Drug Testing and the Olympic Movement: 1960–1999," pp. 65–128 in *Doping in Elite Sport: The Politics of Drugs in the Olympic Movement*, edited by Wayne Wilson and Edward Derse. Champaign, IL: Human Kinetics.
Todd, Terry. 1987. "Anabolic Steroids: The Gremlins of Sport." *Journal of Sport History*, 14 (1):87–107.
Waddington, Ivan. 2006. "Changing Patterns of Drug Use in British Sport from the 1960s," pp. 119–143 in *Drugs, Alcohol and Sport*, edited by Paul Dimeo. London: Routledge.
Wrynn, Alison M. 2006. "A Debt Paid Off in Tears: Science, IOC Politics and the Debate about High Altitude in the 1968 Mexico City Olympics." *The International Journal of the History of Sport*, 23 (7):1152–1172.

Cheating in Sport
Its Meanings and Moral Ambiguities

DANNY ROSENBERG

Cheating in sport is an elusive concept to describe and explain accurately because it contains multiple meanings and various assumptions, its normative content is questionable, and its application to sport examples is not always clear. Numerous questions arise when considering the idea and ethics of cheating in sport. Does cheating require the intentional violation of rules or the violation of any rules at all? Which rules, if any, the written or unwritten ones or both? What sort of advantage is achieved by the cheater and is this gain always unfair? Who benefits from cheating in sport? Is deception a necessary feature of cheating? What normative status does cheating possess and is cheating always wrong? Do athletes have a moral duty not to cheat? What do competitors agree to with regard to cheating? What role do officials play in detecting cheating and cheaters? How important are the purposes and specific contexts of sport to know what counts as cheating?

This essay aims to answer these questions from philosophical and ethical perspectives, but in doing so, it will become evident the answers will be less than conclusive. If one begins by trying to define cheating in sport, most definitions fall short because infallible necessary and sufficient conditions do not exist, and exceptions and counterexamples can be identified to show that not all presumed instances of cheating are in fact cheating cases. Part of the problem lies in characterizing sport itself as a human enterprise comprised of constitutive features, like certain core rules that make sport possible as a distinct practice, and conventional structures that situate and give meaning to sport from historical, social, political and economic vantage points. From these markings arise differing viewpoints about the normative qualities of sport that inscribe its moral standing which can account for expected and acceptable behavior and those actions some call cheating that can be morally censured.

The first section, called "A Characterization of Cheating in Sport," will be a lengthy critique of an article by Feezell (1988) whose analysis of cheating in sport is comprehensive and still relevant. Specific issues like the status of constitutive rules, his expression "prescriptive atmosphere," intention, deception, and latent agreement will be addressed. In the next section, entitled "Three Theories of Sport and Their Implications for Cheating and Fair Play," I will briefly explicate three theories—formalism, conventionalism and broad internalism—that circumscribe and may help explain or perhaps confound the nature of cheating in sport in terms of fair play and its moral standing. The third section, called "Character Types in Sport," will delineate different types of characters who participate in sport to distinguish the motives and conduct of the cheater from other athletes who seek or express alternative purposes when playing. The final section, "Summary and Conclusion," will recap the main features of cheating in sport and suggest why this concept continues to vex sport theorists.

A Characterization of Cheating in Sport

According to Rosenberg (1994), Feezell (1988) intuitively feels those who advocate cheating in sport or see there is nothing morally wrong or unfair with cheating are mistaken (see Leaman 1988; Lehman 1988). Drawing from meanings of cheating based on conventional wisdom and clear-cut cases, Feezell's approach is to describe "what we mean by cheating" and not stipulate "what cheating means" by way of necessary and sufficient conditions (p. 67). He mentions the non-sport examples of the tax-cheat and a child who cheats at cards and concludes, "the concept of cheating will have a great deal to do with breaking rules, the intention to gain an unfair advantage, deception, and issues of character" (p. 58).

At least three assumptions contained in these cases require comment. First, the examples indicate that the unfair advantage favors the cheater, and in most instances this is true. However, someone may cheat so others gain an advantage. Teammates in sport sometimes have the opportunity to do this. Hsu (1999) rightly observes that even here the cheater benefits directly or indirectly because the cheater and teammate share the partisan goal of trying to win. Still, when a loss is a foregone conclusion, there may be instances where cheating for a teammate who is trying to break an individual scoring record does not benefit the cheater. Such a player might be called an altruistic or selfless cheater.

The preceding discussion may lead to the question, when is a person capable of cheating? One can reasonably assume that a child who cheats at cards already comprehends enough of what it means to play the game to then intentionally violate rules, act with deception, undermine tacit agreements and expectations, and perhaps show disrespect to the game and others. The cheat also knows the important connection between winning and adhering to the rules, and if not, she would likely not appreciate the character and integrity (moral) implications from cheating-like conduct. For the young person who is capable of cheating, an explanation of the wrongness of cheating and part of the lesson in moral education might include MacIntyre's (1984) observation, "Now if the child cheats, he or she will be defeating not me, but himself or herself" (p. 188).

Finally, one can presuppose that cheaters only hold a belief that their violations of rules and latent agreements and acts of deception will lead to favorable outcomes (Simon, 1988). This statement is a non-moral one because the intentions of the cheater do not always succeed. Cheating in games usually guarantees momentary or partial unfair gains, whereas overall winning may still elude the cheater. Thus, in many such instances, the general uncertainty of games remains intact until the end of the contest, despite some temporary shifts of advantage due to cheating behavior.

Feezell (1988) then discusses cheating and clear-cut sport-specific cases like unfair score-keeping, violating eligibility rules, hiring biased officials, and tampering with equipment. He is wrong however to count eligibility rule violations as constitutive of sport because even a knowingly ineligible player, while a cheat, when actually playing the game need not engage in any unfair play. This is so because the means by which eligible and ineligible athletes pursue the goals of the game are not necessarily and substantively different. Breaches of the core elements of sport like tampering with equipment or field dimensions or clearly violating proscribed means (e.g., use of the hand in soccer) are usually identified as clearer cases of cheating.

Another feature of cheating in sport beyond the scope of this essay to detail in length, is the one made by Rosenberg (1995) who identifies two general domains where cheating in sport occurs, namely incontest and noncontest forms of cheating. If cheating generally refers to deliberate, deceptive violation of rules that seek unfair gains, then incontest cheating occurs during competitive moments in a contest. Noncontest cheating occurs before, after or during breaks in a contest. Moreover, differently structured sports like team, individual, exhibition and parallel sport contests are aligned with each of these realms of cheating. For example, most team sports offer possibilities for players to engage in incontest cheating that transpire when performing in games. Actions like holding, bumping, touching the net, stepping on boundary lines, trapping balls, feigning an injury and the like can be executed without being detected and may involve cheating. Multiple players, congestion on the field, officiating constraints and dynamic play often create conditions where incontest cheating can occur. Most individual sports, like singles tennis or badminton matches, or exhibition sports like figure skating and diving, or parallel-run sports like swimming and track offer significantly fewer or no opportunities to engage in incontest cheating. Instead, if cheating occurs in these sports it is typically the noncontest variety that ensues before, after or during a break in the competition. It should be noted that these categories of cheating are not mutually exclusive, and in fact, in team sports there is always the opportunity to engage in noncontest forms of cheating. On the other hand, the distinction has greater merit when referring to cheating by officials. Bribed officials in team sports who engage in incontest cheating can steer the course of a game as it unfolds toward a particular result. Corrupt officials in individual, exhibition and parallel-run competitions usually cheat outside of the performance moments of a contest.

Whether one discusses incontest or noncontest forms of cheating in sport, Feezell (1988) recognizes that all cheating occurs in a particular climate. He calls this the "prescriptive atmosphere" of sport. This expression defines "competitive expectations in which the participants may gain a competitive advantage, and perhaps win, only in the context of an underlying equality expressed in the rules" (p. 60). He also says that "the prescriptive atmosphere is only partly constituted by the central, explicit rules of the game in question" (p. 60; see also D'Agostino 1981; Reddiford 1985). This notion tries to account for aspects of sport which are informally accepted and expected as historically "part of the game" or as "tricks of the trade" and may assist in delineating between cheating and noncheating behaviors. In baseball, excessively watering down the base paths, letting the grass grow high, erasing chalk lines so the batter's foot can be positioned outside the box, trapping catches in the outfield, and "framing" pitches by catchers are understood as part of the prescriptive atmosphere of baseball and may not be seen as overt instances of cheating. On the other hand, use of a corked bat would more clearly count as a case of cheating in baseball (Feezell 2004). By contrast, the prescriptive atmosphere of golf is more formal and less fluid and intolerant than baseball because the former in part developed historically as a sport of honor. Yet, how helpful is the prescriptive atmosphere in distinguishing between cheating and noncheating actions in sport, and who decides which actions are deemed "part of the game"?

Feezell (1988) believes the prescriptive atmosphere is useful in distinguishing between acceptable and expected actions in sport and those that are not, even those that are technically illegal. It can also serve as a yardstick or frame of reference, albeit a loose and evolving one, to decide what is or is not cheating. He writes, "With regard to judgments concerning cheating we must decide, based on the central explicit rules and the traditions of the sport that outline certain latent agreements, what sort of behavior is reasonably expected in pursuit of victory" (p. 61). As to who is qualified to make such judgments, he defers to informed and knowledgeable people in the sport community to decide which actions will be tolerated and which will be shunned, perhaps even banned. The prescriptive atmosphere is crucial for understanding the nature of cheating in sport because it shows that cheating behavior is more than simply violating rules.

Examples in sport some call cheating but are not according to Feezell (1988) are numerous. So delay strategies in games, psychological tactics, unruly conduct (e.g., jawing, stare-downs and screaming at officials) and those instances where expected rule violations occur are not genuine instances of cheating. As mentioned, breaking rules is not sufficient for cheating because expected conduct may create no distinct advantage and is part of the latent agreement the sport community accepts. For example, a certain amount of violence via the institutionalization of fighting is expected and accepted in professional male ice hockey. This in turn creates a prescriptive atmosphere whereby some hockey players deliberately try to get away with engaging in other forms of violence to gain strategic advantages. Along the same lines, Feezell (1988) believes the climate in baseball is such that the spitball may not be considered cheating, again, because it is a widely known, expected and accepted part of the game. He therefore concludes, "cheating essentially involves the intent to gain an unfair advantage" (p. 65).

Many writers on the subject define cheating as intentional behavior (Lueschen 1976; McIntosh 1979; Wertz 1981; Thomas 1983; Fraleigh 1984, 1988; Delattre 1988; Pearson 1988; Hsu 1999). Consider Simon's (1991) assertion, "It is natural to identify cheating with violation of the rules of the game but that surely is not enough. Thus, one who unknowingly violates the rules is not a cheater. At the very least, the violation must be intentional, and designed to secure an advantage for the cheater or for some other participant for whom the cheater is concerned" (p. 40). The idea that the cheater commits rule violations deliberately is for many an uncontested condition and Feezell's account assumes as much. The more difficult argument is one which supports the feasibility of unintentional cheating. Wertz (1981) is one author who tries to make this argument by raising a specific example in tennis and in a very detailed analysis that cannot be taken up here. Rosenberg (1995) criticizes Wertz's position by showing the example really involves errors in judgment, and the argument Wertz proposes is circular in two senses, one of which is that cheating is deliberate, much like murder but unlike manslaughter even though murder and manslaughter involve the killing of another human being.

Besides this specific debate, few can deny that, in many instances, especially in sport, it is often impossible to know what players intend or how much they intend when merely observing their conduct. Sometimes asking athletes what they intended in and by their actions remains unclear because of situational factors, lack of attentiveness, or simply reacting too quickly to intend anything specific. Some athletes who genuinely have no intention of cheating in a premeditated sense may find themselves in circumstances where undetected by the officials they knowingly touch the line in football, the ball with the hand in soccer or the net in volleyball, and score a game-winning touchdown, goal or point. Whether intentional or not at the point of wittingly violating a rule, players in this predicament have to decide whether or not to accept or reject the touchdown, goal or point. One could say the preceding decision and subsequent action to admit to the violation or keep silent requires intentional reflection on the part of the player.

While intention is difficult to ascertain with precision, those who cheat in sport more often than not do so in a deliberate manner and know more or less what violations are being committed and what advantages are being sought. And if a significant, game-changing rule violation becomes known to the athlete alone, the matter of cheating may return as a serious consideration to the player in question. In elite sport today, with its pervasive and expansive media coverage and surveillance, athlete behavior is scrutinized in such detail, incontest cheating is sometimes very hard to mask. This last point leads to another contentious element related to cheating in sport, namely, deception.

A number of writers refer to deception as a significant, but not a necessary, feature of cheating (Luschen 1976; McIntosh 1979; Pearson 1988; Fraleigh 1988; Simon 1991). Reddiford (1998) states, "Where cheating is, deceit, fraud, trickery, guile, lying and injustice are often to be found" (p. 227). He describes the cheat as one who seeks gains by often misrepresenting his actions through hiding his real motives, intentions and purposes. In this sense, Connor (2011) asserts, "So cheating is not rule-breaking, which is a normal part of the game, but the pretence of rule-following" (p. 173). Moreover, cheating only succeeds if the victims of such behavior or game officials believe all is well in the particular social circumstance or contest. While many argue deception is an important component of cheating in sport, the idea of open cheating is also discussed. Luschen (1976) for one explains that open cheating can occur when minor violations take place, like wrong calls, disruptive play and interference, and these may transpire as unconcealed forms of cheating when they are effectively ignored by players, officials, coaches and others. More recently, Russell (2014) has challenged the idea that deception is central to an account of cheating in sport as part of his overall critique of the efficacy of the very concept of cheating. He writes, "There are enough different and plausible examples to indicate that any sport-specific or stipulated definition of cheating that incorporates deception as an element will be seriously inadequate and question-begging" (p. 307). For example, if in soccer a handball by a defensive player in her own box goes undetected by the referee and her team wins by a goal, there may be no attempt by the player to deceive anyone. Russell makes the distinction between not be detected and overt conduct by the player to deceive to show that deception need not be part of cheating behavior. This example and others like it may only apply to incontest cheating; perhaps the same could not be said with regard to noncontest cheating.

It may be unreasonable to say that if in advance of a contest one seriously tampers with equipment or field dimensions or bribes officials that not being spotted precludes any active deception on the part of the cheater in these cases. Surely these instances are not conducted openly, and if detected, how could the cheater claim no deception is involved? If we return to the idea of open cheating, Simon (1991) asserts, "A competitor who has power over the other competitors may cheat quite openly" (p. 40). It is not clear from this statement the kind and degree of power this contestant possesses. If employees play golf with the boss and he openly cheats by kicking his ball from the rough onto the fairway due to his power as the boss, this sort of power has nothing to do with sport. On the other hand, a superior or domineering player who expresses his power through performance and openly cheats is a possibility in sport. Legendary professional ice hockey player Gordie Howe has been accused of being such a player (Maggio 2014). Still, open cheating has its limits.

If open cheating of the soccer handball variety mentioned above became widespread, in all likelihood, it would not be tolerated by the sport community in most instances. Grossly undermining the system of rules generally accepted by participants and nonparticipants would terminally influence the institution and practice of sport if cheating involved mostly unconcealed activity. For this reason, Luschen (1976) writes, "the cheater makes every effort to keep the system focused on the goals of the contest, and to keep the means for achieving those goals intact, so that the undetected cheater appears to be protected by the system" (p. 67). Open cheating is a possibility in sport, but it cannot be consistently and widely maintained as part of the sport practices of most athletes. It is more likely then that cheating behavior is carried out deceptively whether in or outside of the contest.

A related point to this discussion concerns the good, professional or strategic foul where a player deliberately and openly violates a rule to incur a penalty. Even as strong a critic of the good foul as Fraleigh (1988) does not label the good foul as an instance of cheating, since, according to his view, the cheater commits rule violations and actively deceives to avoid any penalty. His objection to the good foul rests in part on issues related to the spirit of the rules, actions and tactics which are not positively prescribed, and the agreement all participants comply with to avoid the use of proscribed means while playing and to subscribe to necessary and permitted means only. One may agree with Fraleigh that the good foul is not cheating, yet still find Simon's (1991) analysis of the strategic foul and the function of rules with penalties more cogent and convincing. It would be beyond the scope of this essay to detail Simon's argument here, but his distinction between game penalties as prices rather than as sanctions contains important implications. Therefore, based on the issue of deception, the good foul may have little or nothing to do with cheating, and arguments for its wrongfulness must be based on separate grounds.

The relative importance of deception in the above discussion does not refer to another dimension of cheating seen as a violation against some type of latent agreement held by those in the sport community (Rosenberg 1995). Namely, cheating, which is often secretive, breaches a general understanding that those involved in sport abide by written and unwritten rules that sustain the activity. There is no formal promise-breaking here or a breach of an explicit contract, yet those who cheat undermine tacitly agreed-upon ways and conditions in which a given sport is to be played. Feezell (1988) perhaps overstates the consequences of subverting this latent agreement when he asserts, "Cheating lies in the extreme described by 'destruction of the game,' because it involves such central violations of the game, as defined by written rules and customs" (p. 66). While one can make a case to say cheating doesn't always destroy the game, it can certainly do so in some instances. In many other circumstances though, it may seriously alter the forms of reasonable expected behavior in sport.

In part, these shared expectations are contained in the latent agreement in sport and cheating may not eliminate all these expectations. The type, degree and seriousness of cheating practices obviously enter into this calculation. If cheating mostly occurs as unexpected, rule-violating and deceptive behavior, identifying such conduct may be difficult. Recall, most cheaters want the game to proceed as usual. They act covertly in the system of sport, abide by most of the rules, and this state of affairs protects them from being exposed. As Suits (1978) points out, "[the cheater] continu[es] to operate in terms of the institution [and this] is a necessary condition for his exploitation of the game and of his opponent" (p. 46). Most often, cheaters deliberately try to avoid drawing attention to themselves, and, instead, they create a smokescreen that all is normal in the game. When this effort is successful it is mostly because cheaters rely on the implicit pledge most of the sport community has taken to uphold the latent agreement of a particular game. The latter may indicate and distinguish well enough those actions in the game which are expected, reasonable and permissible, and those that are not.

The tacit agreement issue in general is a difficult one to contend with because at times it can delineate cases where cheating has occurred, but in other situations, it seems no clear answer can be given. Rosenberg (1995) raises the following example and analyzes it. Many decades ago, during day games at home, a major league pitcher was known to wear a white, long-sleeved undershirt so his arm and the ball blended with white sheets and linens hanging from tenement buildings directly behind him outside the stadium. As a result, batters were at a disadvantage because they had no time to "read" the ball once the throw was made. How should such an open, yet unexpected, move that does not violate the rules and creates such an advantage be judged? Perhaps the latent agreement permits this type of behavior? And is this a case of cheating?

Kretchmar (1992) argues that "tricks of the trade" in baseball like in the preceding example demonstrate one's ability to pretend to play the game, since no new novel sport skills are being performed. Further, such "unreadable" pitches exploit inherent weaknesses in baseball in terms of the rules not covering every circumstance, flaws in human perception, and they place a premium on winning by unusual means, and may lead to situations where results are incomparable and victory hollow. As Kretchmar (1992) explains:

> I want our contest to be a fair one. But if you are playing baseball combined with bits of somethings other than baseball, while I am only playing baseball—or if you and I are both playing something other than baseball to different and unpredictable degrees—it is likely in either case that we will literally be playing two different games. You and I will be using two set of means to achieve the same end. And our results will be incomparable. In which case any victory is actually meaningless [p. 11].

While the preceding quote is reasonably cogent, one might ask, why can't all players agree to play baseball combined with bits of something other than baseball? One may presume that if one player has this option, why not all? This may be part of the latent agreement in serious competitive sport, whereby players, coaches and officials agree to follow enough of the rules and goals of a specific sport, but they also agree to accept nonsport elements into the game. This may be sufficient to ensure a fair contest, use of similar means, and comparable results and meaningful victories can still be preserved. Issues related to the kind, degree and amount of nonsport bits a game can tolerate may remain a pressing concern. However, the sport community can monitor, accept and reject how much, to what extent and what types of these bits will enter into games. Thus, the latent agreement element is significant if one holds that cheating is more than just the violation of rules. The agreed-upon way the sport community practices and appreciates games may include episodes where nonskilled sport-specific actions don't permanently or seriously damage the character of sport. Yet, the cheater, in my view, exploits the necessarily unclear parameters of the tacit agreement by stepping outside of this pact in the act of cheating.

Three Theories of Sport and Their Implications for Cheating and Fair Play

There may be other ways to comprehend the nature of cheating in sport by briefly reviewing three theories—formalism, conventionalism and broad internalism—that explain the basic character of sport itself and the notion of fair play. Formalism is the view that the rules alone define sport by prescribing necessary conditions and skills in order to meet the goals of a contest (Fraleigh 2014). Official dimensions of ice rinks and equipment, plus skills such as skating, passing, stickhandling and shooting are required in ice hockey toward the goal of putting the puck in the net. The rules also prohibit certain actions like holding, tripping and slashing that incur penalties. Given this description, formalists hold the basis of cheating involves the intentional violation of rules. Athletes are contracted to abide by the rules and if they intentionally violate them, they are no longer, logically speaking, playing the game and are doing something else. This also means a cheater can never claim to have won a contest (Fraleigh 1984; Morgan 1987; Pearson 1988; McFee 2004; Connor 2011). Fair play is achieved on the formalist account when all players adhere strictly to the rules that define the sport, and, when regulative rules are breached, all players accept the penalties so play may continue under fair conditions for all.

Another popular way to understand sport is to appreciate its historical and social contexts, and the customs and traditions developed within it. This view is sometimes called conventionalism and refers to the ethos of sport and is similar to what Feezell (1988) above calls the "prescriptive atmosphere" (see D'Agostino 1981; Tamburrini 2010). Conventionalists hold that all rule-governed activities like sport develop over time and reflect societal influences and conditions. This means rules are contextualized, interpreted, enforced and may be expressed differently from the rulebook once implemented. For example, under the formal rules basketball is defined as a noncontact sport, yet there is a tremendous amount of contact during the course of play. Conventionalists argue that even intentional rule violations may be unproblematic from a fair play perspective, and cheating may not be such a negative factor in sport (Leaman 1988; Tamburrini 2010; Upton 2011). To test the soundness of this contention, Loland (2005) analyzes intentional ethos violations to determine whether or not they are acceptable, including Maradona's famous "hand of God" goal in the 1986 World Cup final which Tamburrini (2010) supports as morally unproblematic. As a direct criticism of this last point, Connor (2011) explains that a handball in soccer "introduces inanity and unmeaning into the heart of the game, evaporating the consensus that is the only thing that keeps the game in being" (p. 180). Loland concludes that conventionalism (he calls this view contextualism) results in controversial positions like the preceding example and is akin to moral relativism (an outlook that claims there are no objective moral truths). This means issues of fair play are decided primarily in the way sport is practiced and based on its ethos (Sheridan 2003). For example, if the context of major league baseball is replete with all forms of deception, trickery and chicanery not covered by the rules, this kind of play is accepted by most, plus if enough players are rogues and scoundrels who try to and do get away with questionable actions, then fair play is sustained by the conventions of baseball. For die-hard conventionalists it is useless to determine what is fair or unfair by appealing to the written rules of the game, contrary to Hamilton (2004) who tries to do so in the case of baseball.

A third theory that describes and explains the character of sport and has implications for cheating and fair play is known as broad internalism (some call it interpretivism). This concept refers to the recognition "that rules require interpretation by general principles that are as much parts of sport and games as the rules themselves" (Russell 2014:319). On what basis should rules be interpreted? Some broad internalists hold that sport primarily involves the pursuit and comparative worth of athletic excellence and therefore the rules should be interpreted to promote those excellences. Actions that seriously subvert opportunities to display such excellences should be questioned from a moral point of view. Other broad internalists advance additional principles by which rules should be interpreted. For example, respect for rules and one's opponents, and trying one's best to win are or should be mutually held and expressed by all stakeholders invested in competitive sport. In fact, without mutual adherence to some or all of the preceding principles, the best kind of competitive sport is unlikely (Torres and Hager 2013). An interpretivist approach provides a powerful means to ensure competitive fairness and adjudicate between actions that do or do not reflect sport at its best. For example, referees and umpires may interpret rules during a contest to do what's best for the sport and fair to the players. Seriously tampering with equipment or deceptively violating a fundamental rule of a game like a handball in soccer can be called cheating, because these actions do not preserve and encourage the exhibition of sporting excellences, undermine basic rules, and show disrespect for the game and others. The issue of fairness is also maintained by broad internalism which encourages that the best interests of sport and the interpretation of rules be decided by the sport community through open, transparent discourse.

Character Types in Sport

To this point the discussion has covered major components of cheating in sport and three theories that account for the nature of sport, fair play and their implications for cheating conduct. Another useful task is to identify and describe typical characters in sport, including the cheater, to differentiate the varied motives and purposes athletes bring to, develop and express in sport. Based on Morgan, Meier and Schneider (2001), the following is a short summary of six such characters:

1. Good sports possess a certain attitude that upholds respect for the game, are concerned about good play and the well-played game, are gracious in victory and defeat, and share with opponents the values and spirit of sport. Good sports play fairly (to ensure good play) and try their best at all times.
2. Poor sports may play fairly but apply different standards to decide the quality of play. Poor sports take little responsibility for their poor play, and do not acknowledge the good play of opponents. They take too much credit for their good play and are too concerned with their own performance than a well-played game. Poor sports may abandon fair play and resort to cheating, or, if play is going badly, become spoilsports.
3. Gamespersons take up the attitude whereby their concern for winning is foremost. They uphold the letter but the not the spirit of the rules, consider permitted

what is not covered by the rules, and see penalties as prices for breaking rules as found in strategic fouling. Gamespersons maintain fairness by expecting opponents to play the same way they do.

4. Spoilsports deliberately destroy the game for themselves and everyone else. If play is going badly for the child who owns the ball in a game, he or she would take the ball and go home. Among adults, spoilsports would be more subtle by insisting, for example, that technical rules be strictly followed in a friendly game which would disrupt or impede play.

5. Triflers do not care about the means and/or goals of sports. They might be on the court but they make no attempt to either execute appropriate actions and/or try to win. They may even be skilled, unlike novice players who may be less skilled but at least they try.

6. Cheaters show a disregard for fair play. They usually break rules with intent, try or hope not to get caught, and seek unfair advantages usually for themselves. Cheaters are preoccupied with the score, care less about the game, know that normal game conditions often shield them from detection, exploit game flaws and human frailties, and privilege themselves arbitrarily because they often cannot recommend their conduct to others. The behavior and character of cheaters are typically condemned on moral grounds and the breach of principles of fairness.

Conclusion

The last of these six characters of sport summarizes the main features of cheating in sport with regard to breaking rules with intent, deception, lack of fair play, respect for the game and opponents. As for the wrongness of cheating, much depends perhaps on whether or not one is a formalist, conventionalist or broad internalist. In the sport philosophy and ethics literature, no one theory is sound and powerful enough to conclusively decide what counts as cheating in sport and why cheating is wrong. I am empathetic to Russell's (2014) declaration that calling certain conduct in sport cheating neither alleviates imprecision nor justifies moral disapproval, and that its use in everyday language is mostly laden with emotion not conceptual clarity. I am also sensitive to some who see peculiar and bizarre scenes and behaviors in sport and wonder if the "cheating" thing has gotten out of hand, without being certain whether or not cheating exists and is wrong (McNamee 2009). Such skepticism and confusion about cheating in sport with reference to its meanings and moral ambiguities should redouble our resolve to find alternative principles and standards to understand cheating, condemn improper behavior and seek the very best sport has to offer.

Bibliography

Connor, Steven. 2011. *A Philosophy of Sport*. London: Reaktion Books.

D'Agostino, Frank. 1981. "The Ethos of Games." *Journal of the Philosophy of Sport*, 8:7–18.

Delattre, Edwin. 1988. "Some Reflections on Success and Failure in Competitive Athletics," pp. 271–276 in *Philosophic Inquiry in Sport,* edited by William J. Morgan and Klaus V. Meier. Champaign, IL: Human Kinetics.

Feezell, Randolph. 1988. "On the Wrongness of Cheating and Why Cheaters Can't Play the Game." *Journal of the Philosophy of Sport*, 15:57–68.

_____. 2004. "Baseball, Cheating, and Tradition: Would Kant Cork His Bat?" pp. 109–125 in *Baseball and Philosophy: Thinking Outside the Batter's Box,* edited by Eric Bronson. Chicago: Open Court.

Fraleigh, Warren. 1984. *Right Actions in Sport*. Champaign, IL: Human Kinetics.
_____. 1988. "Why the Good Foul Is Not Good," pp. 267–270 in *Philosophic Inquiry in Sport*, edited by William J. Morgan and Klaus V. Meier. Champaign, IL: Human Kinetics.
_____. 2014. "Cheating," pp. 341–343 in *The Bloomsbury Companion to the Philosophy of Sport*, edited by Cesar R. Torres. London: Bloomsbury.
Hamilton, Mark. 2004. "There's No Lying in Baseball (Wink, Wink)," pp. 126–138 in *Baseball and Philosophy: Thinking Outside the Batter's Box*, edited by Eric Bronson. Chicago: Open Court.
Hsu, Leo. 1999. "Cheating and Sport Rules." Paper presented at the 7th International Postgraduate Seminar on Olympic Studies, International Olympic Academy. Retrieved June 25, 2015 (http://www.geocities.ws/olympic_seminar7/papers/hsu.htm).
Leaman, Oliver. 1988. "Cheating and Fair Play," pp. 277–282 in *Philosophic Inquiry in Sport*, edited by William J. Morgan and Klaus V. Meier. Champaign, IL: Human Kinetics.
Lehman, Craig. 1988. "Can Cheaters Play the Game?" pp. 283–287 in *Philosophic Inquiry in Sport*, edited by William J. Morgan and Klaus V. Meier. Champaign, IL: Human Kinetics.
Loland, Sigmund. 2005. "The Varieties of Cheating—Comments on Ethical Analyses in Sport [1]." *Sport in Society*, 8 (1):11–26.
Lueschen, Gunter. 1976. "Cheating in Sport," pp. 67–77 in *Social Problems in Athletics*, edited by Daniel Landers. Urbana: University of Illinois Press.
MacIntyre, Alasdair. 1984. *After Virtue*, 2d ed. Notre Dame: University of Notre Dame Press.
Maggio, Andrew. 2014. "Top 25 Dirtiest Players in NHL History." Retrieved July 2, 2015 (http://www.thesportster.com).
McFee, Graham. 2004. *Sport, Rules and Values: Philosophical Investigations into the Nature of Sport*. London: Routledge.
McIntosh, Peter. 1979. *Fair Play: Ethics in Sport and Education*. London: Heinemann.
McNamee, Mike. 2009. "On Being 'Probably Slightly on the Wrong Side of the Cheating Thing.'" *Sport, Ethics and Philosophy*, 3 (3):283–285.
Morgan, William J. 1987. "The Logical Incompatibility Thesis and Rules: A Reconsideration of Formalism as an Account of Games." *Journal of the Philosophy of Sport*, 14 (1):1–20.
Morgan, William, J., Klaus V. Meier, and Angela J. Schneider. 2001. *Ethics in Sport*. Champaign, IL: Human Kinetics.
Pearson, Kathleen. 1988. "Deception, Sportsmanship, and Ethics," pp. 263–266 in *Philosophic Inquiry in Sport*, edited by William J. Morgan and Klaus V. Meier. Champaign, IL: Human Kinetics.
Reddiford, Gordon. 1985. "Constitutions, Institutions and Games." *Journal of the Philosophy of Sport*, 12:41–51.
_____. 1998. "Cheating and Self-Deception in Sport," pp. 225–239 in *Ethics and Sport*, edited by Mike McNamee and Jim Parry. London: E & FN Spon.
Rosenberg, Danny. 1995. "The Concept of Cheating in Sport." *International Journal of Physical Education*, 32 (2):4–14.
Russell, John. 2014. "Is There a Normatively Distinctive Concept of Cheating in Sport (Or Anywhere Else)?" *Journal of the Philosophy of Sport*, 41 (3):303–323.
Sheridan, Heather. 2003. "Conceptualizing 'Fair Play': A Review of the Literature." *European Physical Education Review*, 9 (2):163–184.
Simon, Robert. 1988. "Good Competition and Drug-Enhanced Performance," pp. 289–296 in *Philosophic Inquiry in Sport*, edited by William J. Morgan and Klaus V. Meier. Champaign, IL: Human Kinetics.
Simon, Robert. 1991. *Fair Play: Sports, Values, and Society*. Boulder: Westview Press.
Suits, Bernard. 1988. "The Elements of Sport," pp. 39–48 in *Philosophic Inquiry in Sport*, edited by William J. Morgan and Klaus V. Meier. Champaign, IL: Human Kinetics.
Tamburrini, Claudio. 2010. "The 'Hand of God,'" pp. 132–144 in *The Ethics of Sport: A Reader*, edited by Mike McNamee. London: Routledge.
Thomas, Carolyn. 1983. *Sport in a Philosophic Context*. Philadelphia: Lea & Febiger.
Torres, Cesar, and Peter Hager. 2013. "Competition, Ethics and, Coaching Youth," pp. 167–184 in *The Ethics of Coaching Sports: Moral, Social, and Legal Issues*, edited by Robert Simon. Boulder: Westview Press.
Upton, Hugh. 2011. "Can There Be a Moral Duty to Cheat in Sport?" *Sport, Ethics and Philosophy*, 5 (2):161–174.
Wertz, Spencer. 1981. "The Varieties of Cheating." *Journal of the Philosophy of Sport*, 8:19–40.

Sports, Leisure and Recreation in Prison

Tim Delaney

As described in "Sportsmanship: A Sociological Perspective," ideals of sportsmanship include a sense of fair play, competitiveness, self-discipline, persistence, trustworthiness, hard work, dedication, and obedience to authority, all of which are tied to a society's cultural morality. Sportsmanship it closely associated to morality because it represents the high standards of expected behavior—to be a good sport and play nicely and fairly with others. Sportsmanship, then, provides a code of acceptable behaviors which members of society should thrive to attain. It is generally believed that sportspersons who engage in behaviors opposite of the ideal may be described as poor sports. It is put forth here that criminals, at least most of them, would represent the polar opposite to the ideals of sportsmanship.

In this essay, we will take a look at the sports, leisure and recreation opportunities of incarcerated persons in United States correctional facilities (prisons) and the role they play within the correctional system. We begin by taking a quick glance at the incarceration rates in the United States.

Incarceration

A great number of Americans are committing crime. In fact, "over the past 20 years, authorities have made more than a quarter of a billion arrests, the Federal Bureau of Investigation estimates. As a result, the FBI currently has 77.7 million individuals on file in its master criminal database—or nearly one out of every three American adults. Between 10,000 and 12,000 new names are added each day" (Fields and Emshwiller 2014). Put another way, "by age 23, almost a third of Americans have been arrested for a crime.... That figure is significantly higher than the 22 percent found in a 1965" (Goode 2011). The Federal Bureau of Investigation (FBI), via its Uniform Crime Reports (UCR), is the nation's leading tracker of arrest statistics. The UCR Program "counts one arrest for each separate instance in which a person is arrested, cited, or summoned for an offense. The UCR Program collects arrest data on 28 offenses" but it does not track data on citations for traffic violations, runaways or "police contact with a juvenile who has not committed an offense" (*Federal Bureau of Investigation* 2015). To reach the near quarter-billion arrest statistic over the past twenty years cited above, the FBI (2015) reports that law enforcement made an estimated 12.4 million arrests in 2011; calculating fluctuations in each of the 20 years during the period equates to roughly a quarter-billion.

To be fair, most Americans are committing petty crime and are not incarcerated (Delaney 2014). Still, no other country in the world has a higher incarceration rate than the United States. "In the past 30 years, the United States has come to rely on imprisonment as its response to all types of crime. Even minor violations of parole or probation often lead to a return to prison" (Hartney 2006). In 2006, the United States had "less than 5 percent of the world's population but over 23 percent of the world's incarcerated people" (Hartney 2006). As reported by the Population Reference Bureau (PRB), prison populations are increasing in some parts of world but they tend to be around 100 prisoners per 100,000 population. Comparably, the PRB cites data from the Bureau of Justice Statistics (BJS) that the incarceration rate in the U.S. is 500 prisoners per 100,000 (Tsai and Scommegna 2012). Most U.S. inmates are males (90 percent), young (highest incarceration rates are for those in their 20s–early 30s), poorly educated (about 70 percent have not completed high school), and black or Latino (Tsai and Scommegna 2012). The Bureau of Justice Statistics (2014) reports that an "estimated 6,899,000 persons were under the supervision of adult correctional systems at year end 2013." This includes the more than 2.3 million Americans incarcerated in some sort of detention facility (e.g., jails and prisons) (Delaney 2014). In 2008, roughly 1.4 million of the then-United States' 2.2 million inmates were in either state or federal prisons (Delaney and Madigan 2009a). The BJS (2014) also reports that "about 1 in 35 adults (2.8 percent) in the United States was under some form of correctional supervision at yearend 2013.... About 1 in 51 adults was on probation or parole at yearend 2013." Interestingly, the 2013 figures cited by the BJS indicate a slight decline in the number of people under supervision, on parole and incarcerated. In 2009, data revealed that there were an estimated total of more than 7.3 million Americans in the corrections systems (Delaney 2012).

The demographics of incarcerated Americans are far more complicated than presented here: for example, drug offenders constitute 33 percent of the prison population (Webb 2009) and more than one in eight prisoners in the United States have a mental illness (Foster, Orr and Laing 2009), but the focus of this essay will be incarcerated males and the role of race on sports and leisure in prison.

Sports, Leisure and Recreation in Prison

My own interest in the role of sports and leisure is multi-faceted. I was born and raised and then moved back to a small Central New York city with the nickname "Prison City." I went to elementary school within a few hundred yards of the maximum-security prison (the inmates were generally among the most notorious violent offenders of the state of New York) and because of the proximity between the two we regularly had "prison break" drills, much like a fire drill. Many students walked by the prison on their way from home to school and back. My ride to school included a drive down the appropriately named Wall Street (the street ran parallel to the prison wall just a few yards away). When I was a child I heard my grandfather, who was once a cook in the prison kitchen, talk about how he got stabbed multiple times during a prison riot. His injuries never quite healed right and his disfigured left leg left a lasting impression with anyone who saw it.

Growing up in Prison City meant that everyone knew someone who worked behind bars. Some of the favorite "watering holes" were located across the street from the prison. The downtown location certainly left quite an impression on anyone who ventured to Prison City. For local residents, the prison was as much a part of the scenery as tall trees, the downtown river and the shops and restaurants. In other words, you didn't pay too much attention to it; that is, until a crisis occurred.

Academically, I've had an interest in what goes on behind closed doors for decades now. As a street gang researcher, I have often written about the role of the prison setting and gangism. Some of the most notorious street gangs have their origin in the correctional facilities of the United States. And certainly, a large number of gang members end up incarcerated. However, while still a graduate student in the early 1990s, I became interested in the prison setting because of my interest in sports and leisure. I analyzed data collected from my fellow University of Nevada–Las Vegas sociology Ph.D. candidate, Bud Brown. Brown had collected extensive research on inmates in the entire Nevada state prison system for different purposes. Brown's questionnaire survey data netted 1,770 respondents. My focus was on the data ascertained from the questions pertaining to sports and leisure. Some of the data results will be shared shortly.

Although I have mostly been using the term "prison" throughout this chapter, the correct contemporary judiciary term is "correctional facility." The two terms essentially mean the same thing, but the implications between the two are quite different. A prison is defined similarly in nearly all dictionaries as a place for the confinement and punishment of persons convicted of crimes, especially felonies. A prison inmate is looked upon as being in captivity, confined to a life of restriction. Prison confinement implies punishment for past illegal (unsporting) behaviors. Correctional facilities, as the root word "correct" would imply, are designed to alter, modify and correct illegal (unsporting) behaviors. According to *U.S. Legal* (2015), a "correctional facility is a term that may be used to refer to a jail, or other place of incarceration by government officials. They serve to confine and rehabilitate prisoners and may be classified as minimum, median, or maximum security facilities, or contain separate divisions for such categories of prisoners." Correctional facilities, like prisons, are places of confinement; however, a prison is designed to punish and correctional facility are designed to rehabilitate. With a focus on rehabilitation, correctional facilities are designed to provide educational and vocational programs as well as industries programs or a work release program. Clearly, for maximum security facilities, which generally contain life-sentenced inmates, work release programs are not an option.

Historically, formal and informal recreation programs in prison were discouraged and most forms of play were prohibited. "Play was not viewed as consistent with a philosophy of punishment that emphasized harsh, personal deprivation" (Frey and Delaney 1996:80). Taking a hard line against inmates had a number of negative consequences in many prison systems, especially the ever-growing over-crowded facilities. One the most significant consequences was the formation of prison gangs. Today, prison gangs are known to be in existence in nearly all correctional facilities in the United States. They are especially prominent in the California and Illinois prison systems which, not coincidentally, are the home states of the four U.S. nation gangs (Crips and Bloods in California and People and Folks in Illinois). Just as the first two nation gangs, the Crips and Bloods, formed in California, so too did most prison gangs first appear in the California corrections systems.

According to Fong (1990), the first prison gang formed in 1950 when a group of prisoners at the Washington Penitentiary in Walla Walla organized and took the name of the Gypsy Jokers. The largest of all prison gangs, the Mexican Mafia, or La Eme (*Eme* is Spanish for the letter "M"), was started around 1957 at Deuel Vocational Institution, a confinement facility for youthful offenders in Tracy, California (Delaney 2014). The original intention of the formation of La Eme was for Mexican-American inmates to have protection from the large number of black inmates. As more Los Angeles Hispanics were sent to prison, they were recruited into La Eme. Before long, Mexican-Americans outnumbered blacks in Los Angeles and in the California prison systems. By the late 1960s, La Eme was so powerful their influence extended to communities outside of prison walls. The Mexican Mafia is associated primarily with the highly populated Southern California (So CAL). They felt the need to not only dominate blacks and whites in prison but also other Mexican-Americans, including those from Northern California (No CAL). The Mexican-Americans in No CAL were mostly migrant workers who worked in rural farmlands. To protect themselves from La Eme, La Nuestra Familia (NF) was formed in Soledad Prison, CA, in the mid–1960s. In response to the organized Mexican-American prison gangs in California, the Black Guerrilla Family (BGF) was formed by former Black Panther member George L. Jackson in 1966 at San Quentin State Prison. Meanwhile, the power advantage that whites generally enjoyed in society (when compared to blacks and Hispanics) did not extend behind prison walls. Instead, whites are greatly outnumbered and as a result, the Aryan Brotherhood (AB) prison gang was formed. Originating in 1964, in San Quentin State Prison, Marin County, California, the early AB members were mostly motorcycle bikers and a few neo-Nazis. In the early 1970s, the Texas Syndicate (TS), also known as Syndicato Tejano, originated in California's notorious Folsom prison. TS was formed in direct response to the other California prison gangs—especially the Aryan Brotherhood and the Mexican Mafia—who were preying on native Texas inmates (Delaney 2014).

By the early 1970s, it became vividly apparent that many correctional facilities had to deal with inmates who were far more violent and had better connections to illicit activities outside prison walls (Welling 1994). Among the solutions floated to solve this new reality was to offer recreational activities as a means of alleviating the monotony of prison life and as a safety valve for inmates to release built-up emotions and tensions. "The National Advisory Commission on Criminal Justice Standards and Goals (1973) established standard policies and practices for recreation programs that included recommending that every institution employ a full-time director of recreation; that every offender be evaluated for interest in leisure services; that recreation programs provide some interaction opportunities with the outside community; and that a wide range of recreational activities be made available to inmates" (Frey and Delaney, 1996:80). What led to this change in philosophy? Proponents argue that sports and leisure programs in prison raise inmate morale, reduce boredom, and provide a "proper" avenue for blowing off or releasing pent-up frustrations. Among the more popular active forms of recreation involved lifting weights "in the yard," touch football, basketball, baseball, boxing, softball, and volleyball. Many inmates enjoy lifting weights because it has the potential to lift self-esteem (Foster 1995). Weightlifting also provided a tangible form of measurable competition and as a result competitions became very common. Weightlifting competitions come in a variety of forms including competitions between inmates and non-inmates, inmates and inmates in the same prison and against inmates from other prisons. In the 1980s a number of prison weightlifting competitions were conducted under the auspices of a National Postal Tournament conducted by mail rather than by face-to-face competition (Telander 1988). Competition officials at various competing prisons would record the scores of competitors (inmates) and mail them off to each other to determine a winner. Today, of course, officials can use computers or smart phones.

During the late 1980s and early 1990s, however, there was a strong movement in the United States among national, state and local politicians to get "tough on crime." Notions of rehabilitation were replaced by penal punitiveness resulting in the elimination of many sports and leisure programs. The number one target of this penal movement was weightlifting, especially free weights. The get "tough on crime" concept included a fear of inmates who were hugely muscular because they were deemed as threats to the correctional officers and the general public if they were released from prison. In addition, the very idea of inmates with so much time on their hands that they could lift weights long enough to the point where they could get as big as so many had become without the assistance of anabolic steroids did not set right with the conservative ideology of this political time period.

It was in this climate that I decided to conduct research on the role of sports and leisure in prison. (Note: After I had conducted the data analysis, my UNLV mentor, James H. Frey, teamed up with me to write an article on my research that would be published in 1996.) As Mahon and Bullock (1991) explained, research on sports and leisure in the prison setting was virtually ignored by most academic disciplines including sociology, criminology, recreation, and physical education; they argued that this reality was unfortunate as such an inquiry could have theoretical and policy implications. Through the early 1990s, sport sociologists had researched a multitude of topics related to deviance in sport including the use of performance-enhancing, incidence of assaults, rapes, and related criminal activities by athletes, and the frequency of violence on-the-field and in the stands. But all these topics were studied in the conventional settings such as educational institutions or sports stadia, not prisons or jails.

There was limited research on sports and leisure activities available from the academic discipline of recreation. The research included the aforementioned idea that sports and leisure programs help to raise inmate morale, provide a relief from boredom, and as a means to displace aggressive behaviors against other inmates. There was also a belief that physical fitness programs could serve as a means of defense against interpersonal violence. Other potential functions of sports and leisure programs researched from the area of recreational studies include the idea that they serve as a valuable treatment for individual rehabilitation (Brayshaw 1974); provide inmates with the opportunity to experience the pleasures associated with non-prison life (Speckman 1981; Williams, 1981); and increase inmate morale by providing healthy activity that stimulates positive attitudes among inmates (Telander 1988). Corrections officials believe that sports can reduce medical expenses by improving the health of inmates (Dobie 2004). Recreation programs may also reduce recidivism because inmates have enhanced their self-esteem by participation in a lifestyle that is acceptable in the outside world (Brayshaw 1978; 1981). Most supporters of sport and recreation in prison argue that these activities serve as a safety valve or a way of "blowing off steam" or displacing aggressive energy in a legitimate manner (Mahon and Bullock 1991; Bartollas 1985; Leonard 1988). Thus, an inmate who vents his aggressive tendencies by exerting considerable energy lifting weights or hitting a baseball is less likely to assault a fellow inmate or correctional officer. Frey and Delaney (1996) state:

> Recreation and leisure programs relate to the safety of the institution by serving as a barometer of prison climate. Guards get a "feel" for the overall prison mood by observing how prisoners group together during leisure time. For example, if the groupings form along clearly racial lines then the possibility for conflict increases. If leisure groupings are racially integrated the climate may be less hostile. When there is extensive congenial interaction among various prisoners during leisure time, the guards know overall tension is low. The observation of recreation patterns gives prison administrators and guards the opportunity to detect potential conflict in the prison population. Tension management, skill enhancement, time management, and mood assessment are functions assigned to the place of sport and leisure in a prison setting. These activities augment prison control measures by providing a mechanism to promote the safety of prisoners and guards within the setting [p. 82].

Prison officials view sports and recreation time as something that has to be "earned." In that way, proper behavior is encouraged, as inmates who want recreation time learn to behave and follow the rules. Conversely, prison officials may take away recreational privileges for improper behavior. These functions of sports and leisure programs are especially important in maximum security facilities for obvious reasons. The prime idea that inmates who are serving life sentences (and especially consecutive life sentences) have little incentive to behave "properly" because officials cannot threaten them with the punishment of further prison time. Threatening to take away something they love to do, sports and leisure opportunities, is a good motivator to encourage sporting behavior.

In my research of the Nevada Department of Prisons, recreational activities were divided into two categories: active activities (weightlifting, jogging, handball and basketball) and passive activities (reading books, visiting other inmates, watching television, and playing cards). Frey and Delaney (1996) report that weightlifting and jogging were the most popular of the active activities. But the percentage of inmates who extensively (defined as more than 10 hours per week) lifted weights was just 18 percent and only 4 percent for those who jogged extensively. Passive activities such as reading, visiting other inmates, and watching television were far more popular than active activities. The percentage of those who engaged in passive activities extensively were led by those who watched television (43 percent), read books (39 percent), and visited other inmates (33 percent). That less than half of all inmates participated in active leisure pursuits puts into question the cathartic effect of recreation on the reduction of aggression. "It is not possible for significant tension release to take place if most inmates are either not participating in recreation or, if they do participate, do so in a passive manner. These results suggest that building friendships and social relationships are the most important outcomes of leisure participation, not tension release. Thus, leisure time can contribute to building solidarity or a sense of community among prisoners" (Frey and Delaney, 1996:84). Still, it was common for most state and federal prisons to have "extensive collections of free weights and weight machines through the 1980s," and inmates were allowed to "spend significant portions of their days bulking up" (Palmer 2011).

The idea of inmates getting big and strong at the taxpayers' expense upset a number of conservative lawmakers and throughout the mid–1990s a number of states introduced legislation to eliminate weightlifting, especially free weights. The 1994 elections gave the Republicans control of the House and the Senate. "Shortly after, Newt Gingrich took over as the new Speaker of the House, Congressman Richard Zimmer (R–New Jersey) introduced his No Frills Prison Act (HR 663), subtitled, 'Amendment to Prevent Luxurious Conditions in Prisons'" (Tepperman 2015:5). HR 663 would lead the charge on the national debate over prisoner privileges and access to weights (Tepperman 2015). Also in 1994, the Pryce-Stupak Amendments to HR 4092 (The Crime Bill) was introduced. Among the specifics of the proposed amendments were: prohibiting strength-training; forbidding prisoners from engaging in any activities designed to increase their physical strength or their fighting ability; and the removal of any equipment that would allow this to happen (*Pryce-Stupak Amendment* 1994). As Foster (1995) explains, in 1995, Freshman Representative Steve Chabot (R–Ohio) introduced an amendment to the No Frills Prison Act that would "put the punishment back into prison by making life behind bars less pleasant. Amenities from cable TV to girlie magazines are under fire, but of all the perks, weight lifting seems to rankle critics the most." Chabot's amendment would require the removal of barbells and weightlifting equipment from all federal prisons. Chabot said, "We need more books in prison and less weight-lifting equipment" (Foster 1995). A 1993 riot at Ohio's maximum-security prison in Lucasville wherein inmates used weights to smash through walls of two supposedly secure stairwells, where they killed an inmate and took three guards hostage, prompted Chabot's desire to eliminate weightlifting equipment from prisons. In March 1994, inmates at Rikers Island jail in New York City attacked guards with weights and benches, injuring 16 (Foster 1995). There were more incidents as well involving riots and the inmate use of weights and equipment that prompted the get tough on prisoners philosophy.

Palmer (2011) adds, "In 1996, an amendment to an appropriations bill expressly prohibited the federal Bureau of Prisons from purchasing 'training equipment for boxing, wrestling, judo, karate, or other martial art, or any bodybuilding or weightlifting equipment of any sort.' Many states, including California, made the same decision, either by statue or policy. These days, whatever free weights you'd find in U.S. prisons are decades old." Palmer adds that the free weights that do exist are generally chained to walls so that inmates cannot use either the free weights or the bars as weapons against other inmates or correctional officers.

Presently (2015), it is common for there to be all sorts of weightlifting and self-defense activities and competitions behind prison walls. There are some precautions, such as no dumbbells lighter than 35 pounds (to discourage attempts to use them as weapons in fights against other inmates or correctional officers) (Genis 2014) and limitations, such as no fancy spa equipment just basic power lifting equipment (Karnes 2013). In fact, there are all sorts of sports, leisure and recreational opportunities for inmates today. "Recreational programming is meant to provide inmates with physical, mental, and emotional outlets to enhance their well-being.... Advocates for prison recreation argue that recreation is used as a therapeutic tool, and it may reduce recidivism. The benefits and skills that inmates obtain from exercise, such as time management, wellness, stress relief, and anger management, will assist them in the community as well" (*Encyclopedia of Prisons & Correctional Facilities* 2012).

Among the many sporting opportunities for inmates today are softball competitions versus teams from outside of prison and prison rodeos. In the remainder of this essay we will look at a case study of a former student of mine who was on a softball team that played against a prison team at Collins Correctional Facility (NY) and the Angola Prison Rodeo which celebrated its 50th anniversary in 2014.

Case Study: Softball in Prison

There are occasions when civilian sports teams are willing, and allowed, to play against prison teams. Naturally, all the games are played on the home turf of the prison squads. It takes a relatively brave group of people to be willing to go inside a correctional facility and come close enough to inmates that they can literally reach out and touch them. Understandably, many civilian teams find it intimidating to play sports behind prison walls. The sound of the big heavy doors slamming shut instills a sudden sense of reality that is quite different from being in the general society. Civilian ball teams want to win when the play prison teams but many players may worry that the inmates may display acts of poor sportsmanship and seek out vengeance against them. Prison team members are unlikely to attack civilian team members because they are very grateful for the opportunity to compete against a team from the conventional society. Prison team members enjoy the privilege of being allowed to play against civilian teams and are unlikely to violate that trust. Furthermore, correctional officers stand-by at the ready in case something happens.

A former student of mine, Carolyn Agle, described to me her experiences as the only female on a softball team that went behind the walls of the Collins Correctional Facility in New York. Collins is a medium-security prison that is co-located with the Gowanda Correctional Facility, another medium-security prison, located north of Gowanda, in Collins, New York, at the southern end of Erie County. Agle was a 20-year-old college student and NCAA softball player at the time of her experience playing softball at Collins. "Although Agle recalls many 'cat calls' from the men (the inmates stood on the third base sideline and they were especially disappointed when she was ruled out on a close play at second base—because she would not find her way to third base) her overall experience was a very positive one" (Delaney and Madigan 2009b:203,206).

In an interview with Agle (which was first published in Delaney and Madigan's co-authored *Sports: Why People Love Them!*), she explained her reaction when she was told that she was going to be playing a game against an inmate team. Agle explained that she never became nervous until the drive to the facility. Team members all made jokes about playing behind prison walls as a coping device for their apprehension. Carolyn's teammate, Matt, the one who set up the game, worked at the facility so he had played games against the inmates before.

When asked whether any of her family members had expressed reservations about her playing a prison team, Agle said that her mom was nervous, especially because she would be the only female on the team. Her mom was especially concerned about the potential verbal abuse Agle would receive from the prisoners. Her dad, on the other hand, thought "it was cool and made jokes about it" and told her to play hard. Agle said that her step-dad tried to introduce a sense of humor about the matter. Carolyn and her teammate Shea were at her house prior to leaving for the game and Carolyn's step dad made some politically incorrect statements such as, "Shea, you better wear your cup backwards to avoid any 'problems,'" referring to him being taken advantage of by the inmates. Carolyn added, "Shea is really good looking and of the teammates knew that the inmates would love him and pick on him the most."

I asked Agle what it was like when she first approached the prison and how she reacted when the gate was locked behind her. Agle explained that she didn't say much and stood close to her friend Shea. Actually walking into the prison, rather than just thinking about it, certainly made the experience real. Agle said that is when she became nervous and anxious. "I think I was just nervous because I didn't know what to expect, and then once we were getting briefed by the woman who coordinates the prisoners' games versus other teams, she told us that once we got into the 'yard' there would be upwards to 500 prisoners out there with us. Then I became very nervous, because I only expected prisoners that we were actually playing to be on the field, but the hours that we were there was also the inmates' free time. When the prison gate locked behind us, I was like, well there's no turning back now." Agle describe the uniqueness of the playing field environment, "The prison setting included several windy tunnels and sidewalks to get to the yard and there were also a lot of brick walls ad barbed wire fences. There were a lot of guard towers as well. However, there were some really nice trees and shrubbery so I was surprised that it actually looked fairly nice and well-kept inside the prison."

As for any special instructions given to the team members by prison officials, Agle said that all their possessions (cleats, sneakers, gloves and any carried-in bags) were checked and that they had to sign many (liability) forms and turn over their driver's licenses in favor of visitor passes. Agle said that the officials made a strong point about making sure they never lost their visitor's pass (they were allowed to take them off while playing in the field). They were also warned that for whatever reason, inmates might try to sneak items into the team members' personal belongings and that it was their responsibility to make sure that did not happen. Agle recalled that the officials also warned them about the inmates taunting (e.g., talking smack) them and that it was all just a part of competition. The guard ended the instructions by saying, "have fun," Agle pointed out.

When asked what it was like to be the only female on the team and whether or not she felt scared or intimidated around the male inmates, Agle said she it was actually fun. Agle explained that males were always underestimating her softball abilities and she was happy to prove them wrong. Agle did admit, however, that were times when she felt intimidated by the inmates because she played right field. "About 20 feet behind where I stood was the caged-in area where the weights were, so the prisoners were working out right behind me. In addition, they would all walk through the outfield to get to the work out area instead of going around and they were walking within 5 feet of me and some of them would make comments, but it was funny." Carolyn sensed that the inmates were trying to intimidate her, but she stood her ground and acted tough. Clearly, she was the right person for the position.

Agle described one incident that kind of "freaked" her out. "When I was in right field and the inmates would walk by her on their way to lift weights some would say things like, 'I hope you guys kick their asses!' and I responded, 'Yeah, me too!' The only thing that really freaked me out though was one of the inmates walked by me and said, 'Hey Carolyn, how are you doing?' I was like, 'Uhhhhh, good.' It really scared me that he knew my name and I was wondering how he could have known that, so that worried me." Other than that, it was mostly the normal-type of banter to be expected between competing teams. Agle did mention one moment she really enjoyed, "The one time I ran down a fly ball and caught it the inmates all went wild—I think it was because a girl got a guy out, that whole gender thing. But it was an awesome feeling." Agle described the time when she singled, much to the delight of the inmates. However, when the next batter hit into a double play when Agle being called out on a close play at second, the inmates lined up on the third base line loudly booed the call. Agle said, "I was confused why they were booing because I thought they wanted to win. When I returned to my dugout all of my teammates were laughing and I asked what was so funny. That is when I learned that the inmates were booing because they didn't want to get thrown out because they wanted to watch me run to third base and remain at third base so that they could 'check me out.' Ha ha ha, so I thought that was kind of funny, typical guy behavior! But at the same time, I was so naïve I didn't realize that was the reason." Agle proudly pointed out that the next four times she got up to bat she also singled and scored all 4 times; thus, giving the inmates something to cheer about.

When asked about overall safety and who won the game, Agle reported that she felt safe nearly the entire time. The teams played a game that consisted of 4 innings of modified pitch and 4 innings of slow pitch. "We lost by a couple of runs. We were all mad that we lost but we knew going into it that the prisoners take these games really seriously and also they play together all the time because they have nothing else to do. So we were happy that we played a close game with them." As for the overall experience, Agle said that she had a lot fun and said that she would do it again. She also recommended the experience to other athletes in other sports under properly supervised conditions.

Agle also expressed that the notion of sportsmanship was on full display as both teams played to win, were competitive and played within the rules. Sports behind prison walls demonstrate that sportsmanship can exist even in the hostile environment of correctional facilities.

Angola Prison Rodeo

That inmates are allowed to participate in sports programs that involve civilians implies a sign of good behavior within the corrections system and such good behavior almost always translates to good sportsmanship during competition. In addition to civilian sports teams playing inmate teams, such as softball described above, as well as a variety of other sports, some prison sports programs are so elaborate that they involve civilian spectators. A great example of such a program is the Angola Prison Rodeo, billed as the "Wildest Show in the South!" Celebrating its 50th anniversary in 2014, the Angola rodeo has long entertained civilians from communities outside of its prison walls. The rodeos take place over one weekend in April and every Sunday in October.

The Angola Prison (Louisiana), known as "The Farm," is the largest maximum security prison in the United States. The facility is located in the marshy midsection of the state of Louisiana—the state with the highest rate of incarceration in the nation (Wertheim 2014; *The Economist* 2014). Louisiana is famous for its harsh sentencing and being stingy with its parole—roughly 73 percent of Angola's 6,250 inmates are serving life without parole sentences and the average sentence for the rest of the inmates is approximately 91 years (Wertheim 2014; *The Economist* 2014).

As for the "wildest show in the south" itself, the Angola Prison Rodeo is the longest running prison rodeo in the nation, having started in 1965 (*Angola Museum* 2015). The first arena, built by inmates, was quite small as the original idea of the rodeo was to provide entertainment for inmates and employees. In 1967, the rodeo first opened to the general public on a limited basis, but there were no stands at this time; instead, visitors sat on apple crates or the hoods of their cars to watch the performances (*Angola Museum* 2015). The 1967 and 1968 shows were so popular that a 4,500-seat arena was built for the

1969 rodeo. Over the years, the rodeo grew in popularity and added sponsorships. In 1972, the official Professional Rodeo Cowboys Association rules were adopted and as a result, the Angola Prison Rodeo is recognized as a professional rodeo. In 1997, spectator capacity increased by 1,000 seats and a roof was added to protect the spectators from the weather (rain or hot sun). Convict-run concessions serve up such southern delights as frogs' legs, crackling (roasted pig skin) and, for $4, fried Coke. Inmates also set up booths and sell their arts and crafts (Wertheim 2014). Concessions and arts and crafts just add to the festive feel of the Angola rodeo events. "Today, the inmate-built arena seats 11,000 and is invariably filled to capacity" (Wertheim 2014:8). The 2014 rodeos drew a total of 70,000 spectators with admission at $15 and car license plates in the parking lot indicates that people come from across the country to see this high level of rodeo competition (Wertheim 2014).

The rodeo participants are inmates dressed in the "old-school" black and white stripped convict uniform. There are 10 rodeo events at the Angola Prison Rodeo, most of which are potentially life-threatening. Among the events are "wild cow milking; guts and glory (inmates try to grab a poker chip tied to the head of a furious bull); and convict poker (four inmates play cards at a table in the arena; the last man to remain seated after a charging bull is released wins)" (*The Economist* 2014).

Detractors of the idea of inmates risking life (there has never been a rodeo fatality) and limb to entertain crowds of civilians compare the Angola Prison Rodeo to gladiators in the Colosseum via "plantation-style entertainment" (Wertheim 2014:8). Critics also point out that most of the participants involved in the rodeo are African American while the spectators are not. Of course, this is true in many American sports. Proponents, however, echo the belief of one of the primary themes of this chapter—that prison officials view sports, leisure and recreation participation opportunities as an incentive to encourage proper behavior (or good sportsmanship, if you will). Burl Cain, the Angola Prison warden since 1995, credits programs like the rodeo as a contributing force with making Angola safer than it used to be (the prison reports that inmate violence is down 80 percent since he took over as warden) (*The Economist* 2014). Specifically addressing the benefits to inmates who participate in the rodeo, Cain states, "They're king" (Wertheim 2014:10). The inmate participants themselves "speak enthusiastically of the fun, the competition and the diversion that attends the rodeo. If they end up in the medical ward, well, perhaps it was worth it" (Wertheim 2014:10). The inmates participate in the rodeo because it makes them feel good about themselves. Their self-esteem is enhanced when conventional citizens cheer their sporting skills.

As a point of interest, the winner of the 2014 All-Around Cowboy award was Gary Lindsey, 46, an inmate serving a 40-year sentence for armed robbery. "He wrestled steer to the ground. He rode a horse bareback. He stayed atop a thrashing bull for eight seconds. And for those few seconds, he was free" (Wertheim 2014:10). He was also given a chance to display acts of good sportsmanship.

Conclusion

There are a wide variety of sports, leisure and recreation opportunities available for inmates behind prison walls. There are active sporting opportunities such as basketball, baseball, softball, jogging, weight-lifting and even rodeos. There are also the more popular passive activities of reading, watching television and visiting other inmates. Prison officials have generally found that offering sports, leisure and recreational programs serves as an enticement to encourage proper and sporting behavior. After all, many inmates face life sentences and there has to be something that corrections officials can offer and then threaten to take away in order to encourage conforming behaviors. Inmates must, therefore, maintain the strictest adherence to the ideals of good sportsmanship or they risk losing all their sports and recreation privileges. The ability of prison officials to be able to dangle this carrot in front of inmates assures their cooperative behavior in general lockup as well.

In the specific case of a 20-year-old female college student who played as the only female on a softball team in a game of softball behind prison walls, it was revealed that the notion of sportsmanship was on full display as both teams played to win, were competitive and played within the rules. The Angola Prison Rodeo involves a great deal of good sportsmanship both on the part of the participating inmates and the civilian spectators.

Sports, leisure and recreation behind prison walls demonstrate that sportsmanship can exist even in the hostile environment of correctional facilities.

Bibliography

Angola Museum. 2015. "Rodeo History." Retrieved April 1, 2015 (http://angolamuseum.org).

Bartollas, Clemens. 1985. *Correctional Treatment Theory and Practice*. Englewood Cliffs, NJ: Prentice-Hall.

Brayhsaw, R. D. 1974. "Leisure Counseling for People in Correctional Institutions." *Leisurability*, 1:10–14.

_____. 1981. "The Future of Correctional Recreation." *Journal of Physical Education, Recreation and Dance*, 52 (4):53,58.

Bureau of Justice Statistics (BJS). 2014. "Correctional Populations in the United States, 2013." December 19. Retrieved April 2, 2015 (http://www.bjs.gov).

Delaney, Tim, and Tim Madigan. 2009a. *The Sociology of Sports: An Introduction*. Jefferson, NC: McFarland.

_____. 2009b. *Sports: Why People Love Them!* Lanham, MD: University Press of America.

_____. 2012. *Connecting Sociology to Our Lives: An Introduction to Sociology*. Boulder: Paradigm.

_____. 2014. *American Street Gangs*, 2d ed. Upper Saddle River, NJ: Pearson.

Dobie, Michael. 2004. "Frequently Asked Questions." *Newsday*, July 11.

The Economist. 2014. "The Angola Prison Rodeo: Life, Death and Raging Bulls." May 10. Retrieved April 3, 2015 (http://www.economist.com).

Encyclopedia of Prisons & Correctional Facilities. 2012. "Recreation Programs." Sage Reference. Retrieved April 4, 2015 (http://www.sagepub.com).

Federal Bureau of Investigation (FBI). 2015. "Uniform Crime Reports: Crime in the United States 2011." Retrieved April 5, 2015 (http://www.fbi.gov).

Fields, Gary, and John. R. Emshwiller. 2014. "As Arrest Records Rise, Americans Find Consequences Can Last a Lifetime." *Wall Street Journal*, August 18. Retrieved April 4, 2015 (http://www.wsj.com).

Fong, Robert S. 1990. "The Organizational Structure of Prison Gangs: A Texas Case Study." *Federal Probation*, 54 (1):36–43.

Foster, Brooke Lea, J. Scott Orr, and Laura Laing. 2009. "The Mentally Ill in Prison." *Parade*, June 28:6.

Foster, David. 1995. "Laws Target Prison Weight-lifters: Officials Wary of Stronger Ex-cons." *Ocala Star-Banner*, March 20:1A.

Frey, James H., and Tim Delaney. 1996. "The Role of Leisure Participation in Prison: A Report from Consumers." *Journal of Offender Rehabilitation*, 23 (1/2):79–89.

Genis, Daniel. 2014. "Barbells Behind Bars." *TNation*, July 30. Retrieved April 5, 2015 (http://www.t-nation.com).

Goode, Erica. 2011. "Many in U.S. Are Arrested by Age 23, Study Finds." *New York Times,* December 19. Retrieved April 5, 2015 (http://www.nytimes.com).

Hartney, Christopher. 2006. "Fact Sheet: U.S. Rates of Incarceration, a Global Perspective." *National Council on Crime and Delinquency.* Retrieved April 22, 2015 (http://www.nccdglobal.org).

Karnes, Chase. 2013. "Kentucky Strong: Prison Strong?" *Elitefts,* July 25. Retrieved April 23, 2015 (http://articles.elitefts.com).

Leonard, Wilbert. M. 1988. *A Sociological Perspective of Sport.* New York: Macmillan.

Mahon, M. J., and C.C. Bullock. 1991. "Recreation and Corrections: A Review of the Literature Over the Past Two Years." *Correctional Recreation Today,* 5: 7–15.

Palmer, Brian. 2011. "Do Prisoners Really Spend All Their Time Lifting Weights?" *Slate,* May 14. Retrieved April 15, 2015 (http://www.slate.com).

Pryce-Stupak Amendment. 1994. "Pryce-Stupak Amendment To HR 4092 (The Crime Bill) 19th and 20th April 1994." Retrieved April 14, 2015 (http://www.strengthtech.com).

Speckman, Ray. 1981. "Recreation in Prison—A Panacea?" *Journal of Physical Education, Recreation and Dance,* 52:46–47.

Telander, Rick. 1988. "Sports Behind the Walls." *Sports Illustrated.* Retrieved April 15, 2015 (http://www.correctionalprograms.com).

Tepperman, Alex. 2015. "We Will NOT Pump You Up: Punishment and Prison Weightlifting in the 1990s." *Academia.edu.* Retrieved April 22, 2015 (http://www.academia.edu).

Tsai, Tyjen, and Paoloa Scommegna. 2012. "U.S. Has World's Highest Incarceration Rate." *Population Reference Bureau.* Retrieved April 22, 2015 (http://www.prb.org).

U.S. Legal. 2015. "Correctional Facility Law and Legal Definitions." Retrieved April 2, 2015 (http://definitions.uslegal.com).

Webb, Jim. 2009. "Why WE Must Fix Our Prisons." *Parade,* March 29: 4–5.

Welling, Dale. 1994. "Experts Unite to Combat Street and Prison Gang Activities." *Corrections Today,* 56 (5):148–149.

Wertheim, L. Jon. 2014. "Prison Break." *Sports Illustrated,* November 17:6–11.

Williams, Larry R. 1981. "Women's Correctional Recreation Services." *Journal of Physical Education, Recreation and Dance,* 52:55–58.

Ethics and Character Formation in Sports
A Philosophical Perspective

Tim Madigan

The philosopher Friedrich Nietzsche (1844–1900) famously proclaimed that "God is dead and we have killed Him." Might one say similarly that in today's "winner take all" society "sportsmanship is dead and we have killed it"? Is the very concept no longer relevant in the modern age of competitive sports? In this essay I will show how three long dead philosophers—Aristotle, Kant, and the aforementioned Nietzsche—still have much to teach us about sportsmanship and its continued relevance for the present day.

Aristotle on Excellence

In a recent ad for *Under Armour* sneakers, the actor Jamie Foxx intones the following: "You know, the Greek philosopher Aristotle said 'You are what you repeatedly do.' Huh—but in our book, we take it a little deeper. We say, 'You are what you repeatedly do when things get hard'" (*Under Armour* 2015). Foxx goes on to say, "My apologies to Aristotle, but excellence doesn't become a habit by running the same path over and over. No, No, No! You know what the excellent ones do? They reinvent the rules altogether. The excellent ones just step up to the line and ask 'What's the record?'" (*Under Armour* 2015).

Since I am a philosopher by profession, it's perhaps not surprising that I cannot help but connect current topics with the age-old wisdom of thinkers of the past. What might they say to this claim that "excellence" is all about reinventing the rules?

While he lived long ago, the ethical writings of the Ancient Greek philosopher Aristotle (384–322 BCE) still have relevance to the present day, particularly when we try to understand the meaning of the term "sportsmanship." As a longtime advocate for finding philosophy in popular culture I was pleasantly surprised to hear his name invoked in a commercial for sneakers. With apologies to Mr. Foxx, though, I'm not sure he really captures the true meaning of Aristotle. First of all, as we shall see, Aristotle's concept of excellence (or *arête*) is not diametrically opposed to that of Mr. Foxx, since he too felt that it involves constantly trying to better one's self, not simply doing the same act over and over. But second and, more importantly, Aristotle would never assert that excellence equals constantly trying to break the record, if by that one means trying to win at all costs. Admitting one's limitations as well as one's abilities is crucial to Aristotle's overall defense of excellence, and it remains an aspect of sports that continues to need stressing. The concept of arête for Aristotle involves the full development of a person's mind and body, with the proper understanding of one's true potentiality as well as one's true limitations. Or, as he put it in his work *The Nichomachean Ethics*, virtue or excellence consists of achieving a balance (or "golden mean") between two vices: "the one of excess and the other of deficiency" (Aristotle 1962:43). In the case of athletics, this involves trying to do what is necessary to achieve one's personal best, both in the physical sense of maximizing one's bodily strengths and in the mental sense of coming to understand one's true nature. Such understanding does not come in a vacuum, however, but rather is achieved by accessing one's abilities through comparisons with other members of one's society. For, as Aristotle stressed throughout his writings, human beings are social animals and cannot thrive independent of social networks.

Sportsmanship and the Civilizing Process

Since we are, by nature, social animals, in Aristotle's view such personal fulfillment can only occur within a communal setting. One judges an individual by the way in which that individual excels, and one judges a community by the role models it holds up as types of citizens who best express that community's ideals. Personal excellence, therefore, is intricately connected with engaging in social activities. Such activities need to be regulated, so that one has a sense of just what is being judged. How, for instance, can you know if you are a good cook if there is no generally accepted sense of what constitutes proper cuisine? How can you know if you are a good mathematician if there are no teachers of mathematics to guide you? While rules can certainly be amended and, if necessary, even overturned, they have to exist in the first place if one is going to make any sort of judgment at all.

It is within this notion of rules of behavior that an Aristotelian defense of "sportsmanship" can be developed. We know, of course, how important sporting activities were to the Ancient Greeks, the founders of the Ancient Olympics. Indeed, in the *Nichomachean Ethics* Aristotle himself gives a "shout out" to a famous athlete of his time, Milo of Croton, whom he uses to exemplify the fact that "the golden mean" differs from person to person: "if ten pounds of food is too much for a man to eat and two pounds little, it does not follow that the trainer will prescribe six pounds, for this may in turn be too much or too little for him to eat; it may be little for Milo and too much for someone who has just begun to take up athletics" (Aristotle 1962:42). In other words, what would constitute just the right amount of food for Milo (and therefore be a virtue) could be a vice for someone else who would find it either excessive or deficient. And notice the stress which Aristotle places on the role of the trainer, whose job is to work with the athlete to ascertain the proper nutrition necessary for the best sort of physical development. He adds: "The same applies to running and wrestling. Thus we see that an expert in a field avoids excess and deficiency, but seeks the median and chooses it—not the median of the object but the median relative to us" (Aristotle 1962:42).

Sport therefore can provide the means for testing one's own abilities through cooperative team activities against worthy opponents, with the support of a community to inspire one to achieve one's best. While, in most sports, winning is the goal (or *telos*), *how* one wins is just as important as achieving the trophy or prize. To win by cheating, or by disparaging an opponent's abilities, or by excessive violent acts, would not be a mark of a worthy character. The winner should not take pride in a task that is achieved through unvirtuous means, and nor should the community treat such a victor as a hero. To do so would be the mark of a vicious, or non-virtuous, society.

The goal of all life, for Aristotle, is to excel through one's abilities within a social framework (or a civilizing process) that channels our energies in fruitful ways by giving us rational guidelines to follow. This theory is known as "Virtue Ethics" and the concept of good sportsmanship is at its very heart. In the *Nichomachean Ethics*, a work he wrote in part as a manual for his son Nichomacheus on how to develop as a virtuous person, Aristotle also discusses the concept of *eudaimonia*. Usually translated from the Greek as "happiness," a better translation would be "self-fulfillment through personal excellence" or "human flourishing." For Aristotle, the good life consists of developing one's natural abilities through the use of reason. A virtuous life is one where proper habits are formed that allow one to reach one's full potential. The word "eudaimonia" itself comes from combining two Greek words—"eu" meaning "good" and "daimonia" meaning "soul" or "spirit." Literally, then, a happy person is one who has achieved a state of fulfillment (or "personal best") and thus demonstrates to others the possession of a "good soul." The "soul" in this regard is the essence of person, or as Jamie Foxx puts it, "you are what you repeatedly do." That is to say, one's essence is determined by one's habits and these habits can be judged to be good (virtues) or bad (vices) in regards to how they relate to the means by which one achieves one's goals. When both a person and a society reach a point where the only thing that matters is winning—by whatever means necessary—then from a moral perspective both the person and the society can be judged to be despicable. There is no honor when records are set by vicious means.

For Aristotle, the struggle to be one's best necessarily involves respect for one's opponent—it is the genuine struggle against a worthy adversary that allows a person to truly understand his or her own abilities. As the old saying goes, when you cheat you're only cheating yourself. How can one really know if one has done one's best if victory involves deception or less-than-worthy means of achieving one's ends? While this may seem an "old-fashioned" view, it is important to note that those modern-day athletes who have been judged to be cheaters or deceivers are not usually admired as persons, nor considered to be proper role models. An Aristotelian perspective still, I would argue, predominates in our love for sporting records that are achieved by following the rules.

Sportsmanship involves fair play, decency, and respect—for oneself, the competitor, and for the sport itself. Ideals of sportsmanship, such as competitiveness, hard work, fair play, obedience to authority, and dedication, are tied to a society's cultural morality. Sportsmanship is tied to morality because it represents an ideal form of behavior—to be a good sport and to play fairly. As philosopher James Keating (2001) explains:

> Sportsmanship is not merely an aggregate of moral qualities comprising a code of specialized behavior; it is also an attitude, a posture, a manner of interpreting what would otherwise be only a legal code. Yet the moral qualities believed to comprise the code have almost monopolized consideration and have proliferated to the point of depriving sportsmanship of any distinctiveness. Truthfulness, courage, Spartan endurance, self-control, self-respect, scorn of luxury, consideration for another's opinions and rights, courtesy, fairness, magnanimity, a high sense of honor, co-operation, generosity. The list seems interminable [p. 12].

Sportsmanship, then, is an expression of morality and provides a code of acceptable behavior for athletes to abide by in their pursuit of fair play. Good sportsmanship involves conduct and attitudes considered befitting to participants, especially in regards to a sense of fair play, courtesy toward teammates and opponents, game officials, and others involved in sporting contests, as well as grace in losing. Good sportsmanship generally implies that participants play sports for the joy of playing. However, it should be noted that because sportsmanship is tied to cultural standards of morality, norms, and values, ideal types may vary from one society to the next. But this involves more than simply following rules—it also implies a *respect* for those rules. To wish to *reinvent* the rules simply because they are inconvenient would seem to be a mark of a poor character. More to the point, most athletes and their supporters expect their opponents to play by the rules, and become enraged when blatant disregard for the rules is demonstrated. Another great philosopher of the past, Immanuel Kant (1724–1804), can offer us some further guidance on the meaning of "sportsmanship" when it comes to following the rules of play.

Kant on Respect for Rules

Imagine the following scenario. A football team just scores a winning touchdown. The hometown crowd goes wild. The opposing team hangs its head in shame. The referees nod sagely that all is well. Just then, the coach rushes up to the referees and says, "I'm sorry, but one of my players was offside. You didn't see it, but I did. You must penalize us for this. I refuse to accept a touchdown that wasn't properly earned." When the announcers alert the crowd in the stands and the viewers at home to this bit of news, how will it likely be received? Will the coach be carried out of the stands in triumph for his strict adherence to the rules? Almost assuredly not.

Following rules is an essential part of any sporting event, and one of the most important roles which coaches fulfill (in addition to plotting strategy, motivating players, and inspiring the fans) is to make sure that such rules are both understood and followed by the athletes. One only has to watch the expression on coaches' faces when the opposing team commits an infraction to see just how important sticking to the rules is to them.

Grantland Rice's famous statement "It's not whether you win or lose, it's how you play the game" is a perfect expression of Immanuel Kant's duty-based approach to ethics. For Kant, one should never allow anticipated consequences to cause one to deviate from following the rules of ethics. For him, a good character is one who practices reciprocity, that is to say treating others in the same manner that one wishes to be treated. If it would be wrong for someone to cut in front of me after I've waited in line for hours to get into my favorite sporting event, why would it be right for me to do the same thing to others? If the rule "one should wait in line before entering an event" is generally accepted, how can I justify being an exception to it? One can only wonder what sort of a coach Kant would have made. His pep talks during half-time might lack the fire of Knute Rockne's exhortations. "Remember team," I can hear him say, "don't ever treat the opposing players as merely a means to an end." Hardly as powerful as "Win this one for the Gipper!" But Kant was always suspicious of motivations based upon appeals to emotion. For him, an action can only be considered moral if it can be universalized. If it is wrong for the opposing team to win the game due to an uncalled penalty, how can it be right for one's own team to do so?

Perhaps the real issue here is that the rules of sporting events are not as hard-and-fast as one might think. Allowance must be made for human fallibility. And often the sheer numbers of possible infractions are such that malicious-minded referees could plausibly penalize the athletes on almost every play, thereby giving both coaches attacks of apoplexy.

The usual stated antithesis to Grantland Rice's motto is that of football coach Vince Lombardi: "Winning isn't everything; it's the only thing." But what Lombardi actually said is rather different: "Winning is not everything, but wanting to win is." Surely even a Kantian coach would have no quarrel with that—if an athlete doesn't desire to win, then he or she should not be on the field. But if a coach knows that victory has occurred due to a lack of diligence on the part of the officials, it makes it rather unsporting to criticize the officials when the same thing happens to the benefit of the opposition. While I don't expect to ever see so dramatic a scenario as that with which I began this section, I can't help but think that a little dose of Kantianism would help restore the virtue of fair play which is so essential to any sporting event. Go out, and win one for the Kanter.

Nietzsche on Pride and Honor

Often, it seems, athletes are driven by other intentions beyond fair play and morality. The pressure to win may compromise the fair play ethos. Athletes may desire fame and recognition, material benefits and self-realization through victory even if it comes at the cost of sportsmanship. The desire to win, sometimes at any cost, causes some athletes to circumvent ideals of good sportsmanship.

Still, victories that occur because of bad calls or unnoticed fouls tend to be long remembered. Interestingly enough, such tainted victories can have their own long-term repercussions and can be motivating factors for those who were wronged. Jennifer Allen, daughter of the legendary Washington Redskins football coach George Allen, published an article in the January 12, 2003, *New York Times* editorial page entitled "Don't Let the Healing Begin." In it, she writes: "My father, George Allen, was a firm believer in keeping open the wounds of unfairness." He was so upset about losing a 1975 game to the St. Louis Cardinals, whose receiver, although credited with a touchdown, was on replay clearly out of bounds (later known as "the phantom catch") that he brooded about it incessantly. "He shared his obsession with the team," his daughter writes. "The cause bound them together and raised their level of play. In the 1976 season, the Redskins swept the Cardinals."

As the philosopher Friedrich Nietzsche well knew, having the right enemy can be a powerful motivating force. He often spoke, in his provocative way, about the struggle for existence and the role which revenge plays in motivating us. In his 1872 essay "Homer's Contest," for instance, he writes about the Ancient Greek concept of the *agon,* or "struggle," and holds that the love for contests of all sort, especially sporting contests, was part and parcel with the desire for glory that motivated all the Greeks. Speaking of Aristotle, he writes: "The greater and more sublime a Greek is, the brighter the flame of ambition that flares out of him, consuming everybody who runs on the same course. Aristotle once made a list of such hostile contests in the grand manner; the most striking of the examples is that even a dead man can still spur a live one to consuming jealousy" (Nietzsche 1979:35). The example is that of the poet Xenophanes of Colophon, driven to be a better poet than the long dead Homer. Xenophanes sought to overshadow his predecessor, or in the words of Jamie Foxx, he stepped up to the line and asked "What's the record?" "We do not understand the full strength of Xenophanes' attack on the national hero of poetry," Nietzsche writes, "unless ... we see that at its root lay an overwhelming craving to assume the place of the overthrown poet and to inherit his fame" (Nietzsche 1979:36). And describing another famed wrestler of the Ancient Greek world, he adds: "How characteristic are question and answer when a noted opponent of Pericles is asked whether he or Pericles is the best wrestler in the city, and answers: 'Even when I throw him down, he denies that he fell and attains his purpose, persuading even those who saw him fall'" (Nietzsche 1979:36).

One can perhaps admire the audacity and indefatigability of Xenophanes and Pericles for taking on the best and refusing to give in. But do they really meet the Aristotelian concept of virtue? One would rather say that Xenophanes is guilty of what Aristotle called *hubris,* or excessive pride—a vice rather than a virtue. While trying to overcome Homer might be a worthy goal for some, it doesn't seem to be such for him—for while everyone has heard of Homer, who remembers Xenophanes? And if Pericles was truly pinned fair and square, denying this fact doesn't change it but rather makes him seem ridiculous, much like the Black Knight in *Monty Python and the Holy Grail,* who keeps saying "it's only a flesh wound" even after his arms and legs are chopped off in a duel. One of the most important aspects of sportsmanship is admitting defeat and accepting it gracefully—notwithstanding the desire to fight again later.

And while some might interpret Nietzsche's advocacy of the *agon* as a defense of victory by any means necessary, it is important to note that he himself valued the ancient Greek concept of honor. To him, the struggle to be one's best necessarily involves respect for one's opponent and for rules. In his 1887 book *The Genealogy of Morals,* Nietzsche addresses the concept of standards of value. What is we truly value? The most admirable person is one who adheres to a code of honor, and respects those who also bind themselves by their word. He is one who is "sparing with his trust but confers *honor* by the very fact of trusting, who gives his word as something that can be relied on, because he knows himself strong enough to keep it even in the teeth of disasters" (Nietzsche 2003:36).

Is Sportsmanship Dead?

One can ask: have the ideals of sportsmanship really disappeared? Or are they often merely overshadowed by incidents of narcissism and a "me first" philosophy? While we can all come up with many examples of athletes who have blatantly violated the rules, or achieved victory through duplicitous means, it is important to note that these are still exceptions, not the general rule. Sportsmanship is not dead. It does, however, at times, take a back seat to other sport priorities; specifically winning and making a profit. Thus, there are times when sportsmanship seems to be in contradiction with the primary goal of sport—winning. This is because sportsmanship, "insofar as it connotes the behavior proper to the athlete, seeks to place certain basic limitations on the rigors of competition" (Keating 2001:15). At times it seems more important in sport to win than to be a good sport.

Ideally, athletes should not need to have "codes of conduct" from sports leagues impressed upon them. One would hope that they already possess internalized codes of restraint and respect for others which obligates them not to harm others or violate the rules for their own benefit. Contemporary moralists ponder whether violent sports have a place in modern civil societies; especially societies which attempt to impose a civilizing protocol among its citizens. Others address the ways in which athletes, coaches and fans can still achieve a virtuous life through their participation in sport. For instance, Aristotle felt that some activities, such as watching plays or engaging in sporting events, can help people to harmlessly release energies which, if directly acted upon, could have a detrimental impact. For example, if one is angry because of feeling slighted, a person could act out that anger directly by deliberately hurting another person through an act of violence. This would be morally unacceptable. But simply bottling up the feeling of anger would not be beneficial. Engaging in vigorous physical activity, though, or even watching others engaged in such activities, can allow one to vicariously release the feelings of anger. He called this *catharsis,* which literally means a cleansing or purging. One could argue that sporting events from both a participatory and spectator perspective fulfill this cathartic goal and allow for civilized individuals to purge themselves of energies that would otherwise be uncivilized or harmful.

As previously mentioned, contemporary individuals should not need "codes of conduct" from sports leagues or official organizations to tell them what the proper way to act should be. Yet it is important to note that most people affiliated with the sports world, including spectators and fans, athletes, coaches, and officials, *do* behave in a civil manner. Contemporary moralists, including both philosophers and sociologists, ponder the ways in which athletes, coaches and fans can still achieve a virtuous life through their participation in sport. Randall Feezell, for instance, is a professor of philosophy at Creighton University as well as an athlete and coach. In discussing the importance of "character" and sportsmanship, he writes:

> First of all, I associate character with a kind of strength that forces one properly to take responsibility for certain negative events that befall a person. Such events might make one look bad in the eyes of others and oneself. It is the courage to take responsibility for defeat and failure when appropriate, to be honest about one's self. I know of no neat virtue term that sums up this quality, but it is obviously a kind of responsibility. It is akin to a kind of self-reliance, and its opposite is the perpetual whiner, blamer, and excuse-monger. John McEnroe's lack of this quality is expressed in his constant paranoid complaints to officials, as if he has experienced more unfair and incompetent officiating than anyone in the history of tennis. Lack of this quality is apparent throughout the sports world when officiating is blamed for defeat [Feezell 2004:139–140].

Many ethicists see a return to an Aristotelian "Virtue Ethics" approach as a rejection of moral theories based simply upon merely learning and applying rules. Virtue Ethics—as identified with Aristotle's teachings—stresses the importance of character development, including the harmonizing of one's personal traits, applying good judgment, and having a sense of pride in doing one's best, rather than necessarily winning or achieving public recognition. While civility may be under attack, it is also clear that athletes, coaches and spectators who violate such norms do receive public criticism and, in extreme cases, are prosecuted for their infractions. It is by no means the case that a "winner take all" attitude permeates modern society to such an extent that boorish behavior, violence and cheating are generally acceptable practices.

Sports and Character Formation

Student athletic participation is an important part of the college experience. This is not simply a matter of achieving a winning record. It also relates to the formation of good character. Students who play a sport are learning discipline and teamwork. These skills can help a student to study. And because the team is depending on each of its players to remain academically eligible, studying and attending class brings with it added importance. Hard work and good grades in high school helps a student reach college. Once in college, the good study habits athletes learned in high school tend to carry over. And on the average, college athletes perform better and achieve higher graduation rates than non-athletes. Thus, the benefits of being involved in sports are vital to the entire college experience. In addition, such bonds often continue to connect alumni to the schools they went to as students, thereby fostering a further communal involvement.

In that connection, I would like to briefly discuss a St. John Fisher College program which I feel should be better known—the Honorary Coach program initiated by the football team's head coach Paul Vosburgh. Since 2005 I have had the privilege of serving every year as an honorary coach for one game each season for the St. John Fisher College Division III football team, the Cardinals. (My "winning" record, in case you're wondering, is 7–3.) The program is open to all Fisher faculty and staff, and each game—including away games—usually has two or more such "honorees." It has been a great learning opportunity for me. I have been able to meet the coaching staff, the players, the parents, the chaplain and other team supporters in a way I could never have done as a fan in the stands or a teacher in the classroom. In particular, I have been able to observe several of my athlete students as they prepare for the big game, work with their coaches and coordinate their team activities. I have thereby learned a great deal about these students which I could not have done if I had only known them in a classroom setting. A few years back I had the memorable experiencing of riding with the team to an away game in Vermont, an 8-hour bus ride. I'm glad to say the Cardinals defeated Norwich University 45 to 6—it would have been a long ride back otherwise!

I would encourage more schools to initiate an honorary coaching program such as Fisher promotes. I was able to incorporate my experience in a Learning Community class I co-taught with a Sports Management professor on "Ethics and Sportsmanship," and I invited Coach Vosburgh to give a presentation to the class on what sportsmanship means to him. Turnabout is fair play—or as Kant would say, this was a case of reciprocity. But I must admit, Coach Vosburgh did a far better job as an honorary professor than I have done as an honorary coach. I didn't actually have to formulate any plays in the field—all I needed to do what bask in the reflected glory of the victories and encourage the students to learn what they could from their defeats. The Honorary Coach program exemplifies the true meaning of "honor" in that it allows academic participants to better understand the hard work and dedication that goes into planning for and participating in the game, and how such activities relate to the formation of the character of student-athletes.

Conclusion

In conclusion, perhaps when it comes to understanding what "sportsmanship" means today, both on college campuses and in other venues as well, the main question is still the one the philosopher Aristotle asked so long ago—what does it mean to be a virtuous person in society?

Aristotle's concept of the noble person, proud of one's personal achievements because they *are* personal achievements while also working within a community to help develop the best traits of that community, remains a living ideal, and stories of good sportsmanship need to be told, to counteract the prevailing focus on disreputable and unprofessional behavior.

Finally, another important question to ask is, when cheating is always an option, why don't most athletes take the opportunity to do so? *Sports Illustrated* columnist Joe Posnanski, in an article about the controversy over Alex Rodriguez's admitted use of illegal performance-enhancing drugs, addresses this nicely. He writes:

> I remember years ago being in a high school accounting class. We had this teacher who let everyone cheat. Nothing subtle about it. Kids would walk up to her desk, copy answers, shout them out for all to hear. She wanted us to cheat—or at the very least did not care—and so it didn't seem like cheating. It felt like what you were supposed to do. Still, I remember one guy who refused. He kept his head down and worked out the numbers. The guy wasn't brilliant or holier than thou. I used to watch him sometimes and wonder what was going on inside his head. I never asked him. I wish I could now. Because, at the end of the sad day, the fall of A-Rod just shows that the real question isn't why some players cheated. The question is why some others didn't [Posnanski 2009:15].

Aristotle's notion of a virtuous victor, while it may sound trite in today's increasingly competitive world, still rings true for all those who love sports—athletes, coaches, support staff, officials, and fans. This is especially the case when one considers how engaging in and given support to athletic competition can help to build character and unite people in a common cause. Kant's defense of reciprocity remains at the heart of why we still, for the most part, respect the rules of engagement. And while Nietzsche's defense of the *agon* is at the heart of today's sports rivalries, his stress upon honorable victory also remains vital. With all due respect to Jamie Foxx (an Academy Award winning actor, for those who keep score), excellence is not about reinventing the rules but rather testing one's abilities in light of those rules.

Bibliography

Allen, Jennifer. 2003. "Don't Let the Healing Begin." *New York Times*, January 12. Retrieved May 5, 2015 (http://www.nytimes.com).

Aristotle. 1962. *Nicomachean Ethics*. Edited and translated by Martin Ostwald. New York: Macmillan/Library of Liberal Arts.

Feezell, Randolph. 2004. *Sport, Play & Ethical Reflection*. Urbana: University of Illinois Press.

Keating, James W. 2001. "Sportsmanship as a Moral Category," pp. 7–20 in *Ethics in Sport*, edited by William J. Morgan, Klaus U. Meier, and Angela J. Schneider. Champaign, IL: Human Kinetics.

Nietzsche, Friedrich. 1979. *The Portable Nietzsche*. Edited and translated by Walter Kaufmann. New York: Penguin.

_____. 2003. *The Genealogy of Morals*. Translated by Horace B. Samuel. New York: Dover.

Posnanski, Joe. "The End of an Era? Alex Rodriguez's Fall Tells Us All We Need to Know about the Steroid Years." *Sports Illustrated*, February 16:8–10.

Under Armour TV Spot. 2015. "Aristotle Got It Wrong" Featuring Jamie Foxx. Retrieved May 10, 2015 (http://www.ispot.tv).

Part B

Learning About Sportsmanship

Sportsmanship, as with nearly all behaviors, is taught through socialization—a process of social development and learning that occurs as individuals interact with one another and learn about society's expectations for acceptable behavior. Learning how to behave properly is primarily accomplished via social learning. Social learning generally takes place through two key methods: conditioning and modeling. Conditioning is a learning process whereby individuals associate certain behaviors with rewards and others with punishments. Modeling takes place through observing the behaviors of others.

Learning about sportsmanship begins with primary groups. Primary groups are those characterized by intimate face-to-face associations and cooperation. The initial primary group for most us is our parents, family members and guardians. Ideally, parents teach their children about the benefits of good sportsmanship even before they begin to play formal sports. Good sportsmanship should be taught during formal youth sport participation via coaches and others closely attached to youth sports and continues as individuals progress to more advanced forms of sporting competition.

In this section of the book, there are essays that address the emphasis of sportsmanship in youth sports, peer groups, coaching and among referees. There are essay that examine the role of sport throughout history with special emphasis on sportsmanship among the Irish, in golf and among Brazilian Ju-Jitsu practitioners.

Sport Participation and Sportsmanship in Youth Sport

TANYIKA MOBLEY

Currently in the United States, there are nearly 50 million youth, between the ages of 6 and 18, participating in sport-based programs (Smoll and Smith 2010). As a result of this increase in sport participation, sport scientists continue examining the ways sport experiences enhance the opportunity for human enrichment (Cox 2012). Particularly, research on whether there is a direct correlation between sports and socialization benefits for youth sports participants has garnered increased interest in recent years, with proponents on both sides of the issue. There are many who believe sports is instrumental in the development of prosocial behaviors, such as increased leadership, self-confidence, intrinsic motivation and positive sportsmanship (Martens 1978; Michener 1976; Smoll and Smith 1995b; Cox 2012).

However, due to a dearth of research in this area, it is difficult to identify whether sports, in isolation, can be attributed as the sole or primary factor influencing socialization behaviors such as sportsmanship. Or rather, is sports merely just one of the many psychosocial factors that can be hypothesized as a contributor to the socialization processes developed by youth. This essay will explore the potential benefits of sport participation and ways it possibly teaches socialization to youth participants, the development and influences to sportsmanship according to research and how these changes have impacted the positive youth sport development movement.

Sports and the Socialization of Children

How many times have you heard "sports build character"? There is a widely held belief by sports enthusiasts that sports have an innate ability to teach participants important socialization behaviors. It is one of the explanations for why youth sports have seen exponential growth over the past few decades (Cox 2012). There is continued support by sport researchers and those working within sport-specific programs, who believe it is imperative to use sport as an educational conduit for socialization opportunities for youth participants. Recently, organized sports and athletic agencies have begun working diligently to find innovative ways of teaching positive prosocial behaviors through the engagement of youth sports participation, hoping to provide leadership strategies that will promote more positive outcomes for youth during their childhood and adolescent developmental stages (Martens 1978; Michener 1976; Smoll and Smith 1995b). It is hoped by proponents of the "sport as a teacher" model that youth participants will develop a systematic way of implementing transferable lessons from sport, implement them into their life skills and build prosocial behaviors, including "sportsmanship." So how do we define such a subjective concept as "sportsmanship," where do we learn it, and why is it important for sport participation?

Learning Sportsmanship and Prosocial Behaviors

As each person lives and breathes, they will undergo organic processes as part of the human development process. One of the most important processes all individuals will undergo is the cultivation and nurturing of their socialization. "Socialization" is the process by which we learn and develop socially, based on our interaction with those around us and society at large (Coakley 2007). It is an interpersonal process whereby individuals determine behavioral and communication patterns, as well as relational and psychosocial outcomes (Kendall 2011). It is those patterns and outcomes that ultimately guides our interactions, choices and engagement with the world around us. We must have an understanding of the various sociocultural factors that influence the socialization process, to better navigate our experiences, including the sport experience. So where do we primarily learn our sport socialization processes and how does this impact youth participation and sportsmanship development?

Quite simply, who we are, how we behave and the choices we make, "starts at home." Individuals' beliefs, motivations and choice behaviors are formed by several demographic factors such as education, socio-economic status, religion, marital status, cultural traditions, and the number of children in the family and community resources (Brustad 1993). Specific to sport participation, literature has suggested extrinsic motivators such as parental encouragement, parental values and beliefs, monetary resources and community athletic resources, as being positively linked with our sports behaviors, perceptions and participation (Brustad 1993; Eccles et al. 2006). These factors are considered the most salient influences on our socialization, especially when assessing athletes' behaviors and participation motives within the sport domain. If an individual were to ask most athletes about their early attitudes toward sports and where they learned how to behave within the game, many would acknowledge that their family, coaches and peers played the most significant role in the facilitation of sports choice and participation (Fredericks and Eccles 2004), as well as how they choose to behave toward their opponents.

Bandura (1997) posited that through observational learning and reinforcement structure, children tend to learn appropriate or inappropriate behaviors Sport socialization of youth athletes is defined as the ways social and environmental climates, as well as external factors, help athletes learn to ascribe meaning to sport. It is also how they determine what the appropriate attitudes and behaviors are during sport engagement (Eccles 1993; Eccles et al. 1998). A large part of sport socialization is learning sportsmanship and how to interact with our teammates, coaches and opponents within the sport domain. "Sportsmanship" is defined as the moral functioning of athletes during performance (Cox 2012). It is the decisions that athletes make about moral behavior within the context of sport play, whether good or bad, regarding rule adherence and fair play participation. Researchers have found that athletes who are more ego-oriented and focused on winning tend to display lower levels of moral functioning and thus, are more likely to break rules to win and engage in poor sportsmanship (Cox 2012).

However, the more moral an athlete chooses to be, the greater likelihood they will act with higher levels of sportsmanship. Duda (1996) also found that positive prosocial attitudes toward sport would typically be demonstrated by athletes whose major reasons for participation are intrinsic in nature. The less an athlete is concerned about external rewards and the more focused on participation for the enjoyment or personal motivation, the more positive sportsmanship they will exhibit.

It has been suggested (Haan, Aerts, and Cooper 1985) that youth sport participants learn by personally experiencing moral dilemmas and discussing possible solutions that benefit themselves and others. A great example of this came when two high school wrestlers, Mitchell McKee and Malik Stewart, made national news with their state wrestling title on the line. Prior to taking the mat, Mitchell, a high school sophomore from St. Michael Albertville High School in Minnesota, had declared he wanted to win the Minnesota state wrestling championship for his father, who was battling terminal cancer, "I prayed 'God help me win this match' so I can go win a state title for my dad" (*ABC News* 2014). With his prayers answered, Mitchell won, taking the Minnesota state wrestling in the 120 lb. weight class. But that's not where the story ended. After shaking hands with the opponent who had just defeated him in what was the biggest match of his life, sophomore wrestler Malik Stewart from Blaine High School went over to Mitchell's father, Steve McKee, to offer a handshake and embrace. Malik didn't stop there, he wanted Mr. McKee to feel encouraged, offering these words, "He was pretty proud, and his dad was pretty proud, so I went over there and I shook his hand. I embraced him a little bit, and told him to stay strong and that everybody loves him" (*ABC News* 2014). In what could only be described as the ultimate display of sportsmanship, Malik's opponent went on to acknowledge what he believed was an act mired in total respect, "It was a big match for him and to be able to hug my dad like that and not be mad and storm off like a lot of kids do. It was really respectful" (*ABC News* 2014).

Sports stories such as the one with Malik and Mitchell raise the questions, "Does sports teach prosocial behaviors and sportsmanship attitudes, and if not, where do participants learn these?" Generally speaking, Vallerand and Losier's (1999) "Integrated Theory of Intrinsic and Extrinsic Motivation Model" best explains sport behaviors and attitudes of athletes. Their model posits that an individuals' psychological need to be satisfied mediates the relationship between the social influences and outcomes in an athlete's experience. Their study's outcomes confirmed that self-efficacy, autonomy, close adult relationships and affective dispositions all influenced athletes' motivations in choice and participation. Essentially, their findings indicated that individuals' beliefs and behaviors are formed by demographics, affective/emotional states and sociocultural factors, such as parents, peers, efficacy beliefs and affective outcomes (Bandura 1997; Vallerand and Losier 1999; Fredericks and Eccles 2004; Eccles 2004), not necessarily the sport experience of the athlete.

Most of a child's time is spent with the family, particularly before they reach their high school years (Eccles 2012), which is why their social and choice behaviors are most heavily biased by their parents' guidance during childhood and early adolescence. Through the informal introduction process of "modeling" sport behaviors, parents have the main pipeline to sway their children values (Eccles 2012). Based on modeling behaviors or specific feedback, parents can influence the sport experience, self-concept and self-efficacy of their youth athletes. Expectations of success and task values are directly affected by parental feedback, as these factors are the most significant predictors of value systems, motivational beliefs and choice behaviors (Eccles 2012). Specific to modeling behaviors, observational learning is one of the primary ways children internalize behaviors and attitudes of parents and family (Bandura 1977; Eccles 2012).

Particularly in sport, research shows that when parents role model behaviors such as coaching, participation in athletics or having fun while playing or observing sports, these behaviors are critical in normalizing involvement in athletics and creating attitudes about sport participation as appropriate behavior for youth (Bandura 1977; Brustad 1996). This is why parents' beliefs about their children's sport are influenced by their social and environmental factors, such as gender stereotypes and beliefs about athletic ability, which will have a direct impact on their children, as it relates to their attitudes about athletics (Frederick and Eccles 2005). By providing positive feedback and encouragement, parents have the potential to positively impact their children's enjoyment of sports and self-concept development and thus, influence attitudes, behaviors and the overall sport experience of their children (Brustad 1993). Since parents act as interpreters of experience, they can potentially influence the process of by which children develop their self-concept and the emotional outcomes relating to choice behaviors (Eccles, Wigfield, Harold, and Blumenfeld 1993). Many parents are engaged in the youth athletic experience, whether it be providing transportation, volunteering as a coach, financing equipment costs, being a spectator or offering encouragement and support during events (Eccles, Wigfield, Harold, and Blumenfeld 1993; Eccles, Fredericks, and Simpkins, 2012). This relationship carries with it a heavy burden, as parental beliefs, values and involvement directly influences the development of attitudes and behaviors. This includes negative behaviors, for instance, parental misbehavior at competitions that are problematic and cause parents to lose attendance privileges. Therefore, it is imperative to have a gatekeeper within the sport context (e.g., a youth sport coach) that can create a buffer between the athlete and the parent, to create more positive affective outcomes for participant.

The youth athlete is subject to the "athletic triangle" (Smith, Smoll, and Smith 1989), which refers to the coach-parent-athlete dynamic consistent for the youth sport participant. This symbiotic relationship guides the interactions that are most prevalent in the psychological development of the youth sport participant. Coaching support in youth sports has a similar role to parents, as encourager and role model. Coaches, recognize that "parents influence children's motivation by being interpreters of experience and providers of experience" (Eccles et al. 1998:148), so it is critical for them to work in concert to educate the parent on best practices for distributing positive feedback and normalizing appropriate behavior (e.g., sportsmanship). Specific to youth sport, coaches are perceived as role models for their athletes, who take their cues about appropriate sportsmanship behaviors through reinforcement and punishment based on their actions. The unique relationship between the coach-athlete, especially during child development stages, is effective when teaching interpersonal variables such as enjoyment or fun, attraction toward coach and teammates, self-confidence, performance anxiety, team cohesion, and sport attrition (Fisher, Mancini, Hirsch, Proulx, and Staurowsky 1982; Smith and Smoll 1995a; Westre and Weiss 1991).

This intentionality by coaches has the potential for increased prosocial behavior development and to decreased incidences of violent adult behavior in the youth sport environment. Coaches often have shifting roles and their support can extend beyond the field of play, specifically helping athletes in their positive character development. When Coach Dean Smith passed away in February 2015, many of his players recalled moments with him, their father figure (*ESPN* 2015). Hubert Davis stated:

> "I remember when he walked into the locker room. I was on the StairMaster and I jumped off and it was him and Coach Guthridge, and I just gave them a big hug," Davis said. "And all the guys in the locker room were like, 'Dang, you're like a little kid, like, that's your dad.' And I was like, 'He is my dad. That's my coach'" [*ESPN*, 2015].

Coaches provide emotional support that increases the confidence of an athlete and assuages concerns about performance and sociocultural factors associated with the challenges of participating in sports. Athletes, as they get older, tend to seek out coaches to play a surrogate "parental" role, when their parents were not able to be present or role model appropriate behavior at events and in life circumstances. The level of trust and connectedness developed between youth athletes and their coaches is significant, similar to that of a parent when building socialization skills; however it is far different than the influence peers have on each other when discussing social development.

Peer influence must be mentioned, as it is a noteworthy factor, particularly in the areas of self-perception, enjoyment of activities and motivation of behaviors. Sport-specific studies have produced encouraging results that show a positive correlation between psychological well-being, positive peer relationships and sport involvement (Scanlan et al. 1993; McDonough and Crocker 2005). Youth sport participation has been cited as one of the best ways to form and strengthen friendships, experience team interaction and supportiveness that contributes to overall sport enjoyment, positive experiences and sportsmanship (Chase and Machida 2011; McDonough and Crocker 2005). Peer social support and peer modeling are powerful influences during adolescence, as youth develop attitudes about appropriate behaviors.

However, there are limitations to the understanding of the sport socialization process, as it is difficult to identify all the factors contributing to the way an individual derives meaning and ascribes it to behavioral intent. In recent years, Coakley (2007) began examining the reasons why individuals become involved, behave and potentially maintain involvement in sport. He found that, generally speaking, there were established factors, which contributed or were indicators of why people participate in sport. Those factors included (a) an individual's perception of their abilities or resources to reach desired outcomes were determinants of sport participation, (b) the influences of one's salient relationships with others indicated whether or not they would participate (specifically, role modeling and support of parents, peers, coaches, teachers or siblings), and (c) an individual having the opportunity to play the sport by having the necessary finances or geographic access to participate and feel personally satisfied with the experience (Coakley 2007). Coakley (2007) explained that these factors were proven to be significant to the sport socialization process, particularly the "introduction and involvement" and the process of "developing a commitment to sport participation" (Coakley 2007:94). However, Coakley (2007) describes what he believed was an issue with researching the sport socialization process, stating, "Studies of socialization into sports must take into account the ways in which sport participation is related to individual development, the organization of social life and the ideologies that are prevalent in a culture" (Coakley 2007:96). He goes on to explain that the ways in which an individual derives social meaning based on race/ethnicity, gender, class, etc., will have a direct influence on their sport participation and behaviors (Coakley 2007).

Benefits of Youth Sport Participation on Socialization

So what happened to sports being "fun" and just about "playing the game," without the complexities of social meaning? Nowadays, you find a vast majority of sports programs promoting the "win at all cost" attitude and, with that, higher levels of sports withdrawals by youth, distress and anxiety and violence involving adults (Cox 2012). As Rick McGuire, Head Track Coach of the University of Missouri–Columbia, stated on May 28, 2006, "Being a part of sport should enhance people's lives. Kids weren't put on earth to become tools of entertainment for adults. Kids are on earth to grow into happy healthy, contributing, fulfilled and satisfied adults and parents" (Walljasper 2006:4B).

Youth sport participation potentially impacts a child's perception about his or her self-concept and may have effects on self-esteem (Horn and Hasbrook 1987). Since it often occurs during the developmental stage when youth are unable to properly assess their competencies, they evaluate their capabilities from both social and non-social cues that may provide inaccuracies about their sport experience. This inaccurate evaluation has the potential to cause anxiety, attrition and burnout and can be damaging to the child's self-esteem (Scanlan 1995).

However, sports have many benefits, when underlying psychological reasons are removed. Youth sport participation creates fun experiences, provides physical challenges, social opportunities, health benefits and teaches new skills. Unfortunately, when an overly competitive environment is introduced, rather than a mastery focused climate, many of the perceived benefits of youth sport participation on socialization become obsolete. Competitive based programs have been linked to producing antisocial behaviors and poor sportsmanship in youth sport programs (Arthur-Banning et al. 2009),while a mastery climate, one focused on youth developing individualized skills to gain empowerment and self-efficacy, has been connected to greater incidences of positive sportsmanship (Cox 2012).

Positive Youth Sport Development

Seeing athletes display acts of sportsmanship are a seeming anomaly rather than the norm, due to a changing cultural attitude of "If you ain't first, you're last" (Ricky Bobby, *Talladega Nights, The Ricky Bobby Story*). Remember a couple of years ago, the high school runner that finished her race, but went back to help her competitor finish after she was injured and couldn't make it to the end? While it was an extraordinary act, epitomizing the essence of sportsmanship, why did it make national headlines? Unfortunately, these acts of sportsmanship have become a rarity in sports, which is now seen by many as "big business," starting with youth sports. There are more stories of youth sports participants running up the scores on opponents, adult violence at youth sports games and even cheating scandals by adults on the largest youth sports. With such negative incidents, adults are leaving a trail of pathologically poor examples of how to behave for youth sports participants. Much of this has to do with a lack of understanding by adults of what motivates youth athletes, the significance of role modeling when fostering attitudes of sportsmanship and no desire by adults and leaders of sport to adhere to social norms in the context of the sports domain. As a result of this ongoing discussion, the positive youth sports development was created.

The positive youth sport development movement, which has gained widespread recognition and support from youth sport based programs, was originated by individuals who wanted to reframe the culture of youth sports. Also, these practitioners wanted to bring the "fun" back to children and remind them of what sports was really about, enjoyment, skill development and social opportunities. It was also developed to educate adults, specifically parents and coaches, on the best ways to engage youth in sports participation and to create consistent positive sport experiences. By educating coaches on strategies for setting high but realistic expectations and positive social norms, they learn ways of optimizing youths' development of good sportsmanship (Eccles and Gootman 2002). The idea was to get youth to engage in caring and supportive relationships with adults and peers to promote the development of personal assets through skill-building activities, leveraged through sport experiences. These programs often times teach life skills through the facilitation of sport and physical activity opportunities, making them transferable lessons that are practical and comprehensive for youth participants. Even more, these programs are designed to provide strategies for increased self-efficacy, self-confidence, friendship, and a mastery climate that facilitates positive sportsmanship development.

Recommendations for Increasing Sportsmanship and Prosocial Behaviors in Youth Sports

When business owners want to determine ways to improve services rendered, where do they glean this information? The consumer or client becomes the expert, as they are the target audience. It is no different when developing youth sport based programs. To understand the ways to improve or bring about change, we must begin with encouraging youth to provide relevant feedback on their sport experiences. By adults, parents and coaches reversing roles and allowing youth to become interpreters of their experience, it is another way of educating themselves on the needs of those served. Based on various studies, by increasing sport experiences that cater to the participation motives of children, there is a greater likelihood they will be willing to role model and be persistent in their motivation to follow the lead of their coaches and parents. When adults create experiences of "fun" and enjoyment, skill development, mastery climate over ego-centered client, social opportunities and a challenging sport environment, youth participants will are more likely to adapt prosocial behaviors, including sportsmanship.

Therefore, when coaches and adults create a motivational climate that focuses on personal improvement and cooperative learning, they will have greater influence over an athletes' sportsperson-like behavior and cultivate a positive behavioral culture for their team (Miller, Roberts, and Ommundsen 2005; Stornes and Ommundsen 2004). Once a positive sport culture and trust has been established by coaches, they have the ability to inspire athletes and influence behaviors such as good sportsmanship through four methods: modeling, reinforcement, teaching, and punishment.

For youth to learn accepted social norms of behavior, they need to witness it. Have you ever heard parents say, "Do as I say, not as I do"? In order to teach young people still in the developmental stages, this cannot be the attitude of those in a position of influences. Coaches and parents must first model good sportsmanship to educate youth sports participants on prosocial behavior when interacting with both teammates and their opponents. The best method for this is through "observational learning," which is one of the primary ways social influence is used when teaching moral development (e.g., Mugno and Feltz 1985; Smith 1978). When adults role model prosocial behaviors, it allows youth to watch interactions in a naturalistic way that helps them acquire these skills organically.

The power of reinforcement has been around since Pavlov and the oft cited study of the salivating dogs (Pavlov 1903). One of the best ways to implement behavior change is through reinforcing another's behavior through positive or negative messages of feedback. To guide youth participants toward good sportsmanship, coaches must reinforce their behavior through a reward system, whether it be positive feedback or increased opportunities for fun or a tangible item. Just as important, antisocial behavior must be met with punishment or poor sportsmanship is likely to increase or will be repeated until addressed (e.g., Mugno and Feltz 1985; Smith 1978). Thus, teaching and educating youth athletes about the importance of good sportsmanship is one of the more salient athletic life skills, which they must learn are transferable skills that can be utilized in other areas of their lives. Coaches have a duty to educate youth sports participants about the nuances of good sportsmanship and how it relates to learning how to manage emotions, accept personal and social responsibility, and show empathy for others beyond the sports environment (Gould and Carson 2008; Gould, Collins, Lauer, and Chung 2007; Weiss and Wiese-Bjornstal 2009). The more coaches and adults find ways to nurture a caring climate of education and fun for youth sports participants and allow children to learn prosocial behaviors through example and experience, the more likely increased sportsmanship opportunities will become the standardized behavioral norms in youth sports.

Conclusion

While anecdotal observations seem to indicate the significant role sports can play in the lives of youth participants, there is no evidence of a direct correlation between sports as an isolated experience that develops or increases prosocial behaviors. Although, it can be reasoned that sport experiences do in fact contribute to a child's self-concept and self-esteem (Horn and Hasbrook 1987; Smoll, Smith, Barnett, and Everett 1993), it is uncertain whether "sports builds character," as often hypothesized (Scanlan 1995). These attitudes derive from both social and nonsocial sources, and this input helps form their self-concept and their evaluative responses to it (i.e., their self-esteem). While there has been some progress to indicate that sports participation can potentially foster both positive and negative moral function and thus, good and bad sportsmanship, there is still a need for more research assessment to link impacts of sport participation on children's prosocial attitudes (Vallerand and Losier 1994; Weiss and Bredemeier 1986, 1991).

There are many other influences that cultivate attitudes and behaviors about fair play and sportsmanship by youth sport participants, including parental, coaching and peer influences. In addition, the mastery climate and motivational regulation are key predictors in sportsmanship behaviors youth athletes and provide indicators for future strategies when hoping to facilitate prosocial behavior (Shields et al. 2007). As best stated by Coakley (2007), "Studies of socialization into sports must take into account the ways in which sport participation is related to individual development, the organization of social life and the ideologies that are prevalent in a culture" (p. 96). In other words, "back to the drawing board."

Bibliography

ABC News. 2014. "High School Wrestler Loses Championship, Wins Crowd with Heartwarming Gesture." Retrieved March 12, 2014 (http://abcnews.go.com).

Arthur-Banning, Skye, Mary S. Wells, Birgitta L. Baker, and Ryan Hegreness. 2009. "Parents Behaving Badly: The Relationship Between the Sportsmanship Behaviors of Adults and Athletes in Youth Basketball Games." *Journal of Sport Behavior*, 32:3–18.

Bandura, Albert. 1977. "Self-Efficacy: Toward a Unifying Theory of Behavioral Change." *Psychological Review*, 84:191–215.

_____. 1997. *Self-Efficacy: The Exercise of Control*. New York: Freeman.

Brustad, Richard J. 1993. "Who Will Go Out and Play? Parental and Psychological Influences on Children's Attraction to Physical Activity." *Pediatric Exercise Science*, 5:210–233.

Chase, Melissa A., and Moe Machida. 2011. "The Role of Sport as a Social Status Determinant for Children: Thirty Years Later." *Research Quarterly for Exercise and Sport*, 82 (4): 731–739.

Coakley, Jay J. 2007. *Sports in Society: Issues and Controversies*, 9th ed. New York, NY: McGraw-Hill.

Cox, Richard. 2012. *Sport Psychology: Concepts and Applications*, 7th ed. New York: McGraw-Hill.

Eccles, Jacquelynne S., Jennifer A. Fredericks, and Sandra A. Simpkins. 2012. "Charting the Eccles' Expectancy-Value Model from Mothers' Beliefs in Childhood to Youths' Activities in Adolescence." *Developmental Psychology*, 48 (4): 1019–1032.

Eccles, Jacquelynne S., and Jennifer A. Gootman. 2002. *Community Programs to Promote Youth Development*. Washington, D.C.: National Academy Press.

Eccles, Jacquelynne S., Allan Wigfield, Rena D. Harold, and Phyllis Blumenfield. 1993. "Ontogeny of Children's Self-perceptions and Subjective Task Values Across Activity Domains During the Early Elementary School Years." *Child Development*, 64:830–847.

Eccles, Jacquelynne S., Allan Wigfield, and Ulrich Schiefele. 1998. "Motivation to Succeed," pp. 1017–1095 in *Handbook of Child Psychology, Social, Emotional, and Personality Development*, 5th ed., edited by William Damon and Nancy Eisenberg. Hoboken, NJ: John Wiley & Sons.

Eccles, Jacquelynne S., Carol A. Wong, and Stephen C. Peck. 2006. "Ethnicity as a Social Context for the Development of African-American Adolescents." *Journal of School Psychology*, 44 (5):407–426.

ESPN. 2015. "Smith's Influence Felt Strongly at UNC." Retrieved February 9, 2015 (http://espn.go.com).

Fisher, A.C., Victor H. Mancini, Ronald L. Hirsch, Thomas J. Proulx, and Ellen J. Staurowsky. 1982. "Coach-Athlete Interactions and Team Climate. *Journal of Sport Psychology*, 4:388–404.

Fredricks, Jennifer A., and Jacquelynne S. Eccles. 2004. "Parental Influences on Youth Involvement in Sports," pp. 145–164 in *Developmental Sport and Exercise Psychology: A Lifespan Perspective*, edited by Maureen R. Weiss. Morgantown, WV: Fitness Information Technology.

_____. 2005. "Family Socialization, Gender, Motivation, and Involvement." *Journal of Sport & Exercise Psychology*, 27:3–31.

Gould, Daniel, and Sarah Carson. 2008. "Life Skills Development Through Sport: Current Status and Future Directions." *International Review of Sport and Exercise Psychology*, 1:58–78.

Gould, Daniel, Karen Collins, Larry Lauer, and Yongchul Chung. 2007. "Coaching Life Skills Through Football: A Study of Award Winning High School Coaches." *Journal of Applied Sport Psychology*, 19:16–37.

Haan, Norma. 1978. "Two Moralities in Action Contexts: Relationship to Thought, Ego Regulation, and Development." *Journal of Personality and Social Psychology*, 36:286–305.

Hellison, Don. 2003. *Teaching Responsibility Through Physical Activity*, 2d ed. Champaign, IL: Human Kinetics.

Horn, Thelma, and Cynthia A. Hasbrook. 1987. "Psychological Characteristics and the Criteria Children Use for Self-Evaluation." *Journal of Sport Psychology*, 9:208–221.

Kendall, Diane. 2011. *Sociology in Our Times*, 8th ed. Belmont, CA: Wadsworth.

Martens, Rainer. 1978. *Joy and Sadness in Children's Sports*. Champaign, IL: Human Kinetics.

McDonough, Meghan H., and Peter R. Crocker. 2005. "Sport Participation Motivation in Young Adolescent Girls: The Role of Friendship Quality and Self-Concept." *Research Quarterly for Exercise and Sport*, 76 (4): 456–467.

Michener, James A. 1976. *Sports in America*. New York: Random House.

Miller, Blake W., Glen C. Roberts, and Yngvar Ommundsen. 2005. "Effect of Perceived Motivational

Climate on Moral Functioning, Team Moral Atmosphere Perceptions, and the Legitimacy of Intentionally Injurious Acts Among Competitive Youth Football Players." *Psychology of Sport and Exercise*, 6:461–477.

Mugno, D'Arrigo, and Deborah L. Feltz. 1985. "The Social Learning of Aggression in Youth Football in the United States." *Canadian Journal of Applied Sports Sciences*, 10:26–35.

Scanlan, Tara K. 1995. "Social Evaluation and the Competition Process: A Developmental Perspective," pp. 298–308 in *Children and Youth in Sport: A Biopsychosocial Perspective*, edited by F. L. Smoll & R. E. Smith. Dubuque: Brown & Benchmark.

Scanlan, Tara K., Jeffrey P. Simons, Paul J. Carpenter, Greg W. Schmidt, and Bruce Keeler. 1993. "The Sport Commitment Model: Measurement Development for the Youth-sport Domain." *Journal of Sport and Exercise Psychology*, 15:16–38.

Smith, Michael D. 1978. "Social Learning of Violence in Minor Hockey," pp. 91–106 in *Psychological Perspectives in Youth Sports*, edited by F. L. Smoll & R. E. Smith. Washington, D.C.: Hemisphere.

Smoll, Frank L., and Ronald E. Smith. 1993. "Educating Youth Sport Coaches: An Applied Sport Psychology Perspective," pp. 36–57 in *Applied Sport Psychology: Personal Growth to Peak Performance*, 2d ed. edited by Jean M. Williams. Mountain View, CA: Mayfield.

Smoll, Frank L., and Ronald E. Smith, eds. 1995a. *Children and Youth in Sport: A Biopsychosocial Perspective*. Dubuque: Brown & Benchmark.

Smoll, Frank L., and Ronald E. Smith. 1995b. "Competitive Anxiety: Sources, Consequences, and Intervention Strategies," pp. 359–380 in *Children and Youth in Sport: A Biopsychosocial Perspective*, edited by F. L. Smoll and R. E. Smith. Dubuque, IA: Brown & Benchmark.

Smith, Ronald. E., and Frank L. Smoll. 2010. *Psychosocial Interventions in Youth Sports*. Dubuque: Brown & Benchmark.

Smith, Ronald E., Frank L. Smoll, and Nathan J. Smith. 1989. *Parents' Complete Guide to Youth Sports*. Reston, VA: American Alliance for Health, Physical Education, Recreation and Dance.

Stornes, T., and Yngvar Ommundsen. 2004. "Achievement Goals, Motivational Climate and Sportspersonship: A Study of Young Handball Players." *Scandinavian Journal of Educational Research*, 48:205–221.

Vallerand, Robert J., and Gaetan F. Losier. 1999. "An Integrative Analysis of Intrinsic and Extrinsic Motivation in Sport." *Journal of Applied Sport Psychology*, 11, 142–169.

Walljasper, Jay. 2006. "More Than a One-Track Mind." *Columbia Daily Tribune*, 4B.

Weiss, Maureen R., and Brenda Jo Bredemeier. 1986. "Moral Development," pp. 374–390 in *Physical Activity and Human Well-Being*, edited by Vern Seefeldt. Reston, VA: American Alliance for Health, Physical Education, Recreation and Dance.

Weiss, Maureen R., and Brenda Jo Bredemeier. 1991. "Moral Development in Sport," pp. 331–378 in *Exercise and Sport Science Reviews* (18), edited by Kent B. Pandolf and John O. Holloszy. Baltimore: Wilkins & Wilkins.

Weiss, Maureen R., and Diane M. Wiese-Bjornstal. 2009. "Promoting Positive Youth Development Through Physical Activity." *President's Council on Physical Fitness and Sports Research Digest*, 10:1–8.

Westre, Kirk R., and Maureen Weiss. 1991. "The Relationship Between Perceived Coaching Behaviors and Group Cohesion in High School Football Teams." *The Sport Psychologist*, 5:41–54.

Emphasizing Sportsmanship in Youth Sport

Todd Harrison

A quick internet search of youth sport leads to a mixture of links promoting youth programming, governing bodies and many stories proclaiming the ills afflicting the games these organizations are producing and protecting. Stories of out of control parents, abusive coaches and demanding schedules are discussed (and complained about) around dinner tables and water coolers yet youth sport participation continues to increase. In 2000, the number of American youth between 6- and 17-years old who played on at least one organized sport team was 54 percent; a number that jumped to 59 percent in a similar study completed five years later looking at a group of kids between ages 10 and 17 (Woods 2011). Similarly, the Sports and Fitness Industry Association (SFIA) completed a study examining youth participation trends and interests and pegged the 2011 participation rate of kids between ages 6 and 17 at 21.47 million kids (Kelley and Carchia 2013).

With all of this attention, and money, being given to organized sport by parents across America, a set of questions arise:

- Why are children so quickly placed into youth sport programs?
- Ideally, how does participation in these games assist in youth development?
- Are the youth sport organizations around the country meeting the needs of their participants?

Discussion of these queries will be advanced in coming sections but there are a number of statistics that focus on the third question and the answers are not often positive. The National Alliance for Sports has reported that while 20 million kids register each year to play hockey, football, baseball, soccer and other competitive sports, 70 percent of them will quit playing these sports by age 13. From burnout and lack of fun, to injuries and attention given to sports, the reasons for dropping out are many. Most of the attention from scholars and practitioners is given to the impact youth sport has on children and this essay will further that examination.

Elena Delle Donne, the 6'5" star of the WNBA's Chicago Sky, hardly looks like a poster-child for the intensity of youth sport success, as she racks up accolades on the court in America's only professional women's basketball league. However, the WNBA's 2013 Rookie of the Year left the University of Connecticut two days after arriving on campus. She was burned out from basketball after years of camps, summer leagues, AAU tournaments, high school seasons and other showcases. The pressure on one of the most highly touted women's basketball recruits ever led her to return to Delaware and a spot on the University of Delaware's volleyball team, where she excelled before returning to the basketball court after a year absence (Longman 2008). But how does this story speak to sportsmanship? The intensity of Elena's pre–18 years old basketball experiences speaks to the historical trend of ratcheted expectations of kids across the country, whether they are the best player in the country or trying to earn a spot on a high school football team.

This essay will examine the shift in cultural norms and social expectations surrounding youth sport and how emphases on sportsmanship in youth sport programs can help salvage some of the wholesome values sought after by parents when signing up their children into sport leagues. There is no major overhaul in sight for youth sport organization and certainly little desire to eliminate sports from the young lives of boys and girls across the country, so how can we work to extend some of the virtues of sport craved by parents for their kids? By emphasizing sportsmanship.

How Did We Get to Today?

Belief is widespread that participation in sport, especially among youth, contributes to development physically (through enhancement of motor skills and fitness) and emotionally/socially (increase in self-confidence, self-image or character development). Through the mid–1800s nearly all youth-focused activity engaged in by American youth was through informal play and recreation but that changed in the post–Civil War era (Wiggins 2013). After 1865, youth sport programs primarily serving boys were developed and managed by religious groups, who were the pillars of local communities and were worried that modern life was being made too easy by industrial development and technological advancements.

By 1920, more of the nation lived in urban areas than anywhere else and the number of highly organized, adult-directed youth sport programs exploded. Many of these programs were led by private organizations that existed separate from education centers and proclaimed a desire to support the development of local youth. Instead they laid the seeds for a "competition culture" so pervasive in those youth sport critiques discussed in the essay introduction (Wiggins 2013).

Through the middle of the 20th century, there was a tug-of-war between the private organizations seeking to extend their development of the baby boom generation and professional health and physical educators who fought to pass legislation condemning overspecialization, an overemphasis on competition and poor coaching which was often provided by fathers of team members. There was a growing sentiment within the country linking the growing competitive economy to the youth sports fields where kids (still mostly male) could earn valuable lessons for later in life.

Formal versus Informal Play

After cultural shifts present themselves, researchers often scurry to gain an understanding of decisions being made, and the youth sport debate has been one framed and reframed by scholars for decades, especially since the late 1970s. What emerged, almost immediately, was a conceptualization of the rise of organized sport as a zero-sum competitor to informal play and the debate regarding child development has grown almost entirely within the confines of a one or the other framework. Work is being done by sport scholars like Bowers and Green (2013) that attempts to view youth sport through the combined experiences within structured environments and unstructured settings that offer a more accurate look at how individual participants are being impacted by sport.

Within this section of the essay an attempt is made to paint a picture of both components of a child's sport experience separately, and there is no intention to paint either formal or informal play as free of problems or carrying all of the problems. While informal play may, in many cases, lead to relatively even teams and allow kids to remedy disagreements, there are certainly many instances of bullying, physical altercations and dissent. Without adult supervision to manage dominant personalities or observe social pecking orders, there is an environment capable of excluding unwanted members and being difficult for kids to be in. Likewise, formal play has provided children a forum to participate in peer interactions and to become a part of an extra-familial group, but has also pushed children towards specialization and led to burnout. Here is a quick overview of both sides of the discussion:

Informal play creates an environment of creativity where participants must reach an agreement on what to play, how to play it and what rules will be used to govern the activity if the game is to even be started. Delaney and Madigan (2009) described the significant characteristics of informal sport as

- activity that is player-controlled;
- activity that involves action, especially that which leads to scoring opportunities;
- activity that maximizes personal involvement in the sport;
- spontaneity of play; that is, the plays do not come from a pre-written "playbook";
- no referees, the youth work out disputes for themselves;
- a close score and relatively even teams, which lead to a competitive sporting activity;
- activity can end at any time, even if it is just because the kids are bored of playing or they are called to dinner;
- opportunities to reaffirm friendships through participation in the sporting activity; and
- seldom impacts the total family life—family schedules are not adjusted so that youths can participate in informal play.

Youth desire to be permitted the freedom to play with little adult interference can be seen in the increase in exposure to extreme/alternative sports. Skateboarding, inline skating and snowboarding have all made marked advancements in participant numbers over the last two decades (600 percent increase since 1990) and led to multiple annual X-Games competitions celebrating the best athletes in those activities. Communities around the country heeded the calls from their local youth and are working to find a balanced use of public spaces that meet the needs of the skaters and will remain viable for a reasonable length of time but also don't infringe too much on the rest of their residents who see skateboarding and bicycling as a hindrance.

Coakley (2009) outlined five changes that were important to the growth of organized youth sports over the last 50 years. They included

- number of families with both parents working outside the home has increased dramatically;

- since 1980's major cultural shift on what it means to be a "good parent" changed to those who can account for their child's whereabouts 24/7;
- growing belief that informal, child-controlled activities inevitably lead to trouble;
- increased media focus on fear-producing stories have led parents to view the world outside home as a dangerous place; and
- visibility of high performance and professional sports has increased people's awareness of organized competitive sports as a valued part of culture.

Each of these cultural developments has pushed youth sport away from backyard play where children often play with family members, neighbors or close friends and control the games without intervention from adults. Sport specific organizations like the Little League and Amateur Athletic Union (AAU) have filled that void, recruiting participants as early as age 5, with other programs organizing kids into sports at the age of three. Mike Wagner, Todd Jones and Jill Riepenhoff from the *Columbus Dispatch* researched the tax returns from groups affiliated with youth sports and reported that the industry saw $5 billion pass through its accounts in 2009, a clear indication of the number of parents who register their kids for formal sport leagues and fully adhere to the trends cited by Coakley earlier in the section.

A consequence, intended or not, of this progression toward formalization is that socio-economic status has furthered its encroachment into the youth development equation. Children from lower-income households are not able to participate at the same rate and notably begin youth sport later in their childhood than those from affluent families. If the household income rises above $100,000, a child's mean age at entry into organized/team sports is 6.3, with that age rising to 8.1 when the child is born into a family making less than $35,000 per year (Sabo 2009).

Recent Trends

While the 50-year relationship between formal and informal play has swung toward organized programming, there have been a number of trends over the last 20 years that have impacted the emphasis sportsmanship and other "character developments" are given to American youth during their formative sporting experiences. Two of these movements deserve more attention as they are indicative of a cultural shift away from the development of the whole child and toward the development of an athlete. They are the *privatization* of youth sports as a whole and the *specialization* of the individuals participating in those programs. Both of these trends are related in many ways and the resulting environment created in many cases deemphasizes lessons like sportsmanship and are the primary focus of youth sport reformers.

Privatization

Compounding that widening income gap of youth sport participants is the movement toward private or commercial sport organizations. While youth sports may have their organizational roots within religious groups and continued through municipal recreation departments, tightening budgets and the desire by parents for the "best" for their children have led to a recipe of private coaches, physical trainers, top-flight equipment and exclusive travel teams that create a system of financial haves and have nots.

Through the 1970s much of the nation's youth sport programming occurred within the municipal recreation department or was associated with the religiously-affiliated groups that started the organized youth sport movement. However, in the 1980's local governments were forced to make budgeting decisions as their state and federal funds began to dry up. Among the first cuts were ancillary programs like youth sports (Coakley 2009). Into this vacuum filled private organizations, some started by groups of parents and others by entrepreneurs seizing an opportunity. From these early clubs have evolved a smorgasbord of private coaches, highly-selective teams, and strength trainers all playing to a parent's desire to offer for their child what the media, their neighbors and other influencers say are important.

Privatization is an extension of the trend toward more formalized sport and exacerbates the same economic and ethnic problems discussed briefly above. Trainers, coaches and programs all come at a cost and the reduction in publically-funded programs tilts the tables away from the disadvantaged.

Specialization

One connection that is not often discussed but plays a role is the impact the prospect of paying for college has on parents' decision-making for their children. Higher education is becoming the national standard, with nearly 90 percent of students hoping to attend college and 75 percent of high school graduates furthering their studies (Ramaley and Leskes 2002). With this trend toward increased college attendance comes increased competition for college acceptances and scholarships. Students must find ways to set themselves apart from their peers, either through academics, community involvement, or sports in order to gain entrance to their desired college. Once and if they make it through admissions, many must find a way to pay the costly tuition. While parents can often help with the burden, most students must still take out loans, work during college, receive grants, earn academic scholarships, or win athletic scholarships.

Many families and students anticipate the expense of tuition and hope to get scholarships, which are very desirable among college-bound students. Many concentrate on obtaining academic scholarships, while others work towards athletic scholarships, often specializing in one sport at an early age with hopes to succeed in high school and to be recruited for college. According to Tom Fakehany, a board chair of the Collegiate Volleyball Officiating Association, early specialization is increasing largely because it is thought to improve the athlete's chances of receiving a collegiate athletic scholarship (1995). Athletes desire to specialize in order to gain more exposure to the sport and to become more advanced more quickly (Susanj and Stewart n.d.).

From Youth Sport History and Trends to Sportsmanship

Up to this point, the focus has been on the organizational structures, cultural trends and history of youth sport. Embedded in each of these topics are the impact sport plays in a child's character development and the role sportsmanship plays as part of that development. However, almost from its outset the relationship between sportsmanship and athletics has been cloudy, with the balance between winning and competition and "behavior of a sportsperson" sometimes running at odds (Hinkle Smith 2008). With a review of youth sport history in our rearview mirror, showing a landscape growing in competitive intensity, the role that an emphasis on sportsmanship plays on youth teams and in gyms and rinks across the country is unclear. The rest of this essay will examine how an emphasis on sportsmanship can play an important role in the sport experience of kids across the country, the challenges a more sportsmanlike field of play face and a specific look at the primary stakeholders who have the ability to create an environment more conducive to the development of sportsmanship.

Sportsmanship as Part of Character Development

Sportsmanship, character development, moral development and training in ethics are all terms to describe the merits of sport participation. However there is plenty of work available questioning whether sports inherently build character and may, perhaps, lead to negative youth development. Many of these observations arise from the difficulty in empirically verifying the "sport builds character" hypothesis which leaves researchers with a handful of anecdotes that link sports and character but do not rule out whether the character traits were already evident in the participants prior playing or why others who display strong character qualities have never played sport before (Sage 2013).

Two social psychologists, David Light Shields and Brenda Light Bredemeier, focused much of their research on the link between character development and sports, and coaches' and teammates' influence on children's social development within sport. They stated in their 1995 piece that

> research does not support either position in the debate over sport building character. If any conclusion is justified, it is that the question as posed is too simplistic. The term character is vague.... More important, sport experience is far from uniform ... the social interactions that are fostered by the sport experience ... varies from sport to sport, from team to team, from one geographical region to another, from one level of competition to another, and so on [p. 178].

The authors continued to discuss their view on the overall importance sport plays in the development of moral character by adding sportspersonship as one of the four virtues of moral character as listed by Shields and Bredemeier (1995). The four virtues include: compassion, fairness, sportspersonship and integrity.

Shields and Bredemeier support the discussion running through this essay that by emphasizing sportsmanship, as part of a focus on a holistic development of youth by sport programs, the greater the likelihood of those children emerging from those experiences as stronger citizens. Coaches and teammates influence children's social development within sport (Coakley 2004; Wylleman 2000); while also playing a key role in whether those children enter or withdraw from participating in sports (Rottensteiner, Laakso, Pihala and Konttinen 2013). As such, a significant amount of influence is laid on these two groups and defining sportsmanship is centered on the pair.

No cut-and-dried definition of sportsmanship has been agreed upon by those who study the topic; however five dimensions have been proposed by experts in child development and sociology and to these scholars, positive sportsmanship should include athletes' and coaches' respect and concern for

- one's full commitment toward sport;
- the rules and officials;

- the opponent;
- the social conventions; and
- avoidance of negative approach toward sport participation [Vallerand et al. 1996; Vallerand et al. 1997].

While the coaches and players are most central to how sportsmanship is conveyed, the way in which sport is structured and framed by all with a hand in the child's sport experience directly impacts their overall development. Next attention is shifted to the sources of sportsmanship modeling, looking at ways an emphasis on sportsmanship can influence youth development and the overall sporting experience.

Sources of Sportsmanship Modeling

Character development values taught within organized youth sports are not just presented to children through a play diagram or YouTube video. Behaviors are modeled and taught by three primary youth sport stakeholders who work together (sometimes the same person plays multiple roles) and is where an emphasis on sportsmanship as part of a coherent strategy has the potential to reverse the trends of unsportsmanlike behavior seen at all ages of sport. These three groups are supported by many others like referees, who have a vast amount of control on every aspect of the contest and can mitigate the emotion pushed forth by overzealous coaches or parents and enforce the norms of the game with the participants (Arthur-Banning, Paisley and Wells 2007). Here is an examination of those stakeholders (League/Organizational Administrators, Coaches, Parents) and how they influence the assimilation of sportsmanlike actions into a child's everyday behavior pattern.

League/Organizational Administrators

While parents, coaches and referees may have a hand in emphasizing, or deemphasizing, sportsmanship day to day, the broader organizational structure in which those practices and games are held sets the culture dictating the actions of the other influencers. Duda, Olson and Templin (1991) and Duda and White (1992) examined the relationships between the goals of a sport program and the sportsmanship shown by its participants. The closer a program was to a win-at-all-costs mentality, the greater the unsportsmanlike attitudes such as cheating and using deception to gain an advantage. Alternatively, as the orientation of the program gravitated towards skill and performance improvement, a positive correlation was found with ethical attitudes toward sport.

This research supports Achievement Goal Theory which posits that individuals will possess different meanings that they attach to a particular context and different goals they try to accomplish when faced with making decisions and behavioral choices in a given situation (Lemyre, Roberts, and Ommundsen 2002). More specifically, there are two major goals that guide behavior, ego involvement and task involvement. As they relate to sportsmanship, the more a person is disposed to ego involvement as a goal, the more likely he or she is to view a game as win-at-all-costs, while a task involved athlete participates for the intrinsic benefits and seeks skill development. For adults, our behaviors are likely set and we see games as competitive or not, but youth, for whom sport is a focal point of their personal development, are much more malleable. Whether the camp or league or team they are playing on is constructed with an eye toward development or toward competition holds great influence over whether that child will see sport as a long-term competitive outlet or as a part of their lifelong development. An emphasis from a camp director or league administrator to their subordinates on the importance of development and sportsmanlike behavior sets the cultural tone of that program and the other influential stakeholder groups are likely to adhere to those boundaries.

Coaches

For many children, their youth sport experiences are modeled by coaches who have not undergone formal training. In fact, less than 20 percent of the 2–4 million "little league" coaches and less than 8 percent of high school coaches have received formal training (Merkel 2013). Coaches who have undergone proper training have been schooled in cognitive development and use of age-appropriate methods, including the balance of competitiveness and development. Using the 2005–2006 Women's Sport Foundation data cited in Kelley and Carchia (2013), 39 percent of boys and 38 percent of girls indicated they quit playing sports because they were not having fun and 22 percent of boys and 18 percent of girls quit because they did not get along with the coach. Additionally, while sport administrators and parents continue to emphasize their desire that coaches exhibit and require sportsmanship, coaches (who are often parents of a player) have been found to be unaware that their actions in the heat of competition could be construed as unsportsmanlike (Barton and Stewart 2005; Stewart 1997; Smith and Smoll 1997).

Much of the foundation for coaching education is built on the Arizona Sports Summit Accord (Stewart 2014). In the agreement, emphasis was given to the need for coaches in training to attain specific skills, including a basic knowledge of the character-building aspects of sport and methods of teaching and enforcing the core values of sportsmanship and good character. Martens (2012) stated that one of the primary functions of a coach is to teach athletes moral and ethical behavioral alternatives, and trained coaches are prepared to instill those lessons in their players, but what about a system where the vast majority of coaches are untrained? This is where the organization and administrators play a vital role in supporting their coaches. Be it through communication with parents, modeling to kids or providing information and training for coaches, the various conduits to the athletes are all important to support coaches who spend 11 hours a week with their teams (Hedstrom and Gould 2004).

Parents

Parents shape their children's psychological development through their involvement in their child's athletic experience, be it as a driver, coach or supporter in the stands (Cote and Hay 2002). Substantial literature suggests that behaviors demonstrated by the significant person in a child's life have a great impact on that person's behavior. Thus, how a parent emphasizes and reinforces winning or skill development can have a major effect on what a child deems as success in sports (Hedstrom and Gould 2004). As such, theory proposes that children's sportsmanship behaviors are correlated to those of their parents (Arthur-Banning, Wells, Baker, and Hegreness 2009).

Parental inclination toward ego or task involvement rubs off on their children, which in turn impacts the anxiety felt by the kids before and after games. Scanlan and Lewthwaite (1984) indicated that "prematch worries about failure and perceived parental pressure to participate" were predictors of pre-match stress (p. 208). Similarly Hellstedt's (1988) study on parental pressure on young ski racers found that those who perceived their parents as supportive and positive had more positive reactions to sport participation.

Connections between parental views/actions and the behaviors exhibited by their children are probably the strongest support for the impact an emphasis on sportsmanship can have on youth development. Again, message symmetry between all of these stakeholders toward competition versus development and reinforcing sportsmanship's place in that relationship is vitally important for it to reach its intended target.

Examples of Good and Bad Sportsmanship

To finalize this overview, it is important to draw these broader, theoretical discussions into examples of bad and good sportsmanship happening across the country. Each of the discussed stakeholders have done right by the children in their care as well as acted in ways that hinder their development and experience. This section will outline one specific occurrence from the last few years where coaches, parents, administrators and referees each demonstrated what happens when youth sport goes wrong as well as when its virtues are accented.

When Youth Sports Go Wrong

Unfortunately, there are plenty of examples to pull from where those in charge of youth sport development have acted in ways that put winning and their own personal interests ahead of the children they are leading. Many of these examples have been thrust into the media spotlight, which has influenced some of these decisions by sensationalizing the win-at-all-costs attitude seen here.

Administrators. The month of August in 2014 saw a group of kids from the South Side of Chicago capture the attention of the country as the Jackie Robinson West team won the Little League U.S. Championship. What was supposedly a celebration of a group of kids from disadvantaged backgrounds overcoming the odds turned into a story of corrupt decision-making when a February 2015 announcement stripped the team of its wins for utilizing players from outside the club's jurisdiction. It was determined that administrators from Jackie Robinson West falsified the boundaries of their territory, leading the President and CEO of Little League International Mr. Stephen D. Keener to say, "This is a heartbreaking decision. What these players accomplished on the field and the memories and lessons they have learned during the Little League World Series tournament is something the kids can be proud of, but it is unfortunate that the actions of adults have led to this outcome" (Little League 2015).

This decision came 13 years after another Little League team from the Bronx was stripped of their championships for using an overaged player. They are two of dozens of similar stories where grown men and women push the limits of, and exceed, rules and regulations in place to ensure fair play and a level playing field. With the desire to win so great that administrators are cheating to accomplish their goals, one can imagine the pressure placed on the shoulders of the players.

Coaches. Part of any coach's job is to create a strategy that helps put their team into a position to win. Two Tennessee high school teams were banned from participation in the postseason for deliberately trying to lose in order to earn a more favorable seeding (Branch 2015). With a game against the defending state champion awaiting the winner, Riverdale High School and Smyrna High School started the game with their backups on the floor. From there, players on both sides passed the ball around with little to no intent to score and when Smyrna's players were instructed to foul to give Riverdale free-throw opportunities, the Riverdale player purposely missed them. Finally, the referees called the coaches together in the third quarter after a player on Smyrna tried to shoot at the wrong basket and then notified the Tennessee Secondary School Athletic Association of his experience which lead to the ultimate decision.

Parents. In probably the most publicized story centered on youth sport-related violence, Thomas Junta attacked and killed his 10-year old son's hockey coach Michael Costin in July 2000. After complaining that the youth hockey practice his son was playing in was too rough and Costin responding that hockey was a tough game, Junta rushed Costin in front of the team and hit the coach mercilessly, rupturing an artery in his neck, causing death. Junta was convicted of involuntary manslaughter and has long been the example of extreme parental behavior.

While the example is heinous and sensational in its violence, overzealous youth sport parent stories can be found throughout the media. They range from verbal assaults of parents on their children, coaches and referees as well as threats of legal action against coaches for decisions made and parent vs. parent fights on the sideline of games around the country. Every story of parental fanatical behavior clouds the impact sport can have on youth development and hinders the role of sportsmanship has in that process.

When Youth Sports Go Right

As the normal sport cycle has grown to a never ending, 24/7 race for the next big headline, attention has been swung wildly to stories with negative angles. As such, what is read in newspapers and on websites, and seen on television broadcasts are often those events that are out of the ordinary, i.e., unsportsmanlike behaviors. What isn't shown often enough on *SportsCenter* and others like it are the everyday sporting acts of decency and the extraordinary events that clearly support the view of sport acting as a character development tool. Below are a handful of real-life examples where youth sport went right.

Administrators. In 1991 a group of local volunteers in Harlem sought an opportunity to engage local youth in sport and allow the inner-city youth to learn the value of teams by offering them opportunities to play and learn. Almost 25 years later, Harlem RBI has a budget of $2.7 million and has evolved to include programs like literacy camps, a regular newsletter and mentoring options (Berlin, et.al. 2007). Harlem RBI's program has many of the principal elements discussed earlier in this essay as vital to maximizing youth development. They include:

- Youth are engaged over many years, not on a seasonal or ad hoc basis;
- programs are group based, providing a support network among peers.
- there are low adult-to-youth ratios, fostering connections between youth and caring role models;
- well-trained staff and volunteers ensure high-quality programming; and

• expectations for all participants, no matter their personal circumstances are high [Berlin et al. 2007].

The results of the structure provided by these elements are impressive. Harlem RBI set out in 2001 to create benchmarks and evaluate the results of their programs. Here is what they found:

• 86 percent of participants of the reading program maintained their reading levels through the summer;
• 92 percent of the kids reading program reported they read more and enjoyed reading more;
• 75 percent improved their ability to praise, motivate and support their peers; and
• average length of engagement with program was 3.9 years [Berlin et al. 2007].

These numbers, and the program as a whole, demonstrate sports ability to create measurable change in youth behaviors and attitudes if organized and supported well with an emphasis on developmental outcomes, not those on the field.

Coaches. On many occasions, when opposing teams reach a friendly agreement there are improprieties involved, but a 2009 interaction between St. Joseph Benton and Maryville High Schools in Missouri led to a shining example of sportsmanship. After running across the field to talk to his counterpart during a timeout late in the game with his team down 46–0, Maryville coach Dan McCamy inserted a player on his team with Down Syndrome into the contest. Matt Ziesel, who hadn't participated in full-contact drills in practice but had been part of the Maryville team, entered the game, received the handoff, and with the St. Joseph Benton players suppressing their own stats to assist with creating a lifelong memory, ran 60 yards untouched for a touchdown.

The play made headlines and there were many people who were critical of the play, but the emphasis placed by both coaches on the experience and development of their players instead of with the final score epitomizes sportsmanlike action.

Parents. In a story not shown much attention through the media, fans of the Vanguard College Preparatory School in Texas attended their boys basketball game with Gainesville State School wearing the black and white colors of Gainesville State rather than the normal green and white of Vanguard. Beyond the team color switch, these patrons cheered for Gainesville State, a correctional facility whose players were not going to have anyone cheering for them at the game. The movement was generated by a couple of Vanguard's players who had discussed their desire to not play the game because of the lack of support enjoyed by the Gainesville players and their belief that this wasn't fair (Branch 2015).

After the contest, Gainesville's coach spoke of how little support and encouragement his players receive at games and was very gracious and appreciative of the gesture. While a seemingly minute story, the actions of the players and parents of Vanguard speak to the impact an emphasis on sportsmanship can have long-term and how positively modeled behaviors impact youth development.

Conclusion

Youth sport is a topic under great scrutiny as more becomes known of the impacts on society's increased attention on organized play, winning and specialization among under-18 kids. Many parents see sports as a means to enhance the physical, emotional and social development of their children and an emphasis on participation and sportsmanship have the potential to meet those parental expectations when signing up their child. However, cultural momentum has trended toward power and performance sports and ego involvement with a prevailing goal on winning rather than that development.

While there are many stories out there chronicling unsportsmanlike behavior, those examples tend to be enflamed by the media and significant research demonstrates those with experiences in sport as youth are equipped with leadership and social skills valuable in an array of careers. How well organizations, their administrators, coaches and referees, as well as the parents of the children model positive sporting behaviors, including sportsmanship, is of great importance to maximizing youth sport's value.

Bibliography

Arthur-Banning Skye, Mary Sara Wells, Birgitta Baker and Ryan Hegreness. 2009. "Parents Behaving Badly? The Relationship Between the Sportsmanship Behaviors of Adults and Athletes in Youth Basketball Games." *Journal of Sport Behavior*, 32 (1):3–18.

Barton, Candace, and C. Craig Stewart. 2005. *Parental Expectations of Coaches: Closing the Communication Gap.* International Society of Biomechanics in Sport, Coach Information Services.

Berlin, Richard A., Aaron Dworkin, Ned Eames, Arn Menconi, and Daniel F. Perkins. 2007. "Examples of Sport-Based Youth Development Programs." *New Directions for Youth Development*, 115:85–106.

Bowers, Matthew, and B. Christine Green. 2013. "Reconstructing the Community-Based Youth Sport Experience: How Children Derive Meaning from Unstructured and Organized Settings." *Journal of Sport Management*, 27:422–438.

Branch, G.E. 2015. "Balance Between Win-At-All-Costs and Sportsmanship Hard to Find." *Diverse Education.* Retrieved May 6, 2015 (http://www.readperiodicals.com).

Coakley, Jay J. 2004. "Burnout Among Adolescent Athletes: A Personal Failure or Social Problem." *Sociology of Sport Journal*, 9:271–285.

_____. 2009. *Sports in Society: Issues and Controversies*, 10th ed. New York: McGraw-Hill Education.

Cote, Jean, and John Hay. 2002. "Family Influences on Youth Sport Performance and Participation," pp. 503–519 in *Psychological Foundations of Sport*, edited by John M. Silva and Diane Stevens. Boston: Allyn and Bacon.

Delaney, Tim, and Tim Madigan. 2009. *The Sociology of Sports: An Introduction.* Jefferson, NC: McFarland.

Duda, Joan J., Linda K. Olson, and Thomas J. Templin. 1991. "The Relationship of Task and Ego-Orientation to Sportsmanship Attitudes and the Perceived Legitimacy of Injurious Acts." *Research Quarterly for Exercise and Sport*, 62:79–85.

Duda, Joan J., and Sally A. White. 1992. "Goal Orientations and Beliefs: About the Causes of Sport Success Among Elite Skiers." *The Sport Psychologist*, 6:334–343.

Fakehany, Tom. 1995. *One-Sport High School Athletes.* Retrieved March 8, 2015 (http://home.earthlink.net/~tfakehany/1sport.html).

Hedstrom, Ryan, and Daniel Gould. 2004. *Research in Youth Sports: Critical Issues Status.* Institute for the Study of Youth Sports.

Hellstedt, Jon C. 1988. "Early Adolescent Perceptions of Parental Pressure in the Sport Environment." *Journal of Sport Behavior*, 13:135–144.

Hinkle Smith, Shelby L. 2008. "Sportsmanship." *Research Starters Education*, online ed. Retrieved March 8, 2015 (http://connection.ebscohost.com).

Kelley, Bruce and Carl Carchia. 2013. "Hey, Data Data—Swing!" *ESPN the Magazine.* Retrieved February 16, 2015 (http://espn.go.com).

Lemyre Pierre-Nicolas, Glyn Roberts, and Yngvar Ommundsen. 2002. "Achievement Goal Orientations, Perceived Ability and Sportspersonship in Youth Soccer." *Journal of Applied Sport Psychology*, 14:120–136.

Little League International. 2015. *Suspensions Handed Out, U.S. Championship Title Revoked, Special District Advisor to be Named.* Retrieved May 29, 2015 (http://www.littleleague.org).

Longman, Jere. 2008. "At Pinnacle, Stepping Away from Basketball." *New York Times*. Retrieved March 8, 2015 (http://www.nytimes.com).

Martens, Rainier. 2012. *Successful Coaching*, 4th ed. Champaign, IL: Human Kinetics.

Merkel, Donna L. 2013. "Youth Sport: Positive and Negative Impact on Young Athletes." *Journal of Sports Medicine*, 4:151–160.

Ramaley, Judith A., and Andrea Leskes 2002. *Greater Expectations Panel Report*. Association of American Colleges and Universities. Washington, D.C.

Sabo, Don. 2009. "The Gender Gap in Youth Sports: Too Many Urban Girls Are Being Left Behind." *Journal of Physical Education, Recreation and Dance*, 80 (8):35–40.

Sage, George. 2013. "Does Sport Affect Character Development in Athletes?" *Journal of Physical Education, Recreation and Dance*, 69 (1):15–18.

Scanlan, Tara K., and Rebecca Lewthwaite. 1984. "Social Psychological Aspects of Competition for Male Youth Sport Participants I. Predictors of Competitive Stress." *Journal of Sport Psychology*, 6:208–226.

Shields, David Light, and Brenda Light Bredemeier. 1995. *Character Development and Physical Activity*. Champaign, IL: Human Kinetics.

Smith, Ronald, and Frank Smoll. 1997. "Coaching the Coaches: Youth Sports as a Scientific and Applied Behavior Setting." *Current Directions in Psychological Science*, 6:16–21.

Stewart, C. Craig 1997. "Parent-Coach Understanding: Another Look." *Physical Educator*, 54:96–104.

_____. 2014. "Sportsmanship, Gamesmanship, and the Implications for Coach Education." *Strategies: A Journal for Physical and Sport Educators*, 27 (5): 3–7.

Susanj, David, and C. Craig Stewart N.d. *Specialization in Sport: How Early.... How Necessary?* Retrieved May 10, 2015 (http://letitflyfootballcamp.com).

Vallerand, Robert J., Nathalie Briere, Celine Blanchard, and Pierre Provencher. 1997. "Development and Validation of the Multidimensional Sportspersonship Orientations Scale." *Journal of Sport and Exercise Psychology*, 19 (2):197–206.

Vallerand, Robert J., Paul Deshaies, Jean-Pierre Cuerrier, Nathalie Briere, and Luc G. Pelletier. 1996. "Toward a Multidimensional Definition of Sportsmanship." *Journal of Applied Sport Psychology*, 8 (1):89–101.

Wiggins David K. 2013. "A Worthwhile Effort? History of Organized Youth Sport in the United States." *Kinesiology Review*, 2:65–75.

Woods, Robert B. 2011. *Social Issues in Sport*, 2d ed. Champaign, IL: Human Kinetics.

Wylleman, Paul. 2000. "Interpersonal Relationships in Sport: Uncharted Territory in Sport Psychology Research." *International Journal of Sport Psychology*, 31:555–572.

Sportsmanship and Cognitive Psychology

STEPHEN A. WURST

When someone mentions "sportsmanship" to you, you probably remember sporting events that are exemplars of what you consider to be good sportsmanship and poor sportsmanship. Below are four examples that illustrate different aspects of sportsmanship:

> In the semi-finals women's match in the 2009 U.S. Open tennis tournament, Kim Clijsters was leading Serena Williams 6–4, 6–5 with Williams serving at 15–30. On her second serve, Williams was called for a foot fault, resulting in an outburst by Williams in which she waved her racquets at the lineswoman and was reported to repeatedly use profanity and threaten to shove the ball down the lineswoman's throat. Williams was called for a code violation for unsportsmanlike conduct, and because of an earlier violation involving racquet abuse, lost an additional point, and therefore the match. Although Williams is widely considered to be the best female tennis player of all time, and her recent behavior has been exemplary, this incident remains a prominent event of her career [Graber 2009].

> In the 2008 World Series, Game 3, between the Tampa Bay Rays and the Philadelphia Phillies, 45-year-old Jamie Moyer, the oldest pitcher to start a World Series game since 1929, is pitching a two-hitter starting the top of the seventh with his Phillies leading 4–1. Carl Crawford leads off the inning for Tampa Bay with a bunt toward the first base line. Moyer races over to the ball, dives to the ground and flips the ball with his glove to first-baseman Ryan Howard, who grabs the ball with his bare hand as Crawford speeds down the line. The first base umpire calls Crawford safe. Numerous replays, however, show that the "throw" beat Crawford's foot touching the bag, and therefore he should have been called out. Moyer, laying on the ground and looking directly at first, would have had the best view of the play. Moyer's reaction was to walk back to the pitcher's mound. His first pitch to the next batter, Dioneer Navarro, was a called strike. The Phillies went on to win the game, and the Series [*The Philadelphia Phillies 2008 World Series Collector's Edition* 2008].

> A similar situation occurred on June 2, 2010, when Detroit Tigers pitcher Armando Gallaraga was one out away from pitching the first perfect game in the history of this storied franchise. Cleveland's Jason Donald hit a ground ball that was fielded by Tigers first baseman Miguel Cabrera. Cabrera ranged to his right, and threw to Gallaraga covering first base. Although replays showed that the throw beat Donald, first base umpire Jim Joyce called Donald safe, thus depriving Gallaraga of a perfect game. Gallaraga started celebrating after the play, until he realized the safe call was made. He made what has been described as a "wry smile" at the umpire, and then returned to the pitcher's mound to face the next batter. He finished the game with a one-hitter, in a game now referred to as the "28-out perfect game" [Castrovince 2011].

> In a Division II women's softball game between Western Oregon and Central Washington on April 26, 2008, that would be instrumental in determining who would advance to the NCAA playoffs, a play occurred that would quickly become the definitive act of sportsmanship. Western Oregon's Sara Tucholsky hit a home run over the fence, the first home run of her career. But as she backtracked to touch first base after initially missing the bag, she tore her ACL and fell to the ground. She was now unable to round the bases. If her teammates helped her, according the umpire, she would be called out. Central Washington teammates Mallory Holtman, who had the most home runs in conference history, and Liz Wallace came out of their dugout and carried Tucholsky around the bases, gently lighting her foot on each base and home plate, making it an official home run. The home run was ultimately the difference in the outcome, with Western Oregon winning 4–2. This play was later awarded the Espy Award for the "Best Sport Moment" of 2008 [Hayes 2015].

These four events have been selected to demonstrate how cognitive psychology can play a role in sportsmanship. In this essay, I will first provide definitions of cognitive psychology and of sportsmanship; then show how cognitive psychology has been used to help athletes cope with acute stressors, and therefore exhibit good sportsmanship and avoid unsportsmanlike behavior; and finally how an analysis of problem solving can be used to lead to good sportsmanship and unsportsmanlike behavior.

Definitions of Key Terms

Although many definitions of cognitive psychology itemize the various aspects of cognition (e.g., Goldstein 2009), a more direct definition is provided by Nevid (2009): Cognitive psychology is the branch of psychology that "explores … how we think, process information, use language, and solve problems" (p. 228). Although all of these processes could play a role in sportsmanship, the present essay will focus on how we can control our thoughts ("cognitive control strategies") and problem solving.

In regard to sportsmanship, most people have a sense of what sportsmanship is, but it is important to have a strong definition. The one most relevant to this essay was devised by Vallerand, Briere, Deshaies, Cuerrier, and Peletier (2007), who conducted a factor analysis to develop their definition of sportsmanship. Their five factors that define sportsmanship are the respect and concern for

- one's full commitment toward sport participation;
- the rules and officials;
- social conventions;
- the opponent; and
- a negative (win at all costs) approach toward sport participation [p. 436].

Vallerand et al. (2007) listed exemplars for each factor. "Shows a temper after losing" was an example of the "Negative Approach" factor, and "not criticizing the referee when he or she makes mistakes" and "remaining calm after making a mistake" were examples of the "Rules and Officials" factor. These exemplars are obviously related to the Williams, Moyer and Gallaraga scenarios mentioned above. For "The Opponent" factor, "refusing to take advantage of an injured opponent" was listed. This would be an understatement as it relates to the Central Washington-Western Oregon softball game.

So how does cognitive psychology relate to sportsmanship given this definition? The commonality in the "Negative Approach" factor and the "Rules and Officials" factor is how the athlete handles bad calls from the officials. Cognitive psychology plays a role here by developing cognitive control strategies that aid the athlete in coping with these situations. Additionally, the topic area of problem solving in cognitive psychology can provide insight as to how some more ambiguous examples of unsportsmanlike behavior occur. For "The Opponent" factor, the process of solving problems can also reveal how sportsmanship can be achieved in novel situations. Each of these will be addressed in turn below.

Cognitive Control Strategies and Sportsmanship

The general psychology literature has a rich history of strategies on how to cope with stress, but it has only been within approximately the last 25 years that this research has been applied to sport. One major model of coping as it applies to sport performance was devised by Anshel (1990). One important aspect of Anshel's research is that he has emphasized the difference between chronic stress and acute stressors. Acute stressors are those that are unpredictable and cause immediate and high levels of stress. Examples of acute stressors are injury, opponent's cheating, bad calls by officials, personal mistakes, criticism from coaches, teammates and parents, negative comments by opponents, and heckling and booing from spectators (Goyen and Anshel 1998). Since many of the high profile examples of unsportsmanlike behavior have been elicited by acute stressors (e.g., numerous outbursts by tennis player John McEnroe in response to calls by officials, NBA player Ron Artest's fight with a spectator after having a beer thrown at him igniting the "Malice in the Palace" in 2004, baseball fights started by a hit-by-pitch, such as Jason Varitek and Alex Rodriguez starting a bench-clearing fight between the Red Sox and Yankees in 2004), this model seems the most appropriate to highlight. Anshel named his strategy the "COPE model" of dealing with acute stressors. COPE is an acronym for the four steps involved in the strategy: Control emotions; Organize input; Plan response; and Execute the next action. Anshel states that an acute stressor results in the "fight or flight response" and the accompanying adrenaline release, so taking a few deep breaths to control this situation is the vital first step. This will help prevent the physiological "upheaval" that will interfere with behavior and prepares the athlete for the subsequent cognitive component. This can take a few seconds to a couple of minutes, depending on the situation and the individual. The "Organize input" step is to use cognitive control techniques to alleviate the stressor. The thought process in the "Plan response" stage is to focus on his/her sport task at hand, knowing that the acute stressor and all related emotions are "history." The last step is executing the task, being focused and assertive. An important point about the COPE strategy is that it can be learned and has been shown to be an effective way of dealing with acute stressors (e.g., Anshel 1990; Anshel, Gregory, and Kaczmarek, 1990).

The major cognitive element in this strategy, and perhaps the most important, is the "Organize Input" stage. Indeed, one study by Anshel (1994) showed no significant difference between the full COPE strategy training and just training on "organizing input," with both being better than the control group. In this stage, Anshel (1990) advises athletes to essentially translate the information at hand. For example, if a coach is yelling criticism that includes name-calling, the athlete needs to concentrate on what the coach's valid criticism is, and filter out the personal negative comments. Other cognitive control strategies that have been reviewed by Bunker, Williams, and Zinsser (1993) can be used in this stage also. Three major cognitive control strategies are thought stoppage, countering, and reframing. Bunker at al. discuss these in order to improve general performance, but certainly these strategies can be used as ways of coping with acute stressors, and therefore avoid unsportsmanlike behavior.

Thought stoppage is the use of a trigger word, such as "Stop!" that can be yelled subvocally, or an action, such as snapping a rubber band, that terminates the negative thoughts that can be elicited by an acute stressor (Bunker et al. 1993). This is important because negative thoughts can escalate, and the loss of control of emotions can follow, which can lead to unsportsmanlike behavior. As Bunker at al. point out, it seems easy to recommend these techniques, but in highly competitive situations, these techniques may be difficult to implement. Therefore, this technique does need to be practiced, but still might not be enough to curtail the resulting stress. What is interesting to note about the Serena Williams example above is that Williams may have tried to do some similar strategy, because she did pause for a few seconds between the foot fault call and her approaching the lineswoman who made the call. So even knowing about these strategies may not be enough to cope with high levels of stress.

The second cognitive control strategy that can reduce unsportsmanlike behavior is countering. Countering is "an internal dialogue that uses facts and reasons to refute the underlying beliefs and assumptions that lead to negative thinking" (Bunker et al. 1993:234). The athlete using this strategy is essentially debating the negative thoughts with positive thoughts. For example, if an official makes a bad call, the athlete might have the negative thoughts of "the ref stinks" and "the ref is against me," that can lead to the athlete yelling at the official. However, if the athlete counters these thoughts with the positive thoughts of "I can't change the call, I have to concentrate on what I can control," then more sportsmanlike behavior should follow. The same idea can happen with criticism from a coach, teammate, or the athlete. Instead of thinking, "Coach/teammate hates me," the athlete can counter with "Coach/teammate is yelling because he/she cares." And instead of "I suck," the athlete can counter with "I'm feeling this way because I don't want to let my team down; I have to get back into the game and show the team I can overcome this."

Reframing is a similar technique to countering, but involves taking the current information and processing it in a positive way (Bunker et al. 1993). Jones (2003) also suggests reframing as a way of controlling emotions in competition. For example, if a soccer player misses any easy shot, he/she can reframe the situation as "I'll get it next time" or "I make many other contributions to the team; this one shot doesn't dictate my performance." Another sport example derives from the classic cognition research on the effect of labeling on decision making. In an oft-cited study, Levin and Gaeth (1988) showed that consumers rated ground beef labeled as "75 percent lean" as less greasy and tastier than ground beef labeled "25 percent fat." An analogous situation in baseball would be if a relief pitcher enters a game in an acutely stressful situation, and is pitching against someone who the pitcher knows is hitting .400 against him/her. The pitcher might have the negative thought of "This batter has a great batting average against me." But reframing takes that same information and puts it in a positive light: "I have a better chance of getting him/her out that he/she getting a hit!"

More recent research has identified other cognitive coping strategies, especially in regard to cognitive appraisal of the situation (is the stressful situation perceived as a "threat" or a "challenge" to the athlete?). Other classifications of responses to stressors include whether the response is an "approach" vs. "avoidance" cognitive strategy (Anshel 2000), or if it is "problem-based" vs. "emotion-based" (e.g., Nicholls, Holt, Polman, and Bloomfield 2006). Anshel (2000) recommends self-talk comments such as "I am in control" and "I can learn from this experience" as examples of "approach based cognitions," while 'The umps are just having a bad day" and "I can laugh about this later" exemplify "avoidance based" cognitions. Examples of "problem-focused coping" fit the COPE model's third stage of "Plan response" such as increasing concentration on the immediate task and correcting the error just made. "Emotion-focused coping" overlaps with the "Control emotion" stage (do relaxation techniques) and "Organize input" (use positive thoughts to reduce stress and using self-deprecating humor).

Although it is speculative at this point, it seems that the Moyer and Gallaraga examples cited above may have entailed coping strategies similar to the COPE model. Moyer was composed emotionally after the bad call, did some cognitive control, and planned and executed the next response (pitching to Navarro). Gallaraga seemed to do the same steps, but may have added some humor (e.g., Giacobbi, Foore, and Weinberg 2004) to his self-talk since he did smile after the bad call.

Subsequent research has also shown how coping strategies are used by children, adolescent and adult athletes, and that gender and racial differences exist in coping strategies, in diverse sports such as basketball (Anshel and Kaissidis 1997), field hockey, basketball, cricket (Goyen and Anshel 1998), rugby (Nicholls, Holt, Polman, and Bloomfield 2006) and golf (Giacobbi et al. 2004). Nicholls and Polman (2006), in their review article, state that older athletes are more effective at controlling stress; that athletes in individual sports use more coping strategies than team athletes; and that individual differences need to be considered when teaching cognitive control strategies. The important conclusion reached by Nicholls and Polman is that coping strategies can be learned, which will help improve individual performance and satisfaction, but will have the added benefit of increasing higher levels of sportsmanship.

Problem Solving and Sportsmanship

Another major topic area in cognitive psychology is problem solving. A problem can be defined as when there is a gap between an initial state and the goal state, without an obvious way of crossing that gap (Hayes 1989). Some well-known problems used in cognitive psychology include the Tower of Hanoi (Goldstein 2009), Duncker's box-candle problem, Maier's two-string problem, and the Nine-dot problem (Hayes 1989). Research using each of these problems has resulted in models about how humans generate solutions, and what impediments can occur when trying to come up with solutions.

One classic model of problem solving was developed by Hayes (1989). According to Hayes, problem solving consists of six steps: (1) Finding the problem; (2) Representing the problem; (3) Planning the solution; (4) Carrying out the plan; (5) Evaluating the solution; and (6) Consolidating gains. Each of these steps will be discussed and related to sportsmanship in general, especially in regard to "representing the problem" and the illuminating case of how problem solving was successfully achieved by Mallory Holtman and Liz Wallace in the Central Washington-Western Oregon softball game.

Finding a problem is exceptionally easy in daily life. In fact, problems tend to find us: How do I get to class on time? How do I make more money? How do I complete the task my boss assigned me? In sports, the list is just as easy: How do I find time to work out? How do I approach the coach with a question? What can I do to play better? It is evident that problems do abound in life and in sports, but the accompanying step is whether the problem is important enough to *you* to try to find a solution for. Hayes (1989), for example, cites a personal example of searching a newspaper for theater listings, but never really considered this a problem worthy enough to try to solve.

According to Hayes (1989), representing the problem has four parts: (1) the goal; (2) the initial state; (3) the operators; and (4) the restrictions on the operators ("the rules"). The Nine-dot problem can be used to demonstrate these steps (Hayes 1989). The "initial state" in this problem is a 3 × 3 array of equally spaced dots. The goal is to have four lines that connect all nine dots. The operator is drawing the lines. The restrictions are (a) the lines must be straight lines; (b) each dot must be touched by at least one of the lines; and (c) you cannot raise your pencil from the paper. (Take a minute to try it out if you have never encountered this problem before!) The Nine-dot problem also highlights an important part of problem solving: People tend to add restrictions that aren't explicitly given. The general term for these impediments to problem solving is "mental set." In this specific example, individuals tend to consider only the area where the dots are as the "playing field." The solution can only be achieved in this case if the individual literally "thinks outside the box" and draws lines beyond the subjective "box" where the nine dots are.

A sport example that has generated ongoing controversy is the problem of a pitcher having a good grip on the baseball on a cold night. The initial state is "not being able to grip the ball" and the goal state is "gripping the ball efficiently." The operator is simply the ball is in the hand and needing to be pitched. How the "restrictions" are interpreted by the individual is the source the controversy and whether the solution is unsportsmanlike. For example, pitchers such as the Yankees Michael Pineda, the Brewers Will Smith, and the Orioles Brian Matusz have been suspended recently for applying a foreign substance (such as pine tar, sunscreen, and resin) to the baseball. Although this solution does seem to be a formal restriction, several commentators and ex-players indicated that this solution is an unwritten acceptable solution. The prevalence of this tactic is exemplified by the Hall of Fame pitcher Gaylord Perry, who has achieved popular culture fame for his perceived use of foreign substances (Madden 2014).

Usually, applying restrictions on the operators that aren't specified can impede problem solving. In situations like the foreign substances on the baseball, it can lead to a solution, but whether it is an appropriate way of getting an advantage, or whether it's bad sportsmanship, can be ambiguous. For example, former NFL linebacker Bill Romanowski has been outspoken about his attempts to test where the restrictions are. Among the tactics he used to gain an advantage was tailoring his uniform and applying Vaseline to it so opponents couldn't grab him; adding silicone to his gloves for a better grip; ingesting substances that would make his body and breathe smell bad; and spitting on an opponent (Babb 2012). These tactics obviously vary in how ambiguous the level of sportsmanship is in each case.

The three "-gates" in the NFL between 2007 and 2015 also highlight how interpreting the restrictions (or ignoring them) can lead to bad sportsmanship (Molloy 2015). "Spygate," the term used for the New England Patriots violating NFL rules on videotaping signals against the New York Jets in 2007, shows how the rules can be explicit but somewhat rationalized away in this case. Similarly, "Deflategate," in 2015, involved the Patriots again, with the footballs used in the AFC Conference final game being at an inflation level below the NFL restricted level. (Details at the time of writing this essay are still being debated). A more flagrant act of bad sportsmanship in 2009 was coined "Bountygate." New Orleans Saints defensive coordinator Gregg Williams organized a monetary award system for players who injured select players from the opposing team, including star veteran quarterbacks such as Kurt Warner and Bret Favre, and emerging stars such as Cam Newton. As opposed to the other two "-gates," Bountygate demonstrates the lack of respect for opponents and the negative approach components of Vallerand et al.'s (2007) definition of sportsmanship. Certainly other topic areas in psychology, such as social psychology, personality, and learning theory, are relevant in determining why these rules would be violated, but the focus of this essay is to illustrate where in the problem solving process bad sportsmanship can occur.

As opposed to the above examples of unsportsmanship behavior, the Hayes model can illustrate how the extraordinary act of good sportsmanship occurred in the Western Oregon-Central Washington softball game (Rinaldi 2009). Step 1 of "finding the problem" is not as obvious as it first appears. That Tucholsky fell and could not round the bases is a problem, but most directly to Tucholsky and her team. What is vital to this act of sportsmanship was that Holtman determined it was *her* problem as well that needed a solution. The second step of "representing the problem" is also crucial to understanding how sportsmanship happened here. The initial state (Tucholsky on the ground at first base unable to walk) and the goal state (getting credit for the home run) needed to be identified. Again, the initial state is obvious, but the goal state needed to be determined by the problem solvers. Next the operators and restrictions were mentally itemized: Each base needed to be touched by Tucholsky; her teammates and coach could not help her; a pinch-runner could be used, but the hit would count as a two-run single. Step 3, planning the solution, was then accomplished. The various solutions were generated and critiqued. Pinch-runner? A "two-run single" doesn't attain the goal state of a home run. Teammates helping? Also rejected because she would be called out. Then the problem solvers "thought outside the box" and creative solutions were generated. In a less publicized, but also incredibly touching, act of sportsmanship, the wife of Western Oregon coach Gary Frederick, Bobbi Frederick, who used a wheelchair because she had ALS, generated the solution of using her wheelchair to transport Tucholsky around the bases (Hayes 2015). Then Holtman's solution "popped into her head," according to Wallace, who then critiqued it by asking the umpires if that would violate any of the restrictions. The umpires verified that it wouldn't (Rinaldi 2009). Steps 4 through 6 were then performed: the plan was then carried out, evaluated (it did accomplish the goal), and gains consolidated (although it ultimately cost us the game and the season, something much greater was achieved).

Conclusion

As reviewed above, cognitive psychology is an important part of sportsmanship. Cognitive control strategies can result in examples of good sportsmanship, while the lack of these strategies can result in unsportsmanlike behavior. Teaching athletes these techniques needs to be implemented at all ages and competition levels. Not only do these techniques encourage good sportsmanship, these strategies will help the athlete's performance and satisfaction. Cognitive psychology can also increase good sportsmanship by analyzing the athlete's problem solving processes. By investigating current sporting events, sport psychologists can elucidate where in the process good sportsmanship can emerge, and where solutions veer off into acts of unsportsmanlike behavior. This knowledge can also help athletes reflect on their problem solving, and encourage good sportsmanship. Although not specified above, these strategies can also be used to increase sportsmanship in the other participants in sports: coaches, spectators, officials, and parents. Lastly, hopefully it was noticeable that excellent acts of sportsmanship were focused on more in this essay than unsportsmanlike acts. (Many high-profile examples of bad sportsmanship that are probably familiar to the reader were deliberately not cited in this essay.) Unfortunately, acts of good sportsmanship are less publicized. For example, one reason the Moyer play was selected was because it did *not* attract media attention, whereas the "Malice in the Palace," which was only mentioned in passing in this paper, garnered days of media attention. An encouraging sign, however, is that the media did highlight the subsequent reaction to the Gallaraga play from both Gallarga and the umpire Joyce. Although it was beyond the focus of this essay to go into detail here, the actions of both men have been widely promoted as examples of exceptional sportsmanship (Nelson 2011). The more cognitive psychology can help increase sportsmanship, perhaps more acts of good sportsmanship will attract more media attention.

Bibliography

Anshel, Mark H. 1990. "Toward Development of a Model for Coping with Acute Stress in Sport." *International Journal of Sport Psychology*, 21:58–83.

_____. 2000. "A Conceptual Model and Implications for Coping with Stressful Events in Police Work." *Criminal Justice and Behavior*, 27, 375–400.

Anshel, Mark H., and Jennifer Delany. 2001. "Sources of Acute Stress, Cognitive Appraisals, and Coping Strategies of the Male and Female Child Athletes." *Journal of Sport Behavior*, 24 (4):329–353.

Anshel, Mark H., W. Larry Gregory, and Margaret Kaczmarek. 1990. "The Effectiveness of a Stress Training Program in Coping with Criticism in Sport: A Test of the COPE Model." *Journal of Sport Behavior*, 13 (4):194–217.

Anshel, Mark H., and Angelo N. Kaissidis. (1997). "Coping Style and Situational Appraisals as Predictors of Coping Strategies Following Stressful Events in Sport as a Function of Gender and Skill Level." *British Journal of Psychology*, 88 (2): 263–276.

Anshel, Mark H., Toto Sutarso, and Colby Jubenville. 2009. "Racial and Gender Differences on Sources of Acute Stress and Coping Style Among Competitive Athletes." *The Journal of Social Psychology*, 149 (2):159–177.

Babb, Kent. 2012. "In Wake of Chargers Stickum Allegations, Some NFL Alums Say Cheating Is Part of the Game." *Washington Post*, October 27. Retrieved June 1, 2015 (http://www.washingtonpost.com).

Bunker, Linda, Jean M. Williams, and Nate Zinsser. 1993. "Cognitive Techniques for Improving Performance and Building Confidence," pp. 225–242 in *Applied Sport Psychology: Personal Growth to Peak Performance*, 2d ed., edited by Jean M. Williams. Mountain View, CA: Mayfield.

Castrovince, Anthony. 2011. "A Year Later, Perfect Memories of Imperfect Game." Retrieved June 30, 2015. (http://m.mlb.com).

Giacobbi, Peter, Jr., B. Foore, and R. S. Weinberg. 2004. "Broken Clubs and Expletives: The Sources of Stress and Coping Responses of Skilled and Moderately Skilled Golfers." *Journal of Applied Sport Psychology*, 16:166–182.

Goldstein, E. Bruce. 2009. *Cognitive Psychology: Connecting, Mind, Research, and Everyday Experience.* Belmont, CA: Thomson/Wadsworth.

Goyen, Michelle, J., and Mar. H. Anshel. 1998. "Sources of Acute Competitive Stress and Use of Coping Strategies as a Function of Age and Gender." *Journal of Applied Developmental Psychology*, 19 (3):469–486.

Graber, Greg. 2009. "Serena's Tirade Abruptly Ends Match." Retrieved May 30, 2015 (http://sports.espn.go.com).
Hayes, Graham. "Holtman Carried Home to Central Washington." *ESPNW,* May 31. Retrieved May 30, 2015 (http://espn.go.com).
Hayes, John R. 1989. *The Complete Problem Solver,* 2d ed. Hillsdale, NJ: Erlbaum.
Jones, Marc V. 2003. "Controlling Emotions In Sport." *The Sport Psychologist*, 17:471–486.
Levin, I.P., and G.J. Gaeth. 1988. "How Consumers Are Affected by the Framing of Attribute Information Before and After Consuming the Product." *Journal of Consumer Research*, 15:374–378.
Madden, Bill. 2014. "Baseball's Most Famous 'Foreign Substance' Abuser Gaylord Perry Says Pine Tar is Definitely a 'Performance Enhancing Substance' … Tony La Russa Agrees." *New York Daily News,* April 25, 2014. Retrieved June 1, 2015 (http://www.nydailynews.com).
Molloy, Parker Marie. 2015. "The Joy of Six: NFL Cheating Scandals from Spygate to Bountygate." *The Guardian*, January 23. Retrieved June 1, 2015 (http://www.theguardian.com).
Nelson, Amy K. 2011. "Searching for Meaning in the Mistake." Retrieved June 30, 2015 (http://sports.espn.go.com).
Nevid, Jeffrey S. 2009. *Essentials of Psychology: Concepts and Applications*, 2d ed. Boston: Houghton Mifflin.
Nicholls, Adam R., and Remco C.J. Polman. 2007. "Coping in Sport: A Systematic Review." *Journal of Sports Sciences*, 25(1): 11–31.
The Philadelphia Phillies 2008 World Series Collector's Edition. 2008. DVD. Major League Baseball Properties.
Rinaldi, Tom. 2009. "Touching Them All." ESPN SportsCenter, September 3. Retrieved June 1, 2015 (https://www.youtube.com).

Sportsmanship Case Study

Reaching for Team Selection in High Performance Sport at the Price of Sportsmanship

Cíara Losty

The topic of teams, teaming, team-building, or leading teams has been a very popular focus in sports psychology literature in recent years. It has been written about in sport psychology textbooks and management journals alike (Moran 2012; Kremer and Moran, 2013). Coaches and athletes want to be involved in a progressive and functioning team. Team cohesion exists where players are united in a common purpose (Cashmore 2002); however when athletes in high performance sports are competing for team selection team cohesion is difficult to develop. There is no consensus on whether a team should be led by one person or consist of a group of star performers. What is a challenge in many sport organizational settings is the delegating of roles for each team member, particularly with individual athletes, e.g., track and field athletes, yet they may still train together for a relay race. One person may hold all of the power and in sporting organizations this is generally the performance director (PD) or head coach. Interestingly in many small and minority sports organizations the PD or head coach are the same individual. This is a potential area where team/athlete/coach conflict can arise, specifically relating to team selection. The vast majority of teams are plagued by a lack of trust, particularly in a squad type scenario and trust is seen as an essential component within team building (Kramer and Moran 2013; Moran 2012). Lack of trust may undermine core sportsmanship behaviors such as respect, graciousness and interconnection. There are many aspects of teaming worthy of research. This essay will provide an insight into an applied sport psychology provider's experience of working with high performance athletes who train, live, socialize together, yet are all competing for squad selection, and how this impacts on sportsmanship-like behaviors.

The process of athlete selection to a team should be a relatively simple process—the best athlete should be selected ahead of another athlete who does not perform as well. But who decides what the criteria are that determines who the better athlete is, how do people get to know what these criteria are, how does this influence sportsmanship-like behavior within a group of athletes and how does this impact on the coach/athlete relationship? How we each compete in sports can have an effect on our personal moral and ethical behavior in a team environment (Hanson and Savage 2012). The National Collegiate Athletic Association (NCAA) (2003) defined the concept of "sportsmanship" as a set of behaviors to be exhibited by athletes, coaches, officials, administrators and fans (parents) in athletic competition. These behaviors are based on such fundamental values as respect, fairness, civility, honesty, and responsibility (p. 15). However these sportsmanlike behaviors are often compromised in high performance competitive sports. Delaney and Madigan (2009) highlighted that "shouldn't winning come *with* sportsmanship and not in spite of it?" (p. 183). High performance sport clearly provides opportunities for positive outcomes, however these positive outcomes are not necessarily automatic (Cote 2006).

The Cuddihy/Mills Olympic Relay Selection Saga

Catriona Cuddihy (25 years of age) was reinstated into Ireland's 4 × 400m Olympic relay squad following a successful appeal. Cuddihy's place was taken by Northern Ireland athlete Joanna Mills, who won her appeal against her omission from the six-strong squad. Teenager Mills (19 years of age) argued that she was the sixth-best 400m runner in Ireland that season and faster than Cuddihy. Cuddihy lodged a counter appeal to the Olympic Council of Ireland. Cuddihy's personal best of 54.59, set on 10 June 2012 in the UK, was slower than Joanna Mills' seasonal best. Mills was fourth in the individual 400m final of the 2011 European Junior Championships and had a personal best of 53.89 set at that event in Estonia. Mills had also spent a week in Helsinki taking part in relay practice in preparation for the Olympic Games. Catriona's older sister Joanne Cuddihy was also selected for the Olympic 400m relay team. Mills' original appeal was upheld by the Athletics Ireland Appeal Panel after it found that the initial selection of Cuddihy had taken too narrow a view of these criteria, ignoring her international performances at youth and junior level. Cuddihy's overall relay experience and overall experience in major championships were the two main criteria on which the appeal and counter-appeal were contested.

Both athletes gave interviews to the press separately and highlighted how upset and anxious they were with the impending decision. These appeals and selection scenarios played out in the Irish press, leading right up until the final selection was announced. With just three days to go until the 2012 Games officially opened, the tribunal's verdict signaled the end of Joanna Mills' hopes of competing in London. Mills, however, had the option of appealing to the Court of Arbitration for Sport but decided not to. Cuddihy joined her sister Joanne, Michelle Carey, Claire Bergin, Marian Heffernan, and Jessie Barr in the Irish squad for London 2012 Games. The team competed at the London games and did not advance past the heat into the semi-finals. Describing the affair as a significant learning experience, Athletics Ireland promised to conduct a post–Olympic review of the selection and appeals processes and their impact on all involved. The confusion regarding the selections were less than an ideal preparation environment for a high performance relay team at the world's biggest sports show.

When Is a Selection Policy Required?

Natural justice activists would probably argue that there should be a policy any time a coach or sporting body has to select one athlete over another. The reality is, however, that this is impractical, as the implication is that the coach of an under-age soccer team would need to have a documented policy setting out how they are going to pick their team to compete in the Saturday morning local mini-football game. It is far more realistic to consider implementing a formal selection policy when representative team selections are to be made. This is the level where athletes are competing against each other for selection to a particular team or event, and often there are more athletes competing for selection than places available as explored in the Cuddihy/Mills 2012 saga above (see box).

Who is eligible for selection? This needs to be clearly stated so that only those who are eligible can be considered for selection. For example, in some cases age eligibility needs to be stated; in other cases it needs to be stated that only athletes who have registered and are financial members of the association will be considered for selection. What happens if an athlete is injured or ill; are they deselected from the competition and who takes their place? Is it simply a case that who is next in ranking should be selected? This seems to be the fairest way of making the decision; however in applied practice this is often not adhered to and can create tension and unsportsmanlike behaviours within a team. It appears that current trends in sport programming are moving towards institutionalization, elitism, early selection, and early specialization (Fraser-Thomas and Côté 2006; Côté and Hay 2002). Fraser-Thomas and Côté (2006) specifically highlight "that the role of the increasingly popular national training centres for youth in developed nations should be re-examined, particularly given current research on children's psychological readiness for competition and subsequent motivation for sport participation" (p.n17). This is an interesting counter argument to a selection and ranking policy which is currently trending in youth developmental sports and teams. It is worth considering: do these types of sports environments and high performance cultures and coaches promote fair play, decency, and respect (Delaney and Madigan 2006)?

The purpose and/or philosophy behind the selection criteria should be clearly articulated at the beginning of the selection policy. For example, is early identification and development of potential athletes a reason for selection? Will preference be given in the selection of athletes to those who have the most potential? Or is selection based on those who will achieve the best possible result (purely ranking scores) for the sporting organization at the impending championships? Obviously there is a different purpose/philosophy behind each of these statements. Under a sportsmanship model, healthy competition is seen as a means of cultivating personal honor, virtue, and character (Hanson and Savage 2012); however if a result and outcome orientated (win at all cost) selection policy is adhered to the opposite often becomes true. By clearly stating the purpose and overall aims of the sports program at the beginning of a selection policy the athlete (or parent) should be left with no uncertainty relating to the orientations of the selection policy.

Who Is Best Suited to Sit on a Selection Panel?

One of the easiest things to get right is to identify who will form the selection panel. This may be one person (for example, the head coach), or it could be a panel of people that may or may not include the coach. Whoever is on the selection panel must be unbiased. Realistically in small sports governing bodies this can be difficult to implement and even more difficult in minority type sports. A lot of governing bodies are groups of individuals who are parents and/or ex-athletes and have some relationship to the athletes who are competing; this may also compromise objectivity from decision-making regarding what athlete competes at specific competitions. In reality coaches may have to break the news to an athlete about de-selecting him or her from a competition and yet within a couple of hours the coach and athlete must train together. Members of the selection panel do not have to be "experts," but ideally the panel should have a range of expertise that can assist in the process of applying the selection policy to a list of potential athletes. Regardless of how many people and who these people are, it is important to identify the selection panel in the selection policy and these individuals must apply fairness and transparency to their team selection. It is also important to include a "conflict of interest" clause that details what will happen if one or more of the selection panel has a potential conflict of interest (for example, is a parent of a child athlete).

How Does an Athlete Get Selected/De-Selected?

Once the purpose/philosophy of the program is established, the criteria that is used to evaluate potential athletes should clearly spell out what an athlete must do (for example, what events they need to compete in and what standards they must achieve) and the policy should also advise what the selection period is, e.g., the performances/personal bests scores must relate to the last 12 months, etc. Ideally these criteria should be as clear and unambiguous as possible. In some sports, most notably individual sports, this should be relatively easier to achieve as there is often an objective standard such as time, distance, finish position or judge's score against which athletes can be directly compared. However as we've seen from the Cuddihy/Mills selection stage this is not always the case. In establishing these criteria, it must be made clear to the reader what events/competitions will be used and whether there is there a timeframe regarding this. It is also essential that when a selection policy is written, it does not use any retrospective results to select athletes; a timeframe for retrospection results must be clearly identified. For many sports, such as team sports, there is no single objective measure that can be used to compare one athlete against another. Often the decision is a subjective one based on many interconnected factors, e.g., a player is a good trainer, the players adds to the cohesiveness of the team, or the coach might want to bring them to the championship but they might not make the starting team. In these situations it is critical that the process, time frames and events/competitions that will be reviewed by the selector/s are well documented, so that the athlete knows where and when they must compete in order to be considered for selection.

In other situations an objective result may be available, but a degree of subjectivity needs to be applied. An example of this could be in the sport of triathlon where a team is being selected for a world championship to be held in hot, hilly terrain and humid conditions. In this situation it may not be relevant to base selection on a particular World Cup competition which was held in cool conditions. It may be best to have the policy that highlights that athletes will be selected on the basis of their performances during multiple World Cup triathlon competitions. The selection panel will especially consider head-to-head performances of the athletes from these World Cup competitions and will pay particular attention to performances in World Cup races that have similar characteristics (heat, humidity, course profile) to those expected at the world championships.

The reality is, however, that as the importance of the selection increases (for example, being selected for an Olympic team), the complexity of the selection document also increases and the need for a clear and selection policy is essential.

De-selection is an essential part of elite sport and its highly competitive nature. The principles of natural justice dictate that everyone should have the right to appeal against a decision that affects them. This does not mean, however, that anyone can appeal against anything. It simply means that if an athlete wishes to appeal against this or her non-selection then there is a detailed process and set of guidelines that must be followed. Generally the grounds for a selection appeal are along the following lines:

- The selectors did not follow the procedures laid out in the policies, rules, regulations and/or criteria of the organization
- There was an error in the information on which the decision was based
- Members of the decision-making group were influenced by bias
- The decision reached was grossly unfair or unreasonable [Holmik, 2015].

An appeal policy should also be well documented and part of the selection/de-selection policy. Many sports attempt to provide mediation or have a number of internal processes to hear an appeal before having the dispute resolved by a higher authority, such as the Court of Arbitration for Sport in Switzerland. This avenue should only be used as a last resort.

Competition, Team Selection and Sportsmanship

Competition is highly linked to sportsmanship. Athletes are often driven by other intentions beyond fair play and morality (Delaney and Madigan 2009). The pressure to win and be selected for a team may compromise the fair play ethos. Athletes may desire fame and recognition. Very often there are lucrative sponsorship deals available; however without team selection these financial rewards become redundant. This win sometimes at-any-costs and selection at all cost mentality may lead to athletes developing an ego orientation perspective. Athletes with ego orientations are concerned with gaining favorable judgments from others and compare their performance to that of competitors (Nicholls 1989). Through winning, ego orientated athletes seek to display their superiority. Athletes with a strong ego orientation, who are driven to win or strive for selection for a team, often achieve this by any means and at all costs. This may mean that an ego orientated athlete will cheat, hurt their opponents or create an unbearable atmosphere within the team to distract or drive out those who they view as their main competitors for team selection. The win-at-all-costs approach is well-documented in the literature of sports psychology. Vallerand and Losier (1994) suggest, “Playing to win at all costs may lead an athlete to cheat in order to reach his or her goal” (p. 230). Furthermore, studies have shown that athletes point to their coach as having a heavy influence on their decisions to win-at-all-costs (Guivernau and Duda 2002). The win-at-all-costs approach may lead athletes to sacrifice all for the cause (Rudd and Mondello 2006; Krumer et al. 2011).

The author has been privy to and asked to intervene amongst bullying between high performance athletes who are competing for selection. At times, the behavior of the athletes was mentally and emotionally harmful and detrimental to accomplishing team/squad goals and needed to be addressed immediately. The bullying behavior took the form of verbal abuse, intimidation, humiliation and threats practiced by one athlete in order to exert some amount of power over another athlete. This behavior was extreme in nature because its purpose was to humiliate and intimidate. It is worth noting that ego orientated athletes are often subjected to pressures from parents and coaches to reach existing and perhaps unrealistic goals (Gallucci 2008). On the other hand, athletes with strong task orientation concentrate their energies not on winning, but on the task at hand. These task orientated athletes choose to enter into competition in order to continually improve their skills. Athletes who are task orientated view their sporting career as developmental and progressive (Gallucci 2008) which is a more favorable approach.

Goldstein (2006) highlighted that when ego orientation is dominant, sportsmanship takes a lesser position. Unfortunately, today's sport culture, especially the model of high performance sports, enhances this view of competition and thereby undermines the development of sportsmanship in athletes. Within high performance sport settings character and moral development are often forgotten. Among some selfish and self-absorbed high performance athletes, gracious losers and winners are hard to find. Instead, in the author's opinion, attempts to cheat, taunt, and physically intimidate are often the norm and this behavior is often reinforced by coaches to create a "competitive like environment." When developmental athletes are constantly exposed to such role models, it is no wonder that they show little sportsmanship and respect for their opponents. Using personal standards of success, the task orientated athletes typically focus on long-term goals, while the ego orientated athletes, measure success by comparison with others and generally employ short-term goals (Cashmore 2002).

Developing a Motivational and Sportsmanship Climate Within a Team

To develop team cohesion there must be an effective team climate (Anshel 2003). This climate is described as the atmosphere, environment, and perceived conditions and interrelationships among the athletes (Cox 2007). Team climate is a psychological construct, a value judgment made by the athletes. To develop a task motivational climate athletes will need emotional support from coaches and their fellow teammates. Drawing from the author's applied experience there must be a balance on stress and the pressure to succeed from the coach. The coach must inspire athletes to seek to new heights, while not encouraging peer comparisons between athletes. The coach must recognize the individual athletes' improvements and successes independently from one another. One of the critical components in developing a task motivational team climate is trust; the athlete trust the coaches' decisions and this trust is reciprocated. Within this trusting environment risk and creativity are tolerated. That must be coupled with fairness for team selection and this will all aid to developing a positive motivational climate and promote sportsmanship-like behavior within the team/squad. Innovation or the allowance for creativity, where an athlete may have input into their own training program, may also support a strong team motivational climate. Task cohesion is exemplified in individuals working together to achieve a specific and identifiable goal (Cox 2007).

Being a team player is a skill all its own (Cashmore 2002). This skill is often underestimated and difficult to measure, yet is highly desirable in practice. Everyone on the team plays a different role, according to their strengths. Athletes can help and encourage one another in training (in a team or individual type sport setting); this can positively translate into an actual increase in performance on the field. Individual athletes must accept, train and play according to the team norms. While being a team player does not have to contradict with individual performance goals or individuality, it is important to use the individual's talent toward team goals and the development of cohesion and synergy of the whole team/squad. There is no necessary incompatibility between being a team player and an individual. Cashmore (2008) discussed that individual excellence is often realized in the context of a team—a point made by basketball coach Pat Riley (1994) in his *The Winner Within: a Life Plan for Team Players.* Another prominent basketball coach, Phil Jackson, once observed of arguably the best individual ever to play basketball: "I had to convince Michael [Jordan] that the route to greatness was in making others better" (cited in Cashmore 2008). When athletes and coaches communicate—whether showing support, or challenging one another's thinking—it's important to stay positive and respectful, particularly if there is a conflict relating to team selection. Sports teams/ squads are perfect examples of how many players working together can achieve much more than one player who is acting alone.

From an applied perspective athletes must be empowered with more authority and responsibility to develop their task cohesion, in developing their own skill and in building this bond with the team. This will develop the team's dynamics and in-house sportsmanship-like behavior. To build a task and positive motivational climate coaches must highlight each individual athlete's strengths; every athlete has something valuable to offer and it's the coach's job to find this. Athletes must find a role within their team that allows them to do what they do well, e.g., some athletes are great at motivating and supporting others, some are better at organizational tasks; it does not matter what their role is, but each athlete must find their niche. This will encourage each athlete to make a meaningful contribution and therefore increase the chances of a better team performance. This may also translate into a much more progressive and pleasant environment for all to be involved and train in.

Socialization is the process by which individual athletes become members of a culture or team (Cashmore 2002). Individuals learn behavior from other team members and adopt the behaviors and norms of that team. If a team celebrates unsportsmanlike behaviors such as encouraging all team members to engage in overly aggressive play when on the court, then new members to that team will also be socialized into learning and displaying those behaviors. Socialization is a learning process. It is social cognition: a learning process that is influenced by an individual's social context, which in this case study is sport. Socialization includes the immersion into a chosen sport and the learning of specialized skills and behaviors relevant to that sport. Groups are dynamic (Eys et al. 2006), and athletes transition in and out of the team. Group members may be in harmony and at times in conflict. Communication may range from excellent to non-existent. Goals and purposes may vary over time and may change where the team is in their season (preseason in comparison to in-competition season); however the team should remain, revealing its cohesive properties. Group cohesion may be based on the basis of task unity (such as a training group for an Olympic Games) or for social purposes (e.g., more recreational type running groups), but all groups have some purpose (Eys et al. 2006). Even in high task-oriented groups, such as high performance sports or the military, social cohesion generally develops as a result of members' instrumental and social interactions. Group integration represents the individual's perception of the group, while individual attractions to the group represent a personal connection and desire to be in the respective group. Each high performance sports program should aim to develop a sense of "*vicarious achievement*" where team members take satisfaction and pleasure from the success of other team members or the team as a whole (Cashmore 2002). When we celebrate each other's success respect amongst athletes is shown (NCAA, 2003), and this may help to promote sportsmanship-like behaviors amongst the group.

Applied Recommendations for Developing Sportsmanship in a High Performance Sport Program

To create a better environment for sports, the author of this essay suggests that providers of high performance sports adopt and integrate the following the practices:

- Developing a team and selection philosophy is desirable. This will require the athletes, coaches, parents, and administrators to adhere to fundamental values such as respect, fairness, civility, honesty, and responsibility. This philosophy of the sports program must be communicated clearly to both the athletes and parents; providing this philosophy in writing is preferable. As highlighted previously in the Cuddihy/Mills case, is preference given in the selection of athletes to those who have the most potential or is the selection based purely on ranking? This is often the most difficult to implement in sport as there are often some "intangibles" that an athlete may bring to the team such as competition experience or the ability to gel and motivate their team mates.
- Measurable standards (A or B standards/fitness test cut offs) should be highlighted within the team. All section policies should require strict adherence to written policies and procedures related to sportsmanship and ethical conduct. Within these policies information and guidelines relating to bullying should also be addressed. These guidelines should provide examples of acceptable and not acceptable types of behaviors within the high performance team setting. These standards should communicate the policies and procedures to the athletes, coaches, officials, parents, and administrators. The policy should also advise what the selection period timeframe also is, what personal best scores will be considered in what timeframe.
- Providing sporting and ethical-conduct education to participants, coaches, officials, parents, and administrators would also be useful. A person who practices good sportsmanship is likely to carry the respect and appreciation of other people into every other aspect of life. Athletes who engage in bullying tactics should understand the impact their behavior has on the rest of the team; this should be highlighted to them in an appropriate setting. If coaches witness or become aware of teasing, exclusion, threats or other forms of bullying, they need to take action. An evaluation should be undertaken which includes a systematic and rigorous monitoring of the effectiveness of the sporting and ethical-conduct education efforts.

Conclusion

Research supports a task motivation environment that promotes fairness and good sportsmanship like behavior amongst team members. The philosophy of the program should consider focusing on the goal of learning rather than achievement. When coaches focus on the goal of improving over time rather than on the goal of performing well quickly or on the outcome, athletes are more likely to maintain their motivation and become more task orientated. In a supportive coaching environment, athletes should be given clear selection criteria. Athlete should be given selection or de-selection performance evaluation criteria and specific, private feedback on what they accomplished well and what aspects of their performance needs improvement. It may be that those who choose to compete as a high performance athlete are more biased to the to win-at-all-costs approach; however the high performance sports coaching environment often promotes and pushes athletes forward and increases their will to win-at-all-costs mentality (Krumer et al. 2011). The harmful impact of an outcome and ego driven motivational climate program on athletes for selection must be given attention. Who is to say that a task motivational climate and a developmental program philosophy would not yield the same results? The gold standard aim should be "vicarious achievement" within a team.

Bibliography

Anshel, Mark. H. 2003. *Sport Psychology: From Theory to Practice*, 4th ed. San Francisco: Benjamin Cummings.

Cashmore, Ellis. 2002. *Sport Psychology: The Key Concepts*. New York: Routledge.

Côté, Jean, and Joseph Hay. 2002. "Children's Involvement in Sport: A Developmental Perspective," pp. 484–502 in *Psychological Foundations of Sport*, edited by J.M. Silva and D.E. Stevens. Boston: Allyn & Bacon.

Cox, Richard, H. 2007. *Sport Psychology: Concepts and Applications*, 6th ed. New York: McGraw-Hill.

Delaney, Tim, and Tim Madigan. 2009. *Sports: Why People Love Them*! Lanham, MD: University Press of America.

Eys, Mark A., Mark R. Beauchamp, and Stephen R. Bray. 2006. "A Review of Team Roles in Sport," pp. 227–256 in *Literature Reviews in Sport Psychology*, edited by Sheldon Hanton and Stephen D. Mellalieu. Hauppauge, NY: Nova Science.

Fraser-Thomas, Jessica, and Jean Côté. 2006. "Youth Sports: Implementing Findings and Moving Forward with Research." *Athletic Insight: The Online Journal of Sport Psychology*. Retrieved May 20, 2015(http://www.athleticinsight.com).

Gallucci, Nicholas. 2008. *Sport Psychology: Performance Enhancement, Performance Inhibition, Individuals, and Teams*. New York: Psychology Press.

Goldstein, Jay. 2006. "Perspectives from Sport Psychology Promoting Sportsmanship in Youth Sports." *Journal of Physical Education, Research and Dance*, 77:7.

Guivernau, Marta, and Joan L. Duda. 2002. "Moral Atmosphere and Athletic Aggressive Tendencies in Young Soccer Players." *Journal of Moral Education*, 31:67–85.

Hanson, Holmi O., and Matt Savage. 2015. "What Role Does Ethics Play in Sports?" Retrieved May 29, 2015 (http://www.scu.edu).

Holmik, Emery. 2015. "The Process of Athlete Selection, Getting It Right: Guidelines for Selection." Available Through ASC Publishing. Retrieved May 29· 2015 (http://www.ausport.gov.au).

Kramer, John, and Aidan Moran. 2013. *Pure Sport, Practical Sport Psychology*. London: Routledge.

Krumer, Alex, Tal Shavit, and Mosi Rosenboim. 2011. "Why do Professional Athletes Have Different Time Preferences than Non-athletes?" *Judgment and Decision Making*, 6:542–551.

Moran, Aidan. 2012. *Sport and Exercise Psychology, A Critical Introduction*, 2d ed.London: Routledge.

National Collegiate Athletic Association (NCAA). 2003. "Report on the Sportsmanship and Fan Behavior Summit." Retrieved May 20, 2015 (http://www.ncaa.org).

Nicholls, John G. 1992. *The Competitive Ethos and Democratic Education*. Cambridge: Harvard University Press.

Riley, Pat. 1994. *The Winner Within: A Life Plan for Team Players*. New York: Berkley .

Rudd, Andrew, and Michael J. Mondello. 2006. "How Do College Coaches Define Character? A Qualitative Study with Division I-A Head Coaches." *Journal of College & Character*, 3:1–10.

Vallerand, Robert J., and Gaeten F. Losier. 1994. "Self-Determined Motivation and Sportsmanship Orientations: An Assessment of Their Temporal Relationship." *Journal of Sport and Exercise Psychology*, 116, 229–245.

Ideals of Sportsmanship Throughout History

SEÁN MORAN

In this essay, we explore the ways in which sporting ideals have changed over the ages: from ancient times to the 21st century. Various historical epochs have conceptualized the ideal sportsperson differently, and understanding some of these views helps us to make more sense of our own era.

Firstly, though, we should consider what is meant by the term "ideals." A suitable place to start is with the Greek philosopher Plato (ca. 428 BCE–ca. 348 BCE), who had much to say about the notion. He conjectured that there is an ideal world composed of the "Forms," each Form (or *eidos* in the Greek) being a flawless archetype of the kind of things we experience in our ordinary life. For instance, in his proposed transcendental domain there is a Form of the square that is more perfect than any square we can actually see, draw or construct. But back in the "real world," if we examine a baseball diamond closely enough, we will undoubtedly find that it departs ever so slightly from being an exact square. Even ignoring the arcs cut out for the bases and the home plate, the markings will always be somewhat out of true alignment. And this is the case with any existing thing: a soccer ball is not perfectly spherical; marathon timekeeping is not one hundred percent accurate; a swimmer's stroke is less than ideal.

To Plato, the visible world in which we apparently live is thus only a pale imitation of this higher realm of the Forms. So, for example, there is an ideal Form of Justice, which is superior to any everyday attempts at justice. Genuine Justice only exists in Plato's idealized world of the Forms: we have merely a poor facsimile of it. Significantly, he argues in the *Republic* that earthly justice often conforms to what the powerful find advantageous rather than partaking of the genuine ideal of Justice (Plato 2005:344c).

We might thus think of ideals as aspirations, or models of how things would be "in an ideal world." Our challenge is to actualize them, but in practice such high standards cannot be achieved completely. Our progress towards them is asymptotic: we can never quite reach perfection. Even the most fleet-footed athlete is lacking in some respect or other (possessing "feet of clay" we could say, were the metaphor not so inappropriate). She might have superb strength but be a poor team player; he might have finely tuned reactions, but lack stamina; they might break records but rely on performance-enhancing drugs.

Achievable or not, though, each era has its own sporting ideals: its particular visions of what constitutes an exemplary sportsperson. However, these are in the plural—ideals—for it depends whose vision of the ideal we are considering. Perfection, like beauty, is in the eye of the beholder. The gladiator in the ancient Roman amphitheatre had a different ideal from a member of the crowd, for example. He naturally valued physical survival above everything else, while the audience wanted brutality and blood. For the gladiator, a perfect bout in the arena was one from which he emerged alive and uninjured (with an enhanced reputation too, ideally), but for the crowd a good day in the amphitheatre was a blood-spattered gorefest.

However, the vision of those in power was far removed from either combatant or spectator. As the former Roman Republic transmuted into a dictatorship under autocratic emperors, the spectacle of the games was used to take the minds of the people off their personal loss of political freedom. It was an instrument of state propaganda. The poet Juvenal memorably encapsulated this phenomenon in his *Satires*. The version often quoted is "Give them bread and circuses [*panem et circenses*] and they will never revolt." But Creekmore's translation gives this as

> For the people, who once bestowed authority, army commands, Consulships, and everything else, today keep their hands to themselves and for just two things do they eagerly yearn: Bread and the games [Juvenal 1963:X].

In either case, though, the policy of "*panem et circenses*" had nothing to do with nutrition or sportsmanship, but was a cynical method of appeasing the populace. In this respect, perhaps the goals of the emperor and the gladiator were not too different after all: both wanted to survive and build their reputations in hostile situations.

Occasionally, though, the ruling elites suffered reversals. In Germany, after Hitler came to power in 1933, the Third Reich notoriously promoted a vision of a white "Aryan" master race. The Nazi ideal of a heroic, blond-haired, blue-eyed athlete, with well-defined musculature, was depicted by sculptors, painters and by filmmakers such as Leni Riefenstahl. The 1936 Berlin Olympic Games were intended to be further propaganda for this supposed Aryan "superiority." But it was not to be. Black American athlete Jesse Owens won four gold medals, a trophy tally that was unsurpassed for almost half a century. Owens achieved gold in the 100m dash, 200m dash, 400m relay and long jump. Famously, another Black American athlete—Carl Lewis—took gold in the same four events in the Los Angeles Olympics of 1984.

Unfortunately the Nazi German chancellor was not a good sport. According to Turnbull (2009), Hitler refused to shake Owens's hand for a photograph, the *führer* yelling: "These Americans should be ashamed of themselves for letting their medals be won by a *neger* [sic] … I would never shake the hand of one." Even though this account is disputed, it is certainly the case that Hitler did not accept the example of Owens as a learning opportunity, renounce his misguided racist beliefs and embrace the notion of an Olympic brotherhood of man. Instead, he went on to engulf the world in war and cause millions of deaths. Nine years later, at the end of World War II, a defeated Hitler committed suicide in a bunker in the same city at which the Olympics had been held: a sore loser to the end.

So there are connections between political ideologies, sporting ideals, and actual sporting performances. These are historically and culturally located, and require some analysis in order to appreciate their key features. To illustrate this, we shall consider the ideals of sportsmanship under four historical headings: (i) The Ancient Greeks, (ii) The

Corinthian Spirit, (iii) The Birth of the Modern Olympics, and (iv) The Present Day. Although the first of these involves events of over 2,500 years ago, and the middle two have their genesis in the 19th century, the competing ideals formed in those eras are still being played out in sport today.

The Ancient Greeks' Sporting Ideals

As well as their intense respect for human reasoning powers, physical activity was also of immense importance to the ancient Greeks. Gymnastics (which equates to our present day "athletics") was the main part of a youth's education, alongside grammar and music, and "continued to be cultivated by persons of all ages" (Smith 1875:579). Part of this emphasis on fitness bespoke a militaristic agenda, but there was also a significant spiritual dimension. Body and soul needed each other. The original Olympic Games—held for the first time in Olympia, Greece in 776 BCE—were first and foremost a religious festival. It was intended that the competitors would honor the god Zeus by their physical achievements, rather than merely seek personal glory. But these activities were not open to all. Until the Roman conquest of 146 BCE, only freeborn, Greek, male athletes were allowed to compete. Furthermore, the competitors were unclothed. "Gymnastics" shares an etymology with the word *gymnós* (naked) and signifies "things done nude."

It is tempting to impute the purest of motives to the ancient Greek athletes. The Games were meant to be a tribute to Zeus: the king of the gods and ruler of Mount Olympus. The victor was considered to have won because of help from the gods, and not just by virtue of his own physical prowess. The Greek poet Pindar expressed this notion beautifully:

> Creatures of a Day! Man is merely a shadow of a dream. But when god-given glory comes upon him in victory, a bright light shines upon us, and our life is sweet [Young 2004:70].

This is very reminiscent of Plato's notion that earthly phenomena are poor facsimiles of a higher world. But in sporting victory the athletes could transcend such limitations—thanks to divine intervention—and partake of more elevated ideals. The physical rewards were seemingly rather paltry though: a palm leaf; a red woollen ribbon; a crown of olive branches. And the majority of the competitors received nothing at all. One spectator, Lucian of Samosata, even questioned the Greeks' sanity, because "they invest large amounts of time and effort in training for athletic contests for which the only reward is a heap of weeds" (Murray 2014:309). We form a picture of selfless athletes, pushing their bodies to the limit as a sacrifice to the gods of Mount Olympus, and hoping for nothing more than an olive crown.

But Lucian went on to explain that they compete for the honor of victory and not for the small worldly prizes, because "the one among them who succeeds in winning is counted equal to the gods" (Murray 2014:309). The athletes took part for the *kudos*, a word that originally meant having earned the favor of the gods and being worthy of respect by the people. Young (2004:71) reports that Pindar considered the Games to be "a microcosm of the general human struggle to pass beyond ordinary human limitations, to effect extraordinary achievements, to do something that humans cannot ordinarily do." These achievements were in three spheres: the agonic (competitive), the ludic (playful) and the esthetic (beautiful). To excel in all three was regarded as a godlike performance.

However, from this apotheosis, real earthly benefits accrued to the victor. Statues would be erected to him, his hometown would welcome him back as a semi-divine hero to be worshiped, and a life of fame and fortune would follow. For example, Milo of Croton—six-times Olympic wrestling champion, according to the International Olympic Committee (IOC 2012:2)—became famous throughout the Greek-speaking world, and was mentioned by both Plato and Aristotle. His legendary strength involved resistance training by reputedly carrying a calf every day until it grew into a full-sized ox, which he then carried on his shoulders through the Olympic stadium. His victories provided him with great wealth, political influence, and the friendship of the philosopher and mathematician Pythagoras.

If these rewards were sometimes enough to contaminate the purity of the sacred sporting ideals, the practices of the athletes were often similarly less than wholesome. In particular, the combat event *pankration*—a free-for-all combination of boxing and wrestling—allowed competitors to make vicious moves against their opponents. Its name derives from *pan* (all) *kratos* (strength), meaning that every unarmed fighting technique was permitted (except biting and gouging). The British Museum in London exhibits ancient vases depicting these contests. One caption reads: "Sostratos, a pankratiast from Sikyon, was famous for breaking his opponent's fingers at the beginning of the contest." In another Olympic bout, in 564 BCE, the fighter Arrachion's opponent

> held Arrachion, hugging him with his legs, and at the same time he squeezed his neck with his hands. Arrachion dislocated his opponent's toe, but expired owing to suffocation; but he who suffocated Arrachion was forced to give in at the same time because of the pain in his toe. The Eleans crowned and proclaimed victor the corpse of Arrachion [Jones and Omerod in Christopoulos 2013:455].

After the Roman invasion, the conquerors—who, as we saw, were more interested in pandering to the crowd than honoring high athletic ideals—made boxers put iron in their gloves to cause more entertaining injuries and bloodshed.

Brutality, distraction techniques, and low cunning seem out of place in Games that had once espoused a high religious tone. But we can also see such a combination of the sacred and the profane in the works of the eighth century BCE Greek poet Homer. In the *Odyssey*, the heroic figure Odysseus achieved victory by trickery and ruthlessness, but with the connivance of the goddess Athena. And in the *Iliad*, the same goddess interfered with a running competition, at the request of Odysseus. Moreover, despite their transcendental pretentions, the Games were founded on the skills of the battleground. The events of these original Olympics can be categorized into running, wrestling, boxing, *pankration*, equestrian competitions, and the pentathlon (running, long jump, discus, javelin and wrestling) (IOC 2012:2–3). We can see how honing these talents could be of much practical use in combat. In the ancient Greek milieu, religious, sporting and martial ideals co-existed quite happily.

There were political benefits associated with the Games, too. A strict truce was imposed between any warring cities, so relations between the various competing states would improve before, during and after the Games. Diplomacy could thrive while the competitions took place, and war was conducted by other means.

But it was the religious nature of the Olympic ideals that led to the demise of the original Games. The Roman Emperor Theodosius I (a convert to Christianity) regarded them as a pagan cult so he abolished them in 393 CE, ending over a thousand years of tradition. It was to be a further millennium and a half before the modern Olympics began a new sporting custom, representing at least some degree of continuity with the ancient festival.

Corinthian Sporting Ideals

We sometimes hear nostalgic talk of the "Corinthian Spirit." This conjures up an era of amateurism in the original sense: a time when players supposedly participated just for the love of their event or game. It was a period in which the notion of a "gentleman" had a particular resonance. This prosperous individual took part in sport, not to win at all costs, nor to attain fame and fortune, but for the sake of the sport itself. He was not a professional, but a dilettante who valued fair play, healthy exercise and camaraderie more than glory. Self-sacrifice and loyalty to the team, rather than personal triumph, characterized the Corinthian sportsman. However, at first sight the word itself looks a somewhat odd choice. As Roybal (2005) remarked:

> "Corinthianize" meant to take it to the limit in decadence and "Corinthian girl" meant a prostitute. The "sin city" capital of the ancient world, this was a people completely given over to pleasure and debauchery [p. 73].

So how did this come to be associated with well-behaved sportsmen? One answer seems to be that "Corinthians" connoted high-born individuals who liked to "slum it" with *hoi polloi.* In Shakespeare's play *Henry IV Part 1* (1597), Prince Hal—a boisterous character who enjoys carousing with the drunkard Falstaff—sees himself as "a Corinthian, a lad of mettle." By 1821, this trope was well established, when the original Tom and Jerry featured in Pierce Egan's splendidly-titled *The day and night scenes of Jerry Hawthorn, esq., and his elegant friend, Corinthian Tom, accompanied by Bob Logic, the Oxonian, in their rambles and sprees through the metropolis.* In this illustrated monthly publication, high society rubbed shoulders with London low life. The Corinthian ideal thus involved mixing with those "beneath" one in the social order.

Another explanation derives from St Paul's first letter to the Corinthians in the Christian *New Testament.* In Paul's day, Corinth, Greece, was the location for the biennial Isthmian Games, so he used imagery that would be familiar to his readership: "Athletes exercise self-control in all things; they do it to receive a perishable wreath, but we [do it for] an imperishable one" (1 Corinthians 9:25). In effect, Paul promises eternal life to those residents of "sin city" who are self-controlled, and he dismisses earthly prizes as unimportant and ephemeral. Good behavior in a naughty world and disdain for material reward are the way to salvation.

The first sporting usage of the term was by the Royal Corinthian Yacht Club (UK) in 1872. The Seawanhaka Yacht Club of New York could have claimed precedence—being founded in 1871 on Corinthian principles—had it not waited ten years to add the word "Corinthian" explicitly to its name. The epithet carries an implication that the wealthy yacht owners would crew their vessels side-by-side with the hired hands. The latter were not allowed in the clubhouse, though, and eventually yachting competition rules prohibited their employment at all during races. The collegial mingling of the social classes had its limits.

The 1932 Los Angeles Olympic Code for yachting was drafted by the Royal Corinthian Yacht Club. It defined Corinthianism in yachting as

> that attribute which represents participation in sport as distinct from gain and which also involves the acquirement of nautical experience through the love of the sport rather than through necessity or the hope of gain [Corinthian Yacht Club of San Francisco (CYCSF) 2015].

Here we see two essential attributes of the Corinthian spirit. It valorizes amateurism, in the sense of doing something for love—the Latin for "lover" being *amator*—and it forbids the motive of hoping to profit from the activity. Ironically, an echo of the days of competing for nothing—for love—can still be heard in the scoring system of multi-million dollar tennis tournaments. A score of fifteen-nothing is reported by the umpire as "fifteen-love."

In soccer, the amateur ideal was typified by the formation of the Corinthian Football Club (London, England) in 1882. Its founder, N. Lane Jackson, described the characteristics of the "Corinthian breed" as

> one who has not merely braced his muscles and developed his endurance by the exercise of some great sport, but has, in the pursuit of that exercise, learnt to control his anger, to be considerate to his fellow men, to take no mean advantage, to resent as dishonor the very suspicion of trickery, to bear aloft a cheerful countenance under disappointment, and never to own himself defeated until the last breath is out of his body [Federation International de Football Association (FIFA) 2012].

We may suppress a wry smile at the presence of these sentiments on the FIFA website, but to the 19th century Corinthians they were intended as more than a merely vacuous aspiration. Evidence that there might have been genuine uptake of these tenets can be found in their attitude to penalties, which were introduced in 1891 at the suggestion of an Irishman, William "Master Willie" McCrum. One of the Corinthians decried this addition to the rule-book as "a standing insult to sports men," whom—so he felt—the new law assumed to "behave like cads of the most unscrupulous kidney" (Charles B. Fry in Doyle 2011). Tellingly, though, he went on to complain that "the lines marking the penalty area are a disgrace to the playing fields of a public school." In England, "public schools" are in fact private schools (such as Eton, Harrow and Winchester) that charge hefty fees to educate the children of the privileged, so there is a strong class element at play here. We see this in the snobbish denunciations in some newspapers of the day of the "Irishman's motion" or the "death penalty" (Hume 2014). That this elitism was accompanied by a measure of hypocrisy is shown by "the first-class travel on expenses, the boot money and testimonial games, [and] the social apartheid suffered by artisans and mechanics" (Polley 2006:454).

Putting this to one side, though, there were some admirable aspects not just of the Corinthian ideals but also of their practices. For example, if a penalty was awarded against the Corinthians, their goalkeeper would abandon his position in the goal-mouth so that his opponent could score unimpeded; if a player of the opposing team was sent off, a Corinthian would also leave the pitch to keep things fair.

The working class, professional teams of Northern England (such as Blackburn Rovers and Preston North End) played a more robust style of soccer, and these "cads" regarded the Corinthians as "toffs." The 1883 constitution of the Corinthians required that players "shall not compete for any challenge cup or any prize of any description," but they decisively beat the then FA Cup holders, Blackburn Rovers, in 1884 (8–0) and the League Champions, Preston North End, in 1889 (5–0) in friendly matches. This amateur team even defeated Manchester United 11–3 in 1904.

But by the 1930s, the Corinthians had faded into obscurity. This was perhaps an inevitable consequence of the inexorable rise of professionalism in sport—a process not confined to soccer. With the final "Gentleman vs. Players" cricket match of 1962 "a whole era in English sport had come to an end," according to Taylor (2010:1).

The ideal did not vanish completely, though, and a folk memory of the noble principles sometimes re-emerges. For example, the famous African soccer player Eusébio, who died in 2014, was praised in obituaries for his "Corinthian spirit." Many of these referred to one outstanding example of his sportsmanship, in which he had generously and fulsomely congratulated the opposing goalkeeper, Alex Stepney, for saving Eusébio's shot: a blast at goal in the closing minutes of the game that could have won the 1968 European cup final for Benfica against Manchester United at Wembley, London.

And the Little League baseball competitions of the United States can, at their best, still foster an innocent love of the sport. The movement was founded in 1939 in Williamsport, Pennsylvania, initially for boys only. Nolan Ryan, Jr., erstwhile Major League pitcher, commented, "Little League was a great period of my life. We never won a championship, but we tried real hard. I guess that's what the little league is all about" (Van Auken 2001:14). Perhaps that, too, is what the authentic Corinthian spirit is all about. The Little League's logo contains the words "Character, Courage, Loyalty"—which we can take to be amongst its cherished ideals—and these would not look out of place on the crest of a 19th century gentleman's sporting club. Winning is not all that counts. Somewhat counter-intuitively, the organization states that its mission is "not to develop exceptional ball players" but rather to teach children "how to accept success and deal with failure, while learning about sportsmanship, competition and accountability." Here, the link to aspects of the wider American culture is clear—particularly the justification that "today's Little Leaguers are tomorrow's leaders" (Little League n.d.a). But a less thrusting set of principles is also cited: the "ideals of sportsmanship, fair play and teamwork" (Little League n.d.b).

In Ireland, the Gaelic Athletic Association (GAA, established 1884) oversees hurling and Gaelic football competitions between amateur teams. It originates from an era when Ireland was part of the British Empire, and its first patron—the archbishop of Cashel—saw it as an antidote against what he termed English "effeminate follies" (Kirby n.d.:19). This nationalistic element is still present in the current *Official Guide*:

> Those who control its destinies see in the GAA a means of consolidating our Irish identity.... The primary purpose of the GAA is the organization of native pastimes and the promotion of athletic fitness as a means to create a disciplined, self-reliant, national-minded manhood [GAA 2012:4].

In keeping with its wider cultural ideals, the GAA *Scór* competition is held outside of the sporting season, and comprises eight events: céilí dancing, solo singing, instrumental music, recitation, ballad group, novelty act, question time and set dancing. The use of the Irish language is also promoted throughout the year—including the rule that team-sheets must list players' names in Irish (a requirement that leads to imaginative renderings of the names of "new Irish" youngsters such as Jiao-long, Muhammad and Wojciech).

Although it is the best-attended sporting organization in Ireland, and boasts revenues in the tens of millions of Euro, the GAA ethos remains strictly amateur. The rules state that

> a player, team, official or member shall not accept payment in cash or in kind in conjunction with the playing of Gaelic Games ... [and] may not participate in full-time training [GAA 2012:7].

There are occasional rumblings in newspapers, though, about over-training, star players receiving various benefits in kind, and unsporting "professional" conduct on the field. Nevertheless, the very fact that such things are even remarked upon demonstrates the enduring appeal of high ideals—even if some players fail to live up to them.

The Birth of the Modern Olympics

We associate the ideals of the modern Olympic Games with the French aristocrat Baron de Coubertin. There had been Games modeled on the ancient Greek concept before, including Robert Dover's Olympic Games (UK 1612); the Montréal Olympic Games (Canada 1844); and the New York Olympic Games (USA 1853) (Weiler 2004:429). In common with the original Greek Olympics, the Much Wenlock Olympian Games (UK 1850) awarded olive crowns for some events, but the winner of the "old woman race" received a pound of tea, and the prize for the "blindfolded wheelbarrow race" goes unrecorded (Wenlock Olympian Society 2015).

However it was Coubertin's vision that led to the first modern global Olympic Games of 1896 that have since continued on a four-yearly cycle—excepting 1916, 1940 and 1944, when war stopped play—to the present day. Coubertin advanced an amateur, non-commercial vision of the Games, that he hoped would promote international harmony and not succumb to the degradations of the Roman *circenses*:

> It is vital that athletics retain the noble and chivalrous quality which distinguished it in the past.... Human imperfection tends always to transform the Olympian athlete into a circus gladiator. To defend oneself against the spirit of lucre and professionalism which threatens to invade them ... [t]he re-establishment of the Olympic Games ... would bring together, every four years, representatives of the nations of the world, and ... these peaceful, courteous contests constitute the best form of internationalism [Müller 2000:301].

This expresses an extrinsic motivation for the restoration of the tradition; one that focuses on the benefits to the world, rather than to the sportspeople themselves qua athletes. Coubertin did, however, also pay full attention to the intrinsic advantages of sporting activity, and altered Juvenal's Latin tag "*mens sana in corpore sano*" (a sound mind in a healthy body) to "*mens fervida in corpore lacertoso*" (a fervent mind in a well-trained body). Participation was enough to achieve these internal desiderata, and ultimately the external gains for humanity:

> The important thing in the Olympic Games is not to win, but to take part, the important thing in life is not the triumph but the struggle, the essential thing is not to have conquered but to have fought well. To spread these precepts is to build up a stronger and more valiant and above all more scrupulous and more generous humanity [Coubertin in Toohey and Veal 2007:64].

But having said this, Coubertin recognized that without a sort of driven quality, the competitors would not give of their best: "Athletes need 'freedom of excess.' That is why their motto is *citius, altius, fortius*: higher, faster, stronger, the motto of anyone who dares to try to beat a record" (McNamee and Parry 2013:112). And this excess is not confined to the duration of the competitions: victory and overnight fame are built on decades of rigorous dedication, in which many ordinary pleasures are eschewed in the interests of serious training. However, this sets up a degree of tension between the competing ideals that athletes are expected to follow. If athletes really felt that taking part was enough, and that their role was to foster a more benevolent spirit in the world by such participation, they would perhaps not develop the finely honed competitive edge that the events require. But on the other hand, if an excessive determination to go higher, faster and stronger was the sole driving principle, then any means—no matter how unsporting—could be appropriated to this end.

Perhaps these demands could be tempered by an aesthetic and even theological sensibility. In a reference to the primarily religious (and secondarily military) culture of the ancient Greek games, Curtius reminded us of the

> important and irrefutable demand of the gods: physical health, beauty of form, a sure and light step, sprightly elegance and power of momentum in the limbs, endurance in running and in battle, a bright and courageous eye and the level-headedness and presence of mind that is acquired only in the daily presence of danger [Weiler 2004:431].

This would rule out the unhealthy, ugly and hubristic practices that sometimes infect our contemporary Games. The transcendental experience of pushing one's body harder than ever before cannot be bought cheaply, and to achieve this by illicit means is to go through a counterfeit version. Having said this, we note that chosen Greek competitors in ancient times were alleged to have had performance-enhancing assistance from the gods of Mount Olympus.

De Coubertin's noble ideals for the Olympics were well intended. But it is perhaps in the nature of international competition that tribal loyalties can take precedence over fine rhetoric about the brotherhood of man and the sacred Olympic spirit. Orwell (1945:42) grumbled about

> the nations who work themselves into furies over these absurd contests, and seriously believe—at any rate for short periods—that running, jumping and kicking a ball are tests of national virtue.

Moreover, while the enormous international crowd—both real and virtual—is watching the athletes, the advertisers are keenly observing this audience of potential customers. To the public relations sections of globalized industries, the extrinsic benefits of the Olympics are clear to see: bewitched onlookers who will associate their sugary drink or sweatshop-made shoe with noble victories.

The Present Day

This section is shorter than those dealing with earlier eras, because other chapters in this book address the current state of play. It is tempting to hark back to a "golden age" in which the highest ideals of fair play were upheld: a time before bloated salaries, match fixing, ball tampering, "diving" to claim a penalty, blood doping, the use of performance-enhancing pharmaceuticals, and so on. Earlier, we discussed Plato's view that ideals such as justice are often made to align with what the powerful find congenial, rather than truly partaking of the transcendental ideal of Justice (Plato 2005:344c). Unfortunately, this is sometimes also the case with sporting ideals. Powerful vested interests—including dubious states looking to burnish their images, and rapacious multinational corporations wishing to be associated with winners—re-appropriate and distort the original ideals. We might even say that *circenses* and free *panem* are no longer just used, as in Roman times, to subdue criticism, but modern *circenses* now actively promote sales of our contemporary *panem*—fast food—together with footwear, consumer electronics products and so on. We may complain that commercial motives to increase gate receipts, sell more merchandising, auction television rights to the highest bidder, and attract lucrative corporate sponsorship have nothing to do with the noble principles of sport.

But it would be a mistake to conclude that sporting ideals have disappeared in our day. The fact that we can recognize the non-ideal character of the litany of ills just mentioned suggests that we still hold an image of what the ideals actually are. They may now only exist in a Platonic transcendental realm of the Forms, but perhaps they always did: that is the nature of ideals. There was conceivably a more innocent age of sport for its own sake, but that was long ago and far away. By the end of World War II, Orwell felt that the days of playing for fun were all but over:

> Nearly all the sports practiced nowadays are competitive. You play to win, and the game has little meaning unless you do your utmost to win. On the village green, where you pick up sides and no feeling of local patriotism is involved, it is possible to play simply for the fun and exercise: but as soon as the question of prestige arises, as soon as you feel that you and some larger unit will be disgraced if you lose, the most savage combative instincts are aroused [Orwell 1945:41].

In contrast to the amateur Corinthian ideal of the 19th century, 20th century soccer became increasingly professionalized. Bill Shankly, who managed Liverpool FC in the 1960s and 1970s, famously decreed that "if a player is not interfering with play or seeking to gain an advantage, then he should be" (Hassall 2009). The object was to win at all costs, a principle redolent of the Homeric hero Odysseus. Fair play counted for nothing: skill, cunning, play-acting and deception were all available to the professional player, as long as he could escape detection by the referee.

Off the playing field, too, sporting ideals sometimes gave way to naked self-interest. The international governing body for soccer, FIFA, became mired in a corruption scandal in 2015. Key officials allegedly received more than $150 million in bribes and kickbacks, and World Cup tournaments were controversially allocated to Russia in 2018 and to Qatar in 2022. The latter is an oil-rich emirate of just over two million people, with no history of top-flight soccer and a climate that is unsuitable for international games.

But let us not forget the enormous gains in sporting ideals during our times. Unlike the restriction on competitors in the ancient Games to freeborn, male Greek citizens who worshiped Zeus—and the Corinthians' valorizing of upper class, white, Christian gentlemen—access has opened up significantly in today's world. For example, Little League Baseball claims that it "does not limit participation in its activities on the basis of disability, race, color, creed, national origin, gender, sexual preference or religious preference" (Little League n.d.c). Women's participation in sport is now commonplace, and there are Special Olympics and Paralympics to widen the opportunities for sportspersons of differing abilities. Fun runs and marathons are frequent events and the "Sport for All" movement promotes healthy physical exercise for everyone:

> The practice of sport is a human right, and every individual must have the possibility of practicing it without discrimination. Sport not only enables people to live more active and fulfilling lives, but can also teach vital life skills and values, while making a contribution to improving quality of life [Rogge 2013:5].

These are high ideals, with which one would not want to argue. Putting them into practice could benefit not only the individual person, but also the wider society in which he or she lives, works and plays.

Conclusion

We began this essay by considering the notion of "the ideal" in Plato's sense: an unattainable aspiration that is present only in the transcendental world of the Forms. But perhaps there is no Platonic form of (say) the ideal soccer match: it is just a practice with its own intrinsic goods, continuously defined and re-defined by the players, spectators and commentators. When we earlier examined ancient Greek, Corinthian, modern Olympic and present-day sporting ideals, we found that some were more honored in the breach than the observance.

Plato's student Aristotle proposed a "doctrine of the mean," and this may provide us with a more down to earth way of viewing sporting ideals. To Aristotle, the flourishing life aims not for the heights but merely for a happy medium. Neither excessive nor deficient ambition is desirable. Exactly where the midpoint lies will depend both on the individual, and on the attribute we are considering. By way of example, Aristotle (2004:1106b) makes the point that a moderate diet for Milo the wrestler would represent gluttony for a normal person. But in the international sporting arena, such a rejection of an excessive "will to win" would set up mediocrity as an ambition. The elite athlete, like the top-flight concert pianist, must lead an unbalanced life, or a rival performer who is willing to train obsessively will displace him or her.

But it may be that seeking an Aristotelian happy medium is more likely to lead to personal flourishing than excessive sporting zeal. Here we might draw a distinction between watching spectator sports and taking part in healthy exercise. We can perhaps let the elite athletes lead unbalanced lives on our behalf, while the rest of us enjoy the spectacle and participate in less extreme ways. The two sets of ideals can co-exist happily.

Bibliography

Aristotle. 2004. *Nicomachean Ethics.* Translated by James A.K. Thompson. London: Penguin.
Christopoulos, Lucas. 2013. "Greek Combat Sports and their Transmission to Central and East Asia." *Classical World*, 106 (3):431–459.
Corinthian Yacht Club of San Francisco (CYCSF). 2015. "What Is Corinthian?" Retrieved June 6, 2015 (http://www.cyc.org).
Doyle, Paul. 2011. "Why the Penalty Laws Should Change." *The Guardian*. April 20. Retrieved May 10, 2015 (http://www.theguardian.com).
Egan, Pierce. 2010. *The Day and Night Scenes of Jerry Hawthorn, esq., and His Elegant Friend, Corinthian Tom, Accompanied by Bob Logic, the Oxonian, in Their Rambles and Sprees Through the Metropolis.* Charleston, SC: Nabu Press.
FIFA. 2012. "Fair Play Reigned for Football's First Corinthians." Retrieved May 5, 2015 (http://www.fifa.com).
GAA. 2012. *Official Guide–Parts 1 and 2.* Dublin: Central Council of the Gaelic Athletic Association.
Hassall, Paul. 2009. "Bill Shankly in Quotes." Retrieved June 1, 2015 (http://www.liverpoolfc.com).
Hume, Robert. 2014. "Irishman Put Football on Spot with Penalties." *Irish Examiner*. June 17.
IOC. 2012. *The Olympic Games of Antiquity*. Lausanne: International Olympic Committee.
Juvenal. 1963. *The Satires.* Translated by Hubert Creekmore. New York: New American Library.
Kirby, Brian. n.d. *The GAA to 1891.* Dublin: National Library of Ireland in Association with the National Council for Curriculum and Assessment.
Little League (n.d.a) "Local League's 'Call to Action' Speech for Parents." Retrieved May 18, 2015 (www.littleleague.org).
Little League (n.d.b) "History of Little League." Retrieved May 18, 2015 (http://www.littleleague.org).
Little League (n.d.c) "Little League Player Registration Form." Retrieved May 18, 2015 (www.eglittleleague.org).
McNamee, Mike, and Jim Parry. 2013. *Olympic Ethics and Philosophy.* New York: Routledge.

Müller, Norbert. 2000. *Pierre de Coubertin (1863–1937). Olympism. Selected Writings.* Lausanne: International Olympic Committee.
Murray, Sarah C. 2014. "The Role of Religion in Greek Sport," pp. 309–319 in *A Companion to Sport and Spectacle in Greek and Roman Antiquity*, edited by Paul Christesen and Donald G. Kyle. Malden, MA: John Wiley & Sons.
Orwell, George. 1968. "The Sporting Spirit," pp. 40–43 in *The Collected Essays, Journalism and Letters of George Orwell 1945–1950*, edited by Sonia Orwell and Ian Angus. London: Martin Seeker & Warburg Limited.
Plato. 2005. *Republic.* Translated by Paul Shorey, pp. 575–844 in *Plato: Collected Dialogues,* nineteenth printing, edited by Edith Hamilton and Huntingdon Cairns. Princeton: Princeton University Press.
Polley, Martin. 2006. "The Amateur Ideal and British Sports Diplomacy, 1900–1945." *Sport in History*, 26 (3):450–467
Rogge, Jacques. 2013. *15th IOC World Conference on Sport for All, Lima.* Lausanne: International Olympic Committee.
Roybal, Rory. 2010. *Miracles or Magic?* Los Gatos, CA: Smashwords.
Smith, William. 1875. *A Dictionary of Greek and Roman Antiquities.* London: John Murray.
Taylor, David J. 2010. *On The Corinthian Spirit: The Decline of Amateurism in Sport.* London: Yellow Jersey Press.
Toohey, Kristine, and Anthony J. Veal. Editors 2007. *The Olympic Games: A Social Science Perspective.* Cambridge, MA: CABI.
Turnbull, Simon. 2009. "Hitler Was There. But Jesse Had Gone to Fulfil a Dream." *The Independent*, August 11.
Van Auken, Lance. 2001. *"Play Ball!" The Story of Little League Baseball.* University Park: Pennsylvania State University Press
Weiler, Ingomar. 2004. "The Predecessors of the Olympic Movement, and Pierre de Coubertin." *European Review*, 12 (3):427–443.
Wenlock Olympian Society. 2015. "Much Wenlock & The Olympian Connection." Retrieved June 6, 2015 (http://www.wenlock-olympian-society.org.uk).
Young, David C. 2004. *A Brief History of the Olympic Games.* Oxford: Blackwell.

Amataeurism and Professsionalism

Sportsmanship and the Irish

JEAN MCARDLE

The concept of amateurism and the philosophical link to sportsmanship make a good vantage point from which to examine sport in Ireland. On quick examination the intrinsic values attributed to amateurism in the past seem to have little alignment to modern elite sport today. The ethos of amateurism that was once dominant within the Olympic Games and in the early formation of organized sport has for the most part long since been abandoned. When athletes participate in sport for no payment there is a suggestion that they do so for recreational or health reasons, whereas in professional sport athletes get paid (in the case of English soccer, for instance, Wayne Rooney earns up to $432,912 per week). Sports stars have become celebrities and endorsement deals have increased their financial status and worth (Moran 2001), which may impact on the ethos of sportsmanship. Ireland from a sporting perspective has one anomaly, the GAA (Gaelic Athletic Association), the only mass spectator sport in the world that is still organized on an amateur basis. GAA and rugby are highly successful and much loved sports within Ireland and provide a forum from which to debate the notion of sportsmanship and the relationship to amateurism and professionalism.

The historical development of a sporting culture in Ireland, like many other cultural pursuits, is a reflection of the political, social and cultural history of the island as a whole. Sport and recreational pursuits in Ireland, when examined, show a story of an uneasy relationship between accommodation and resistance intertwined in the historical and political history of Ireland. As Mike Cronin (1999) observes, "until there is only one idea of Irish nationalism, and a singular and commonly shared expression of identity, then sport will continue to reflect the multifaceted and ever changing nature of Irishness" (p. 190). The story of the development of Irish sport can be said to resemble one of at least three different Irelands. Using history and political change as a format to timeline the development of sport in Ireland we can break it down into the following phases. There is the pre-partition or pre–Independence (1921) era, Sport in the Republic of Ireland (Irish Free State) post-partition, and sport in Northern Ireland (six counties). This story can be contextualized further with the prevalence of two main religions, the Catholic and Protestant faiths, urban and rural Ireland, social class divisions, traditional and modern Ireland and finally professional and amateur sport.

Claims that Ireland possesses a rich and ancient sporting heritage are regularly asserted by commentators but this is possibly no different to most societies. While there are definite accounts of striking games (early forms of Hurling) and some forms of football type games the same could be said of most countries. Yet, like many nations surrounding England, the sporting revolution and codifying of games had an impact on Ireland in a number of ways. Sports became more formal and available (soccer, rugby, athletics and cricket) but there was also a nationalist response which led to the development of some of the dominant sporting codes in Ireland today.

As Bairner (2005) states, "Prior to the mid-nineteenth century the concept of sport in Ireland had another meaning far removed from the rough and tumble activities of the agricultural laboring class" (p. 192). The distinction between the gentleman (Anglo-Irish gentry) and the everyday man in Ireland was clear. Like their English counterparts, the Irish gentry's class enjoyed field sports such as rugby, cricket, tennis, bowls and croquet, along with recreational activities such as hunting and fishing. This section of Irish society would be the first to experience and be affected by the changes taking place in England in sport. The geography and politics between Ireland and the United Kingdom in the later 19th century meant that while Britain was forging its way as the "creator" of the modern sporting world, particularly in team games, Ireland was well represented in these formative years. The geography and the politics that bound the two countries together helped forge a cultural exchange. A reason for the changing face of sport in Ireland, particularly with the gentry's classes, was the considerable ties and links that had developed with England for generations, which manifested itself in the education of the younger generations. For decades the sons (but not too many of the daughters) of the wealthier classes (both Catholic and Protestant) had been traveling to England to utilize the well-established public school and university systems. Hence, there was an inevitability that the developments and changes taking place within England would transfer back to Ireland. The games, laws and ethics, and of course the concept of sportsmanship, developed within these educational environments and became entrenched within Irish society over time. Within the later part of the 19th century there was an increase in the amount of people playing cricket in Ireland, with one of the first games taking place in 1792 between the Irish Militia and the Gentlemen of Ireland. By the mid–1850s the game had expanded to the point where it was the largest and most popular sport in Ireland. In fact, its success was such that the first team to represent Ireland beat their English counterparts in 1855. Largely a victim of class and politics, cricket went in to sharp decline with the growth of nationalist sentiment within Irish political and social systems. Interestingly, two of the country's most dominant nationalist leaders were seasoned cricket players: Charles Stewart Parnell and John Redmond. Contemporary ideals and values aligned to sport in Ireland at this time were closely linked to the Victorian ideals of amateurism and masculinity which were entrenched in the dominant social and political classes in Ireland with the diffusion of Anglo-centric sports. In essence it was a middle and upper class urban affair. Whereas in sharp contrast rural Ireland, post-famine era and in the throws of a "land war" experienced a different sporting culture.

With the increase in political and social upheaval in Ireland at the later part of the 19th century and with the formation of the GAA a growing antipathy towards English sports and what was seen to be the influence of English imperialism started to emerge. The idea that sport was being used as a form of cultural imperialism and a way to further entrench British rule in Ireland was something that could be used to enhance nationalist ideals. The wider sporting revolution that was taking place in Ireland was curtailed to the middle and upper classes, with one exception: Association Football (soccer). Soccer was spreading rapidly into working class areas, particularly in Belfast (Northern Ireland). An examination of the demographics of the developing Ireland in the late 19th century showed Belfast closely resembled a Northern English town. The growth of sports like soccer saw a working class sporting culture align with a professional league which was in stark contrast to leafy suburban Dublin, home to tennis and golf clubs with rugby and cricket becoming increasingly popular.

By the 1880s organized sport had become a significant part of Irish social life. The Victorian ideals associated with sports, such as amateurism, gamesmanship, fair play, honor, teamwork, strength of character and will, were all characteristics identified with these ideals. These ideals had been developed within the English education system and became key components of the philosophy and ideals of sport throughout Europe. Yet, if we think about sportsmanship today as a form of conduct one in which players "stick to the rules, keep faith with their team, athletes keep fit, do not lose their temper, keep play free from brutality, keep pride in victory, a firm heart in loss and a sound and clean mind and body" (Keating 1995:146), a paradox appears. The paradox being that in the elite modern world of sport we ask athletes to engage in a deadly serious emotional and physical competition and behave as if they are to enjoy the activity like a pleasant recreational game of tennis and not the final of Wimbledon. To ask an athlete, particularly a professional athlete but also a full time amateur athlete, to act with fairness in a contest with modesty in victory and admirable composure in defeat is to demand a great deal. Sport in England was to be used to build the character of the upper to middle-class elite and develop the patriarchal role models for the future. However in Ireland particularly in the GAA, sport was to become a tool to assert independence and nationalism while still adhering to English sporting rules.

Ireland has been a country of competing sporting identities from as far back as the late 1800s. With the formation of the GAA (Gaelic Athletic Association) in 1884 this concept of identity took on a new meaning with cultural nationalism aligning itself intricately with a national sporting governing body. As stated previously sports such as soccer, rugby and cricket were becoming popular with the Anglo-Irish gentry classes and the middle and upper middle classes within Ireland. Particularly the latter two were codified, well organized amateur activities that upheld the Victorian principles of sportsmanship. The formation of the GAA saw an amateur sport develop more in line with the rough and tumble working class characteristics of the developing game of soccer.

History of the GAA

Michael Cusack (1847–1906) was a national school Irish language teacher with a keen interest in sport; involved in athletics (track and field) in 1882 he became a member of the newly established Dublin hurling club which was formed with the intention of re-establishing the "national game." He was engaged in the activities of the Gaelic revival and became a member of the Gaelic League which aligned with his nationalist political views. A game of hurling between the Dublin Metropolitan team—a team founded by Cusack—and a Galway team from Kilimor highlighted to Cusack the regional differences in this ancient indigenous sport that had developed with no formal structures, rules, and regulations. Cusack believed that not only did the rules of the game need to be standardized but that a governing body must be established to manage Irish sports. On the 1st of November 1884, the "Gaelic Athletic Association for the Preservation and Cultivation of National Pastimes" was created (Croke Park 2015a). The primary objective of the organization was to revive and promote a range of Irish cultural practices, amongst them hurling and Gaelic football but also including athletics and handball. The socio-political and cultural importance of the foundation of the GAA was that it would now serve as a vehicle for the transmission of a counter-hegemonic cultural and political ideology whilst maintaining the Victorian ideals of sportsmanship with the ideals of amateurism deeply entrenched within the organization. "Amateurism, Christian values and character formation were at least as cherished by the leadership of this nationalist sporting organisation as they had been by the muscular Christians of the English public schools some years earlier" (Bairner 2005:195).

While there is no doubt that Gaelic Football and Hurling are indigenous Irish sports and acted to provide Ireland with a distinctive sporting identity, the definitive history of both sports is intertwined with the sporting revolution that was taking place in Britain and spreading worldwide. A decision made by the GAA executive which would have long-lasting effects on the psyche of the Irish public in relation to sports was the introduction of a number of "bans" which were entwined within the nationalist sentiment of the GAA. The bans were aimed at preventing GAA members from playing and watching "foreign" sports and to disallow others from partaking in GAA. Two of the most controversial rules, rule 21 (banning members of the British forces and the RUC from playing Gaelic games) and rule 42 (banning the playing of non-Gaelic sports on GAA grounds), were only modified and changed in 2001 and 2005, respectively. The relevance of this was that post-partition there was the development of a dichotomous sporting identity in Ireland, that of the GAA and other sports and sport within the Irish Republic and Northern Ireland. Sport over the following decades within the Republic of Ireland centered on Gaelic Games with both rugby and soccer becoming dominant activities amongst the general public. What developed is that the GAA became a distinctive indigenous sporting culture that has been detrimental to Ireland competing on a world stage. However, with an ever increasing diaspora and the decision by Sky Sports to show Gaelic Games, international interest in Gaelic games would seem to be on the rise. Both soccer and rugby, along with numerous other sports such as boxing, athletics, swimming and equestrian sports, have become popular and relatively successful activities both in Ireland and on an international stage. However, the three main sports in the Republic of Ireland today are still GAA, soccer, and rugby from both a participatory and spectator perspective.

History of the IRFU

Trinity College Dublin founded a rugby team in 1854, which was the first organized football club in Ireland. Students at the university had first learned the game while at such English public schools as Cheltenham and Rugby. The sport was brought back to Ireland and while technically not affected by partition, it was already marginalized due to its alignment with British cultural traditions. This marginalization occurred due to both locality and, for the most part, social class. Therefore, what we see with the development of rugby in Ireland was that it was entrenched in the social, cultural and political traditions of Britain. Rugby Union from its early inception had promoted and heralded the amateur ethos aligned to the Victorian ideals of the British education system, yet this changed after nearly a century when Rugby Union turned professional and declared itself open. For most of its history, rugby was a strictly amateur football code, and the sport's administrators frequently imposed bans and restrictions on players whom they viewed as professional. Rugby league was created to allow players to be paid which was contradictory to the ethos of how the game of rugby and the philosophy of the game developed. In 1995, Rugby Union was declared an "open" game, and thus professionalism was sanctioned, alterations from the older Victorian ideals and the concepts of sportsmanship became apparent.

Initially there were two bodies in existence managing the sport of Rugby in Ireland, due to the political issues within the country, but in 1879 the two Unions agreed to amalgamate. Rugby Union was now organized on an All-Ireland level, and provincial branches were organized initially in Leinster, Munster and Ulster followed at a later date by Connaught (1885). Like with the GAA, the IRFU (Irish Rugby Football Union) was not devoid of political undertones; pre-partition, with increased nationalist sentiments developing in Ireland throughout the island, Rugby Union was more anti-nationalist than pro-nationalist. These sentiments did not end post-partition, particularly when it came to the flying of a national flag. Pre-partition the Union Jack was flown over the many pitches across the country; this was replaced in the Republic with the Tricolor and the issue was only resolved in 1925 with the creation of a new IRFU flag. The Tricolor is now only flown when games are played in the Republic of Ireland and a flag with the arms of the four provinces of Ireland with the shamrock in the center is flown alongside the Irish Tricolor in Dublin, and is used exclusively when playing elsewhere. Other political issues related to the singing of the Irish National Anthem culminated in 1995 with the composition of "Ireland's Call" which was to either replace or to be used alongside "Amhrán na bhFiann," the National Anthem of the Republic of Ireland. This was to help placate political tensions within the Union. Ireland's Call is now used by a number of other All-Ireland governing bodies such as cricket and hockey.

In Northern Ireland sport developed in a slightly more divisive manner with Gaelic and British games along with religious, social, cultural and economic impacts affecting participation. Simply put, Catholics played and participated in Gaelic Games while Protestants more often played rugby and cricket amongst other anglicized sports. While these are generalizations, they are indicative of the two major traditions and largely still apply (Bairner 2005). The GAA in the past did little to transcend these cultural divides and the same applied to sports such as soccer, rugby, hockey and cricket. Soccer in Northern Ireland was affected more by social class then by religion although religion still particularly affected the divisive nature of some of the dominant teams in the six counties. Working class urban nationalists and unionists were both equally drawn to soccer while middle-class nationalists tended to be drawn to Gaelic Games. Middle-class unionists were drawn more to rugby, cricket and hockey which are more dominant activities in the Protestant school system.

For the purpose of this essay an examination of amateurism and professionalism in the GAA and the IRFU will be explored. These two sports align with the evolution of the modern nation of Ireland; however, social, political and cultural changes in Ireland meant that they evolved differently. The focal question for the remainder of this essay is to see whether in the modern elite game we can distinguish whether GAA (amateur indigenous games) or Rugby Union, (internationalized and professional) differ in moral and ethical alignment to the ideals of sportsmanship.

GAA and Amateurism

The GAA is organized on a 32-county basis across the whole of the island of Ireland with competitive teams also in London and New York who regularly compete in the provincial championships. The organization has a presence on all five continents due to the vast Irish diaspora and is Ireland's largest sporting organization which is celebrated as one of the greatest and most prolific amateur sporting organizations in the world. The GAA is volunteer led and community based and has become an integral part of the Irish consciousness, playing an influential role in Irish society that extends far beyond the basic aim of promoting Gaelic games. The final nail-biting games of the season are played in Croke Park, an internationally acclaimed stadium that hosts up to 82,000 spectators which will fill every seat come All-Ireland final day. And yet the players who perform in this arena to a full capacity crowd are not paid and many will have to put aside the highs and lows of a win or loss in Croke Park on a Sunday and get up for work on a Monday morning to earn their living. The GAA as a national organization takes pride in its amateur status with section 1.10 of the GAA constitution, stating:

> The Association is an Amateur Association. A player, team, official or member shall not accept payment in cash or in kind in conjunction with the playing of Gaelic Games. A player, team, official or member shall not contract himself/itself to any agent other than those officially approved by Central Council. Expenses paid to all officials, players, and members shall not exceed the standard rates laid down by the Central Council. Members of the Association may not participate in full-time training. This Rule shall not prohibit the payment of salaries or wages to employees of the Association. Penalty: Twenty four weeks Suspension or Expulsion [GAA 2013:7].

The GAA is organized on provincial and county lines and has been widely credited with enshrining and enhancing the status of both entities within Irish life. The Provincial Councils are organized alongside historical lines with Leinster catering for the 12 counties in the east, Ulster nine in the north, Munster six in the south and Connacht five in the west. The All-Ireland national competition is contested by 32 teams in both hurling and football at different grades. There is a tiered system in place, with dominant teams in both codes competing at different levels with the same end goal: the All-Ireland championship. Players on senior inter county teams commit to play with first and foremost their club teams (parish teams) which serve as the backbone to everything the GAA stands for: loyalty, locality, community, parish and love of the game. If selected, they also commit to training and competitive structures with the senior county team, which for most young players is the dream, like a high-school baseball player hoping to end up playing with the New York Yankees. Adherence to the senior panel means up to three extra field sessions of training a week, combined with daily strength and conditioning sessions on top of their club training (usually two nights a week with a game at the weekend) with many players' full-time students or holding down full-time jobs.

Demands on players today are well documented by the press and GAA commentators, with national, provincial newspapers and broadcasters regularly leading with headlines such as "Is Too Much Being Asked of Our GAA players?" (Cormic 2015). Considering that in the 1950s players on a senior panel only came together for two weeks before an All-Ireland final. Much has been discussed about the concept of Senior County GAA players as "indentured slaves" with the assertion that managers at all levels have imported professional practices into an amateur sport and players young and old are finding it difficult to keep up not unlike Collegiate American football. Players are not being paid to endure the same level of training and competition as professional athletes yet this is the current level of expectation. Therefore, a common occurrence today are issues related to foul play, gambling and a more recent problem of performance enhancing substances being used by players with supplement use becoming a staple part of their training.

The backroom staff of a senior county panel has grown from a manager and two selectors, to a manager, two selectors (if not more), a physical trainer, physiotherapist, doctor, sports psychologist, nutritionist and a kit man amongst others, mirroring a professional sports team organization. These changes have not taken place overnight but have been simmering and developing for many years. A deal with Sky Sports in 2014 saw the GAA sign over the rights of 20 games in the football and hurling championships and caused controversy amongst players, spectators and commentators alike, with one player highlighting that on an All-Ireland final day the only people *not* getting paid are the players. The players may receive a stipend, will more than likely (if they are on the winning side) receive a foreign holiday for themselves and their family, food is provided post training and post matches, along with a free sports kit, a travel allowance for training and, in some individual cases, a player may be on the receiving end of a relatively lucrative (in Irish sporting circles) sponsorship deal. Yet the players and the organization still adhere to an amateur ethos in principle. One particularly ironic and regularly debated issue within the GAA is the fact that the organization has signed up to WADA (World Anti Doping Agency). The irony being that they are amateur athletes, and while many of these players train and play on sub-standard facilities on a weekly basis, inter-county players are subjected to drug tests, in cold, damp and sometimes humiliating conditions. An organization which started from humble, mainly working class roots, has developed into a professional structure in everything but name and money.

Managers at inter-county level also make for an interesting study in that by Croke Park decree they should not be receiving a salary from the county however it is a well-known secret that they are indeed financially reimbursed for their involvement and time (Lawlor 2014).

> I've been in dressing rooms where the only people not getting paid were the players. Everyone from the video man, the fitness gurus, the physios and the manager are all being paid. It's being done surreptitiously and it's a blemish on the organisation with some people pulling down between €30,000 and €60,000 for training teams [Whelan, 2009].

According to Sean Potts from the GPA (Gaelic Players Association), he believes that the GAA need to face up to these issues as denial is damaging to its reputation:

> It's the elephant in the room and it needs to be out in the open and monitored. Ignoring it is just compounding the problem and transparency and acknowledging that people need to be reimbursed is no threat to the GAA's amateur status and will not lead to players knocking on the door to go professional or be paid [Whelan 2009].

This statement highlights the alterations in the modern GAA; a call for transparency on issues that go against the constitution, a breaking of rules; but an issue that needs to be addressed. The changing structures, commercial interests and a more professionalized organization being driven by managers, businesses, the media and players has meant that while the amateur ethos is still alive it has increasingly more to do with tradition than necessity.

The core philosophy of the GAA is based on local community, club and parish devised to enhance pride within the locality and pride within your county. However, the GAA, like any sporting body, is subject to regular deviant actions; on pitch fighting, brutal and deliberate tackles intended to injure, gambling, referee abuse and many more. This is an organization that incites local and national passions and hence the philosophy of sportsmanship can regularly be ignored in the heat of the moment. The history and development of the GAA as an organization was created using the ideals of amateurism which can be seen as integral to the philosophy of sportsmanship. Therefore, an examination of the modern senior county game shows a deviation from amateurism in everything other than name and payment to players like the Olympic Games! An ironic juxtaposition led in part and encouraged by the GAA central council that wants to enhance the quality of the product while still adhering to what some would see as antiquated laws and conventions.

Rugby and Professionalism

Interest and support for Rugby Union in Ireland has flourished since it became "open" in 1995. Numbers playing and supporting both the National and provincial teams have increased since the early 2000s, particularly with European Club success and success for the National team on the international stage. Following a disastrous World Cup campaign in 1999, a decision to invest heavily in keeping the best players at home rather than letting them be lured to England, and to a lesser extent France, was the turning point for Irish Rugby. From there on Irish players trained here, had their playing schedules managed here, played here and lived here. An off-shoot of this success is the creation of visible sporting heroes; Brian O'Driscoll, the former Irish captain, being a perfect example. Irish success in international club-rugby (which involves the four provinces of Ulster, Munster, Leinster and Connaught) in the 2000s has generated sporting heroes whose success is traced to amateur commitment to place and community despite rugby's professionalization in 1995. This attribution offered a vision of a nationally sustainable professional game where player professionalism was driven by local rootedness, despite the provinces' regional rather than traditional club status.

However, paid sportsmen make unstable heroic objects of investment. Extensively publicized refusals of national selection by high-profile players have highlighted the fragility of projections of national heroism and have shown how the economic power and cultural significance of clubs as employers conflict with those of international competition. By contrast, journalists and other commentators in the Irish media depicted rugby's crossing of amateur/professional, middle/working-class, urban/rural, and North/South divides as the successful national integration of multiple masculinities, aligning with the GAA yet not necessarily precise (Free 2013).

Growth in participation rates in rugby have been documented at an approximate 10 percent increase per annum in recent years; thus from a situation in 2005 where there were some 98,000 registered players there is now currently in excess of 150,000. The game of rugby had been predominantly a middle-class game linked to a sub-cultural component of Irish society, that of the upper middle and gentry classes. The development of the game has been promoted by international success and increased media coverage, which has had the effect of increasing spectatorship, putting Rugby Union on a par with Senior County GAA and soccer in the hearts and minds of the Irish sports spectator. From a cultural standpoint this would not have been the case even fifty years previously. Particularly with the GAA bans still in place which also had the impact of stopping the cross-pollination of sports viewing and participation in Ireland.

In the initial stages of "open" play many Irish players were bought by English rugby clubs, with players happy to leave for a more advanced pay check than they would receive staying in the Irish structure, which was still figuring out how it was going to fund this new open league. Professionalism lured away many a dominant Irish player and the lack of success at international level meant that this exodus of talent would continue. While Rugby Union embraced professionalism it was still the last international sport in Ireland to set aside its amateur status. "Rugby as a healthy, manly pursuit had evolved and prospered on the dedication, hard work and goodwill of successive generations, yet overnight it went from being a game to a business" (Moran 2001:277). While the business of rugby has flourished on a provincial and International level, with estimates on salaries of top Irish professionals ranging from $112,000 to $280,000 per annum which can be enhanced with prolific sponsorship deals. The club game has suffered with the pay to play ethos that became particularly popular in the boom years in Ireland, which has caused what has been estimated at approximately $23 million in debt, suggesting that continuation of this structure is not viable.

Rugby has become a business: in business contracts are shorter, players are put under increasing levels of pressure to be fit, to raise their game, there is pressure on management to perform, and increased media speculation about the players, their personal lives and their families. Rugby, while it does not generate the same kind of financial stipend that many other high profile sports do, particularly in the United States; still makes enough money and generates enough interest for it to have made celebrities out of the players and for the players to utilize this fame to amass personal fortunes. There are also numerous offshoot businesses that have derived from the game and like with other mediated, professional sports, control belongs less and less to the players and the teams and more to the organizations and businesses backing the game. A far cry from the gentleman's game that was lauded for generations for its ethical and philosophical adherence to the ideals of amateurism aligned to its status amongst the upper echelons of Irish society.

High profile deviant acts have been committed by many of the National Irish rugby team in the past, with such examples being eye gouging, claw stamping (deliberate stamping on someone's hand), gambling debts, six month bans, and inter-provincial rivalries that were not always rectified when it came to national selection and playing for the national team. The pressure players are under to maintain their place, their fitness and their salary is partially due to their love of the game but also linked to a hubris that exists within the game of rugby. Hubris that they are the tough guys the players who can brush off serious tackles and injuries and continue to play. Brian O'Driscoll makes for a good example, who after experiencing a life-threatening tackle returned to the game for another eight years after a six month hiatus; a product of the demands of the modern professionalized game or the inner strength of the player? Offshoots from the professional game have been stories of some talented high-school student-athletes who have been found taking performance-enhancing substances with increasing pressure being placed on them if they want to make it to the academy stage and then on to have pro-careers. Research has shown that professionalism has an impact on the amount of injuries within the professional and the amateur game (Garraway et al. 2000), emphasizing the allure of the professional game and what athletes and coaches will do to access that arena. A win at all costs attitude, one which counteracts the ideals of sportsmanship in many ways.

Table 1.1 provides a synopsis of some of the main characteristics that apply to both Rugby and GAA. However, the reality is that bar the internationalism and pay for play structures in rugby, the attributes ascribed to both activities; amateur and professional are increasingly similar.

Table 1.1: Professional versus Amateur Attributes: A Comparison of Rugby and GAA

Rugby	***GAA***
Status	*Status*
Professional (National and Provincial) Since 1995	Amateur (At All Levels)
Attributes (Intrinsic)	*Attributes (Intrinsic)*
Dedication	Pride (County / Jersey)
Employment	Loyalty
Internationalism	Local (Community)
Culture	Culture
Extrinsic Rewards	*Extrinsic Rewards*
Pay for Play	Limited Sponsorship
Sponsorship (Team and Individual)	Local Support

The key components of sportsmanship align with both sports, and the concept of amateurism in the GAA for some is only lip service, yet the idea that players will dedicate their time, bodies and lives to a sport that has become increasingly demanding on them for the "love of the jersey" still overrides the intrinsic and extrinsic qualities attributed to professional sports. Increasingly we are seeing Senior County GAA players moving to rugby and soccer with the allure of being able to do something that you love and being paid for it. The Victorian ideals associated with both of these sports are still in existence with characteristics like teamwork, honor, strength of character and will in abundance. Yet we return to our opening questions does the status of amateur and professional have an impact on sportsmanship in Ireland? From the social, political and historical analysis of both codes it would seem that the idealism of the past and the ethos of amateurism is diminishing for both; one due to the impact of professionalism on the game (rugby) even though internal financial factors are calling its viability into question at a local club level; and the other (GAA) due to the demands of the counties, management, media, players and the spectators who want to see heightened competition and value for money. Both of these sports at local and community level maintain the same level of amateurism that always existed, where volunteerism and community spirit are dominant factors in how these sports are played and organized, but at the national level the story is different. Therefore we are left with something akin to an answer in the case of sport in Ireland; contrasting pasts and recent social and cultural developments in the amateur and professional ethos would suggest that the philosophy of sportsmanship is not necessarily affected by changes in the standing of the sport but increasingly on the pressures placed on them by the modern world.

Bibliography

Bairner, Alan. 2005. *Sport and the Irish: Histories, Identities and Issues.* Dublin: University College Press.

Cleary, Joe, and Claire Connolly. *The Cambridge Companion to Modern Irish Culture.* Cambridge: Cambridge University Press.

Coakley, Jay, and Elizabeth Pike. 2009. *Sports in Society: Issues and Controversies.* New York: McGraw-Hill.

Cormic, Eoghan. 2015. "Is Too Much Being Asked of Our GAA Players?" Retrieved January 17, 2015 (http://www.irishexaminer.com).

Croke Park. 2015a. "About the GAA." Retrieved April 9, 2015 (https://www.gaa.ie).

Croke Park. 2015b. "A Biography of Michael Cusack." Retrieved April 9, 2015(http://www.crokepark.ie).

Cronin, Mike. 1999. *Sport, Nationalism in Ireland. Gaelic Games, Soccer and Irish Identity Since 1884.* Dublin: Four Courts Press.

Do Chara. 2010. "Rugby in Ireland." Retrieved April 9, 2015 (http://www.dochara.com).

Free, Marcus. 2013. "Diaspora and Rootedness, Amateurism and Professionalism in Media Discourses of Irish Soccer and Rugby in the 1990s and 2000s." *Éire-Ireland*, 48 (1&2): 211–229. Retrieved April 9, 2015(https://muse.jhu.edu/).

Garraway, William, Mandy Lee, Sean Hutton, Eoin Russell, and Donald Macleod. 2000. "Impact of Professionalism on Injuries in Rugby Union." *British Journal of Sports Medicine.* 34:348–351.

Gaelic Athletic Association. 2013. *Official Guide–Part 1.* Dublin 3. Published by the Central Council of the Association Croke Park.

Independent Newspaper. 1997. "Rugby Union: France Call Foul on Ireland Retrieved February 19, 2015 (http://www.independent.co.uk).

Irish Times. 2011. "World Cup Final Eye Gouging: McCaw Points the Finger at Rougerie." Retrieved February 19. 2015 (http://www.irishtimes.com).

Lawlor, Damien. 2014. "Should GAA Wage War on Payments to Managers, or Just Make It Official?" Retrieved May 22, 2015 (http://www.independent.ie).

Moran, Sean. 2001 "The Gaelic Athletic Association and Professionalism in Irish Sport." *Irish Quarterly Review*, 90 (359):276–282.

Morgan, William J., and Klaus Meier. *Philosophic Inquiry in Sport.* Champaign, IL: Human Kinetics.

Rouse, Paul. 2014. "Sports Rights Commercialization Revisited: Sky and the GAA by History and Policy Opinion." Retrieved June 1, 2015 (http://historyhub.ie).

Sugden, John, and Alan Bairner. 1993. *Sport, Sectarianism and Society in a Divided Ireland.* Leicester: Leicester University Press.

Whelan, John. 2009. "GAA Shamed by Hypocrisy of €20m Tax Free Payments to Managers." Retrieved June 1, 2015 (http://www.wiredwithwhelan.com).

Warrior, Patriot, Statesman

Irish Sportsmanship and Irish Identity

Denis Brennan

There is no more doubt about the influence of sports in the Republic of Ireland's culture than there is for the influence of sports in the United States. In both nations, major sporting events receive sophisticated and widespread attention and, whether it is the Super Bowl in the U.S. or the All Ireland Senior Hurling Championship, new national holidays have been created and are regularly celebrated. Sports stars are treated with deference and respect which, for some observers, seems well out of proportion with their status in society; after all, while athletes are certainly entitled to political opinions or to comment on social controversy, what makes social or political observations voiced by a LeBron James or a Roy Keane more relevant or especially valuable? The modern world of sports is a far cry from the power or sway sports exerted in either nation around the turn of the 20th century. Regardless, both countries followed somewhat similar paths as sports became dominant influences; but, there was a fundamental distinction—one, the United States, was a conservative effort to maintain a dominant social and cultural ideology, the other, Ireland, was a radical effort to undermine the dominant cultural ideology and restore a fast-eroding traditional culture threatened with imminent eradication.

In the closing decades of the 19th century and the early decades of the twentieth, sport was transformed in the U.S. and pre-partition Ireland. The founding of the Gaelic Athletic Association (GAA) followed in the wake of the Great Famine (*an Gorta Mor*), which had contributed to an amplification of Anglicization as traditional Irish culture became increasingly moribund. The GAA was founded to promote traditional Irish games, especially hurling and Gaelic football, to help stimulate pride in Irish national traditions, and to challenge growing British sporting influence among the nation's youth. In the United States around the same time, a combination of factors, including: recognition of post–Civil War divisions, industrialization, urbanization, global economic expansion, and the end of the frontier provoked a perceived need for a new means of teaching American national identity. The values associated with that identity (i.e., rugged individualism, free enterprise, open society) were founded in the nation's agrarian-republican experience, but were now to be taught to American youth in sports, especially baseball and collegiate football. Additionally, creation myths, or "invented traditions," particularly for baseball in the United States and hurling in Ireland, linked national games to cultural anchors in order to promote a sense of continuity for national identity. Finally, in both countries, communication and transportation improvements provided a means for the successful popularization, promotion, and development of these changes.

However, while sports played an increasingly important role in U.S. society at the end of the 19th century and found acceptance both as an instrument of instruction and as a means for inculcating "American" values, sports in Ireland around the same time was decidedly more radical. Baseball and football in the U.S. were a means to restore and uphold a traditional understanding of what it meant to be an American; hurling and Gaelic football were weapons meant to undermine and destroy the expanding British hegemonic control of a native people. Hurlers and footballers became more than athletes or icons of national identity; they were warriors in a battle for independence, symbols of patriotic nationalism, and statesmen urging radical political transformation.

Sports, Nationalism and Myth in the United States

Three years after the United States Census Department announced that a fixed line demarcating the American frontier could no longer be drawn, Frederick Jackson Turner delivered his famous address, "The Significance of the Frontier in American History." For Turner, the frontier was more than a space on a map; its existence since the earliest colonial times had defined the rugged independent character of the American individual, i.e., self-reliant, optimistic, adaptable, and ingenious. Ominously, he warned that with the loss of the frontier, the nation required a new means of defining American character (Dorsey 2007). Concurrent with this development, the last decades of the 19th century witnessed a desire to define American nationalism for its burgeoning industrial era. Partially driven by the post–Civil War effort to re-unite a people torn apart, it was also driven by the celebration, in 1876, of the nation's first century, the initial flowerings of a real industrial revolution, a reaction to the enormous influx of immigrants, and the impulses of globalization. Earlier conceptions of American identity no longer applied as accurately as they once had.

J. Hector St. John de Crèvecour had offered a definition of "What Is an American" in his famous letters from the late 18th century. Even today Americans embrace his notion that "we are the most perfect society now existing in the world ... free as [we] ought to be" and unencumbered by powerful governmental strictures; however, his description of Americans as "a people of cultivators scattered over an immense territory" was clearly no longer as apt as it once had been (St. John Crèvecour 1782; 2013:29). The nation was "immense" and people "scattered" but the end of the frontier, industrialization, and urbanization were quickly undermining the image of the American people as "cultivators." Furthermore, while the forces of change encouraged economic development, industrial expansion, and material progress some feared that the changes wrought by new social and cultural systems, especially without regulation, threatened to undermine the shared values and shared identity which Americans had embraced in the past. The benefit of economic growth in the "Gilded Age" was not shared equitably; a few found much greater reward than most. "In an increasingly heterogeneous society," according to historian S. W. Pope, "many Americans found it difficult to define the precise nature of their national identity" (Pope 1997:9). At this time, intellectuals, politicians, social leaders, and many in the growing middle class recognized this dilemma and found that "the rise of modern athletics" could provide "new expressions of nationalism" which could provide unity to a nation divided by class, cultural, ethnic, and even racial distinctions (Pope 1997:11).

Long distained, especially by those who held Victorian values, athletic activity and organized sports developed during this period into an institution with a vital social purpose. Victorian sensibility had esteemed duty, integrity, hard work, and moral certitude above all. These characteristics were, Victorians believed, incompatible with the profane world of sport, where excesses of immorality (i.e., swearing, gambling, and alcohol) were common. However, as the 19th century waned, urban, middle-class men and women in particular increasingly envisioned sport not as detrimental, but as an activity that taught the values fundamental to American identity, the values of a frontier society, the values of the rugged individual, of free enterprise, of community, of adaptability, of creativity, and of success. In the 19th century, this blending of sports with national identity created what has been called a "sporting republic" which "combined ideas about the power of athletics to shape human beings with the enduring theory that republics are the best of all forms of government" (Dyreson 1998:14). The United States at the end of the 19th century was threatened by the forces of modernity (industrialization, economic stratification, labor unrest, and an emerging leisure class) as well as the changes produced by urbanization and immigration. A republic founded and defined by its agrarian ideas required redefinition and the tool chosen by progressives, intellectuals, writers, sports entrepreneurs, and many political leaders was athletics and sports (Dyreson 1998). The intertwining of sport and American identity, whether by class, gender, ethnicity, or race, only deepened throughout the 20th century.

Chief among the politicians who epitomized the importance of athletics and the "sporting republic" was Theodore Roosevelt. In 1899, while Governor of New York, he avowed a need for Americans to embrace "the life of toil and effort, of labor and strife" without which success and triumph as both an individual and a nation was not feasible (Roosevelt 2004:755). Roosevelt was remarkably consistent in describing the meaning of "Americanism," which included the need for moral character, the willingness to share equality, but "chief among those founding elements was physical vigor" (Dorsey 2007:19). Despite the brutality associated with collegiate American football, which muckrakers vilified widely in the early 20th century, Roosevelt believed that aggressive sports built the kind of leadership character needed for a successful future for the United States. To face the challenge of modernization, loss of an agrarian foundation, and the potential threats from other nations and other societies, Americans needed the discipline, teamwork, aggression, and work ethic found in Dyreson's "sporting republic." The nation faced new challenges and the strength to face them would be found in the traditional values of Crevecour's "American"; what was needed was a new means of teaching those values—that new means was sports.

Arguably the most notable example of the link between American nationalism and sports came from Albert Spalding's decades-long effort to demonstrate that baseball was more than the undisputed "national pastime"; he sought to prove that it was distinctly and purely American in origin. The "game" of baseball for Spalding was only part of the reason that Americans were enthralled by the sport; the game had a significant role in "developing character and its demonstration of the importance of organization, professionalism, and individual strength for achieving success" (Levine 1985:115). Spalding waxed philosophic about the influence of the game in his own history of baseball; "no other sport," he wrote, "is the exponent of American Courage, Confidence, Combativeness; American Dash, Discipline, Determination; American Energy, Eagerness, Enthusiasm; American Pluck, Persistency, Performance; American Spirit, Sagacity, Success; American Vim, Vigor, Virility" (Spalding 1992; 1911:4).

When the purely American origins of baseball was once again challenged, Spalding "attacked" the heresy in the 1905 edition of *Spalding's Official Baseball Guide* and proposed a commission to find the truth. Under his careful guidance and with the serendipitous recollections of Abner Graves, the commission dutifully proclaimed the purely American origins of baseball three years later. In response to the commission's plea for evidence about the game's origins, Graves had written that as a child he witnessed Abner Doubleday scratch a diamond in the sand of a Cooperstown, NY road and explain the rules of the game in 1839. Without corroboration, the commission embraced the story as "the final step in the evolution of the game" (Spalding 1992; 1911:39). No small measure of that embrace was enhanced by the fact that young Abner Doubleday became Major General Abner Doubleday and had risen to national hero status with his defense of Fort Sumter in 1861 and his later service for the Union during the Civil War. In 1908, Spalding understood that the "Gilded Age" image of the independent, self-made, individualistic American whose strength emerged from an agrarian society did not fit with the reality of an increasingly capitalist, industrialized, and urbanized society. However, the story of a young future Civil War hero designing "America's game" in the dirt of small town rural America most certainly resonated and fit that image. A myth and legend was born.

Sport and Myth in Ireland

The myths and legends of ancient Ireland have preserved many stories and arguably none is more important to modern Irish sport than a legend associated with the Irish warrior hero, Setanta (later known as Cúchulainn). From the earliest days of the GAA there was a desire, in a fashion not completely dissimilar to Spalding's efforts, to demonstrate the uniqueness of sport and games in Ireland. Gaelic football had, supposedly, developed completely independent of the English version, but more importantly, "Hurling was traced back to the days of Cúchulain and vested with legendary grandeur" (Mandle 1977:424). The full story can be found in the Irish epic known as *The Táin* (or *Cattle Raid*) which is set in first century BCE Ireland. Setanta was a powerful youngster and an extraordinary athlete who defeated all who challenged him at any game of prowess, including ancient versions of Irish hurling. He was invited by King Conchur to attend a great feast but stayed behind to finish his game and promised to follow later. The feast was at the home of Culann, a blacksmith who owned a great hound to guard his estate. The powerful beast required three chains with three men on each chain to restraint him. King Conchur arrived and forgetting the Setanta was to come later, told Culann that his whole entourage was with him and since no one else was expected, Culann locked the gates and ordered the hound loosed from his chains (Kinsella 1970).

When Setanta approached Culann's gates, he carried, as was his practice, his hurley and sliotar—always prepared to use the stick and ball to practice his hurling skills. With no warning, Culann's fearsome hound attacked. Setanta reacted instinctively; he swung his hurley and struck the sliotar with such great force and accuracy that it became buried deep in the hound's throat and the terrifying animal chocked to death; the great warrior was unharmed. The hound's baying reminded King Conchur that Setanta has yet to arrive and the guests rushed from Culann's compound fearing a gruesome sight and were stunned but pleased to find the young boy unscathed. Culann expressed remorse for the hound's actions but lamented the loss of his awesome protector. Setanta regretted the killing and promised to remain and guard Culann's home until a new hound could be trained. In thanks, Culann gave Setanta a new name, Cúchulainn or the Hound of Culann (Kinsella, 1970). This story about a legendary warrior's triumphant but politic response was crucial, at the end of the 19th century, to the promotion of an understanding of the centrality of hurling to Irish culture and of the importance and need to protect Ireland's cultural identity that was being threatened with extinction by British intransigence.

There are aspects of the mythic story of Cúchulainn which parallel the popular "creation myth" about baseball in the United States: both legends have no basis in fact; the protagonist in each is a young man whose reputation later in life rested on military success; and, finally, both emerged in the late 19th century as elements of cultural nationalist sentiment associated with sport. Arguably just as striking are the differences: a young Abner Doubleday's scratching a diamond in the dirt of a Cooperstown road hardly equates with the power and courage Cúchulainn demonstrated; the Doubleday myth was of recent vintage, while the epic Irish myth had been told or read for centuries; and finally, the former was quickly judged trivial, even frivolous while the latter was part of a very serious, indeed even radical, challenge to cultural and political hegemony. The Doubleday myth supposedly demonstrated that baseball was a purely American game and finally put to rest a debate between Albert Spalding and Henry Chadwick, often called the "father of baseball," about the origins of the game. Chadwick lost a debate which he later described as "a joke between us" (Levine 1985:115). On the other hand, though Spalding certainly relished his victory as a demonstration of American nationalism at a time when the United States was emerging on the international stage, it was also linked to the growth and commercial success of organized baseball. For the Irish, however, hurling was not just a game, nor a commercial entity and certainly not a joke, but rather a part of their cultural identity which was threatened with extinction. It was not simply an issue of national patriotism or national pride but an issue of national survival, and the individuals involved in that struggle for survival were not simply players on a field but advocates and instruments of revolution.

Sport and Nationalism in Ireland

At the same time as baseball was becoming commercialized, professionalized, and nationalized, Michael Cusack and others organized a revival of traditional Irish sports, like hurling and Gaelic football, not for profit but as a new dynamic in the centuries-old battle against British authority. Cusack was a schoolteacher who taught at schools in Kilkenny and Kildare before founding his own school in Dublin in 1877, at which "sport was an essential part of the activities" (Rouse 2009:49). An avid sportsman all his life, Cusack particularly enjoyed English sports, cricket and rugby, before the early 1880s; in combination, his school and his participation in Dublin sporting societies had made him a person of some renown. In the 1880s Cusack commenced a new career in journalism and established a reputation as a skillful and effective "letter-writer, reporter, columnist, editor, owner, and historian" (Rouse 2009:51). It was in this career that Cusack emerged as the champion of Irish sports. Eschewing cricket, by the end of 1882, he was pleading for a return to "the game he termed Ireland's 'national pastime'—the game of hurling" (Rouse 2009:51).

Like many of his time, Cusack was part of a post-famine generation whose nationalism was shaped by the terrible consequences of *an Gorta Mor*, during which more than a million died while more than a million emigrated. In the decades following the famine, traditional cultural practices not only declined but many were threatened with extinction. Kevin Whelan examined the cultural changes which followed the famine in four aspects of Irish traditional culture: devotional practices, the keen (public grieving by women after a death), dance, and hurling. He has clearly demonstrated that the famine "marked a watershed in many areas of Irish life—demographics, economics, society, [and] culture" and further asserted that as a result, "Ireland remained culturally comatose in the immediate post–Famine period" (Whelan 2005:138) With regard to hurling, the landed gentry's support for the game, both as spectators and gamblers, had begun to decline before the famine. The French Revolution had exacerbated class differences in Ireland, which discouraged landowners' prior encouragement and involvement with the sport. This decline accelerated in the wake of the famine as the game "degenerated into crudity," as reflected, in the opinion of the English elite, by the way the game was being played by lower class Irish peasants (Whelan 2005:146). Further undermining hurling's acceptance was a growing antipathy to the game by the Catholic ministry and the rising Catholic middle class, as well as the imposition and enforcement of legal restrictions against hurling matches. In the face of growing challenges, the years succeeding the famine saw participation in hurling continue to fall swiftly until it reached near a point of extinction (Whelan 2005).

The GAA and the Birth of Irish Athletic Nationalism

Sport in Ireland had followed an historical narrative not much different than sports' history in the rest of Europe. Bat and ball-type games, like the hurling of Cúchulainn, and football-type games, such as *caid,* had been commonly played for eons. However, when the English sporting revolution reached Ireland in the post-famine years, their growth and ability to displace traditional games "provoked a response from Irish nationalists" like Cusack (Bairner 2005:192). The influence of the Anglo-Irish ascendancy had been powerful for a long time, but after the 1840s it increased significantly as the Irish people were driven "from their trysting-places at the cross-roads and hurling fields back to their cabins" and increasingly abandoned traditional Irish pastimes (Mandle 1977, 418). English sports like cricket and rugby were played with alarming frequency not only in Protestant circles but in Catholic circles as well. In light of this fact, Irish nationalists viewed these sports not simply as games, but as attempts by British educational and military administrations to promote "English sport imperialism" (Bairner 2005:193).

What quickly became the Gaelic Athletic Association (GAA) emerged from Cusack's journalistic response to this perception of British domination and his letter published in *United Ireland* on October 11, 1884, "A Word About Irish Athletics." Athletics and games in Ireland, he asserted, were currently dominated by the Amateur Athletic Association of England; it was time for the Irish to displace foreign influence and revive their own ancient traditions and pastimes (Cronin, Duncan, and Rouse 2009:53). On November 1, 1884, less than a month after "A Word About Irish Athletics" was published, Michael Cusack and several other men (reports vary from seven to thirteen) met at Miss Hayes'

Hotel in Thurles, County Tipperary and the Gaelic Athletic Association was born (McDonnell 2009). Despite what appeared to be an unpretentious creation, the GAA experienced quick and significant growth, not the least due to the fact that from the day of its founding, the GAA radiated Irish nationalism. In addition to Cusack, Maurice Davin, perhaps the most well-known Irish athlete of the day, attended the meeting, along with several men who were active members of the Irish Republican Brotherhood (IRB), an organization formed in Dublin in 1848 and devoted to revolutionary nationalism. Soon afterward, Archbishop Thomas Croke, a strong voice for Irish nationalism in the church hierarchy, Charles Stewart Parnell, the political force behind the parliamentary movement for Irish Home Rule, and Michael Davitt, the radical nationalist founder of the Land League were invited and accepted positions as patrons to the new organization (Garnham 2004). In his letter of acceptance, Archbishop Croke strongly criticized the fact the Ireland "had begun importing from England not only manufactured goods but also fashions, literature, mannerisms, and 'alien' game pastimes." Organizations like the GAA were, Croke asserted, vital in the struggle to reverse these efforts to destroy Irish culture (Byrne, Coleman, and King 2008:359).

Expansion of the GAA

In stark contrast to today's GAA, the GAA's early public success was not initially built on hurling and Gaelic football, although they were important, since they represented a direct link to centuries-old Irish cultural tradition. Rather its popularity was established in a controversy which developed between the GAA and several well-established athletic clubs in Dublin, most notably over track and field events. Jealous of the GAA's quick growth, mixed with personal animosity toward Cusack, the clubs banded together to form the Irish Amateur Athletic Association (IAAA); their organization's primary goal was "to quash the Gaelic Union" (Cronin et al. 2009:40). The conflict was played out widely in the Irish press and, with the IAAA's decision to abide by the standards and rules established by the British Amateur Athletic Association, made the central issue appear to be a simple choice between support for Ireland's own culture or the acceptance of British regulations and authority. For most people in Ireland, the choice was stark: "by the end of 1885 the GAA was in control of Irish athletics, its meetings drawing huge crowds in towns across Ireland" (Cronin et al. 2009:40).

By the middle of 1887, GAA membership had surpassed 50,000 and by the end of the year there were over 400 affiliated clubs in operation across the country (Garnham 2004:65). Many of the clubs expressed an unabashed nationalism by naming their clubs after Irish nationalist heroes. Beyond the appeal of revitalizing nationalism, the GAA also promoted local competition on a county by county basis with the goal of county teams competing for national titles. This structure stimulated press coverage of the competitions as well as widespread interest in and speculation regarding competition for the title of national champion. What was more, those amateurs competing in these events were generally young Catholic men from lower class or lower middle class Irish society and the games were played on Sundays, the only day in the week when they could compete. By inviting into the system those who, because of their status in society, were excluded in the past, popular support for GAA activities grew (Garnham 2004).

Cultural and political attitudes and actions had invigorated a revival of Irish nationalism that by the 1870s and 1880s exerted pressure to once again seek to undermine British domination in every aspect of Irish life, including sport. By 1880 agitation over land policies developed into an outright land war with demands for the destruction of the long-lived landlord system. Supported by the Irish Republican Brotherhood, emboldened by the mounting political influence of Parnell, and encouraged by the founding of Davitt's Land League, agrarian agitators resorted first to resistance against British land policies and eventually to violence when resistance proved insufficient. British police, military, and political leaders attempted to suppress the outbreak but in 1881 concessions were made which at least temporarily restored some semblance of quiet. Most importantly, British prime minister William Gladstone's government granted the Land League's principal demand for free sale, fixity of tenure, and fixed rent in land policy. The Land War would reignite in the years to come, but the campaign of 1879–1881 had resurrected Irish nationalist sentiment, regenerated debate about Home Rule, and revived flagging consideration of partition, which the experience and aftermath of the famine had undermined (Killeen 2004). The revival of Irish sports, as reflected in the GAA, involved more than the advocacy of a few men, no matter how passionate or committed, and did not emerge in a vacuum. Creation of the GAA was one element of a burgeoning movement in the late 19th century toward resurrecting Irish culture, including the Irish language, dance, music, and sport, all of which had suffered under the growing influence of English culture.

Beyond Home: Globalizing the GAA

This movement was not bound by the small island's borders; the GAA sought also to forge connections and influence with the Irish diaspora "across the pond." In September 1888, fifty athletes representing "the cream of Irish athletics and hurling" were selected to "undertake a sporting invasion of America" as international statesmen for Irish nationalism (Cronin 2007:191). The idea was proposed by Michael Davitt, led by Maurice Davin, and organized with the full support of the GAA leadership. Given the success in its first few years of existence and the growth of cultural pride in Ireland, many believed the "invasion" would both raise funds for other cultural events at home and re-energize Irish cultural heritage among Irish in the U.S. Curiously, the GAA tour took place at the same time that Albert Spalding organized a more ambitious *world* tour with two teams of elite baseball players; he sought to demonstrate the athletic/cultural preeminence of the U.S. And, coincidently, Spalding's tourists played the final foreign game of their tour in Dublin, where the teams received a reception "more enthusiastic" than in any country they visited—less because of Irish eagerness to learn baseball and more because of the Irish heritage of many of Spalding's players (Lamster 2006:29) Neither tour accomplished their goal. Spalding aroused little interest in what appeared for many to be a complex and confusing game. Poor planning and poor weather plagued Davin's tour; rather than expanding the GAA's treasury, the tour added considerable debt, seventeen of his athletes chose to remain in the U.S. rather than return home, and any notion of rekindling Irish cultural sporting heritage in America was diminished (Cronin 2007). Nevertheless, both tours represent willful use of sport as a cultural tool for cultural definition: in the case of the U.S. to demonstrate a semi-imperialist drive for influence, and in the case of Ireland to rekindle tradition and forestall imperial domination.

Although the GAA tour failed in its larger objectives, Irish sports did make some inroads within some Irish communities in the U.S., primarily in urban centers with substantial Irish immigrant enclaves, such as New York, Boston, and Chicago. In these cities, GAA clubs were formed and often named for the county that was home to a majority of members, while others were named, as in Ireland, for national heroes. The clubs and the games were certainly a means of reconnecting the Irish in America with the national struggle for independence at home, but were also part of the process of adaptation and assimilation to their new life in their new country—especially in a country which for most of the final decades of the 19th century "possessed a hostile Anglo-Saxon Protestant establishment" that was rather unwelcoming (Darby 2009:66). However, while GAA sports may have provided some comfort to recent immigrants, their children connected more directly and successfully with other sports in their new home, perhaps most notably at first in boxing. From James "Yankee" Sullivan to John Morrisey to John L. Sullivan to James "Gentleman Jim" Corbett, the boxing ring provided an opportunity for tough Irish Americans to fight, quite literally, their way out of poverty. In addition, after the Civil War, baseball, the American "pastime," came under widespread Gaelic influence. In fact as the 19th century ended and the 20th century began, "Irish stars dominated baseball and its greatest teams" (Baldassaro 2002:55) If they did not bring the same level of Irish nationalism that drove the GAA, they did bring a similar passion and intensity; the likes of John McGraw, Mike "King" Kelly, Roger Conner, and Connie Mack brought a combativeness to the game which matched the combativeness of the GAA athletes in their efforts to thwart British authority in the home of their ancestors.

Conclusion: The GAA and Radical Athletic Nationalism

Beginning on that day in November 1884 when the GAA was formed, good reason existed for British authorities at Dublin Castle, the locus of British authority in Ireland until 1922, to consider the organization threatening and subversive. Almost immediately, the Royal Irish Constabulary began monitoring GAA activities, infiltrating the organization with informants, and providing thorough reports to Dublin authorities. Indeed, many of the men at the founding meeting were members or suspected to be members of the IRB which, with its American-based sister organization, the Fenian Brotherhood, aimed "to rid Ireland of English rule by providing American money and manpower to encourage insurrection" (Lee and Casey 2006:290). Both organizations were secret and anonymous societies, although keeping the secret was not their strongest suit. Failure to maintain secrecy doomed an ill-advised and poorly organized "rising" in early 1867; it was a complete disaster and certainly left in question the military expertise of the Fenians or the IRB, although their commitment to the cause of Irish independence remained clear and undeniable. However, while there was no denying the nationalist inclinations of Cusack, Davin, and the other organizers of the GAA, the initial influence of the IRB many have been somewhat overstated. "The reality," according to Mike Cronin, one of Ireland's most noted sports historians, "was that the Thurles meeting was the product of the desire ... to change how sport was organized in Ireland" (Cronin et al. 2009:4). Nevertheless, if the power of the IRB was not as strong as suspected early in the GAA's existence, its influence soon became more substantive.

At the GAA convention in 1885, the newly elected committee of officers for the organization included five Fenians; over the next four years the IRB elements within the GAA expanded their influence, which enabled the IRB to assume "full control at the 23 January 1889 convention" (Mandle 1977:438). In the early 1890s, internal conflicts within the association between the IRB, church supported GAA clubs, and clubs which preferred to remain unaffiliated, as well as national political struggles contributed to a declining membership in the GAA. A resurgence later in the decade restored membership as the IRB muted its advocacy, but "left no one in any doubt as to where [the GAA's] allegiance lay" (Mandle 1977:438). In the 20th century, as GAA activities became increasing significant in Irish life, membership continued to grow chiefly because the IRB became more restrained in its approach toward control of the GAA; it focused its efforts less toward direct recruitment of IRB members and more toward maintaining leadership in the GAA Central Council and county associations. Thus, membership reached about 170,000 by the time of the 1916 Easter Rebellion. Most members clearly supported Irish Home Rule but only a fraction advocated force, although many of that fraction were involved on that Easter Day. Perhaps as many as 300 GAA members participated, five of the sixteen men executed "had GAA connections," and many in the GAA leadership were radical nationalists; however, they were not representative of the "political views of the national membership of the GAA in 1916" (McElligott 2013:99). The IRB exerted its strongest involvement, at this time, with the GAA in County Kerry but "the vast majority of GAA members nationally and locally had little idea that an insurrection was being contemplated" (McElligott 2013:98). The brutal response to the Easter Rising by the British authorities would dramatically change this situation and revitalize an aggressive and radical athletic nationalism.

The initial public reaction to the Rising was hardly supportive and the destruction wrought by a seemingly futile and poorly executed operation only contributed to its unpopularity. British reaction, however, appeared, for many Irish, well out of proportion. Martial law was declared in Dublin on Easter Monday and extended to the entire country the next day. Next, a sweeping round up of suspects was ordered and very quickly over 3,500 men and women from across the country were detained; over half, mostly ordinary citizens, innocent of any involvement with the Rising, were interned for further investigation. Meanwhile, the admitted leaders of the Rising were tried in secret courts martial and sixteen executed within a month. While it is possible to consider these actions as understandable given the authorities fear of the threat of continuing insurrection, they were perceived as callous and unnecessarily cruel. Anger toward the rebels was quickly redirected toward Dublin Castle (Vaughan 1996).

Meanwhile, the GAA directly felt the effects of the British response because those arrested and interned included "hundreds of ordinary members of the GAA," the vast majority of whom had little or no connect with the IRB, much less the Rising itself (McGilligott 2013:101). The prisons made excellent indoctrination camps, where GAA members mingled with and were indoctrinated by committed revolutionaries. Additionally, Gaelic sports were played during free time, both as a form of distraction from the boredom of prison life and as a means of creating a stronger link between Irish nationalism, hatred for British rule, and the importance of traditional Irish sporting culture as an instrument of rebellion. Outside the camps, the GAA became increasingly and willingly associated with the political actions of Sinn Féin as its influence grew in 1917 and 1918. Local GAA clubs sponsored tournaments to raise funds to provide support for nationalist prisoners and matches, at both local and national levels, routinely included visible demonstrations of support for independence (Cronin et al. 2009). British efforts to conscript Irishmen for military service in 1918 was met with an immediate declaration of opposition from the GAA: "we pledge ourselves to resist ... the attempted conscription of Irish manhood" (McGilligott 2013:108). When GAA matches became threatened by British bans against public gatherings, the association organized what became known as "Gaelic Sunday" in resistance. On April 4, 1918, between 50,000 and 100,000 participated in GAA games across the country; British authorities had neither the manpower nor the will to counter the concerted actions of so many and simply capitulated (Cronin et al. 2009). Within three years' time, the GAA, an already nationalist-minded organization, was further transformed, radicalized, and "firmly committed to Sinn Féin's aspiration of establishing an Irish republic" (McGilligott 2013:111). That commitment would not flag during the battle to achieve independence. The unique warrior, patriot, statesmen relationship between Irish sport, Irish nationalism, and Irish identity remains palpable and strong; arguably, it will remain so until "All-Ireland" in the annual GAA finals is "All-Island" and represents a nation no longer partitioned.

Bibliography

Bairner, Alan. 2005. "Irish Sport," pp. 190–205 in *The Cambridge Companion to Modern Irish Culture,* edited by Joe Cleary and Claire Connolly. Cambridge: Cambridge University Press.

Baldassaro, Lawrence, and Richard A. Johnson, eds. 2002. *The American Game: Baseball and Ethnicity.* Carbondale: Southern Illinois University Press.

Barrett, James R. 2012. *The Irish Way: Becoming American in the Multiethnic City.* New York: Penguin.

Byrne, James P., Philip Coleman, and Jason King, eds. 2008. *Ireland and the Americas: Culture, Politics, and History: A Multidisciplinary Encyclopedia.* Transatlantic Relations Series, Vol. 2. Santa Barbara: ABC-CLIO.

Byron, Reginald. 1999. *Irish America.* Oxford: Oxford University Press.

Cronin, Mike. 2007. "The Gaelic Athletic Association's Invasion of America, 1888: Travel Narratives, Microhistory and the Irish American 'Other.'" *Sport in History,* 27 (2): 190–216.

Cronin, Mike, Mark Duncan, and Paul Rouse. 2009. *The GAA: A People's History.* Wilton, Cork: Collins.

Darby, Paul. 2009. *Gaelic Games, Nationalism and the Irish Diaspora in the United States.* Dublin: University College Dublin Press.

Dorsey, Leroy G. 2007. *We are all Americans, Pure and Simple: Theodore Roosevelt and the Myth of Americanism.* Tuscaloosa: University of Alabama Press.

Dyreson, Mark. 1998. *Making the American Team: Sport, Culture, and the Olympic Experience.* Sport and Society. Urbana: University of Illinois Press.

Garnham, Neal. 2004. "Accounting for the Early Success of the Gaelic Athletic Association." *Irish Historical Studies,* 34 (133): 65–78.

Killeen, Richard. 2010. *A Brief History of Ireland.* London: Robinson.

Kinsella, Thomas. 1970. *The Táin.* Translated from the Irish Epic *Tain Bo Cuailnge.* London: Oxford University Press.

Lamster, Mark. 2006. *Spalding's World Tour: The Epic Adventure that Took Baseball Around the Globe—and made it America's Game.* New York: Public Affairs.

Lee, Joseph, and Marion R. Casey, eds. 2006. *Making the Irish American: History and Heritage of the Irish in the United States.* New York: New York University Press.

Levine, Peter. 1985. *A.G. Spalding and the Rise of Baseball: The Promise of American Sport.* New York: Oxford University Press.

Mandle, W. F. 1977. "The I.R.B. and the Beginnings of the Gaelic Athletic Association." *Irish Historical Studies,* 20 (80): 418–438.

McDonnell, Vincent. 2009. *The Story of the GAA.* Wilton, Cork: Collins.

McElligott, R. 2013. "1916 and the Radicalization of the Gaelic Athletic Association." *Éire-Ireland,* 48 (1): 95–111. Irish-American Cultural Institute.

Pope, S. W. 1997. *Patriotic Games: Sporting Traditions in the American Imagination, 1876–1926*. Sports and History. New York: Oxford University Press.

Roosevelt, Theodore. 2004. *Letters and Speeches*. Library of America, Vol. 154. New York: Library of America.

Rouse, Paul. 2009. "Michael Cusack: Sportsman and Journalist," pp. 47–59 in *The Gaelic Athletic Association, 1884–2009*, edited by Mike Cronin, William Murphy, and Paul Rouse. Dublin: Irish Academic Press.

St. John de Crèvecoeur, J. Hector. 2013; 1782. *Letters from an American Farmer and Other Essays*. The John Harvard Library, edited by Dennis D. Moore. Cambridge: Belknap Press of Harvard University Press.

Spalding, A. G., and with Introduction by Benjamin G. Rader. 1992; 1911. *America's National Game: Historic Facts Concerning the Beginning, Evolution, Development, and Popularity of Base Ball, with Personal Reminiscences of its Vicissitudes, Its Victories, and Its Votaries*. Lincoln: University of Nebraska Press.

Vaughan. W.E., ed. 1996. *A New History of Ireland: Ireland Under the Union, II*, Vol. VI. Oxford: Clarendon Press.

Whelan, Kevin. 2005. "The Cultural Effects of the Famine," pp. 137–154 in *The Cambridge Companion to Modern Irish Culture*, edited by Joe Cleary and Claire Connolly. Cambridge: Cambridge University Press.

A Coaching Perspective on Sportsmanship

Christopher Parks

Perhaps you are a coach, perhaps you are not. Regardless of the answer, there is a high percentage chance that you have seen athletic contests and been witness to acts of sportsmanship or the lack of it. Maybe you have been moved by genuine displays of sportsmanship. Maybe you have sat aghast as unsportsmanlike behavior has occurred before your eyes. The common thread is the knowledge and recognition of true sportsmanship when you see it. Sportsmanship can be as simple as helping an opponent to his feet after a hard fought play. Or maybe you acknowledge the outfielder, who just made a ridiculous diving catch to rob you of a tremendous hit, with a tip of your cap as you head back to the dugout. Or, perhaps, sportsmanship is silence and calm as a player ignores the jeers and inflammatory chants of an opposing crowd. Sportsmanship could be the positive cheering of fans for their own team, rather than negative chants directed at the opposing team. A coach may start substituting players in early rather than running up the score when a game has become lopsided. Or, maybe, sportsmanship is not a visible act; so much as it is an everyday way of acting. What follows from here is not an indisputable "How to..." or "How not to..." essay. Rather, it is the reflection of a coach who has seen and been a part of many situations when sportsmanship has been the topic. It is a coach's perspective on knowing something, building something, having a family, playing for someone, celebrating, being counter-cultural, and honoring someone or something. It is a testimony that sportsmanship matters.

Know the Landscape

The concept that "sports builds character" is an acceptable slogan for many sports advocates (Green and Gabbard 1999), and the general public has believed for quite some time that participating in sports not only builds character, but also fosters friendships by promoting sportsmanship among opponents (Rudd 1998). In contrast, some may proclaim that "sports builds characters," based on displays of poor sportsmanship often witnessed at sporting events or, seen later by many more, via news and social media. Therefore, if sports are to be considered a positive microcosm of society (Boxill 2003), then they should include positive behaviors that society would desire. The popularity and visibility of sports have become so great, that, desired or not, the expectations of its participants have increased as well. According to Delaney and Madigan (2009), "Organized sports are supposed to be a setting that encourages cooperation with others and a willingness to accept society's rules" (p. 107). At its ideal, sports should be as simple as players play, coaches coach, officials officiate, fans cheer, and contests are played out enthusiastically and ethically. Yes, isn't life grand? The reality is that players, coaches, officials, and fans all make mistakes. Furthermore, mistakes oftentimes result in what we will call "poor reactions," by players, coaches, and fans. Indeed, coaches and fans are responsible for their own behavior. Yet, there exists a lynchpin reality. Coach's Perspective: When athletes display sportsmanship or a lack of it and fans and opponents alike criticize them for it, there is an inextricable link to one important individual ... the coach.

The Power and Responsibility to Build Something

As sportsmanship becomes a greater focus and emphasis in society, the role of the coach is critically linked to its progress and success. If sportsmanship can be taught to athletes, coaches must be able to teach the lesson. According to Ehrman (2011), "The awesome power and responsibility of coaching: You give your players memories, for better or worse, that stay with them until the day they die" (p. 47). With that in mind, the coach's role as a model of behavior may be that which serves to most greatly impact athletes. A coach's visible behavior can model sportsmanship for athletes, and, in turn, educate athletes in how to compete with decency, respect, and commitment. Likewise, a coach's negative behavior can do irreparable harm to the character development of an athlete. Or as the National Association for Sport and Physical Education stated (2008), "The quality of a participant's experience in amateur sports is largely dependent on the environment created by the coach" (p. 10).

So there it is: Coaches have the incredible and daunting power and influence to create an environment that may ultimately develop or ruin an athlete's character. Don't screw it up. All melodrama aside, the fact is that a coach's perspective on sportsmanship is critical to that of the development of a player's perspective. Both a coach's actions and words are ways to model behavior for athletes. The players are watching, and they are learning much more than techniques, drills, and plays. Players are learning how to interact with officials. Players are learning how to handle the taunts of fans. Players are learning how to respond to the intense play of opponents. We have heard the expression "With great power comes great responsibility." Coach's Perspective: We have the power and responsibility to build character.

Family First

Rutten, Stams, Biesta, Schuengel, Dirks, and Hoeksma (2007) found that student-athletes learn valuable skills and knowledge and sport-related rules and norms. "Adolescents do not engage in sports in order to be educated, yet each social practice in which they participate could have an educational influence" (Rutten et al. 2007:258). Recognizing the influence of the coach on student-athletes, Rutten et al. (2007) focused on the environment created by coaches, suggested that coaches who maintain good relationships with their athletes reduce anti-social behavior, and further discovered that coaches' influence could even be greater than in the family and school context.

Let's face it, on average, many athletes spend more time with their teams and coaches than they do with their own family members. Likewise, as coaches, our teams are our second families. In some cases, the two become so interwoven that, rather than a second family, the team becomes the extended family. We love our families don't we? Sure, every family has its version of a crazy uncle or an annoying cousin that means well but tests the patience of everybody else in the family. And of course, there is usually the relative that is way too enthusiastic about family gatherings and holidays. Do not forget the one relative that always arrives so late that the family starts telling him an arrival time of thirty minutes earlier than the actual time of the party. Well, welcome to the team. If you can create a genuine family dynamic within your team, then you can build anything for and with them.

Each year my current high school team has the benefit of going on an overnight retreat together. Ask the players and coaching staff and they will give you the same response: What occurs in those forty-eight hours is more meaningful than any championship we have ever won. In fact, one season scheduling conflicts prevented us from being able to go on the retreat. To this day, players from that team still point to the "non-retreat" as the one thing that they would go back and change if they could. What's the point? The retreat is not some group therapy session. The retreat is the point where we tune everything else out and we establish our family. We tell the players, "Family members argue. Family members fight. Family members get frustrated and angry with one another. But no matter what, we are always family, and family is forever." I know, it sounds like a greeting card. The reality is, it is the single most effective thing we have ever implemented in our program. If you recognize, appreciate, and emphasize the family nature of a team, then what you want to build together and for one another is incredibly meaningful and effective. From there, you can build character. From character, you can build, strengthen, and value sportsmanship. Coach's Perspective: Character and sportsmanship are family values.

Would You Want Your Son or Daughter to Play for You?

Gut check. Reciprocal determinism holds that "expectations, self-perceptions, goals, and ... environmental events in the form of modeling, instruction, and social persuasion affect the person, and the person in turn evokes different reactions from the environment" (Grusec 1992:782–783). Experience gives individuals self-regulatory and self-efficacy beliefs, and in turn they affect what experiences individuals maintain and repeat (Grusec 1992). Thus, a coach that consistently models sportsmanship and sportsmanlike behaviors is more likely to positively impact the sportsmanlike behavior of his or her athletes. So what kind of coach are you? Or more importantly, what is it that you model for athletes? Indeed, our ethics are the moral principles that define us. They establish who we are and what we stand for. Let us return to the idea that sportsmanship may not be an act so much as a way of acting. When coaching, what is it we expect of our players? What do we model? What do we teach? Do we want athletic juggernauts that vanquish their opponents with extreme focus and tenacity? Do we seek to train dominant athletes that will indeed take part in the ceremonious shaking of hands but then sacrifice sportsmanship for victory? The hopeful response to these questions is "No." However, time and time again coaches have led by example and modeled unsportsmanlike behavior either by their action or inaction. So when a player shows a lack of effort, care, or sportsmanlike behavior, what is it that has been modeled for them? Or, from a family perspective, perhaps the apple doesn't fall far from the tree.

Consequently, coaches should have clear expectations of sportsmanship, and players should know what those expectations look like. Sportsmanship should include full commitment to participation, respect and concern for opponents, rules and officials, and social conventions, and avoiding poor attitudes toward participation (Vallerand and Losier 1994). Full commitment to participation is demonstrated by showing up for practice on time, working hard during all practices and games, and acknowledging one's mistakes and trying to improve. Demonstrating full commitment suggests a strong focus by the student-athlete to become better in all aspects of a game. Examples of full commitment to participation would be a baseball player running hard to first base on a ground ball, a basketball player hustling back to play defense after scoring a basket, and a hockey player skating to the opponent's net to be present in case of a rebounded puck. A half-hearted effort or commitment is not representative of sportsmanship.

"Respect for others, the cornerstone of sportsmanlike behavior, requires first and foremost the perspective to see things from the other's point of view" (Clifford and Feezell 2010:25). Respect and concern for the opponent is sometimes the most easily visible demonstration of sportsmanship. Many times while coaching soccer, our team or an opponent's team would sacrifice possession and kick the ball out of bounds to stop the game when they realized that one of the opposing players was on the ground with an injury. Upon restarting the game, the team with the injured player would in turn sacrifice possession by throwing the ball back in to the opposing team. On a more public scale, Central Washington University women's softball team provided a tremendous example of respect and concern for an opponent. In the second game of a doubleheader against Western Oregon University, WOU's Sara Tucholsky slammed what appeared to be a three-run homer over the centerfield fence, the senior's first in either high school or college. But Tucholsky wrenched her knee at first base and collapsed. Umpires ruled that a pinch-runner could replace Tucholsky, but she would be credited with a single and only two runs would count. After being assured there was no rule against it, Central Washington first baseman Mallory Holtman and shortstop Liz Wallace carried Tucholsky around the bases, completing her homer and adding a run to a 4–2 loss that eliminated the Wildcats from postseason. Where did they learn that? Obviously, their coach never taught them that specific gesture, but it is fair to say that those players practiced and competed in a culture of sportsmanship and character modeled by their coach. Another example of respect and concern for an opponent occurred at the state 4A track and field championships on May 23, 2008 in Pasco, Washington. Nicole Cochran, a senior at Bellarmine Prep in Tacoma, won the 3200-meter title by 3.05 seconds. However, a judge disqualified her, and stated that she had illegally stepped outside of her lane. Almost everyone, including Cochran's competitors, disagreed with the judge, and a video of the race proved that the judge had made an error. After the eight medal winners were recognized, the first-place medal winner, Andrea Nelson of Shadle Park High in Spokane, walked off the podium and placed the medal around Cochran's neck. Each of the remaining seven medal winners then gave her medal to the corresponding runner that had finished ahead of her. Cochran had been treated with respect and concern by her opponents, and in turn she acted similarly when she finished eighth in a later race and presented her medal to the runner who had given up the eighth place medal in the 3200m race. Whether it is the simple gesture of helping an opponent to his feet, or carrying her around the bases, sportsmanship spawns from a culture created and fostered by the coach and lived by the players and coaches.

Respect for and concern for rules and officials is a fundamental aspect of sportsmanship. Rules establish a structure and order that govern organized sports and the correct way to play a specific sport. Officials interpret and apply the rules of the game with the intention of ensuring sportsmanship and fair play. Without rules and officials, organized sports would be subject to the will and varying interpretations of the competitors and coaches and could quickly deteriorate into a "free-for-all." A player that demonstrates sportsmanship does not attempt to cheat or "bend the rules." Likewise, that player respects the rules of the game and does not try to find loopholes to circumvent them. The player respects game officials as the authority on the interpretation and application of the rules. The player does not argue or insult the officials or the rules of the game in either word or action, and is bothered if another player or coach does. Tennis professional Andy Roddick provided an exceptional example of respect for the rules and officials of tennis. Roddick was on the way to the quarterfinals of the Rome Masters tournament, when he asked the chair umpire to reverse a line judge's call that had given him the victory. The gesture of good sportsmanship ended up costing Roddick the match. Roddick's acceptance and following of the rules demonstrated the importance that should be placed on the rules of the game. Roddick showed respect for the rules of the game and officials by putting them before his own interest in winning.

Respect and concern for social conventions, as perceived by society as what is "appropriate and polite," may be simply demonstrated by shaking hands with the opponent or recognizing the opponent's good play. Additionally, a player's pride in appearance, clean uniform, and full effort in warm-ups may demonstrate respect. In the course of competition, the mindful refraining from taunting, excessive celebration, or negative interactions with spectators further demonstrates respect. A positive response by a professional athlete may be the willingness to grant a news interview after a bad game or difficult loss. A student-athlete response that demonstrates respect and concern for social conventions may be as simple as, after competing, genuinely congratulating the opponent.

Examples of avoiding poor attitudes toward participation are avoiding a win-at-all-costs approach, controlling one's temper after a mistake, and competing for more than just individual accolades. Positive attitudes toward participation would be demonstrated by cheering for your teammates, being on time for practices and contests, being prepared for practices and contests, and congratulating teammates and even opponents on a job well done. As the late Dean Smith (2004) once said, "Sometimes we played very well and still lost. Those are the times you shake your opponent's hand, congratulate him, and make a vow to improve" (p. 47).

Do we see players live out all of these ideals? As coaches, do we create and foster a culture that recognizes and values these ideals? We want our players to have the intrinsic motivation to do the right thing. "One of the most effective ways to encourage intrinsic motivation is through modeling" (Duke 2014:109). It is not always easy to do the decent and generous thing, especially in the heat of competition. Coach's Perspective: Observe the sportsmanlike or unsportsmanlike behavior of athletes and look to the bench to see what is being modeled for them.

Celebrate the Players

I have had a long standing belief that you should catch your players doing something good. In laymen's terms: let them know when they have done something well. Does congratulating a player ensure sportsmanship? Absolutely not. What it does is help create that culture of sportsmanship that is strengthened by showing care and concern through positive and respectful interactions. Or as we were told when we were growing up: "Treat people how you want to be treated." Give players a reason to look forward to hearing your voice. If all they ever know is the sound of you correcting them, then you are modeling an authoritative and critical behavior. Don't get me wrong. This isn't kindergarten Frisbee toss with ribbons for everyone for participating. What it is, is letting players know that just going out and doing what is expected of them is important, appreciated and valued. They will come to know and live in a culture of valuing one another and treating one another with respect. They will pick each other up. They will cheer for one another in victory. They will support one another in loss. They will push each other to become better. They will fully embrace the concept of full commitment to the responsibilities of their sport and their team/family. We often hear people talk about "Doing the right thing" in situations. Establish, emphasize, reinforce, and expect sportsmanship in all things that a team does and it will become what they know, expect, and demonstrate. Simply stated, they will learn sportsmanship as a natural way of proceeding.

The more players know that a coach believes in them, the greater their confidence and, most likely, the greater their performance. However, you just can't tell players "You're awesome." That won't help a thing. First of all, they can tell if you're just blowing sunshine at them. If that is the case, then you will completely lose credibility with them. Secondly, if they truly are awesome in a game, their fans and friends will tell them that anyway. As a coach, there are two tremendously powerful things that players will never forget: "I am proud of you" and "I believe in you." Do not say them haphazardly or without genuine reason to. Again, credibility will be forfeited. Instead, speak from the heart if you find the occasion to say these words, and know that the impact of a coach is enduring and sometimes immeasurable. You will impact their lives in ways that you may never realize. While the wording has been changed as it has been passed on over the years, the version I heard from one of my graduate school professors rings true: "Players don't care what you know, until they know that you care." Coach's Perspective: Care about your players and celebrate them when you can.

Be Counter-Cultural

Let's face it, people want to win. Obviously, if a coach stood up and said "Hey! Let's lose this thing!" he or she wouldn't be very successful or have a job for very long. So does being counter-cultural mean that you cannot create a winning culture? Absolutely not. What it means is that winning is not what is emphasized. Emphasize sportsmanship. But how? Indeed, Etzioni (1998) called for schools and school districts to self-examine their sports programs and to involve their teachers and coaches in character education for the betterment of their students. The importance of modeling behavior was recognized as paramount to positively impacting the sportsmanship of players. While school-wide or district-wide programs may be a popular approach, I would suggest a simpler and more straightforward one: Establish expectations of sportsmanship on the first day of practice. Make sportsmanship the main focus. There will be plenty of time for skills and drills, and you will come up with new ones as the season progresses and as different game situations dictate. You cannot go back and redo sportsmanship. Clearly communicate sportsmanship as the number one priority of the team. It doesn't mean you don't want to win. It means you want to compete, win or lose the right way. Too many coaches and teams will quickly trade sportsmanship for victory. Instead, create a culture of "Sportsmanship at all costs." Wouldn't that make a neat pregame t-shirt? Yet, it isn't enough to just talk about sportsmanship. Model it. Expect it in practice and other team activities. Doing so will greatly ensure that it will happen in games. Treat your players, coaching staff, officials, and fans with respect. If you earn the respect of your players "the language you use around them will become a part of their way of looking at things" (Clifford and Feezell 2010:26). Or as Duke (2014) stated, "Amazing things happen when you enter into the lives of your athletes and start to see extrinsic motivation shift towards the more meaningful intrinsic motivation" (p. 109). Remember, the players are watching, and they are learning far more than skills and drills. They are learning sportsmanship … if you are modeling it. We have heard the old saying "Character is doing the right thing when no one else is watching." I would offer that sportsmanship is how a team conducts itself, when the coach isn't there to tell them how. If players have learned it, then they will live it, and you will recognize it. Coach's Perspective: Create a clearly defined and understood culture of sportsmanship and stand by it. Your players will stand with you.

Honor

One of my favorite coaching memories occurred during a boys' high school volleyball tournament. Our team was battling back and forth with one of the top teams in our area. During a lengthy rally, the opposing team's hitter went up and hit a ball that clearly landed out of bounds, giving our team a point. Before the official could give our team the ball, one of our players, a senior, looked at the scoreboard, walked over to the official and told him that he had touched the ball with his fingertip when he had jumped to attempt to block it. The official looked at him and asked, "Are you sure?" Our player responded politely but firmly, "Yes, sir. I definitely touched it." The official thanked him, reversed the call and awarded the point to our opponent. This act of sportsmanship on our player's part made us proud to be his coaches. However, the significance of the situation was even greater than a simple gesture. When our player looked at the scoreboard, he saw that if he made the "honor call," it would give our opponent the final and winning point. Knowing that his sportsmanship would result in a team loss, he chose to do the right thing anyway. Yet, even after the official blew the whistle indicating we had now lost, the most memorable part of the whole situation occurred. His teammates hugged him, patted him on the back, and shook his hand. Several minutes later when a player from another team asked him why he had done what he did, our player responded, "Because we make 'honor calls.'" As a coaching staff, we could not have been prouder of him.

My other favorite memory occurred during a girls' high school volleyball match. Early on in the season, one of our players hit a ball that landed out of bounds. Our team saw it and the opposing team saw it, but the officials did not see it and the fans thought the ball had landed "in." After deliberation by the officials, they determined that they were not certain if the ball landed in or out, because neither of them had a clear look at the play. However, they were going to call it "in." Our team was awarded the point and the serve. We called a time out and explained to our players that the ball had clearly landed out of bounds, and that we did not deserve the point or the serve. Our players all agreed, but understood that the officials had decided to give us the point anyway. We explained to the team that our player now scheduled to serve was going to toss the ball up in the air and let it land at her feet, thereby resulting in a service violation and awarding a point and the ball back to our opponent. The players all nodded in agreement, cheered at the end of the timeout, and then returned to the court. The official blew the whistle, and our player did exactly as we had instructed her to do. The officials and opposing coaches nodded their understanding and the contest went on from there. At the time we were very proud of the sportsmanship displayed by the team. However, the prouder moment came later in the season, when a similar situation occurred involving our team getting an undeserved point. As I was beginning to call for a time out, our server got my attention, smiled, and said, "Don't call time out coach. I know what to do." She tossed the ball up in the air, let it land at her feet, and rolled the ball back to the other team. Appropriately, she was chosen as our most valuable player at the end of the year. Coach's Perspective: Win with humility. Lose with grace. ALWAYS compete with honor.

Conclusion

An old military saying is "The main thing is to keep the main thing the main thing." When it comes to sports, sportsmanship is the main thing. Sportsmanship matters. Though there are and will be many obstacles to the focus and emphasis on sportsmanship along the way, it is a coach's responsibility to establish, emphasize, reinforce, model, and ensure that sportsmanship is always the number one priority of the team. Whether by demonstrating respect and concern for players, coaches, officials, and fans, or by practicing and playing hard, we demonstrate sportsmanship and respect for the game itself. "Without sportsmanship, sport is no longer sport; the game is no longer a game" (Clifford and Feezell 2010:29). Indeed, if sportsmanship is lost, what do we have? Enter the significance of the coach. Coaching is a powerful and rewarding responsibility. It is a blessing and a gift to be called "Coach," because a coach contributes to the formation of a player's character. It is the coach's responsibility to make certain that sportsmanship does not get pushed aside in the name of training and winning. Instead, sportsmanship must be part of training, training not only for sport but for life. When sportsmanship is no longer considered as an individual act or display of character and is instead, an everyday way of acting, then victory is truly achieved. The player will draw strength of character from the team, and the team will be stronger because of each player's character. However, in the end sportsmanship and character are formed and modeled by the coach, and coaches must never lose sight of that. If you are not a coach, then I hope that this reflection from a coach's perspective has been helpful and enlightening. If you are a coach, then I hope that this perspective is one which you can identify with and perhaps draw from as you continue to form lives. And if in either case you find yourself saying, "You're preaching to the choir." Coach's Perspective: Well, when it comes to sportsmanship, the fact is every day is choir practice. In the end, "sportsmanship, while a battered concept, remains a worthy virtue ... alive and well in the twenty-first century" (Delaney and Madigan 2009:207).

Bibliography

Bandura, Albert. 1986. *Social Foundations of Thought and Action: A Social Cognitive Theory*. Englewood Cliffs, NJ: Prentice Hall.

Boxill, Jan. 2003. *Sports Ethics an Anthology*. Malden, MA: Blackwell.

Clifford, Craig, and Randolph M. Feezell. 2010. *Sport and Character: Reclaiming the Principles of Sportsmanship*. Champaign, IL: Human Kinetics.

Delaney, Tim, and Tim Madigan. 2009. *Sports: Why People Love Them!* Lanham, MD: University Press of America.

Duke, Jeff. 2014. *3D Coach: Capturing the Heart Behind the Jersey*. Ventura, CA: Regal.

Erhmann, Joe. 2011. *InSideOut Coaching: How Sports Can Transform Lives*. New York: Simon & Schuster.

Etzioni, Amitai. 1998. "On a Character Education Journey." *School Administrator*, 55 (5): 35–37.

Green, Thomas, and Carl Gabbard. 1999. "Do We Need Sportsmanship Education in Secondary School Athletics?" *Physical Educator*, 56 (2): 98–104.

Grusec, Joan. 1992. "Social Learning Theory and Developmental Psychology: The Legacies of Robert Sears and Albert Bandura." *Developmental Psychology*, 28 (5): 776–786.

National Association for Sport and Physical Education. 2008. *National Coaching Report*. Reston, VA: National Association for Sport and Physical Education.

Rudd, Andrew. 1998. *Sport's Perceived Ability to Build Character*. Unpublished doctoral dissertation, University of Idaho, Moscow.

Rutten, Esther, Geert Stams, Gert Biesta, Carlo Schuengel, Evelien Dirks, and JanHoeksma. 2007. "The Contribution of Organized Youth Sport to Antisocial and Prosocial Behavior in Adolescent Athletes." *Journal of Youth Adolescence*, 36: 255–264.

Smith, Dean, Gerald Bell, and John Kilgo. 2004. *The Carolina Way: Leadership Lessons from a Life in Coaching*. New York: Penguin.

Vallerand, Robert, and Gaetan Losier. 1994. "Self-determined Motivation and Sportsmanship Orientations: An Assessment of Their Temporal Relationship." *Journal of Sport & Exercise Psychology*, 16: 229–24.

Sportsmanship from a Referee's Perspective

A Case Study of Four Sports

TOM WEBB *and* MIKE RAYNER

> "Exactly what do you mean by 'guts'?"
> "I mean, grace under pressure."
> —Dorothy Parker interviewing Ernest Hemingway

While the author Ernest Hemingway in his interview with Dorothy Parker in November 1926, was not discussing sport, his comments have tangible contemporary 21st century relevance when exploring the existence of sportsmanship in the current sporting landscape. Historically, the term "sportsmanship" has been a symbol of character that originated out of the development of sports and games through the Weberian construction of rules or regulations. The division of rules and regulations creates an accepted level of moral obligation in sport to promise to play by agreed rules and the match officials are the arbiters of these regulations in practice.

Although the creation of rules have enabled regular sporting contests to occur, participants must follow a basic acceptance of these rules, or perpetual rule breaking would result in the end of play (Suits 1998). The term "sportsmanship" is defined within the literature as "an attitude, a posture, a manner of interpreting what would otherwise be only a legal code" (Keating 2007:145). However, since we are by nature social animals, sportsmanship is more easily measured through judgments regarding performance and the reflection of individuals in how they express their commitment to adhering to the rules within sport. Sport provides the opportunity for athletes to test their abilities against worthy opponents. To win by cheating, or by disparaging an opponent's abilities, or by excessive violent acts, would not be a mark of a worthy character and would not express notions of "sportsmanship" (Madigan 2014). The argument exists that the very concept or definition of sportsmanship differs from sport to sport and that this then directly affects and impacts upon the match officials. These referees, umpires and adjudicators are attempting to implement and uphold the law and sprit of the game in question and therefore the associated sporting nature of the game. This essay considers the concept of sportsmanship from the perspective of the referee/umpire/match official within four sports. Interviews were conducted with elite level competition officials within the sports of cricket, squash, rugby union and Ultimate Frisbee. The sports selected for this essay have been chosen due to their different approaches to officiating historically and in recent years.

For example, cricket is, in some ways, a very traditional sport; the Marylebone Cricket Club (MCC) only allowed women members in 1999 which ended 212 years of men only exclusivity (MCC women n.d.), players are still required to wear whites for five day test matches and many of the conventions of the game have been maintained to this day, especially in the five day format of the sport. Nevertheless, cricket is somewhat of a paradox when considering the historical and cultural ethos of the game. Juxtaposed with the five-day format of international test cricket is the limited over game, such as 40 or 50 over cricket or 20 over cricket, commonly known as twenty twenty cricket or T20. In these versions of the game players wear multi colored uniforms, there is a white ball instead of the traditional red ball utilized in the five day test format of the sport, music plays in between overs and when a batsmen is dismissed in the 20 over format there are often cheerleaders and other forms of entertainment on display for spectators.

There is however one constant acceptance across all forms of the game of cricket: the introduction and adoption of technological support for the umpires. Despite the traditional view of cricket in the five-day test format, cricket has been quick to embrace new technology. The introduction of limited over cricket was through the media organization of Kerry Packer in the 1970s and early 1980s. Kerry Packer was the head of an Australian Television company and wanted to screen cricket exclusively for five years. The cricket authorities would not sanction Packer's plans and as a result Packer created an alternative tournament, signed players to contracts and created an alternative test series in direct competition with the official test series sanctioned by the International Cricket Council. Packer's series had additional cameras, matches played under floodlights, colored clothing, white and yellow cricket balls and microphones introduced to hear what was happening on the pitch. These adaptations to the game of cricket provide early evidence of the power of television and signified a shift to a more modern form of the game which had remained mostly unchanged since the formation of the MCC in 1787 (Cashmore 2005; Rowe 2004; Whannel 2008). The relationship between sports, technology and the media and also the impact that this relationship has on sportsmanship is considered further in this chapter. In essence the growth of media, and the related increase in the money or "cash nexus" evident in sports, created through either professionalism, media rights or sponsorship, has meant an increased role of technology and media within sport: "media's increasing involvement in, and control over, sport and sports organizations has put it in a powerful position to dictate the characteristics of events, or, indeed even to change fundamental aspects of a sport (e.g., its rules)" (Stead 2003:333).

All four of the sports selected for analysis here are in different stages of development, in terms of their prominence and popularity at both domestic and international levels of competition. The sports of cricket, rugby union, squash and Ultimate Frisbee have been deliberately selected due to the different involvement and developing nature of the role of match officials throughout the duration of a particular match or fixture. For example, in squash the nature of the game dictates that the referee must be situated off the court or playing area. The game is played in a confined space and as such there is no practical space for an on court adjudicator and therefore referees are positioned off court. Cricket, meanwhile, has on field umpires that stand at one end of the wicket and also adjacent to the "square" or playing area that the bowler and batsmen inhabit. Rugby union uses a more traditional "on-field" referee with support from assistants providing support from the side-lines in addition to the television match official. In comparison the sport of Ultimate Frisbee was conceived without the attendance of any on or off field match officials, the game, historically, has been regulated and managed by the on field players themselves, particularly at participant level. Therefore, the importance of the players also becomes important when considering sportsmanship and the relationship between match officials and those participating in the sport.

In cricket players are permitted to appeal to the umpire when they believe that an opposition player should be given out. Players can also "walk" from the wicket and admit if they have hit the ball and been caught, therefore meaning that the umpire does not in effect have to make a decision and give the player out. This is seen as a form of good sportsmanship in cricket, but is becoming much rarer in the professionalized format of the game (Bull 2011). Whereas in rugby union, the referee's opinion is final and the sport has been depicted throughout history as the epitome of the "gentleman's" game due to this relationship both with the referee and amongst the players. However, since the introduction of professionalism in 1995 rugby union has seen instances where this relationship has been challenged to the point where its existence is questioned in the modern landscape of rugby union. In squash players also appeal to the referee if they believe a "stroke" or a "let" should be played and that their opponent has infringed the laws of the game in some way. Lower down the performance pathway this appeal is often to the opposing players themselves, or the opposing player will volunteer the award of a 'stroke' or 'let' on the court. However, in Ultimate Frisbee any foul has, historically, been decided solely between the players on the field of play, at varying levels of participation. An appeal might be made, a conversation may ensue between the players involved and a consensus is then achieved in order for the game to continue. Ultimate Frisbee is player governed, and is one of the only sports played today that still has this at varying levels of the continuum.

This essay considers contemporary views on sportsmanship, changes to the ethos of the game and developments in these sports over time caused by the continued commercialization and commodification of sport and the increased influence of television companies, sponsors and the media more generally (Cashmore 2005; Giulianotti and Robertson 2004, 2009; Smart 2005, 2007). In order to achieve this, the essay is constructed around the themes and general dimensions that have emerged through the interview process. Furthermore, the anonymity of the participants was ensured through the use of pseudonyms to establish and maintain levels of confidentiality.

Sportsmanship and the Role of the Match Official

Research in the area of sportsmanship is wide ranging currently, from a philosophical viewpoint debating the notion of sportsmanship (McNamee 2008; Keating 2007; Morgan 2007), to more practical, specific studies examining sportsmanship in particular sporting settings (Buford May 2010; Robbins 2004; Wells, Ellis, Paisley, and Arthur-Banning 2005) and also sportsmanship as a concept (Delaney 2010; Delaney and Madigan 2009; Madigan 2014). However, this essay seeks to examine the subject area with specific reference to a variety of sports rather than just one sporting example. Before the notion of sportsmanship from a match official perspective is considered in these sports a definition of the role of the match official and their role in the sportsmanship narrative is imperative.

The role of the match official in upholding sporting values in a competitive sporting environment differs from sport to sport. Within Ultimate Frisbee, for example, the very presence of a referee differs between competitions and countries and therefore the concept of sportsmanship in Ultimate Frisbee is rooted in the very notion of the way that the game is played and how the players themselves adhere to the notion of sportsmanship that the game was, in part, founded upon. There is a debate amongst those in positions of authority within Ultimate Frisbee over how central the concept of sportsmanship was when the sport was founded:

> The sport started in the mid 70's in a university car park somewhere in America. Some of the early founders of the sport ended up with this system [no referees] because there were no officials, no one to do it, and they all wanted to play. So they ended up coming up with a system of rules which enabled them to play without a referee, but it wasn't originally a deliberate ethos ... the ethos grew from the fact that it started with no referees for practical reasons but then the ethos grew because people enjoyed it that way. A lot of people find that hard to take, and that the founding fathers of the sport must have decided they did not want any referees. So there is a bit of a debate in the sport about whether it was always planned to be like this [Trevor].

Despite the debate within Ultimate Frisbee concerning the very nature of sportsmanship and how essential it was to the development of the game, it is still a central component (Thornton 2004; Rinehart and Sydnor 2003) and it is also something, alongside the absence of on field/on court match officials, which separates the sport from squash, rugby union and cricket. Although squash does have referees, these referees are not on court. Nevertheless, at lower levels of squash competition, match officials are not evident and players agree penalty stokes and replayed points between themselves. This differs again from sports such as cricket and rugby union with both sports dependent on umpires/referees in order to facilitate the respective sports regardless of playing standard. In cricket, importance is given to the umpires upholding sportsmanship beyond the written rules within a game setting. This action is considered directly relatable to the ability of the umpires to "manage" the players in the professional game and therefore operate empathetically and effectively to ensure players behave:

> What makes a top official is the way you manage the players in a professional environment and the manner in which you apply the regulations. It's all about management, perspectives, empathy everything except the technical side because you have to take it as a given that they've [umpires] got the knowledge and technical skills. Can they put those into the professional circuit and train for the environment? [Henry].

In squash, when a match official is present the nature of the game becomes similar to the atmosphere noted in their professional counterparts. There is an increase in the number of appeals made and furthermore these appeals are towards the match official rather than in negotiation with their opponents:

> You appeal if you think your opponent say got in your way, the referee will then give you a yes let. This means the referee can now give you one of three things a yes let which means play the rally again or a stroke which means you've been awarded the point or a no let which means it is over ruled and you can't have the point [Arthur].

The increase in competition standard or indeed the pressure on players in professionalized sports has developed a "need-to-win" ethos as a central component of modern sport, and this has been evidence to have impacted upon the notion of "sportsmanship" from the referee's perspective.

Sportsmanship and the Impact of Professionalization and Increasing Rewards

In the early 19th century the professional sportsman was regarded as the social inferior and for the amateur it was essential that sport was not associated with labor. The identity of the amateur was synonymous with the concept of the gentleman, an individual who did not need to seek reward for playing sport. The amateur played the game vigorously and intensely but never took the outcome too seriously (Baker 2004). Amateurism in the 19th century was described by G. Lacy Hiller in the following terms:

> The sportsman, then, is the man who has an amusement which may cost him something, but which must not bring him in anything, for an amusement which brings him in anything is not a sport but a business [G. Lacy Hillier quoted in Mangan 2001:1].

Mangan (2001) illustrates a clear distinction between the terms "amateur" and "professional." To remain nominally amateur suggests that participation in a sporting activity was purely for the "love" of the game without any need for excellence or success. Whereas being a professional refers to a "profession" or "livelihood" as a result of training and expertise within sport and more importantly the opportunity to be paid.

The introduction of professionalism during the twentieth and twenty-first centuries created a new landscape for sport and developed a significant relationship between sport and the media. Sport's growing popularity in the first half of the 20th century persuaded the governing bodies to bring their organizations more in line with the ways of a modern, commercially oriented society, rather than remain rooted in their traditional "amateur" configurations. Cricket removed its classifications of the gentlemen (amateurs) and players (professionals) in 1962; rugby union and athletics were the only sports deciding to remain nominally amateur at the time although rugby union eventually allowed the game to accept "open" professionalism in 1995. While originally relying solely on gate revenues to maintain financial viability, professional sport now generates income from television and a range of other media constructed commercial revenue streams (Bellamy 1988; Bernstein and Blain 2002). The increase in popularity that sport experienced in the latter half of the 20th century signifies the entwined evolution of media and sport that was driven by advances in media technology and an increase in consumer purchasing power (Horne, Tomlinson, and Whannel 1999). The increase in profile and exposure of sport attracted rising levels of sponsorship, which according to Collins (2013:120) was most evident in the "former bastion of amateurism the IOC, which had learnt in the 1980s that the quickest way to riches was to sell every conceivable space and service to corporate donors and their brands." At the onset of the 21st century, the economic value of sport could be measured in billions and it had developed a truly global identity.

The speed and scale of the transformation of sport throughout the twentieth and twenty-first centuries illustrates a change in the philosophy of sport. While Mangan (2001) alludes to an ethos of playing for fun as a defining principle of amateurism during the 19th century, this interpretation aligned to sport is almost diluted in the modern sporting professionalized arena:

> The values of amateurism were most evident in the game at the weekend, the Army vs. Navy Match. Yes there were 81,000 watching and it was live on TV but all the players were just proud to be there and represent their service. The attitude was different; they spoke more eloquently, rarely spoke out of turn or even questioned my judgment. In the professional game, they are

starting to question everything, developing a must win attitude but then again some of them have million pound mortgages on the line [Jack].

The pressure for success within the paradigm of professional sports has created a distortion in the interpretation of sportsmanship. As has been previously noted, sports are defined by rules, but these rules have to be interpreted for games to be realized in practice and sportsmanship is the exemplified application of these regulations by the players themselves (Loland 1998). Within cricket and rugby union the match officials are seeing an increase in gamesmanship and an eradication of sportsmanship within their respective sports. While there were conflicting reports from the match officials within all four sports, what is evident is that professional or financially driven athletes will do what ever it takes to win:

> People talk about golf for example where there is enormous money involved but the stern of honesty is very strong and people will call penalties on themselves. They see it as a pinnacle example of the application of sportsmanship and people have suggested that Ultimate [Frisbee] could go down that route; I've got my doubts about that. Golf is different in that it's very relaxed you're not running around getting a high blood pressure or adrenaline. So for that reason it's probably a little easier to remain relaxed and calm, whereas I can't really picture a sport with people running around playing for prize money which is going to maintain the spirit of the game [Trevor].

It is the notion of money within sport that the match officials have noted as impacting upon the overriding concept of sportsmanship. Ultimate Frisbee predominately relies on the interpretation of the rules by the players themselves, unless it is in a competition that involves money or within the professional leagues in the United States of America. However, the use of a match official within Ultimate Frisbee is not one that has been welcomed by the entire Ultimate Frisbee community as one respondent suggests:

> Professional leagues are running with on field referees, they've done that for exactly the reason you said, that is if there is money involved do you need a referee? They have partially done it because they won't watch or won't believe it if there wasn't a referee. I think it's really disappointing and it shows a lack of ambition really. The sports marketplace is super crowded and if we have referees in our sport we are just like the other games but with a flat ball. Whereas if the game is completely self-governed, and part of the sport and part of the spectacle is this sort of fair play question and the process of players dealing with that, then the sport stands a chance of standing out from the others [Geoff].

The introduction of match officials into Ultimate Frisbee has been suggested as an erosion of the "spirit of the game" inevitably diluting the opportunity for sportsmanship to exist in the sport (Griggs 2011). However, sportsmanship is one of the core values in both Ultimate Frisbee and rugby union and the later has found a way to encourage sportsmanship despite the professionalized nature of the elite game:

> It certainly is one of the core values ... look rugby is a family, the majority of people both in the amateur and professional game find a way to stay involved when their playing days are over. Look at all of us here, we all succumbed to injury whilst playing and now we're referees. There are examples of that throughout rugby from coaches, Directors of Rugby, Boards of Directors and even owners. We want to look after the rugby game, and while we allude to examples of bad sportsmanship or even gamesmanship the ethos of our sport is based on sportsmanship and I see it in every game I officiate, obviously to different degrees. Rugby had to find its place when it professionalized in 1995 and I believe that sportsmanship is one of its USP's [John].

The concept of sportsmanship in squash is still considered something that is worth pursuing. Arthur, one of the interview respondents, argues that despite the increased money and personal financial rewards that are now available for the best players in the international game sportsmanship "is still important within the game.... I think it still has a place in our sport" (Arthur). Despite the apparent importance still placed on the notion of sportsmansip in squash, it is also acknowledged that as players progress and play at a higher level dissent towards the match official does increase, "there is an amount of dissent towards officials because the players disagree with decisions made" (Arthur). The intimation here is that as more money ultimately becomes part of the sport and players have more to win and lose potentially, so the relationship with the match official changes.

The Referee, Sportsmanship, the Media and Technology

To this point we have already considered the increasing role of professionalization and the associated impact of increased rewards on the very concept of sportsmanship and how this relationship can affect the attitude of players towards match officials and, the attitude and perspectives of the match officials themselves. Also impacting and affecting the relationships between players and match officials and the very nature of sportsmanship, as has considered throughout this chapter, is the involvement of the media.

Through various alterations of rules and competition structures in the second half of the 20th century, sport has been adapted and designed around spectators, media and commercial interests. The pressure to make sport more "entertaining" coincided with the increasing involvement of the mass media within the sport, particularly television. Widespread television coverage of sport from the 1970s attracted new levels of sponsorship and advertising to the game and this new relationship required alterations to the sporting "product" to increase appeal and entertainment value for new spectating audiences. For example, since the introduction of professionalism rugby union has regularly made further alterations to the game through experimental law variations, alterations to fixture scheduling and changes to "kick-off" times to develop appeal and to fit in with television schedules.

Furthermore, the media has affected sport directly through television deals and the money, or cash nexus that is now evident in professional sports. As money has flowed into sporting organizations, leagues, national governing bodies and clubs/teams so the dependence on the media has increased. The more income is supplemented and provided through media organizations, the greater the dependency level associated with this income becomes. Television rights deals are often directly related to the number of times a club/team is televised throughout a season, so the more the team is featured, the greater the amount of income they can generate. Alongside this, player salaries have increased dramatically over the past 30 years, due at least in part, to the increasing television and sponsorship deals that are common place in professional sports today.

The income generated from these negotiated deals with television companies and other associated media outlets has significantly increased the financial capabilities of clubs/teams and professional sports people. In turn, this has meant that there is more at stake for these organizations and the players and coaches that represent them. The difference between winning and losing in professional sport is becoming greater in terms of the financial benefits and the profile that can be associated with successful teams and players. The relationship between sport, media and money suggests that there is little room for the existence of sportsmanship at the elite level of sport: however this is highly contested by the subjects in this research process as one respondent suggests:

> The media dictates the very essence of sportsmanship. While we can note some positive examples, the media very rarely do. They have to sell sport and instances of sportsmanship do not make the front page or the 6'oclock news: sex or crime does that! Sport and especially rugby union had to adapt to create appeal, that's why there are Friday night and Sunday games, more 7s events and a major drive to get the sport into the Olympics. But believe me, I see examples of sportsmanship each week and without sounding corporate, without it rugby union would just be another mass marketed and commercial sport [Joseph].

Increasing customer expectations of quality, value for money and entertainment have forced National Governing Bodies and sports clubs to become increasingly innovative, efficient and customer focused. It is suggested that spectators require an entertaining product with an element of uncertainty and the ability to identify with success while the broadcasters and commercial investors require their investment to have maximal exposure across a range of media platforms (El-Hodiri and Quirk 1971). For example broadcasters have used their levels of power to insist on changes to package the competitions more attractively for television audiences which has included alterations to the timing of matches, the branding of the teams, the rules of play and even the structure of the competitions.

The media can also impact upon sportsmanship in another way: namely the provision of technology for a particular sport. For example, in cricket, technology is provided to assist the umpires in making on-field decisions, which may affect the outcome of a match. The umpire can decide to consult the available technology if they wish, and players can also call upon the technology and challenge a decision made by the umpire if they believe that the decision was incorrect. The availability of additional technology in cricket has meant, at the top level of the game, that there is more control for the umpires regarding the decisions that they make during a match:

> Since the review system has been used in test matches it has had a positive impact on dissent [at the professional level] there's no doubt about that. Wrongly I think the onus is on the players to appeal his [the umpire] decision. If a player wants to he can say we'll review that but I know it's wrong. I don't think that's right but that's neither here nor there. It should be in the hands of the umpire and they can review anything they need to, that's the fairest way to do it but that's not the way it is [Henry].

Henry believes that in elite level professional cricket, the introduction of technology, although flawed in its application at times, has had an impact on the levels of dissent to which umpires can be subjected. Nevertheless, there have been issues with the reliability of some of the technology that has been introduced to the professional game of cricket such as "Hotspot." This technology was introduced into the game as a direct result of broadcasters, such as Sky, using the technology during their live broadcasts to further examine decisions given by on-field umpires. This technology was not available to the umpires but was latterly adopted by cricket governing bodies. "Hotspot" was adjudged to be unreliable with batsmen allegedly using tape on their bats to deceive the technology (Booth 2013) and as such has been withdrawn from regular international fixtures (Hoult 2013). Despite some issues with technology in cricket the game generally has embraced additional technology. This technology can have a negative impact on the lower levels of the game and this can be seen by a reduction in sportsmanship and a more negative relationship between the players and umpires:

> If you go further down to non-professional cricket like counties, they're [the players] seeing things on telly and reviewing it, but they can't review it so they challenge the umpire a little bit more forcefully. Inevitably using technology has shifted the way people think in terms of what is out and what is not out or anything where there is an opinion needed [Henry].

Additionally, Henry suggests that players are now questioning umpires more forcefully due to the fact that they can see what they view as comparable decisions and outcomes in the professional game. Henry believes that the introduction of technology and the changes to the game that this has brought has led to a change in the way that players at a lower level view the game, the laws of the game and the decisions of the umpire. In effect players believe that it is more acceptable to challenge the umpire, or at least appeal much more vociferously than they would historically. This is arguably a significant shift in the historic ethos of the game and is impacting upon opportunities for sportsmanship to be evident within the cricket.

There are other sports, despite some of the issues identified in cricket related to media involvement and the introduction of technology, that want to increase their relationship with the media and introduce or intensify the technology utilized at the elite level of the game. For example, squash has introduced technology as the game attempts to evolve and appeal to broadcasters, as well as become an attractive proposition for sponsors and the Olympic movement as squash strives to become an Olympic sport (Ziegler 2013). The central aim regarding the introduction of technology in squash was to make the game more dynamic in order to appeal to television (Matthew 2013) with players permitted to review decisions, "its one video review per game, so if you've got 3,4 or 5 games its one review per game" (Arthur).

Squash is not the only sport that believes there are benefits that additional technology and an increased relationship with the media can bring. Those involved in Ultimate Frisbee believe that in the future the game needs to embrace the influence of the media and additional technology:

> I think in the very long term in a stadium with 20,000 people, I think it would be excellent to have the players stop, call a foul and then look at the screen. It would be fantastic to have the two players with microphones so you can hear them discussing the decision [Trevor].

Ultimate Frisbee is considering how the use of technology and further media relationships would develop the sport. However, it is also the changes these developing relationships would enforce upon the wider game that should be considered. Arguably the effects on Ultimate Frisbee could be far reaching and influence the very ethos of the game. The impact of the media can be seen throughout history and much depends on the willingness of the sport in question to embrace this relationship and the additional technology that this can bring.

Conclusion

Sportsmanship, while a debated and contested concept, remains a worthy virtue from the referee's perspective. The officials interviewed throughout this research process, have provided evidence of situations where sportsmanship has not always been evident and yet they have also been forthright in providing some examples of sportsmanship in action. It is important to note that the majority of individuals engaged in the world of sport, such as athletes, fans, coaches and the match officials' act in accordance with the rules and regulations of their sports and those that govern wider society. The individuals who violate such codes of conduct receive public criticism and are punished for their transgressions. A recent example in 2015, saw an England rugby union international player, Manu Tuilagi, appear before magistrates, having been charged with two counts of assaulting a police officer, assault by beating and causing criminal damage. Tuilagi was fined £6,205 and banned from participation at the 2015 Rugby World Cup by the national governing body (Mairs 2015). Nonetheless, sportsmanship in the 21st century despite sport's increasing relationships with technology, media and money is a value that the officials believe is a defining factor within sport and something that, when the opportunity allows, should be promoted to wider society to ensure a lasting legacy and also maintain the role of sportsmanship within sport.

Bibliography

Arthur-Banning, Skye G., Karen Paisley, and Sara Mary Wells. 2007. "Promoting Sportsmanship in Youth Basketball Players: The Effect of Referees' Prosocial Behavior Techniques." *Journal of Par and Recreation Administration*, 25 (1):96–114.

Baker, Norman. 2004. "Whose Hegemony? The Origins of the Amateur Ethos in Nineteenth Century English Society." *Sport in History*, 24 (1):1–16.

Bellamy, Jr., Robert V. 1988. "Impact of the Television Marketplace on the Structure of Major League Baseball." *Journal of Broadcasting and Electronic Media*, 32 (1):73–87.

Bernstein, Alina, and Neil Blain. 2002. "Sport and the Media: The Emergence of a Major Research Field." *Sport in Society*, 5 (3):1–30.

Booth, Lawrence. 2013. "Ashes Batsmen 'Using Tape on Bats to Interfere with HotSpot on DRS Referrals.'" Retrieved May 19, 2015 (http://www.dailymail.co.uk).

Buford May, Reuben. A. 2010. "The Sticky Situation of Sportsmanship: Contexts and Contradictions in Sportsmanship Among High School Boys Basketball Players." *Journal of Sport and Social Issues*, 25 (4):372–389.

Bull, Andy. 2011. *A Good Walk Spoiled*. Retrieved May 23, 2015 (http://www.theguardian.com).

Cashmore, Ellis. 2005. *Making Sense of Sports*, 4th ed. London: Routledge.

Collins, Tony. 2013. *Sport in Capitalist Society: A Short History*. Oxon: Routledge.

Delaney, Tim. 2010. "Humanism and Sportsmanship in an Uncivil Society." *International Journal of the Humanities*, 8 (1): 23–32.

Delaney, Tim, and Tim Madigan. 2009. *Sports: Why People Love Them!* Lanham, MD: University Press of America.

El-Hodiri, Mohamed, and James Quirk. 1971. "An Economic Model of a Professional Sports League." *The Journal of Political Economy*, 1302–1319.

Giulianotti, Richard, and Roland Robertson. 2004. "The Globalization of Football: A Study in the Globalization of the 'Serious Life.'" *The British Journal of Sociology*, 55 (4):545–568.

_____. 2009. *Globalization & Football*. London: Sage.

Griggs, Gerald. 2011. "'This Must Be the Only Sport in the World Where Most of the Players Don't Know the Rules': Operationalizing Self-Refereeing and the Spirit of the Game in UK Ultimate Frisbee." *Sport in Society*, 14 (1):97–110.

Horne, John, Alan Tomlinson, and Gary Whannel. 1999. *Understanding Sport: An Introduction to the Sociological and Cultural Analysis of Sport*. London: E & FN Spon.

Hoult, Nick. 2013. "Ashes 2013–14: DRS Controversy Hits Series as Snicko and Hotspot Fail England's Joe Root." Retrieved May 19, 2015 (http://www.telegraph.co.uk).

Keating, James. W. 1964. "Sportsmanship as a Moral Category." *Ethics*, 75 (1):25–35.

_____. 2007. "Sportsmanship as a Moral Category," pp. 141–152 in *Ethics in Sport*, 2d ed., edited by William John Morgan. Leeds: Human Kinetics.

Loland, Sigmund. 1998. "Fair Play: Historical Anachronism or Topical Ideal?" pp. 79–113 in *Ethics and Sport*, edited by Mike McNamee and Jim Parry. London: Routledge.

_____. 2002. *Fair Play in Sport: A Moral Norm System*. New York: Routledge.

_____. 2005. "The Varieties of Cheating—Comments on Ethical Analyses in Sport [1]." *Sport in Society*, 8 (1):11–26.

Madigan, Tim. 2014. "Developing One's Character: An Aristotelian Defense of Sportsmanship." *Verbum*, 7 (1):83–90.
Mairs, Gavin. 2015. *Manu Tuilagi Assaults Female Police Officer and Ruled Out of Rugby World Cup*. Retrieved May 19, 2015 (http://www.telegraph.co.uk).
Mangan, J, A. 2001. "Series Editors' Foreword," pp. 1–3 in *Amateurism in Sport*, edited by Allison Lincoln. London: Frank Cass.
Matthew, Nick. 2013. *Why it's Time to Squeeze Squash into the 2020 Olympic Games*. Retrieved May 19, 2015 (http://www.theguardian.com).
MCC women. (n.d.). Retrieved May 19, 2015 (http://www.lords.org/mcc/the-club/mcc-women/).
McNamee, Mike. 2008. *Sports, Virtues and Vices: Morality Plays*. London: Routledge.
Morgan, William, John. 2007. *Ethics in Sport*, 2d ed. Leeds: Human Kinetics.
Rinehart, Robert E., and Synthia Sydnor, eds. 2003. *To the Extreme: Alternative Sports, Inside and Out*. Albany: SUNY Press.
Robins, Blaine. 2004. "'That's Cheap': The Rational Invocation of Norms, Practices, and an Ethos in Ultimate Frisbee." *Journal of Sport and Social Issues*, 28 (3):314–337.
Rowe, David. 2004. *Sport, Culture and the Media*, 2d ed. Maidenhead: Open University Press.
Smart, Barry. 2005. *The Sport Star: Modern Sport and the Cultural Economy of Sporting Celebrity*. London: Sage.
_____. 2007. "Not Playing Around: Global Capitalism, Modern Sport and Consumer Culture." *Global Networks*, 7 (2):113–134.
Stead, David. 2008. "Sport and the Media," pp. 328–347 In *Sport and Society: A Student Introduction*, 2d ed., edited by Barry Houlihan. London: Sage.
Suits, Bernard. 1998. *The Grasshopper: Games, Life and Utopia*. Peterborough, Ontario: Broadview.
Thornton, Andrew. 2004. "'Anyone can Play This Game': Ultimate Frisbee, Identity and Difference" pp. 175–196 In *Understanding Lifestyle Sports: Consumption, Identity and Difference*, edited by Belinda Wheaton. London: Routledge.
Wells, Mary Sara, Gary D. Ellis, Karen P. Paisley, and Skye G. Arthur-Banning. 2005. "Development and Evaluation of a Program to Promote Sportsmanship in Youth Sports." *Journal of Park and Recreation Administration*, 23 (1):1–17.
Whannel, Gary. 2008. *Culture, Politics and Sport*. London: Routledge.
Ziegler, Martyn. 2013, September 8. "Olympics: Wrestling Fends off Squash and Baseball to Earn 2020 Return Less Than a Year After Being Dropped." Retrieved 19 May, 2015 (http://www.independent.co.uk).

Francis Ouimet and Sportsmanship in Golf

CHRIS MACK

Arguably, the single greatest spur to the growth of golf as a popular sport in America came on a soggy afternoon on September 19, 1913. On the par four, 17th hole of the Country Club in Brookline, Massachusetts, a twenty-year old amateur golfer, Francis Ouimet, drained a slippery 20 foot, down-hill, side-hill birdie putt that put him in a tie for the lead and forced a playoff in the 19th United States Golf Association's Open Championship (Frost 2002:371). Even more remarkable, in the playoff that ensued on the following day, Ouimet bested the two greatest professional golfers in the world, Britain's Harry Vardon and Edward "Ted" Ray. Ouimet's improbable victory almost single-handedly transformed golf from a sport reserved for the wealthy and leisured elite to one ardently pursued by enthusiasts across all segments of American society.

Even more important was the manner in which Ouimet, Vardon, and Ray conducted themselves during the tournament. For their actions demonstrated to all that no matter the pressure of the situation, the enormity of the event, or the effects of the outcome, the principles of fair play and good sportsmanship provide the very foundation of golf. As a result, "the greatest game ever played" marked not only a singular moment in the history of the sport, but an important one in the development of sportsmanship and proper conduct in American sports overall.

Ouimet, in particular, became recognized as a pillar of proper sportsmanship throughout the golfing world. Indeed, his character and sense of fair play ultimately stood him in good stead when he was temporarily banned from the game by the United States Golf Association (USGA), accused of being a professional despite his declared amateur status. Golfers from around the world rallied to his defense, and Ouimet proved vindicated. The USGA reinstated his amateur status and Ouimet became a beacon of good sportsmanship and a much-beloved ambassador of American golf for the remainder of his lifetime.

Thus, the events of the 19th U.S. Open golf championship and Ouimet's subsequent conduct in his showdown with the USGA, offered testimony to the central importance of good sportsmanship to the game of golf and its adherents. Indeed, good sportsmanship proved triumphant over national jingoism, prejudicial class distinctions, and the institutional power of the USGA.

Good Sportsmanship in the 1913 U.S. Open

To appreciate the tremendous pressure that the golfers experienced during the 1913 U.S. Open, and, correspondingly, the tremendous strain that could have eroded the competitors' good sportsmanship, it is necessary to provide a bit more background information.

Harry Vardon, aged 43 at the time of the 1913 Open, was the world's preeminent golfer. He had already won the U.S. Open in 1900 and four British Open championships (Frost 2002:77). As a celebrated champion, Vardon had toured much of the United States and dominated the over one hundred exhibitions and matches that he played against American professionals and amateurs. His smooth swing and unflappable demeanor won him the nickname "the Greyhound" for his uncanny ability to seemingly effortlessly come from behind to overtake any rivals who might temporarily get ahead of him in a match. Because of his firm self-control, impeccable dress and manners, and ability to deliver unbelievably accurate golf shots time and again under pressure, Vardon intimidated almost all of his challengers.

However, by 1913 illness had somewhat weakened Vardon's armor. Stricken with tuberculosis in 1903, Vardon battled the illness for six years before he achieved a near complete recovery—yet, a sometimes severe tremor in his right hand remained to hinder him ever after. It appeared at the most inopportune moments and forever threatened the once invincible Vardon's ability to easily hole out short pressure putts (Frost 2002:116). Nevertheless, by 1913 it appeared Vardon had returned to form and he prepared to embark on another tour of the United States, culminating with his appearance in the Open at Brookline in the autumn.

Vardon's companion on the 1913 tour was Ted Ray—a long-time friend from Vardon's home island of Jersey. A big bear of a man, Ray crushed the golf ball like no other during his era. His long drives were complemented by a deft short game. The combination of the two allowed Ray to become one of Vardon's premier challengers. Ray won the 1912 British Open at the daunting Muirfield course in Scotland and later won the 1920 U.S. Open. Thus, when Vardon and Ray arrived at the Country Club in September for the 1913 U.S. Open, they were tournament tested and very familiar with the demands of top flight tournament golf.

To turn up the pressure yet another notch, the patron of Vardon's and Ray's tour and participation in the U.S. Open was Alfred Harmsworth, Lord Northcliffe. A publishing magnate and golf fancier, in 1904, Northcliffe witnessed an Australian-born, naturalized American citizen, Walter J. Travis, win the British Amateur championship. Northcliffe feared, despite the dominance of Vardon and others, that Travis's victory might mark the beginning of the end of British supremacy in international golf. He burned for revenge and hoped Vardon and Ray would soundly thrash all American comers at Brookline in 1913.

Excoriated by Northcliffe's newspapers in Britain, Travis, editor of an early American golf magazine, *The American Golfer*, got in his own swipes in favor of good sportsmanship—and cries of foul against the British. He held:

> It is an easy thing to be a good winner, but to be a good loser calls for much soul discipline, much humbling of the spirit and, above all, an eager and appreciative eye for the good qualities of the "other fellow" and a warm heart for their generous acknowledgment; in short, for that

> particular quality known the world over as sportsmanship—which, we are told, is distilled only in its virgin purity in the British Isles and in which, as winners, the English are magnificent. As losers, however, it is quite another story [Travis 1911:376].

Indeed, Travis, perhaps because of the ill-treatment he received from Northcliffe and other British chest-thumpers, championed sportsmanship whenever possible. In another issue of *The American Golfer* he offered his "Golf Ethics":

> Of all games which disclose the petty weaknesses of human nature its frailties on the one hand, and sterling, manly attributes and admirable qualities of true sportsmanship on the other, golf stands pre-eminent. All of a man's best and worst traits are luminously brought forth and exposed to view in all their nakedness. It is one thing to be a good winner ... easy, very, very easy for most; but to be a good loser is quite a different affair. To be a generous loser, to freely own up that defeat has been brought about by the better play of one's opponent rather than to luck or accidents of play, or failure to rise to the occasion on the part of the worsted, means the possession of almost divine qualities [Travis 1909:460].

Travis's appeal to golfers to dampen their patriotic enthusiasms and recall the sportsmanship the game favored was echoed by many.

Beyond Travis's editorial comments, the pages of *The American Golfer* trumpeted the virtues of golf and its function as a conduit of good sportsmanship and forge of good character. Often, such uplifting proselytizing appeared in verse, such as S. Keith Evans "Winning at Golf" (1911):

> To win at golf
> is not so much the test of a man's golf
> as it is a test of the man.
> It is not so much a test of physique
> as it is a test of temperament and a
> man's hold on himself.
> It is not so much a test of his bulldog tenacity as it is a test of his
> sportsmanship.
> A good loser is sure to be a winner,
> because to lose a stroke cheerfully is
> to make the next stroke good.
> No mean or selfish man can ever
> win at golf.
> He may even
> by the exhibition of these qualities
> beat his opponent and carry away the cup,
> but he does not really win
> because golf is not played to win cups.
> It is played
> to win friends.
> He who wins a cup in any division
> from the first to the last and also wins
> a friend evens up the match, because
> the loser of the cup has won a friend.
> Thus you will perceive that golf can
> be a game where all the contestants
> win and none lose [p. 454].

Similar sentiments and counsel appeared in *The American Golfer* (1910) in a second poem, "The Two Great Games":

Life and Gold are, game for game,
Pretty much about the same;
In both you'll find the course you play
Is full of hazards out the way;
Grim bunkers loom along the wake
To catch each shot or bad mistake;
And he who plays in each will find
The winner is not of the kind
Who hits the ball with hardest force,
But he who keeps
straight down the course.
Life and Golf both have their pits
To trap the one who poorly hits;
In both good sportsmanship counts
more
Than any win or any score;
Bad lies abound at every turn
And to succeed one has to learn
To hold the open fairway through
And play well out of Trouble too.
In both you'll quickly find that Luck
Counts some—but not as much as
Pluck;
In both games you'll soon find, forlorn,
That you're more often "off" than
"on";
One day the "break" will be O. K.
And next there's nothing comes your
way;
So it will happen in the strife
And play of Golf as well as Life;
And at the end, O Mortal Soul,
You wind each game up
in a "hole."

Clearly, the popular ideal, however romantic and maudlin, was that golf should foster our better angels and serve as an antidote to the strife and tumult of politics, business, and divisions between people of all kinds.

Still, national sentiments proved hard to dissolve. For example, Northcliffe's rampant British patriotism provoked one of America's early golfing phenoms, John J. McDermott. The United States' first native-born U.S. Open champion, McDermott won back-to-back U.S. Open's at the Chicago Golf Club in 1911 and the Country Club of Buffalo in 1912 (USGA 2010). He won his first national championship at age nineteen, a record that still stands. The son of a Philadelphia mailman, and a self-made man among the society swells of country club golf, McDermott played with a chip on his shoulder. A rather diminutive man, but a fiery, almost demonic, competitor, McDermott torqued himself into a berserker fury on the course. His inner rage allowed him to become America's premier champion, but no one's friend. In addition, McDermott did not figure as a paragon of sportsmanship and fair play.

In the run-up to the U.S. Open, Vardon and Ray squared off against McDermott and other professionals in a tournament at the Shawnee Resort in the Pocono Mountains of Pennsylvania. McDermott won the tournament and when he accepted the winner's trophy he also held aloft his U.S. Open trophy and openly taunted Vardon and Ray. He said, "Mr. Vardon, I understand you won this baby once before. But let me tell you this: you are not going to take our cup back!" (Frost 2002:161). In response to McDermott's provocation, Vardon offered only a laconic smile. The USGA held McDermott's outburst a severe breach of decorum and good sportsmanship and officially reprimanded the young American hot-head. Thus, between McDermott and Lord Northcliffe, the heat of national pride burned as the U.S. Open at the Country Club began.

No one expected Francis Ouimet to present a challenge to Vardon and Ray. No one expected him to even make it into the final qualifying for the competition. Ouimet had no national reputation and no previous experience in the U.S. Open. He did have an intimate knowledge of the Country Club and its testy golf course, for he lived directly across the street from the 17th hole and had worked as a caddie at the club for many years. Thus, he knew the course far better than most of his competitors.

And, despite his lack of renown, Ouimet was not a complete golf novice. In the summer of 1913 he won the Massachusetts state amateur title. He also played well in the USGA's National Amateur Championship in Garden City, Long Island during the first week of September 1913. Squaring off against three-time amateur champion Jerry Travers, Ouimet lost the match 3–2, but, in an act of tremendous sportsmanship, Travers consoled Ouimet by going over the round shot by shot with him after the match, explaining his errors both in thought and execution. Thus, Travers' generous and sporting instruction provided Ouimet with invaluable advice that he could draw on two weeks later against even stronger foes. And perhaps just as significant, he gave Ouimet confidence that he had the ability to one day be a champion (Frost 2002:144). Still, Ouimet lacked big-time tournament experience and despite his potential, didn't think he was ready for U.S. Open play—even if the tournament was across the street and held on a course he knew like no other. Bowing to his perceived reality, reinforced by the loss to Travers in Garden City, Ouimet didn't even bother to enter the U.S. Open at Brookline. Instead, he planned to return to his job at Wright & Ditson's Sporting Goods store and try tournament golf again the following year.

Yet, without Ouimet's knowledge, the president of the USGA, Robert Watson, entered Ouimet in the upcoming tournament. Watson had witnessed Ouimet's match against Travers in the U.S. Amateur and thought Ouimet possessed a strong enough game to well represent the nation's amateurs in the tournament (Frost 2002:146). Watson contacted Ouimet's boss, George Wright (a Hall of Fame pitcher for the Boston Red Stockings and golf nut) and arranged for Ouimet to have the time off for practice and participation in the Open at the Country Club (Frost 2002:146).

Ouimet did all his supporters wanted and more. In his opening qualifying round Ouimet turned in the second best score, trailing Vardon by only one stroke *(New York Times*, 9/17/1913). Still, nearly everyone except Ouimet and his caddie, ten year old Eddie Lowery, thought the green youngster would fold once he fully experienced the pressure cooker of actual Open competition.

Indeed, after the first day of competition (two rounds—the U.S. Open was then contested over two days, with 36 holes played on each day), Ouimet trailed Vardon by four strokes and Ray by two (*New York Times*, September 19, 1913). He still sat tied for fourth place, with many big names behind him, but most thought the ensuing day's play would see Ouimet crumble.

Remarkably, he didn't. In the morning eighteen holes Ouimet posted the best score of the round, shooting an even par 74 on the soggy Country Club course. Even more amazingly, Vardon shot a 78 and was now tied with Ouimet! He led Ted Ray by two. The press applauded his efforts, but did not believe he could keep pace with the great British duo (Frost 2002. He did falter, as the rain turned portions of the course to mud, Vardon and Ray caught Ouimet—thus requiring his heroics at the 17th green mentioned at the beginning of the chapter. After his tying birdie at 17, Ouimet parred the 18th hole and forced the next day's eighteen hole playoff. A raucous celebration by the thousands of fans that surrounded the green ensued:

> Instantly a yell went up, which must have been heard in Boston. The gallery swept past ropes and guards and closed in on Ouimet in a solid phalanx. He was lifted to the shoulders of the advance guard and carried toward the clubhouse surrounded by several thousand cheering, yelling golfers, who forgot their golf in the enthusiasm of being just Americans cheering an American victory [*New York Times*, September 20, 1913].

In an ironic twist, given Ouimet's later ouster by the USGA under the charge of professionalism, the crowd attempted to shower Ouimet with a profusion of cash:

> Many, not realizing that Ouimet was an amateur and not a professional, thrust bills of large denominations at him only to be met with a smile and shake of the head, which took the sting out of the refusal made necessary by their mistake [*New York Times*, September 20, 1913].

Thus, the stage was set for Ouimet's improbable triumph over his celebrated and highly-favored opponents.

What remains notable is how the players treated one another during the hotly contested playoff. Fierce competitors all, each wanted to win. But each wanted to win the right way, by demonstrating the highest degree of sportsmanship *and* competitive fire. The tone was set by Vardon and Ray just after Ouimet tied them for the lead and forced the playoff. When reporters asked for his reaction to Ouimet's performance, Vardon said, "We must all take our hats off to his remarkable achievement. And we greatly look forward to meeting Mr. Ouimet in the playoff tomorrow morning." Ray added, "That was the greatest demonstration of skill and nerve I have ever seen in golf" (Frost 2002:375). Both men were amazed by Ouimet's putt on the 17th hole. "Coming when it did," Vardon commented, "I count it as one of the master strokes of golf." Not to be outdone in the sportsmanship department, Ray enthused, "Only perfect judgment could have put that ball in the cup. I've never seen a putt more confidently played" (Frost 2002:375). The next morning, as the players and their caddies gathered to begin the round, Vardon shook Ouimet's hand and said, "Congratulations, well played yesterday." Ouimet, replied, "Thank you, sir. And the best of luck to you today" (Frost 2002:391). Yet, despite being cordial, Ouimet did not want to be intimidated. He recalled the advice Vardon gave in his 1905 instruction book, *The Complete Golfer*, "Treat your opponent, with all due respect, as a non-entity" (Frost 2002:391). Ouimet met the master with the respect he deserved, but he did not cower before him.

Henry Leach, a British journalist who witnessed the match, later reinforced the importance of Ouimet's character and temperament for his victory. Leach (1916) held that

> we must look to other things than the peculiarities of his strokes for the reason of his success. There is his amazing confidence, his surpassing temperament. It is magnificent. I doubt if there is a player with a temperament that is better. It needs no other testimonial than that it gave itself in the contest with Ray and Vardon at Brookline [p. 262].

Indeed, to Leach it was Ouimet's concentration and focus that not only helped him to win, but helped him to attain the highest degree of sportsmanship as well. He maintained that "at Brookline he kept his eye on his own ball all the time, and looked not at the others until he found them somewhere in the region of the hole on the putting green. A temperament like this is never ruffled, and it induces sportsmanship of a very high order" (Leach 1916:262). It seems then, that in no small part, Ouimet's character and dedication to sportsmanship helped to steel him against the pressure of the U.S. Open. He followed the principles of good sportsmanship and that allowed him to stay within himself, focus on his own game, and insulated him from the dangers of being swept up and carried away by the swirling tides of excessive competition.

Ouimet's intense concentration, composure, and the attitude fostered by his good sportsmanship enabled him to hit all eighteen fairways during the playoff round—as well as to avoid all of the dangerous bunkers that mined the course. He never three-putted a single green. As a result, Ouimet shot a two-under par 72 for the playoff, five shots better than Vardon and six better than Ray (*New York Times*, September 21, 1913).

Both Ray and Vardon accepted Ouimet's victory, and their defeat, with grace and equanimity. During the awards ceremony that followed the match, Ray demonstrated his firm embrace of golf's sporting principles. To the assembled crowd he said: "It gives me the greatest pleasure to congratulate Mr. Ouimet on his splendid victory.... His was the best golf I have ever seen in my time in America. It was an honor to play with him and no dishonor to lose to him" (Frost 2002:424).

Vardon echoed and expanded on Ray's sentiments. Vardon humbly accepted Ouimet's superior play and victory: "We have no excuses to make today, for we were both defeated by the highest class of golf. We made mistakes and Mr. Ouimet, like a wise and good golfer, took advantage of every one of them. His play was so excellent, so steady, all hope was kept out. We do not begrudge him this victory.... He has proved himself to be a superior golfer and a courageous fighter" (Frost 2002:425). Vardon concluded his comments to the crowd by, in no small measure, repudiating the rabid nationalist and patriotic harangues of his patron, Lord Northcliffe. Vardon held that

> there exists a special bond between our two countries, and it is my firm belief that this great sport played in the spirit of friendly competition over time can only make it stronger. This is my second time in America, which I count as one of the great privileges of my life. I hope it is not my last, and for the great kindnesses and hospitality accorded me, I wish to thank all of you. I assure you that, for my part, they are returned with nothing but the deepest and most lasting affections [Frost 2002:425].

The crowd roared its approval.

Reactions to Ouimet's Victory

In the immediate aftermath of the match, the reaction of the British press to Ouimet's victory was one of astonishment, praise, and in some measure relief that, at least, John J. McDermott had not retained the trophy. Lord Northcliffe's own *Daily Mail* reported that "golfers at this moment are engaged, all the world over, in a single, simultaneous, and irrepressible act. They are taking off their hats with a flourish of profound respect. The contest will live in the history of the game as long as it is played" (*New York Times*, September 22, 1913). Another British newspaper, *The Standard*, offered similar sentiments: "We must join with his vanquished adversaries in offering hearty congratulations to the victor whose well-earned success, humiliating as it may be to Britons, is very much to his credit" (*New York Times*, September 22, 1913).

Not all British commentators were so forthcoming in their praise of Ouimet's victory. J.H. Taylor, winner of five British Open titles, claimed that the Brookline youngster's triumph was "humiliating." He went on to argue that Ouimet won, in part, because, blessed by youth and inexperience, he did not comprehend the enormity of his task:

> Youth has no nerves.... Ouimet is a splendid golfer, endowed with splendid nerves. At the same time, my impression is that he had everything to gain and nothing to lose. Vardon and Ray on the other hand knew they carried on their shoulders the golf reputation of this country. That did not make their task easier. It is much more easy to make a reputation at golf than it is to maintain it [*New York Times*, September 23, 1913].

Other British champions, both professional and amateur, like George Duncan, James Sherlock and Tom Ball, agreed with Taylor. Ball said, "From my own experiences in support of them [Vardon and Ray] ... it is harder to keep on top of the ladder than to climb it" (*New York Times*, September 23, 1913). So, for these illustrious British golfers, only time would tell if Ouimet's triumph was that of an accomplished and worthy golfer, or just a fluke, a one-off that wouldn't be repeated.

In 1914, in an effort to prove himself and test his mettle against Europe's finest, Ouimet sailed to Britain and played in a number of tournaments. Although he did well and impressed his foes and detractors, Ouimet did not win any titles, losing both the British Amateur championship and the British Open—finishing well behind the eventual winner, Harry Vardon (*New York Times*, June 20, 1914). Ouimet did, however, win the French Amateur Championship, besting fellow American Henry J. Topping (*New York Times*, May 29, 1914). Still, he acquitted himself well and secured his reputation as one of America's leading amateur golfers and proponents of good sportsmanship.

Thus, the great and humble champions of Britain, and the lowly amateur, son of a laborer, demonstrated the highest principles and taught the world a most valuable lesson. Ouimet's victory at the 1913 United States Open rocketed golf to new heights of popularity and reinforced the importance not of winning, but of properly playing the game.

Ouimet and the Calumny of the USGA

Yet, despite his exploits on the course and his unabashed humility, good character and emphasis on proper sportsmanship, Ouimet ran afoul of the leaders of the USGA. In 1916, the USGA moved to declare anyone who derived revenue from their exploits as a golfer a professional. In January 1916, Ouimet and another outstanding amateur golfer, John H. Sullivan, Jr., opened a sporting goods store in Boston. In an interview in *The New York Times*, Ouimet was asked if he would violate the USGA's new rule. Ouimet argued that he and Sullivan were not in violation of the rule, for "neither Sullivan nor myself are relying on any fame as an amateur golfer to sell goods. We are going into the business because we believe we are good salesmen, not because of our skill on the links" (*New York Times*, January 16, 1916).

Ouimet's reasoning, however persuasive, did not win over USGA President, Frank L. Woodward. Woodward and the USGA took a hard-line on professionalism. Woodward declared:

> There are two and only two classes of occupations that golfers are permitted to engage in for pay and still retain their amateur standing. One is literary work.... The other line of effort for which an amateur golfer may receive pay is work in the direction of what is known as golf architecture—the laying out, remodeling or construction of golf courses [*New York Times*, February 27, 1916].

Woodward made no bones about the fact that Ouimet, Sullivan, and other well-known amateurs would be stripped of their amateur status. As word began to spread of Woodward and the USGA's decision to strictly enforce the letter of the law, a great cry of protest swept through country clubs around the nation. In the pages of *The American Golfer*, Walter Travis asked for his readers' opinion of the ruling against Ouimet. Without exception, his fellow golfers backed Ouimet and testified to his character. An example of the laudatory praise heaped upon the young champion came from Charles Evans, Jr., of the Edgewater Club:

> Personally, I am glad to say that I know no man in the country with a finer amateur spirit than Francis Ouimet. There is not a single word in the British definition of a professional to make him one. A fine, clean young sportsman is needed in every game. The golf career of Francis Ouimet is one to which we can point with pride, as an example for all younger players. He has shunned the nineteenth hole and in every respect he has acted as a true sportsman and a gentleman. Earning an honest living in a way that can add nothing to one's skill in the game ought not to interfere with a man's amateur standing in a democratic country like America. It does not do so even in aristocratic England [Evans 1916].

Other commentators in the *New York Times* held that the actions of the USGA and Woodward smacked of elitism and social prejudice: "The decision of the golf association is too much in line with the tendency to make golf a millionaire's game. It is a snobbish policy" (*New York Times*, February 14, 1916).

Buoyed by the sheer number of such sentiments, Ouimet and Sullivan's home club, The Woodland Golf Club of Newton, MA, defied the USGA and demanded several meetings with USGA leaders to address the situation of its most famous members.

Despite the club's pleas, the USGA refused to relent, prompting further defiance from the leaders of The Woodland Golf Club. Ultimately, in July 1916, the USGA ousted the club and all of its members from the USGA and refused them the right to participate in any USGA-sanctioned events (*New York Times*, July 14, 1916). Not ready to back down, the leaders of the Woodland Golf Club made alliances with disaffected golf clubs and associations throughout the northeast and the country. Ultimately, they forced a showdown at the USGA's annual meeting in New York City on January 12, 1917. After much debate, the matter was put to a vote and the USGA Executive Committee prevailed, 80–12. The strict amateur rule and Ouimet's ban remained in force (*New York Times*, January 14, 1917).

Commentators on the decision held that the leaders of the Woodland Golf Club adopted a failed strategy of attacking the USGA's President, Frank Woodward, and the Executive Committee and threatening the legitimacy and existence of the organization as a whole. When faced with the prospect of dissolving the USGA as the governing body of the game of golf in the United States, most delegates balked. So the leaders of the pro-Ouimet camp overplayed their hand and lost soundly as a result (*New York Times*, January 15, 1917). For his part, Ouimet largely stayed out of the affair. He continued to calmly argue that he had been in the sporting goods business long before he became a golfer of renown and therefore he merely traded on his acumen as a salesman, not his notoriety as a champion golfer. He continued to make headlines for his golfing exploits, but for breaking course records, not for winning titles in USGA matches.

On June 18, 1917, Ouimet and Sullivan met with the USGA's new president, Howard Perrin, and the Executive Committee to present their case for reinstatement (*New York Times*, June 19, 1917). Perrin and the Executive Committee refused to rule on the matter immediately. Ouimet and Sullivan received notice on July 5, 1917, that the USGA Executive Committee had rejected their appeal. The USGA argued that since Ouimet and Sullivan still sold golf supplies at their sporting goods store, then they still violated the rules and could not have their amateur status restored (*New York Times*, July 6, 1917). Ouimet responded defiantly by traveling to Chicago to play, as an amateur, in the Western Open, sponsored by the Western Golf Association which flouted the rule of the USGA and its stranglehold over golf in the U.S. Ouimet won the tournament over a star-studded field, including a young Bobby Jones, by one shot. Still, the stalemate with the USGA continued unabated.

As the reality of the United States entrance into World War I began to hit home, and the country began to furiously prepare for combat in Europe, Ouimet demonstrated his character once again. While many golfers from the elite country club set sought deferments to avoid or mitigate military service, Ouimet did his duty and entered the military draft. He joined the army in 1917 and served at Fort Devens, MA. His service included playing exhibition matches to raise money for the Red Cross and the war effort. For his efforts, Ouimet received a Red Cross Prize Medal for his contributions during the war.

The looming threat of combat and the desire to bring the country together in the face of war, as well as two years' worth of exhaustion and bitterness prompted by his controversial ban, prompted the USGA to revisit Ouimet's expulsion. At the USGA's annual meeting in Philadelphia on January 25, 1918, the USGA announced that it rescinded Ouimet's ban and reinstated his amateur status:

> Whereas, Francis Ouimet, upon entering the service of the United States, severed his connection with the management of the firm Ouimet & Sullivan, and thereby discontinued the practices which were decided to be in violation of the amateur rule of the United States Golf Association. Therefore, be it resolved by the Executive Committee of the United States Golf Association, that he be, and hereby is, reinstated as an amateur golfer [*New York Times*, January 26, 1918].

The resolution was unanimously approved by the delegates who attended the general meeting.

After two years of internecine conflict, the USGA and its leadership found a way to end the affair and begin to put the rancor behind them. For his part, Ouimet welcomed the decision and continued to do his duty, rising to the rank of Second Lieutenant in the United States Army. When the war ended, Ouimet returned to the links. and as a consummate good sport, buried the hatchet with the USGA. He never returned to the sporting goods business; instead, he became a banker, financial advisor, and for a time served as president of the Boston Bruins and as a vice president of the Boston Braves, the city's National League baseball team. He continued to win numerous amateur titles throughout his life, culminating in his second U.S. Amateur championship in 1931 at the Beverly Country Club outside Chicago (USGA 2009).

Conclusion

Clearly, the events of the 19th U.S. Open golf championship and Ouimet's subsequent conduct in his showdown with the USGA, offered testimony to the central importance of good sportsmanship to the game of golf and its adherents. Indeed, good sportsmanship proved triumphant over national jingoism, prejudicial class distinctions, and the institutional power of the USGA. Ouimet, Vardon and Ray all demonstrated the virtues of good sportsmanship that the game trumpeted and held in such great esteem. On the other hand, the USGA's conduct when it accused Ouimet of professionalism and stripped him of his amateur status smacks of extreme poor sportsmanship. The leaders of the USGA, scions of the elite, unfairly moved against those from less privileged backgrounds, like Ouimet, who sought to distinguish themselves in the game of golf. Ouimet's willingness to endure the unjust punishment of the USGA and take the moral high ground in the dispute redounds to his credit. Without doubt, Ouimet especially deserves praise, for he not only won "the greatest game ever played," and made golf a popular sport in America, but his shining example of proper sportsmanship and personal character justifies the title given to him upon his induction into the World Golf Hall of Fame in 1974: "The Father of American Golf."

Bibliography

Evan, S. Keith. 1911. "Winning At Golf." *The American Golfer*, April: 454.
Evans, Jr., Charles. 1916. "Ouimet's Case." *The American Golfer*, 28–29.
Frost, Mark. 2002. *The Greatest Game Ever Played*. New York: Hyperion.
Leach, Henry. 1912. "The U.S. National Amateur Championship." *The American Golfer*, October: 515–531.
_____. 1913. "The United States Amateur Championship." *The American Golfer*, July: 547–567.
_____. 1914. "Some Second Thoughts." *The American Golfer*, March: 371–377.
_____. 1916. "Players of the Period–IX. Edward Ray." *The American Golfer*, April: 392–404.
_____. 1916. "Ouimet Explained." *The American Golfer*, August: 252–266.
_____. 1916. "The Scientific Hilton." *The American Golfer*, December: 86–103.
_____. 1917. "The Human Vardon." *The American Golfer*, January: 172–192.
The American Golfer. 1910. "The Two Great Games." November: 15.
New York Times. 1913. "Ouimet Captures French Golf Title." May 29: 13.
_____. 1913. "Vardon Golf Champion." June 20: 6.
_____. "Vardon Leads in National Open Golf." September 17: 10.
_____. 1913. "Vardon and Reid Lead Big Golf Field." September 19: 10.
_____. 1913. "Ouimet Ties Great English Golfers." September 20: 7.
_____. 1913. "Ouimet's Triumph." September 21: 14.
_____. 1913. "Victory of Ouimet Staggers Britain." September 22: 4.
_____. 1913. "Ouimet's Golf Victory." September 23: 12.
_____. 1916. "Ouimet to Open Store." January 16: 45.
_____. 1916. "Protests Against Ruling On Ouimet." February 14: 10.
_____. 1916. "Commercial Line Drawn Hard in Golf." February 27: 47.
_____. 1916. "Ouimet's Club Barred." July 14: 9.
_____. 1917. "Rigid Amateurism is Golfers' Ideal." January 14: 47.
_____. 1917. "Comment on Current Events in Sports." January 15: 6.
_____. 1917. "Ouimet Presents Case." June 19: 17.
_____. 1917. "U.S.G.A. Will Not Reinstate Ouimet." July 6: 12.
_____. 1918. "United States Golf Association Declares Francis Ouimet Again an Amateur." January 26: 15.
Ouimet, Francis. 1913. "Winning the Open." *The American Golfer*, October: 590–594.
_____. 1914. "America's Chances Abroad." *Golf Illustrated & Outdoor America*, May: 10–11.

______. 1914. "First Impressions of British Golf." *Golf Illustrated & Outdoor America,* June: 14–15.
______. 1914. "Impressions of the British Open." *Golf Illustrated & Outdoor America,* August: 44, 46.
______. 1914. "Impressions of the Amateur Championship." *Golf Illustrated & Outdoor America,* September 1914: 30–31.
Travers, Jerome D., and Francis Ouimet. 1914. "Impressions of the British Amateur Championship." *Golf Illustrated & Outdoor America,* July: 34–37.
Travis, Walter J. 1909. "Golf Ethics." *American Golfer,* June: 460.
______. 1911. "British Sportsmanship—For Home and Foreign Use." March: 376.
United States Golf Association (USGA). 2009. "U.S. Amateur: Past Champions." Retrieved February, 14, 2015 (http://www.usamateur.org).
______. 2010. "U.S. Open: Past Champions." Retrieved August, 25, 2010 (http://usga.usopen.com).

Trust and Training

Sparring Norms and Sportsmanship Among Brazilian Ju-Jitsu Practitioners

Rick A. Matthews *and* Stephen Lyng

Issues of sportsmanship are most often viewed as belonging to the domain of sporting events, with individuals or teams competing against one another or engaging in noncompetitive transactions structured by the organizing principles of a sport. Sportsmanship is rarely regarded as a significant issue in the training activities of participants in competitive and noncompetitive sports. Yet as competitive pressures on professional athletes have intensified in recent decades and new biotechnologies provide more opportunities to gain an edge on one's competitors, the moral dimensions of sports training and performance have become an increasing concern in the world of sport. Although training regimens are structured by instrumental goals primarily, they are also guided by less obvious normative principles, especially when training requires the interaction of training partners whose actions may pose some risk of injury to one another. This latter type of training is rooted in a basic sense of trust between training partners, a belief that neither party will approach training as an opportunity to intentionally injure one's partner.

In this paper, we focus on a sport requiring an especially intense form of training that carries a significant risk of injury between training partners. The sport of Brazilian Ju-Jitsu (BJJ) has been growing in popularity in recent years, both as fighting discipline that has been influential among professional fighters competing in the Ultimate Fighting Championship (UFC) series and as part of the general fitness movement in most Western societies. While BJJ's influence in the UFC is clearly linked to the success of its practitioners in the professional arena (Abramson and Modzelewski 2007; Green 2011), its expanding popularity within the lay population is rather puzzling when one considers the nature of the training regimen required to participate in this sport—as noted, training for BJJ is extremely intense and often exposes participants to the potential for serious pain and injury. Thus, the increasing popularity of BJJ is difficult to explain when one considers the high physical and emotional risks involved in the sport and the need to trust in the probity of the training partners who can impose these risks. This connection between risk and trust is the principle theoretical theme of the present study.

A Sociological Conception of Trust

With sociology's traditional disciplinary concern with the role of moral sentiments and normative constraints in social life, it is surprising that the problem of trust has only recently become a specific focus of sociological study. The first systematic sociological treatments of trust did not appear until the late 1970s and early 1980s with the publication of two important books: Niklas Luhmann's *Trust and Power* (1979) and Bernard Barber's *The Logic and Limits of Trust* (1983). These initial efforts were followed by other notable contributions to the sociology of trust (Lewis and Weigert 1985; Sztompka 1999; Seligman 2000), but perhaps the most innovative sociological theorizing about the role of trust in contemporary social life was undertaken by Anthony Giddens in *The Consequences of Modernity* (1990). While this book was not devoted specifically to developing a sociological theory of trust, Giddens' unique view of the transitions and discontinuities of the modern social universe provides some powerful theoretical insights about the nature of trust in social life. Since one of the key goals of our analysis is to understand how the late modern experience of trust relates to the practices of BJJ participants, Giddens' framework is well-suited for our analysis.

Trust and Risk in Late Modernity

While our primary concern in the present study is the problem of interpersonal trust among members of the BJJ community, it is necessary first to consider Giddens' (1990) analysis of the role of trust in the functioning of modern social systems. A key point in his examination of this problem is that trust must be understood as a distinctly modern phenomenon. In the pre-modern world, where life experience is highly ordered by kinship relations, local community practices, religious cosmologies, and traditional routines and rituals, there is less uncertainty and contingency in one's dealings with individuals and social environments that would require a general willingness to trust (Giddens 1990). By contrast, the processes of modern institutions make the trust response a basic requirement of daily living.

Giddens (1990) defines trust as "confidence in the reliability of a person or [abstract] system, regarding a given set of outcomes or events, where that confidence expresses a faith in the probity or love of another, or in the correctness of abstract principles (technical knowledge)" (p. 34). Thus, trust can be directed to either people or abstract systems and it is the prevalence of the latter in the modern institutional environment that makes trust an essential part of the fabric of everyday life. This conceptualization of trust also points to the important connection between trust and *risk*. In the case of abstract systems in particular, trust always depends on some calculation of "acceptable risk," even though this calculation must rely on the "weak inductive knowledge" that laypersons possess about the issues of concern (1990:35). Moreover, in the late modern condition, trust not only relates to the actions of individuals, but also to the unprecedented "environments of risk" we face today—the humanly-produced dangers that can impact large populations of people or the world population as a whole (i.e., the effects of global warming, global financial collapse, nuclear war, etc.). If trust can be seen as a response to either the "contingent actions of others" (Sztompka 1999:41) or the global dangers confronted by all humankind, then we must acknowledge Giddens' (1990) basic assertion that trust is always intertwined with risk.

Intimacy, Trust and Reflexive Community

Although Giddens stresses that trust in impersonal principles and anonymous others is a necessary part of everyday life in late modernity, he acknowledges that this is connected to a deficit of "basic" trust: "There is a strong psychological need to find others to trust," but the institutions from earlier historical periods that provided such opportunities no longer exist (1990:120). However, the personal realm is not merely overwhelmed by the impersonally organized systems of modern society; it is transformed by them because "Personal life and the social ties it involves [have become] deeply intertwined with the most far-reaching of abstract systems" (Giddens 1990:120–121).

In describing the transformation of personal life by the globalizing forces of late modernity, Giddens focuses on two primary domains of personal relations—friendship and erotic relationships. While friendship existed in the pre-modern world, its highly institutionalized form bears little resemblance to modern friendship. Pre-modern friendship served the practical purposes of creating alliances against mutual enemies or allowing groups to pursue risky endeavors when manpower requirements could not be fulfilled by local kinship or community networks. In contrast, modern friendship is primarily focused on the emotional needs of individuals, the intent of which is to create an experience of emotional intimacy. The same can be said about modern erotic relationships. Although the emotions of an erotic/love relationship are typically more intense than emotions tied to friendship, both types of relationship are rooted in a commitment to the emotional well-being of the two individuals.

The transformation of friendship and erotic relations in late modernity has also reshaped the character of personal trust. When trust could no longer be directed to personal relations within the local community and kinship networks and shifted to relations between friends and lovers, trust became much more "active" in nature. That is, trust is not merely pre-given; it is something that must be actively created by both parties. Moreover, one of the most important aspects of the "work" that is done in generating personal trust is the *mutual process of self-disclosure*. Referring specifically to erotic relations, Giddens highlights the importance in love relationships of pursuing a progressive path of mutual discovery, in which "a process of self-realization on the part of the lover is as much a part of the experience as increasing intimacy with the loved one. Personal trust, therefore, has to be established through the process of self-inquiry: the discovery of oneself becomes a project directly involved with the reflexivity of modernity" (1990:122).

Finally, to complete the discussion of the theoretical framework guiding our analysis of the BJJ phenomenon, we turn to the concept of *reflexive community*. While this concept is generally compatible with the ideas previously discussed, it is not a formal part of Giddens' theoretical framework. Indeed, it is an idea that was introduced as part of Scott Lash's *critique* of a general perspective on late modernity that Giddens shares with the German theorist Ulrich Beck (see Beck, Giddens, and Lash 1994). As we will see, the idea of reflexive community can be usefully applied to important aspects of the BJJ movement.

Lash's reflections on the work of Giddens and Beck relate to his analysis of the experience of the "we" in late modernity, which is stimulated by key deficit he finds in the general perspective they share. He points out that the emphasis on the "individualization process" in this perspective seems to ignore ample evidence of a repressed "we" expressed in the patterns of ethnic cleansing and the "emergent 'neo-tribalism' and ethnocentrism of ethical-aesthetic communities" in recent decades (1994:111, 143). These patterns indicate that the individualization process has by no means eliminated the phenomenon of community, although it is possible that the ontological foundations of community life have shifted. Lash introduces the idea of *reflexive community* to capture this trend: "if we are 'thrown' into the collective meanings and practices of the being-in-the-world of simple community, we reflexively 'throw ourselves' into the communal world of youth subculture, as we decide to become involved in, or even with others come to have a hand in creating them" (1994:147). Even if subcultures in the late modern era are reflexive because they are selected and/or created by their members, they still offer their members a sense of community because they involved shared embodied practices and products on many different levels.

In a further development of his ideas on reflexive community, Lash explores Pierre Bourdieu's approach to reflexivity in order to identify the sources of the "we" that are most difficult to observe. In Bourdieu's conceptualization, reflexivity refers to the systematic uncovering of the "unthought categories," which consist of predispositions, orientations, and habits that are deeply inscribed in the body, making up a shared "habitus" of routine practices and background activities. Elements of habitus are "the learned, yet unthought, techniques of the body—such as swimming, ways of walking, playing tennis—which [are also] foundational for conscious conduct" (1994:155). Thus, the creation of reflexive communities can be regarded as another domain of personal relations comparable to friendship and erotic relations but different from these forms because they are rooted in the experience of the communal "we" as opposed to the individualistically-oriented dyad. However, even with this important distinction, trust assumes the same character in reflexive communities as it does in friendship and love dyads: trust is a project, something to be *worked on* and *won* through a process of collective self-disclosure (that may be either verbal or performative) and ultimately intertwined with a shared program of self-realization and self-discovery on the part of all participants.

Method and Data

The BJJ community is best viewed as a core of dedicated practitioners with varying levels of technical expertise that is surrounded by a transient periphery. While the boundaries between the core and periphery are permeable, with more people in the periphery than the core, we defined the core as anyone with more than a year of steady practice (typically an advanced white belt, or beginning blue belt). These core members see themselves as having undergone an intense rite of passage to achieve their status in the gym's hierarchy, are versed in the subculture of BJJ, and to varying degrees, live what is termed "the BJJ lifestyle." The BJJ lifestyle is a term used within the community to describe several important practices by its members, including a commitment to training regularly, extending the lessons (and values of BJJ) to areas of life outside the gym, eating properly, and being a good representative of the sport (e.g., using one's fighting skills only for self-defense).

As we talked to participants, it became clear that the core members had the experience, knowledge, and insight to speak directly to the normative values, practices, and rituals that define the community. After preliminary observations and exploratory conversations with the members of the gym, we conducted semi-structured interviews with twenty of them over a six-month period.

We conducted most of the fieldwork for our study at a single gym, and all but four of those we interviewed trained there full-time. People we interviewed trained two to three times per week, and self-described as being "serious" about pursuing their personal goals in BJJ. While all of the participants we interviewed had been training regularly for at least one year, some had more than ten years of experience.

The members in the gym we interviewed were diverse in terms of their educational attainment, socioeconomic status, and age, but fairly homogenous in terms of ethnicity and sex. For example, at least three members of the gym who we interviewed had achieved an advanced degree (two master's, and one J.D.). Socioeconomic class ranged from traditional blue-collar working class (e.g., construction worker) to an attorney. The age range for those we interviewed was twenty-four to forty-nine.

Our sample was not diverse in terms of ethnicity or sex (e.g., we were only able to interview five females, and three Latinos). Given that the current literature on mixed martial arts (MMA) and BJJ is largely ethnographic, it is difficult to make strong claims about the characteristics of the population of practitioners. At the same time, the first author has trained at several gyms throughout the Midwest, noting the predominance of whites and males at these gyms (even in communities that are more ethnically diverse). Finally, it appears that the population in the gym we studied is similar to those described in other ethnographic studies of mixed martial artists (Abramson and Modzelewski 2011; Downey 2007; Green 2011; Spencer 2009; Vacarro, Schroke, and McCabe 2011).

In addition to the data gathered from our interviews, we also draw on observational field notes, as well as the first author's experiences participating in BJJ for the past six years. In order to maintain confidentiality, we have replaced the names of all participants—either from field notes or interviews—with pseudonyms.

The Gym as Reflective Community

> *"I think that jujitsu provides many things that are lacking for modern humans ... jujitsu creates communities that are very rare to find in modern life."*
>
> —*Brian*

The core members of the gym share a deep sense of reflexive community, as being part of something larger and more intimate like a "family," or "tribe." Such references to familial ties are common within the larger BJJ community. For example, the slogan for Gracie Barra, which is a BJJ affiliation that traces its origins to Carlos Gracie, Jr., is, "organized like a team, fighting like a family." Other affiliations have similar slogans that emphasize familial identity like "Team Carlson Gracie," or "Team Brasa." Many within the BJJ community can trace the lineage of their academy affiliation to Helio and Carlson Gracie who are credited with creating BJJ after studying under the Japanese Judoka Mitsuyo Maeda (Peligro 2003). Some practitioners note with pride their black belt instructor's place in the "Gracie family" lineage. Given the role that Helio and Carlson Gracie played in the development of BJJ, it is common to see pictures of them in gyms, with some teams respectfully bowing to them before and after class (as was the case in the gym we studied). This shared sense of obligation and inheritance with the past is important part of the subculture of BJJ.

Gym affiliation and lineage can be the source of conflict (e.g., some members of one affiliation leaving a gym to start their own). However, there is a broad sense of shared experiential identity within the BJJ community that transcends gym affiliation. As one member who had been practicing BJJ for the past five years put it, "Every time I meet someone from another academy [who is also a purple belt], I feel like I know him because we've been through the same things to get where we're at." Even though instructors at gyms under different affiliations may emphasize preferred types of techniques or styles of BJJ, the years of intense physical training and technical expertise necessary to be promoted to an intermediate belt like purple creates a bond across gyms. As such, those who practice BJJ see themselves as members of both a local and global community. Brianna, an advanced white belt, put it this way: "We all come from different backgrounds. Whatever our jobs are, whatever our race is, whatever our background is, when we get on that mat, we are all one person. We are all the same, and you feel like a family down there."

These ties to the larger BJJ community can be expressed in a variety of physical, material, and cultural forms. Physically, for example, it is common for someone who has practiced BJJ for several years to develop permanent features like "cauliflower ears" or joint disfiguration in their hands. Cauliflower ear, as it is commonly called, results from blunt trauma to the outer ear that produces severe swelling. Left untreated, such swelling creates intense pain and pressure in the ear, which might burst. Even after draining, such swelling produces lumps in the outer that look like cauliflower. Practicing BJJJ can also be particularly hard on one's finger joints, given the amount of pulling and grasping of the gi (i.e., uniform that is typically made from heavy cotton). Physical features like cauliflower ears are recognized within the community as markers of experience and credibility, and someone who has "spent time on the mats." While material objects like t-shirts, gis, or cultural references like BJJ-specific lingo can be adopted by anyone, the physical markers—and the mat time they represent—are viewed by core members as being "real" symbols of commitment to the sport. As one experienced member of the gym put it when a new member came to class showing off his new gi, "that thing isn't going to make your jujitsu any better."

The corporeal demands of BJJ eventually discourage those who join as consumers of popular culture, seeking only to identify themselves with the cultural popularity of BJJ or MMA. As the owner of the gym told the first author one day, "I started this gym almost eight years ago. I have a stack of liability waivers that's nearly two inches thick. It's amazing how many people have joined this gym and quit within the first six months." Unlike some other communities in late modern society, one cannot simply become a core member of the BJJ community based on the consumption of cultural markers like t-shirts alone.

While there are several important cultural symbols and markers that define the BJJ community as reflexive, we have chosen to focus on the corporeal (i.e., habitus) and material (e.g., the physical space in which that habitus formed) arenas in which projects of trust are undertaken. Our contention is that the corporeal and material sites in which BJJ is practiced are the defining features of this reflexive community, and it is only within the embodied practice of BJJ that one can develop the trust that is required in to minimize (but not eliminate) the risk of serious injury. Avoiding the risk of serious injury, in turn, is necessary for practitioners so that they may continue developing the habitus that is necessary to become more skilled, and thus provides the very foundation for the reflexive community itself.

On the Mats

The primary requisites for a BJJ gym are mats to train on, a qualified instructor, and good training partners. Since BJJ is a grappling-based martial art where practitioners spend a lot of time perfecting their skills in ground fighting, the mats provide protection against bruises, scrapes, and other injuries that might occur from practicing on a hard surface. The sites of intense physical effort, it is also important to keep the mats clean to protect practitioners from debris that might fall from dirty shoes, as well as any bacteria or fungi. Once entered into a gym, bacteria like anti-biotic resistant staph can spread quickly, posing serious risk to everyone in the community. Because of this, practitioners enter the mats barefoot, leaving their shoes (or sandals) on the floor at the edge. Keeping the mats clean is a commonly shared goal by members of the core, and they are quick to admonish newcomers (or visitors) to remove their shoes before entering the mats.

The mats themselves are both a real and symbolic border between the "outside" world and the "inner" world of the reflexive community. Bowing before and after leaving the mats is an important practice that reinforces the idea that one is making a transition from one world to the other. Several students we talked to referred to the mats as possessing a sacred quality, referring to them as a "sanctuary." One member referred to the mats as "his church," noting, "some people go to church to find religion, but I come here."

Developing Habitus Within a Reflexive Community

After a period of warming up with calisthenics and other exercises, most classes are structured the same way: instruction, drilling, and rolling. During instruction, the head instructor—who is most often a black belt—shows the class one or two techniques by demonstrating them with a volunteer from the class. The technique is shown to the class in both words and movement, and often times the instructor will add verbal details to emphasize the importance of particular body movements (e.g., "when doing this choke, you want to place your hand here, so it cuts off the flow of blood to the brain"). Since BJJ relies heavily on developing the sensory feel of subtle details like hand placement when choking, it is sometimes difficult to convey techniques in words. If the technique is particularly dangerous, which means there is little room for error in not causing injury, the instructor will admonish the inexperienced students in the class to be careful when practicing with their partners. Students then pair up to "drill" (i.e., repetitively practice) the technique with each other.

The practice of BJJ relies on specific body movements and mechanics, and most members believe that drilling is an important way to create the "muscle memory" that is necessary to learn the technique. There is no argument that one's path to developing the BJJ habitus begins with basic large motor skills that every student learns on the first day of class (e.g., the "hip escape"). At he same time, the value of drilling likely lies in its role in creating—through continuous repetition and feedback—the development of the habitus that is an essential element to making the practitioner a trusted training partner. As Hogeveen (2014) writes, technical proficiency in BJJ requires learning "the fine gradations of feel and leverage that render the technique effective and efficient" (p. 81). He goes on to note that because such feel and leverage are invisible (and are often difficult to put into words), they must be "discerned through a body that is acting and reacting to stimulus" (Hogeveen 2014:81). While drilling is a potentially dangerous activity that is important to developing both habitus and projects of trust, our focus here is on sparring itself.

Rolling and Projects of Trust

Like the practice of drilling, students are left to pair up during the live rolling portion of class, and it is possible for new members to spar with advanced belts during this time. While the social, corporeal, and behavioral dynamics that regulate the interactions between advanced students and beginners provide unique insight into the difficult path one must take to develop the habitus of a core member, our focus in this essay lies primarily with the role that trust plays in the interactions of core members. At the same time core members relish the opportunity to roll, they also recognize that rolling increases their risk of injury. As we discuss later, this paradox is one that lies at the core of developing trust amongst serious participants within this reflexive community.

Most intermediate and advanced practitioners view the rolling portion of class as enjoyable and rewarding, largely because they see rolling as an opportunity to practice techniques with partners who are actively trying to resist them. "Catching" an accomplished peer (or even senior belt) with a submission—particularly one that's been learned recently, or one that is considered "advanced"—is especially valued. Even so, these practitioners understand that their safety (and the safety of their partners) is more important than catching a submission, and it would be difficult to find a serious member of the BJJ community who would knowingly injure his or her training partners.

Nevertheless, John Danaher (2014), a BJJ black belt who has also earned a Ph.D. in philosophy from Columbia University, has referred to BJJ as an embodied "zero sum game" where "the way to achieve victory is to solve the problems [created by your partner] more rapidly and efficiently than they can create them for you." Like Danaher, many within the BJJ community view rolling as a richly complex and embodied game of chess that contains an extraordinary number of moves and countermoves. Like chess players, BJJ practitioners have a deep understanding of the "game," a large repertoire of "moves," and strategies they employ in pursuit of their goals. Thus, while no serious practitioner would consciously seek injure a training partner, only one person can win.

On the surface, the reasons for not wanting to injure training partners might seem obvious, but the deeper significance of such concern is tied to the role that trust plays in this reflexive enterprise. For example, core members who view their participation in BJJ as part of a larger project of self-improvement recognize that the only way to become better at BJJ is to spend time on the mats drilling and rolling. Injuries are viewed as obstacles to mat time, and practitioners want to avoid them for that reason. Relatedly, they also understand that developing the reputation as someone who injures their training partners will make them a less desirable partner, which will in turn limit their own progress. As Dennis, a blue belt with three years of experience put it, "if you're unsafe and people can't trust you, they won't roll with you. That's not good, because you're not going to get any better if nobody rolls with you."

Beneath this layer of self-interest, however, lies yet another important dimension of the corporeal experience of BJJ that comes from mastering the embodied techniques that are used when rolling. As mentioned earlier, skilled practitioners do not "think" their way through submissions. Rather, they use subtle physical cues to apply the submission, subsequently communicating important information to their partner. For example, the casual observer who sees an experienced practitioner tapping out to another experienced practitioner might believe that the cause of the submission is that he or she is in pain (or injured), but that is rarely the case. Rather, experienced practitioners understand what is happening to them and believe they have no option to escape the submission before an injury occurs. Likewise, an experienced practitioner will stop applying a submission before their partner is injured, unless they believe their partner understands what is happening well enough to be consenting (by not tapping out) to whatever pain or injury follows.

Tapping out is a form of self-disclosure wherein one person admits they "cannot solve" the problem at hand, and understand the risk of injury that will follow from denying it. Admitting that one lacks the skill to avoid or escape a submission can be emotionally charged. Advanced practitioners, therefore, talk frequently about the importance of "leaving one's ego at the door" when rolling, emphasizing that getting tapped out is an important part of the learning process. Mutually invested in such a project of personal growth and self-discovery, such reciprocal understanding between training partners is essential to the development of trust within the community.

The development of the habitus necessary to become a proficient practitioner of BJJ presents an opportunity to build trust that reduces (but doesn't entirely eliminate) risk of injury when rolling. Becoming a trusted rolling partner is an achieved status that emerges only from the continued development of habitus within a community of other like-minded practitioners who are also attempting to navigate similar physical and emotional risks. Such trust lies in a mutual understanding of the physical cues that are used to communicate risk and danger (e.g., submissions), and the reciprocal understanding that each partner has a responsibility to be in control of their own bodies (Danaher 2014). The failure to develop the requisite habitus to perform techniques safely, and the inability to control a natural impulse in such a situation (like exploding out of the technique) can exponentially increase the odds of injury. Most often, the person who is injured in training is the one who fails to understand the physical risk either they, or their partner, has been placed in.

To illustrate this point, many advanced practitioners are careful not to apply advanced submissions like heel hooks on beginners because beginners are likely to injure themselves trying to escape. Because beginners do not understand the biomechanical disadvantage they have been placed in, and the potential for serious injury, they might simply "explode" out of such a submission. The problem, however, is that using non-technical and explosive movements are rarely the best answer "to the problem that's being posed to them," to paraphrase Danaher (2014).

Advanced practitioners, on the other hand, solve such problems using technical competence embedded in habitus. Reading the patterns of movement, leverage, pressure, and contact of their partner, such players can quickly sense whether the person might move explosively (therefore identifying themselves as not being trustworthy). Trustworthy partners are also capable of sending clear indicators to their partners: i.e., "I have the technical answer to the problem you're trying to pose to me." One develops this ability to trust another practitioner in much in the same way they develop the physical habitus that allows them to not "think" about their movements. As such, the project of trust is deeply intertwined and embedded within the project of habitus, developing at the site of intense physicality between similarly motivated participants.

Conclusion

> *"I think that another thing that jujitsu adds for me specifically is that in life it's very difficult to see progression. I think that most people go to their job and they put in their 40 hours a week, and they hold their little stick, and push their little button, and it's just the same stuff over and over again. And it's difficult to see one's development, right? In jujitsu, and for me specifically, it's useful to see my own progression, to see that I am a better jujitsu player today than I was a year ago."*
>
> *—Brian*

Giddens (1990) and others have argued that late modern society is characterized by risk and uncertainty. While it would seem paradoxical for people under such circumstances to join communities that might increase their level of risk, it is very likely that participation in reflexive communities like BJJ offer a significant outlet to better navigate a world filled with the risks imposed by abstract systems. Indeed, many of the participants in our study talked about how their participation in BJJ has helped them in all areas of life, from marital problems to home foreclosure. As one participant noted, "if you can handle the stress of someone trying to choke you unconscious, you can handle anything life throws at you." Thus, while very few of the practitioners we talked to had used their fighting skills outside the gym, they universally agreed that the habitus they had developed in BJJ had increased their ability to handle the contingencies of modern life.

While the skills themselves were important to practitioners, equally important were the development of those skills within the reflexive community. The idea of a future self that was more competent as a BJJ practitioner (and that such competence is measured "honestly" on the mats) can be seen in sentiments of Dennis who said, "The mats don't lie. There's nowhere to hide on the mats. Either your jujitsu works, or it doesn't."

We suggest that the habitus required to deal with such risk is developed within a reflexive community that is bound together by mutually reinforcing projects of trust that are necessary to propel participants forward. As Crawford (2015) has noted, projects of self-improvement that involve the development of skills that are not easy to master are necessary to what he terms "a life of flourishing." The co-presence of social actors engaged such practices who are attending to projects while participating in a potentially dangerous activity likely represents an intensely rewarding feature of the community itself. While it is necessary to examine other sports that contain the potential for significant injury in this light, we believe such lines of inquiry might add significant insight to the literature on risk taking more generally.

Bibliography

Abramson, Corey M., and Darren Modzelewski. 2011. "Caged Morality: Moral Worlds, Subculture, and Stratification Among Middle-Class Cage Fighters." *Qualitative Sociology*, 34:143–175.

Barber, Bernard. 1983. *The Logic and Limits of Trust*. New Brunswick: Rutgers University Press.

Beck, Ulrich, Anthony Giddens, and Scott Lash. 1994. *Reflexive Modernization: Politics, Tradition, and Aesthetics in the Modern Social Order*. Stanford: Stanford University Press.

Crawford, Matthew. 2015. *The World Beyond Your Head: On Becoming an Individual in the Age of Distraction*. New York: Farrar, Straus, and Giroux.

Danaher, John. 2014. Control (9 to Fight). https://www.youtube.com/.

Downey, Greg. 2007. "Producing Pain: Techniques and Technologies in No-Holds Barred Fighting." *Social Studies of Science*, 37 (2):201–226.

Garcia, Raul Sanchez, and Dale C. Spencer, eds. 2014. *Fighting Scholars: Habitus and Ethnographies of Martial Arts and Combat Sports*. New York: Anthem Press.
Giddens, Anthony. 1990. *The Consequences of Modernity*. Stanford: Stanford University Press.
Giddens, Anthony. 1986. *The Constitution of Society: An Outline of the Theory of Structuration*. Berkeley: University of California Press.
Green, Kyle. 2011. "It Hurts So It Is Real: Sensing the Seduction of Mixed Martial Arts." *Social and Cultural Geography*, 12 (4): 377–396.
Hebdige, Dick. 1979. *Subculture: The Meaning of Style*. London: Methuen.
Hoffman, Steve G. 2006. "How to Punch Someone and Stay Friends: An Inductive Theory of Simulation." *Sociological Theory*, 24 (2):170–193.
Hogeveen, Bryan. 2014. "It is About Your Body Recognizing the Move and Automatically Doing it: Merleau-Ponty, Habit and Brazilian Jiu-jitsu," pp. 79–94 in *Fighting Scholars: Habitus and Ethnographies of Martial Arts and Combat Sports*, edited by R.S. Garcia and D.C. Spencer. New York: Anthem Press.
Lash, Scott. 1994. "Reflexivity and its Doubles: Structure, Aesthetics, Community," pp. 110–73 in *Reflexive Modernization: Politics, Tradition, and Aesthetics in the Modern Social Order*, edited by U. Beck, A. Giddens and S. Lash. Stanford: Stanford University Press.
Lewis, David J., and Andrew Weigert. 1985. "Trust as a Social Reality." *Social Forces*, 63 (4):967–985.
Luhmann, Niklas. 1979. *Trust and Power*. Hoboken, NJ: Wiley.
Peligro, Kid. 2003. *The Gracie Way: An Illustrated History of the World's Greatest Martial Arts Family*. Montpelier: Invisible Cities Press.
Seligman, Adam B. 2000. *The Problem of Trust*. Princeton: Princeton University Press.
Spencer, Dale. 2009. "Habit(us), Body Techniques and Body Callusing: An Ethnography of Mixed Martial Arts." *Body and Society* 15(4):119–143.
Sztompka, Piotr. 1999. *Trust: A Sociological Theory*. Cambridge: Cambridge University Press.
Vacarro, Christian A., Douglas P. Schroke, and Janice M. McCabe. 2011. "Managing Manhood: Fighting and Fostering Fear in Mixed Martial Arts." *Social Psychology Quarterly* 74 (4):414–437.
Wacquant, Loic. 2004. *Body & Soul: Notebooks of an Apprentice Boxer*. New York: Oxford University Press.
_____. 2005. "Carnal Connections: On Embodiment, Membership and Apprenticeship." *Qualitative Sociology*, 28 (4):445–74.

Part C

Sportsmanship and Social Institutions

Social institutions are forms of organizations that perform basic functions in a society and are strongly supported by a society's culture. Social institutions include, among others, gender, race/ethnicity, economics, commercialization, sports journalism and social media. Thus, social institutions are not buildings or places but rather structures of relationships, roles, obligations, entities that reinforce cultural values, norms and social expectations.

While most previous essays contained influences from social institutions on the sportsmanship ideal, the essays in this section address such specific social institutions as gender, race, economics, sports journalism, and social media.

Man Up?
Gender and Sportsmanship On and Off the Field

EVELYN A. CLARK

In the climatic scene of Pixar's *Cars* (2006) we see the hero, "Lightening McQueen," give up the chance to win the coveted "Piston Cup" in order to help a fellow retiring racer who was pushed off the road by his nemesis, "Chip Hicks." Hicks and McQueen represent two types of sportsman, both striving to become the best but taking very different routes to become champion. Although both characters embrace traditional characteristics of American masculinity, Hicks uses brute force and underhanded techniques to get to the top. McQueen on the other hand, uses pure skill, ingenuity, and intelligence, and through the course of the film learns to use cooperation as the road to success. In the climax, the audience, both within and outside the film, is meant not only to respect but to be moved by McQueen for his incredible display of sportsmanship. Therefore, while he wins the race, Hicks is really declared the loser as he is unceremoniously thrown his cup while the camera and our attention reverts to our hero McQueen, who has learned the real meaning of sportsmanship and the love of racing. In addition to celebrating sportsmanship, *Cars* explored the world of racing, demonstrating notions of masculinity, competitiveness, community, and friendship. Sports, in this case racing, is a place where people bond; boys learn to be masculine; and, above all, that there is a proper way for winning that should not come at the expense of integrity. Cultural constructions like this film often emphasize the importance of sportsmanship in our celebration of sports. However, what we mean by sportsmanship is not easily defined; and the way in which sportsmanship shapes those who participate and which morals and behaviors it champions varies within and between cultures.

Over the past thirty years, many theorists have begun to wonder if the values of sportsmanship are being challenged or at least changed as sports becomes a business honor the idea of sportsmanship; but, perhaps like any ideal or value, notions of what constitutes fair play vary over time and space. In the past, sports and the rules of conduct and ethics associated with it were seen as a place for men. As women and other minorities became active members of the sports community the ethics of sports changed as well as notions of gender equality, fair play, and competitiveness. Throughout history, sportsmanship has been a means of distinguishing different types of athletes by promoting ethical and moral expectations among those who participate in sports. However, sportsmanship is also a means of dividing participants and limiting their access to privilege and prestige. We may reward winners and those who excel at sports, but only certain types of winners who meet up to our ideals of sportsmanship. Therefore, it is through the ideals and application of sportsmanship that society and culture often reinforce gender, class, race and sexual inequalities.

There is little doubt that sports plays an ever-increasing part of American culture and that, as an institution, its impact on defining ethics is a powerful one. Delaney and Madigan (2009a:183) argue that sportsmanship relates to "fair play, decency, respect—for oneself, the competitor, and the sport itself. Ideals of sportsmanship such as competitiveness, hard work, fair play, obedience to authority, and dedication, are tied to a society's cultural morality." Sportsmanship shapes the norms of sports and can be used to define who belongs in sports and who doesn't. Sportsmanship, like the institution of sports itself, also denotes values and norms that shape and are shaped by race, class, sexuality and gender. Therefore, by exploring how sports and sportsmanship reinforce and shape gender, we can have a better understanding of the institution and its prevailing ethics in addition to the ways in which sports impact how gender is socially constructed within our society.

Understanding Gender, Sports and Sportsmanship

> Organized Sports is a "gendered institution"—an institution constructed by gender relations. As such, its structures and values (rules, formal organization, competition, etc.) reflect dominant conceptions of masculinity and femininity. Organized sports is also a "gendering institution"—an institution that helps to construct the current gender order. Part of this construction of gender is accomplished through the "masculinizing" of male bodies and minds [Messner 1995:112].

Sport is an institution that both shapes and is shaped by gender relations within our society. In sports, boys learn how to be men, albeit a certain kind of man. Girls, on the other hand, often find themselves excluded or devalued within the institution. Although even after the 1960s with the implementation of Title IX of the Civil Rights Act which sought to give women more equal access to the world of sports, girls and women find they must adapt to new types of behaviors and values in order to succeed in the world of sports (Messner 2005). Studying sports and the ethics of the institution, thus, must include an understanding, not only of how the institution divides women and men within our society, but also of how it reinforces cultural notions of how to be men and women within the game and within the broader culture. Sociologists and feminist theorists have long distinguished between sex which include biological differences between males and females from the social construction of gender, which includes the cultural associations of roles, identity, and performances of men and women. Although men and women may have different genitalia, chromosomes, and at times, hormones, most sociologists argue society divides men and women through constructions of masculinity and femininity through socialization. One primary way men and women are socialized to be different is through sports and conceived notions of men's athletic abilities (Crawley, Foley, and Shehan 2008).

Although many critics and researchers in sports and sportsmanship have found that gender is an important dynamic in understanding who plays sports and how they behave, it is also important to include other dynamics that impact how we do gender in sports, or what distinguishes the sexes within the institution. Collins (2000) reminds us that simply discussing gender differences apart from other inequalities including class, race, and sexuality often misses the nuances of prejudice and discrimination and negates the social forces that shape peoples access to property, power and prestige. Collins and Andersen (2016) encourage us to understand not only the gains made within our society that might lead us to celebrate the end of racism, sexism, classism, etc., but also to look deeper into social relationships that divide people and how these social constructions overlap and influence each other. Because sport is an institution that not only shapes roles and relationships between men and women, it is important to understand how it impacts class, sexuality, and race/ethnicity as well. Thus, we can ask which men play and how do they behave? Which women participate and emphasize sportsmanship's ethical and behavior standards?

As sportsmanship is at heart a question of ethics and normative behavior in the context of what participants do on and off the field (Delaney and Madigan 2009a; Keating 2001), sportsmanship becomes a means of determining deviance within the institution and, at times, within a larger culture. Defining deviance within any culture is of course complicated and problematic. While in general, deviance can be viewed as a violation of a social norm, Becker (1963) argues that it isn't the act of violation itself but rather how others react to the violation that constitutes deviance. Although we often think about behaviors (women playing football or men cheerleading) as what constitutes deviance, Becker argues that any profession or status has certain characteristics associated with them that tie to individual. Therefore, people in those professions who do not have those characteristics are deviance regardless of their behavior. For example, he asks, what makes a doctor? Technically any person with a medical degree who passes the boards and gets certified would be a doctor. However, Becker notes that it isn't simply the qualification that makes someone a doctor, but that we associate doctors with other individual traits. In the 1960s it was with men, who were white, and protestant. Those who didn't have those characteristics were labeled as deviant. In this case women and men of color would not have been assumed to be competent doctors even if they did have the requisite qualifications.

In the field of sports, what characteristics do we attribute to athletes? We tend to think of men, and depending on the sport, a certain type of man. Golf is often associated with upper class men of privilege, despite its growing popularity in the 20th century (Varner and Knottnerus 2002). NASCAR racing is associated with men from lower class backgrounds, with other characteristics and lifestyles. Until the mid–20th century, sports were deemed an institution for men, so what happened to the women who entered various sports? Women athletes faced ridicule, violence, and were labeled in various ways because they were seen as invaders or usurpers in sports unless characterized as women's sports (Delaney and Madigan 2009b). Thus, women are not deviant when they participate in cheerleading, gymnastics, volleyball, etc., whereas men might be. Men who do not meet our assumptions about particular sports may also receive the deviant label (Bemiller 2009). Due to racism and perceived assumptions of racial superiority, black men were banned from baseball and boxing and still may face ridicule or violence, or at best be labeled different and unique today when participating in sports like hockey, soccer, and golf.

In terms of sportsmanship, particular ethics and behaviors seem to distinguish the game and those who play them. In addition, the term itself creates and reinforces assumptions about sex and gender. Although in English, traditionally, the term "man" has been allowed to represent both men and women in the general, this rule itself has reinforced the notion that men are the norm in society. The continued use of sportsmanship continues to reinforce traditional associations of sports as being a man's world, with certain masculine qualities. Many theorists and researchers have opted for sportspersonship as an alternative to the masculine association; however, in popular vernacular we may refer to "fair play." Yet many within the American culture continue to use "sportsmanship" to denote the ethics and proper code of conduct in the institution.

Culture and the media also reinforce gender bias by who they honor with accolades. For example, since its inception in 1954, *Sports Illustrated* has been naming a sportsman of the year. The award "honors the athlete, team coach or individual who, by virtue of performance and character on and off the field, transcended the year in sports" (SI.com 2014). In 2014, SI.com even encouraged readers to vote for the person who embodied sportsmanship for the year (SI.com Staff 2014). In the past 60 years, only eight women or women's teams have been honored with the award. Of the eight, only three, including the 1999 Women's World Cup Champion Soccer team, runner Mary Decker in 1983, and tennis champion Chris Evert in 1976, have earned the honor in their own right and not had to share with a sportsman of the year. In contrast, only eight men have had to share the title with either a sportswoman or other sportsman (SI.com 2014). ESPN is much more equitable in its awards for top athletes as it recognizes outstanding athletes for both men and women equally in a variety of categories.

Gender and Sports

> Sport, then, is a site in which the performance and surveillance of masculinity and femininity are rampant. And, we argue, a site where gender becomes "real"—that is, where male-bodied people are encouraged far more than female-bodied people to perform and learn bodily competence and as a result, where men are more likely to feel and become larger, more competent, and expectant that they can use their bodies to accomplish goals [Crawley et al. 2008:57].

Sport since the 20th century is one of the main institutions where boys and men learn masculinity (Connell 1990; Kimmel 1990; Messner 2005). Much of masculinity as noted above is related to the body. Boys learn to be strong and to push their physical abilities (Connell 1990). Boys are also taught not to be girls. According to Kimmel (1990), teaching masculinity became harder to do in industrial, modern societies due to the changing nature of work because of machines and the introduction of women into the productive labor force. Thus, displaying masculinity through strength and economic success became less important, and sports and athletics became a new way for middle-class men to demonstrate their masculinity. The construction of masculinity in modern day sports, however, is complex. Emphasis on body and performance often associate masculinity with violence, heterosexuality, and above all distinction from femininity of any kind. Nevertheless, while still promoting male dominance and privilege, there are contradictions within these constructions which continually face challenges from women and minority men (Messner 2005). Boys in sports are often told not to cry, or to throw like a girl, and to man-up. In addition, men's masculinity is proven by good performance, trying hard, and above all through sportsmanship.

Sports often not only separate men from women but from other men as well. Nineteenth century sports were introduced into British schools in order to separate the nobility from the common men of the society as well as from native men in British Colonies (Mangan and Walvin 1986). In the United States, organized sports emerged at a time when, not only was there a fear of the "feminization of society," but also when middle-class men held racist fears and sought to distinguish themselves from both women and incoming immigrants (Kimmel 1987, 1990; Crosset 1990). In addition, sports become dominated by anti-gay sentiment. However, as notions of masculinity change, which masculinities are valued changes as well. Despite growing acceptance of racial equality and homosexuality in American culture, hegemonic notions of masculinity continue to promote racial and sexual inequalities (Messner 2005).

Ferber (2016) notes that while sport is an institution where racial minorities, African American men in particular, have been able to find equality of participation and success, the ways in which the media portray black athletes, the lack of access to positions of power, and the emphasis on racial myths continue to reinforce racial inequality within our society. Black athletes are often associated with their "natural" ability as opposed to their intelligence or willingness to cooperate (Coakley 2006). For example, in many sports commentaries black athletes are described as "athletic" with "natural talent" whereas white players are often described as "intelligent" players. Black athletes' bodies and abilities are admired by the culture at large but only when they are in the positions of less power and are being adequately controlled by white coaches and managers (Collins 2005). Thus, while sports represents a place where various types of men can participate, certain men are rewarded by positions of power over the rest, and we continue to find racial divisions between participants.

Traditionally, sports has been an institution for men where both biological and social associations discouraged women's participation either because it would make them less feminine or women's biology made them incapable of playing sports well (Delaney and Madigan 2009b; Morgan, Meier, and Schneider 2001). Throughout Western history, although limited and controlled, women have participated in sports including their own games in early Olympics to honor Hera, horseback riding, dancing, skating and eventually bicycling, bowling and baseball (Delaney and Madigan 2009b). In all cases, women were expected to wear particular clothes, behave in feminine ways, and not become too masculine (Sabo 1985). Prior to the 20th century, sports became increasingly important for both men and women to distinguish themselves in the elite classes by playing particular sports that stressed the dominant values of the upper classes and events that allowed for socialization of the right people (Stanley 1996). Whereas men were pushed to prove their masculinity through competition, women, on the other hand, were meant to ensure that they remained feminine (Sabo 1985).

Since the mid–20th century, concerted efforts have been made to include women's sports and include women athletes. Starting in the early 1900s, women's athletic organizations flourished and international competitions including the Olympics in 1912 began to promote women's sports. Attitudes and acceptance of female athletes became the norm in Western countries like England and the United States. Moreover, in the United States starting in the 1970s new concerted efforts began to promote equality within sports. First, Title IX pushed equal access and participation for women in collegiate sports. Second, there were already Female "trailblazers" who were already competing and excelling in sports. Hence there was an explosion of the number of girls and women competing in sports in all levels (Delaney and Madigan 2009b). However, many researchers have found that despite growing numbers participating sports, they still face discrimination. Their sports continue to be devalued; and they continue to face obstacles for success in their sports (Crawley et al. 2008; Messner 2005).

If indeed, it is men who are *sportsmen*, what happens to women who enter this arena? Although attitudes now recognize women's sports as legitimate and see the benefits of sports for women, women athletes still can be labeled deviant, especially if they compete in male-dominated fields. How do we label female athletes? Well of course it depends on the sport. Sports like figure skating and gymnastics tend to emphasize skills that are traditionally defined as feminine. Girls, however, who play football, hockey, or basketball may be labeled deviant as they exhibit talents and skills that are too closely related to more traditionally defined masculine qualities (Mesner 2005). Since the 1970s, two trends regarding women who compete in male-dominated sports have occurred: often their gender and even their sex get challenged or they are perceived as being homosexual. Women continue today to be labeled either for playing the wrong sport or being too good at sports. What happens to them once they are labeled? As deviants, Becker (1963) argues that they will be seen as something different and suffer stigma and isolation. In some cases, they face violence. This is especially true for women who enter sports designated as men's. Kathrine Switzer was the first women in 1967 to register for and finish the Boston Marathon. Although she started the race with lots of encouragement from other male participants, she met hostility and resistance and she was physically accosted and attacked during the race (Switzer 2007).

If women participate in sports, they are often considered unfeminine. But if individual women tend to be good, or even better than men, then we not only question their femininity but whether they are women at all. Although tennis is not necessarily considered a male sport, female tennis stars often face labeling when they excel. For example, Serena Williams faced rumors of being a man early in her career due to her success in both singles and doubles tennis. Both she and her sister got media attention when the head of the Russian Tennis Federation referred to them as the "Williams Bothers and scary to look at." Although Tarpischev was condemned by the community and suspended and fined by World Tennis Association (WTA), media attention served as a means to shame and delegitimize the tennis stars (Associated Press 2014). While the culture of sports celebrates winning for men, the implication for women is that if they are too good they must be men. Brittney Griner is one of the country's best basketball players. In 2012, she led Baylor to an undefeated season and won the Women's NCAA championship. She not only was voted the most valuable player in college basketball but was also recognized with LeBron James as the athlete of the year by ESPN. With that of course came rumors that she is actually a man that got so persistent they were denounced in public by her coach (Associated Press 2012).

In addition to their gender and sex coming into question, women find their sexuality is defined by the labeling process. Women athletes oftentimes are assumed to be homosexual, especially if they play on team sports. Often when both men and women within our culture violate gender roles their sexuality is also questioned. Thus women are labeled butch or lesbians (Blinde and Taub 1992; Lenskyj 1990). Although there have been significant gains made by gays and lesbians within our culture, it is still considered a deviant label that receives a stigma, discrimination, and often violence at one end, if not morbid curiosity at the other (Pharr 1988; Lenskyj 1991). Men in female-dominated sports like ice-skating and cheerleading often face this as well (Bemiller 2009). We often see such men assumed to be gay. Studies on both women and men have found that they will change their behaviors both during play and off the field to counter the homosexual label. This includes having multiple sexual partners and using homophobic language and jokes to prove their heterosexuality (Bemiller 2009; Blinde and Taub 2009). Women on teams find that the label prevents them from bonding with teammates because close friendships would confirm the homosexual label.

As a result of this labeling process within the media and sports arena, women athletes lose out on many of the benefits of sports participation. Sports offers athletes the chance of empowerment through creativity and physicality. We think of men as champions and heroes. Women athletes may fear success and hence may not try as hard. Physicality is another benefit not only in terms of health but also appearance. Exercise and sports are ways to gain strength and self-esteem (Theberge 1987; Birell 1988). These are often denied to women since when they succeed they are labeled deviant. In addition, team sports offer men chances of bonding with teammates. These are important friendships and bonds that improve social and physical abilities for those who participate (Cobban 1982). Because of the deviant label, female athletes may choose to forgo these benefits.

Gender and Sportsmanship

Sportsmanship emerges as a way to distinguish between men on class and race. Brute force and winning at all costs became devalued in favor of a sense of civility. In Western sports, this began as early as the 12th century and continued as the nobility emphasized leisure activities to distinguish between themselves and commoners (Delaney and Madigan 2009b). Civility in sports emphasized particular behavior associated with the upper classes, including a strong sense of controlled behavior and decorum in all circumstances and an absence of uncontrolled violent behavior (Varner and Knottnerus 2002). Slowly over time sportsmanship included not only proper behavior but strict guidelines and penalties for misbehavior even by the sports of the masses. By the 20th century most sports are civilized in "adhering to a set of written rules, established sanctions for violating the rules, referees and officials to enforce the code of conduct specific to each sport, and a governing body to oversee the entire process" (Delaney and Madigan 2009a:195). The amount of control over behavior of participants and spectators of sports varies and often continues to reinforce class differences (Delaney and Madigan 2009b; Varner and Knottnerus 2002).

Research for the past thirty years also emphasizes that senses of fair play and sportsmanship are being challenged by values of winning and the growing industry of the sports as a business (Bockrath and Franke 1995; Grough 1997). Many argue that "winner takes all" and the financial and cultural awards of sports beginning in the past thirty years have started to challenge older notions of sportsmanship which emphasized fair play and adhering to the rules as being as important as finishing first. Athletes, managers, and coaches are under more pressure to win and earn big bonuses or lose jobs on performance and the ability to win championships (Volkwein 1995). Pressure to cheat, to push rule limits in hopes of not getting caught, to take steroids, and at times, to lie about the age of participants to enhance a team's performance are all common in sports and violate the rules and norms of competition (Delaney and Madigan 2009b). The goals of sportsmanship and wining at all costs are contradictory and require participants to juggle between playing by the rules and playing to win. This becomes especially hard on some male athletes as so much of their identity is encompassed by both ideals. Buford Mae (2001) found that the male, African American high school basketball players must define and negotiate this paradox within particular games and contexts depending on where they play and whom. Racism and classism, whether perceived or real, within the context of the game impacted how the players defined what good sportsmanship is and how they behaved in each game. Class, race, and gender intersect in the sense that at times we value winners but only certain types of winners, and sportsmanship matters only in the context of who is the sportsman.

Sportsmanship can also be a means of reinforcing racial stereotypes and racism especially in the media (Ferber 2016; Coakley 2006). Collins (2005) argues that there is a racial component to the ways in which the media portrays African American male athletes. Traditionally, black men have found themselves depicted as overly sexual, violent, and in need of control. In sports we see the emergence of the "bad boy" athlete who flouts the rules of sportsmanship. Often they are portrayed as disrespectful, not coachable and sometimes violent. Media disproportionately cover when these athletes are arrested for violent or sexual assaults over the white male athletes and contribute to emphasizing some of these athletes that the public "love to hate." Nevertheless, research finds that white athletes are just as likely to commit violent and sexual assaults as minority athletes (Collins 2005; Messner 2005). Figures like Charles Barkley, Dennis Rodman, and Barry Bonds all seem to be portrayed as athletic but are not sportsman in the ethical or moral sense of the word.

In addition to separating men by class and race, Messner (1995) notes that sportsmanship is important in the construction of masculinity because it provides a way to distinguish men from femininity as connected to intimate unity with others. "The rule-bound, competitive, hierarchal world of sports offers boys an attractive means of establishing an emotionally distant (and thus 'safe') connection with others" (p. 112). However, although we may distinguish between good sportsman (good winner, plays by the rules, etc.) as a means of elevating behaviors of certain types of men, there is an inherent contradiction. Messner continues, "Yet as boys begin to define themselves as 'athletes' they learn that in order to be accepted (to have connection) through sports, they must be winners. And in order to be winners, they must construct relationships with others (and within themselves) that are consistent with the competitive and hierarchal values and structure of the sports world" (p. 112).

Social psychologists interested in sports and morality have found consistent links with gender differences in the perception of sportsmanship behavior and values. Studies on athletes in various sports in both high school and college find that women athletes tend to score higher on moral behavioral scales (Bredemeier and Shields 1984; Kavussanu and Roberts 2001; Miller, Roberts, and Ommundsen 2005). Other studies have found that female athletes are much more likely to condemn violent, aggressive behavior in various situations as opposed to male athletes who at times might see them as legitimate behaviors (Silva 1983; Conroy et al. 2001). More recent findings also suggest that younger and female athletes are more likely to condemn cheating and more unsportsmanship behavior (Lee, Whitehead, and Ntoumanis 2007; Duda, Olson, and Themplin 1991).

Women's softball has offered two example of sportspersonship of note. The first occurred in 2008 when Division II teams Western Oregon met Central Washington in their first appearance in a NCAA, Division II doubleheader postseason conference matchup, one of the last games of the season. Senior Sara Tucholsky of Western Oregon hit the first homerun of her career in the top of the second inning with two runners on base. Tucholsky missed first base in her trot and had to double back to hit the base when her knee gave out with a torn knee ligament. Unable to finish the run around the bases to take a three run lead, coaches and umpires began working out how to avoid Tucholsky receiving an out if assisted by trainers or coaches. The rules allow for a pinch runner, but that would mean Tucholsky would be credited with a two run single instead of a three run homer. Just as coach Knox of Western Oregon was about to make the substitution, opponent Mallory Holtman, Central Washington's senior offensive star, volunteered to carry Tucholsky to allow her to keep her homerun. She and shortstop Liz Wallace carried Tucholsky around the bases to a standing ovation from the crowd. Western Oregon would go on to win the game 4–2 (Hays 2008). Almost to the day six years later, in the last matchup for the season for Division II Florida Southern College and Ekerdt College in a double header, pitcher Chelsea Oglevie would help carry her opponent Kara Oberer over the plate. Oberer was hurt earlier in the game trying to win the one game necessary to give Ekerdt its first winning season since the program started in 1985. Oberer, one of the team's strongest hitter, opted to hit in the Seventh to give the team a chance to overcome a 2–1 deficit with two runners on base. She went on to hit the home run and began to hobble to first base when Oglevie, who was pitching the last game of her career, and second baseman Leah Pemberton chose to carry her around the bases and give Ekerdt the win it needed (Hays 2014).

Recent research, however, is finding that that the relationship between gender and sportsman-like attitudes and behaviors may be overstated or diminishing. Although some previous studies did find that women athletes were more likely than men to condemn aggressive behavior in sports, Kaye and Ward (2010) found that there were no gender differences in lower moral attitudes in sports. Men were more likely to accept aggressive behavior but not because of ethical reasoning but rather because of experience with aggressive acts in sports. Indeed, when experiencing the same sport experience and socialization, it has been found that women can be as much or even more unsportsmanlike than men (Miller, Roberts, and Ommundsen 2004).

However, while there is contradictory evidence that gender impacts support of unsportsmanship behavior, rules and conduct do impact female athletes in a slightly different way than impact male athletes, related to a sense of fair play. Within the history of modern sports, the question of what makes a female athlete and its connection to cheating has made the sense of winning a problem for some female athletes From early on, successful female athletes have been challenged as being like men and have had to prove their womanhood in a variety of ways. For a sense of fair play, we have consistently needed to decide who gets to compete and what constitutes an unfair advantage. Thus very early on, sports organizations used the distinction of sex in deciding on who got to compete with each other. Can women fairly compete with men if they have perceived physical advantages? Is it fair to judge women and men equally if they are different? One way to deal with this was to establish women's teams as a way in which to reduce men's perceived physical and biological advantages. For example in tennis we get men's, women's, doubles and mixed doubles events. Title IX meant not only to promote women's opportunities in sports but to give them equal access to resources within higher education. However, once sports for men and women emerged, who is eligible to compete in these events, i.e., measuring sex, becomes a much more salient category to determine fair competition.

Throughout the history of individual events, like tennis, something emerged that highlights the complexity of sex and gender, and what really makes a man and a woman. Is it our sex organs, our hormones, chromosomes, that make us men and women? What about individuals who are innersex or have extra chromosomes? In essence, what makes you female and would some male athletes pass as women in order to win? As technology has advanced the answer to these questions has become more complex and various athletic organizations have gone to testing for chromosome, hormones, as a means of determining who is eligible to participate. Due to worries of cheating, the International Associations of Athletics Federation (IAAF) began chromosomal testing in 1950 order to determine sex. Most international competitions used similar measures starting in the 1960s when female sports became more predominate. Fueled by media accounts of men cheating by participating in women's events, the Olympics began testing in 1968 and continued for thirty years. However, due to lack of equipment and the problematic nature of this type of testing, both the Olympics IAAF have ceased using this type of determination (Elsas et al. 2000). Currently determining sex for competition is more complicated than ever. Hormonal testing is now the current practice. However, female levels of testosterone and the tests themselves seem to be as problematic at determining sex as other forms of verification. Female athletes who fail these tests are subjected to disqualification and must go through hormone replacement treatment to reenter the sport. Most female athletes report that testing is humiliating and alienating them from sports (Jordan-Young and Karkazis 2012).

On the surface, this sense of allowing for fair competition seems in line with sportsmanship and would protect both male and female athletes from cheating. However, the application of the rule gets to the hidden assumptions of both sex/gender and sportsmanship in its application. When men excel at sports, or at least when some men do, it is assumed to be a natural part of their identity. Granted some men are accused and sometimes found guilty of cheating, perhaps using steroids, to explain great performances. But what happens to women who are too good? Some may be accused of cheating and they are tested in a much more intimate way than are men. Their sex identity is questioned and tested. The assumption is that if they are really good at sports, they really aren't women and must be men in disguise (Dreger 2009).

One current example of the intersection of gender and sex played out in the London Olympic Games in 2012. The case involved runner Caster Semenaya of South Africa. In 2009, she became world champion in the 800 meters, shaving 8 seconds off her personal best and leaving the competition behind. She was then forced to submit to genetic and hormonal testing to prove her gender/sex and failed. She was banned from the IAAF for nine months afterwards (Dreger 2009). In order to compete in the 2012 Olympics she had to undergo natural testosterone testing. Experts do not agree on whether testosterone levels really determine sex or an unfair advantage in competition. However, this type of test was deemed more appropriate in determining sex then previous methods. In the past, it included making women athletes walk naked in front of a committee and chromosome testing, both of which were deemed insufficient in determining womanhood. Her results showed she did have high levels of testosterone so in order to compete she had to go through hormone replacement therapy and shaming. What is interesting is that there is no equivalent for men who compete in men's sports. Men who have natural biological enhancements such as double-jointed ankles like Michael Phelps or larger hearts like Lance Armstrong are argued to have unfair advantages in competition. But these advantages do not make them ineligible and more importantly does not seem to violate a sense of fair play (Jordan-Young and Karkazis 2012). The use of genetic and other testing, almost primarily done on women, demonstrates that being the winner does not always trump sportsmanship. Close monitoring implies that at least in this context fair play is more important than being the winner.

Conclusion

Despite changing cultural values that emphasize winning in sports, sportsmanship continues to play a pivotal role in understanding who competes and how they do so in sports today. Cultural and media representations such as Pixar's *Cars* continue to value ideas of fair play, being a good sport, and standards of decorum and decency. However, while adhering to the rules, denouncing cheating, and expecting certain etiquette on and off the field are all ways of making sports more equitable and enjoyable, sportsmanship also reinforces norms and values that certain individuals may not be able to equally obtain. As sportsmanship becomes the ways in which participants, spectators, officials, and the media define deviance, sportsmanship is a means of dividing athletes by class, race, gender, and sexuality. The word itself, although challenged more than ever, confirms our associations with proper athletes being men coming from specific class and racial backgrounds.

Sports, as an institution, continues to define and be defined by gender, race, class and sexuality in a variety of ways. While women and minority men have increased their presence and importance in most organized sports, they continue to find discrimination and a culture that labels them different if not deviant. Often, this labeling process is under the guise of sportsmanship or playing by the rules. At other times, it is media representations of those who play that confirm whether or not an individual or group of athletes are indeed sportsmen. As cultural ideals of deviance in sports and in society as a whole evolve to allow for more participation, ideals of fair play and who is a sportsman will continue to evolve. However, it is important to continue to challenge ideals in order for fair play not only to ensure the rules but that all are welcome to adhere to them.

Bibliography

Associated Press. 2014. "Serena: Comments 'In a Bulling Way.'" ESPN.com. Retrieved March 15, 2015 (http://espn.go.com).

_____. 2012. "Kim Molkey Bothered by Taunts." ESPN.com. Retrieved March 15, 2015 (http://espn.go.com).

Andersen, Margaret L., and Patricia Hill Collins. 2016. "Why Race, Class, and Gender Still Matter," pp. 1–14 in *Race, Class & Gender An Anthology*, edited by Margaret L. Andersen and Patricia Hill Collins. Boston: Cengage Learning.

Bemiller, Michele. 2009. "Men Who Cheer," pp. 324–336 in *Constructions of Deviance Social Power, Context, and Interaction*, edited by Patricia A. Adler and Peter Adler. Boston: Wadsworth.

Birrell, Susan. 1988. "Discourses on the Gender/Sport Relationship: From Women in Sport to Gender Relations," pp. 459–502 in *Exercise and Sport Science Reviews*, Vol. 16 edited by K.B. Pandolf. New York: Macmillan.

Blinde, Elaine M., and Diane E. Taub. 2009. "Homophobia and Women's Sport," pp. 196–206 in *Constructions of Deviance Social Power, Context, and Interaction*, edited by Patricia A. Adler and Peter Adler. Boston: Wadsworth.

_____ 1992. "Women Athletes as Falsely Accused Deviants: Managing the Lesbian Stigma." *The Sociological Quarterly*, 33:521–533.

Bredemeier, Brenda Joe, and David L. Shields. 1984 "Divergence in Moral Reasoning About Sport and Life." *Sociology of Sport*, 1:348–357.
Brockrath, Franz, and Elk Franke. 1995. "Is There Any Value in Sports? About the Ethical Importance of Sports Activities." *International Review for the Sociology of Sports*, 30(3–4):283–310.
Buford May, Rueben A. 2001. "The Sticky Situation of Sportsmanship Contexts and Contradictions in Sportsmanship Among High School Boy Basketball Players." *Journal of Sports and Social Issues*, 25:372–389.
Coakley, Jay. 2006. *Sports in Society: Issues and Controversies*. New York: McGraw-Hill.
Cobban, Linn Ni. 1982. "Lesbians in Physical Education and Sport," pp. 179–186 in *Lesbian Studies: Present and Future*, edited by Margaret Cruikshank. New York: Feminist Press.
Collins, Patricia Hill. 2000. *Black Feminist Thought: Knowledge, Consciousness, and Empowerment*. New York: Routledge.
_____. 2005. *Black Sexual Politics: African Americans, Gender, and the New Racism*. New York: Routledge.
Connell, R.W. 1990. "An Iron Man: The Body and Some Contradictions of Hegemonic Masculinity," pp. 83–95 in *Sport, Gender Men and the Social Order: Critical feminist Perspectives*, edited by Michael A Messner, and Don Sabo. Champaign, IL: Human Kinetics.
Conroy, David E., John M. Silva, R. Renee Newcomer, Brent W. Walker, and Matthew S. Johnson, 2001. "Personal and Participatory Socializers of the Perceived Legitimacy of Aggressive Behavior in Sport." *Aggressive Behavior*, 27:405–418.
Crawley, Sara L., Lara J. Foley, and Constance L. Shehan. 2008. *Gendering Bodies*. Lanham, MD: Rowman & Littlefield.
Crossett, Todd. 1990. "Masculinity, Sexuality, and the Development of Early Modern Sport," pp. 45–54 in *Sport, Gender Men and the Social Order: Critical Feminist Perspectives*, edited by Michael A Messner, and Don Sabo. Champaign, IL: Human Kinetics.
Delaney, Tim, and Tim Madigan. 2009a. *Sports: Why People Love Them!* Lanham, MD: University Press of America.
_____. 2009b. *The Sociology of Sports: An Introduction*. Jefferson, NC: McFarland.
Dreger, Alice. 2009. "Where's the Rulebook for Sex Verification?" *New York Times*, August 21, Retrieved April 28, 2015 (http://www.nytimes.com).
Duda, Joan L., Linda K. Olson, and Thomas J. Templin. 1991. "The Relationship of Task and Ego Orientation to Sportsmanship Attitudes and the Perceived Legitimacy of Injurious Acts." *Quarterly for Exercise and Sport*, 62:79–87.
Elsas, Louis J., Arne Ljungqvist, Malcolm A. Ferguson-Smith, Joe Leigh Simpson, Joe Leigh, Myron Genel, Alison S. Carlson, Elizabeth Ferris, Albert De la Chapelle, and Anke A. Ehrhardt. 2000. "Gender Verification of Female Athletes." *Genetics in Medicine*, 2(4):249–254.
Ferber, Abby L. 2016. "The Construction of Black Masculinity White Supremacy Now and Then," pp. 392–398 in *Race, Class & Gender An Anthology*, edited by Margaret L. Andersen and Patricia Hill Collins. Boston: Cengage Learning.
Gough, Russell W. 1997. *Character Is Everything: Promoting Excellence in Sports*. New York: Harcourt Brace College.
Hays, Graham. 2008. "Central Washington Offers the Ultimate Act of Sportsmanship." Espn.com. April 30. Retrieved January 3, 2015. (http://sports.espn.go.com631)
_____. 2014. "Six Years Later, Integrity Wins Again." Espn.com. April 28. Retrieved January 3, 2015 (http://espn.go.com).
Jordan-Young, Rebecca, and Katrina Karkazis. 2012. "You Say You're a Woman? That Should be Enough." *New York Times*. June 27. Retrieved April 28, 2015 (http://www.nytimes.com).
Kaye, Miranda P., and Kevin P. Ward. 2010. "Participant-Related Differences in High School Athletes' Moral Behavior." *Athletic Insight*, 10(1). Retrieved April 15, 2015 (http://www.athleticinsight.com).
Keating, James W. 2001. "Sportsmanship as a Moral Category," pp. 7–20 in *Ethics in Sport*, edited by William J. Morgan, Klaus U. Meier, Angela J. Schneider. Champaign, IL: Human Kinetics.
Kimmel, Michael S. 1987. "Men's Responses to Feminism at the turn of the Century." *Gender and Society*, 1:261–283.
_____. 1990. "Baseball and the Reconstitution of American Masculinity: 1890–1920," pp. 55–65 in *Sport, Men and the Gender Order: Critical Feminist Perspectives*. Champaign, IL: Human Kinetics.

Lenskyj, Helen. 1990. "Power and Play: Gender and Sexuality Issues in Sport and Physical Activity." *International Review for Sociology of Sport*, 25:235–245.
_____. 1991. "Combating Homophobia in Sport and Physical Education." *Sociology of Sport*, 8:61–69.
Mangan, J.A. 1986. *The Games Ethic and Imperialism Aspects of the Diffusion of an Ideal.* London: Frank Cass.
Messner, Michael A. 2005. "Still a Man's World? Studying Masculinities in Sports," pp. 313–325 in *Handbook of Men and Masculinities*, edited by Michael S. Kimmel, Jeff Hern and R.W. Connell. Thousand Oaks: Sage.
_____ 1995. "Boyhood, Organized Sports, and the Construction of Masculinities," pp. 102–114 in *Men's Lives*, 3d ed., edited by Michael S. Kimmel and Michael A. Messner. Boston: Allyn and Bacon.
Miller, Blake W., Glyn C. Roberts, and Yngvar Ommundsen. 2004. "Effect of Motivational Climate on Sportspersonship Among Competitive Youth Male and Female Football Players." *Scandinavian Journal of Medicine and Science in Sports*, 14:193–202.
Morgan, William, Klaus Meier, and Angela Schneider. 2001. *Ethics in Sport.* Champaign, IL: Human Kinetics.
Pharr, Suzanne. 1988. *Homophobia: A Weapon of Sexism*. Inverness, CA: Clurdon.
Sabo, Don. 1985. "Sports, Patriarchy, & Male Identity." *Arena Review*, 9(2):1–30.
SI.com. 2014. "Every Sportsman of the Year." SportsIllustrated.com. Retrieved April 1, 2014 (http://www.si.com).
SI.com Staff. 2014. "Vote Now, Who Should be *SI's* 2014 Sportsman of the Year?"
Sportsllustrated.com, December 2. Retrieved April 1, 2015 (http://www.si.com).
Silva, John M. 1983. "The Perceived Legitimacy of Rule Violating Behavior in Sport." *Journal of Sport Psychology*, 5:438–448.
Stanley, Gregory Kent. 1996. *The Rise and Fall of the Sportswoman: Women's Health, Fitness, and Athletics 1860–1940*. New York: Peter Lang.
Theberge, Nancy. 1987. "Sports and Women's Empowerment." *Women's Studies International Forum*, 10:387–393.
Varner, Monica K., and J. David Knottnerus. 2002. "Civility Rituals and Exclusion: The Emergence of American Gold During the Late 19th and Early 20th Centuries." *Sociological Inquiry*, 72(3):426–441.
Volkwein, Karin A.E. 1995. "Ethics and Top-Level Sport-A Paradox?" *International Review For the Sociology of Sports*, 30 (3–4):311–320.

The Economics of Sportsmanship

Clair Smith

Cheaters never win and winners never cheat. Most children have heard this simple admonition at some point. It is truly unfortunate that it is not true. Sometimes athletes cheat and win, at least for a while. But it is rarely a good long-term strategy. And given the desire to win evident in athletes at all levels, maybe we should not be surprised at the occasional act of cheating, but rather at the rampant cooperation and sportsmanship that in fact transpires each day in professional sports stadium, high school and college facilities, and parks and sandlots across America. In this essay, we will use the tools of economics to examine and explain this epidemic of sportsmanship and good behavior.

Why Economics?

What does economics have to do with sportsmanship? Perhaps more than you think. Economics is much more than stock prices and GDP. Economics is the study of constrained choice in all aspects of life. As Alfred Marshall described in his 1890 textbook, "Economics is a study of mankind in the ordinary business of life" (Marshall 1890:1). Ludwig von Mises named his book on the subject simply but accurately *Human Action* (von Mises 1996 [1949]). Both of these definitions highlight the broad subject matter of economics. When a basketball player makes a split-second decision on whether to drive to the hoop, to pull up and shoot, or to pass to a teammate, she is weighing the expected costs and benefits of various actions—and making a decision we can analyze with the tools of economics. When the tennis player chooses whether to return the ball hard to the back corner of the court or to tap the ball over close to the net, he too is making an economic decision based on the expected benefits and costs of each course of action. Similarly, when neighborhood kids playing first base on the sandlot honestly call the ball fair or lie and say it was foul, they too are making an economic decision.

So how does economics have room for sportsmanship? Economists just preach self-interest, greed, and ruthless competition, right? In the 1987 movie *Wall Street*, Gordon Gekko gives a now famous speech about greed.

> The point is, ladies and gentleman, that greed, for lack of a better word, is good. Greed is right, greed works. Greed clarifies, cuts through, and captures the essence of the evolutionary spirit. Greed, in all of its forms; greed for life, for money, for love, knowledge has marked the upward surge of mankind. And greed, you mark my words, will not only save Teldar Paper, but that

other malfunctioning corporation called the USA. Thank you very much [Stone and Weiser 1987].

Adam Smith is often considered the father of modern economics, and writes extensively in his 1776 treatise *The Wealth of Nations* about the importance of self-interest.

> It is not from the benevolence of the butcher, the brewer, or the baker that we expect our dinner, but from their regard to their own interest. We address ourselves, not to their humanity, but to their self-love, and never talk to them of our own necessities, but of their advantages [Smith 1981 (1776):26–27].

Economists, following in Smith's tradition, continue to emphasize the role of rational self-interest in describing human action and the functioning of the economy. Economists generally assume that people make purposeful choices in an effort to make themselves better off. But the economist's nuanced understanding of self-interest is often incorrectly reduced in popular perception or understanding to an elevation of visceral greed. This common but misguided caricature of Smith and subsequent economists ignores most of what he discussed in both the *Wealth of Nations* (1776) and his previous book, *The Theory of Moral Sentiments* (1759).

What Adam Smith Really Said

Many people think they know what Adam Smith says, but few have actually read his work. That is at least understandable, if not excusable, as *The Wealth of Nations* alone runs over 900 pages. And that does not include the 300 pages of important foundation laid in *The Theory of Moral Sentiments*. In these works he does not condone the idea of greed; Readers will not find Gordon Gekko's ode to greed in any of Smith's work. Instead of a ruthless, win-at-any-cost competition, Smith describes a furthering of one's personal interest—both financial and otherwise—within the bounds of moral and ethical conduct. And while not all economists embrace the totality of Smith's views, the concept of self-interest in economics is quite broad and garners near-universal acceptance. Self-interest encompasses monetary gain as well as acts of charity and other good works that a person finds worthwhile. Economists of all stripes believe that individuals can maximize their well-being on many margins, not just financial. Some may seek money, power, or fame, while others seek health, spiritual fulfillment, or clean water for residents of third-world nations. And within the bounds of moral conduct, all of these are consistent with the economic idea of self-interest that Smith described and generations of economic thinkers since have espoused.

Thinking like an economist does not require that one adopt a win-at-all cost view of competition. The pursuit of self-interest allows for the inclusion of additional goals, like fair play and good sportsmanship. One way that Smith articulates a moral constraint on competitive behavior is through his "Impartial Spectator." In describing how we can ascertain the moral appropriateness of our conduct, he envisions that we reflect upon our conduct as if from an impartial third-party perspective:

> We suppose ourselves the spectators of our own behavior, and endeavor to imagine what effect it would, in this light, produce upon us. This is the only looking-glass by which we can, in some measure, with the eyes of other people, scrutinize the propriety of our own conduct. If in this view it pleases us, we are tolerably satisfied [Smith 1982 (1759):112].

This is essentially a Smithian version of the Golden Rule: Treat others as you wish to be treated. Or perhaps more precisely, treat others in a way that an impartial third-party spectator would find to be acceptable conduct.

The world of sports at all levels—from neighborhood sandlots to professional arenas—works better and provides greater benefits when operating on the foundation of ethical action that Smith espoused. It is good to work hard for oneself and one's team, but one should do so within the bounds of legal and moral conduct. One might sum up what Smith describes with phrases more likely to come from scores of coaches at all levels across the land: "Play hard; Follow the rules." But saying that economics allows for good sportsmanship and that good sportsmanship is a great idea still does not explain why we see so much of it. For that we need to continue our discussion of economics.

One More Economist: F.A. Hayek

Another important economist that should be considered in this discussion on economics and sportsmanship is Friedrich A. Hayek. Hayek is less known than Smith, but he surely is no lightweight, winning the Nobel Prize in Economics in 1974. His thoughts are especially relevant here because of his extensive consideration of moral, social, or cultural constraints on human activity.

Hayek makes a careful distinction between what he calls law and legislation. For Hayek, legislation is manmade rules, like state and federal statutes and regulations. The "Clean Air Act," speed limits, parking regulations, and local zoning ordinances, all constitute examples of legislation. Sports are also riddled with official regulations, or in Hayek's classification, legislation. Examples of sports regulations include the official National Collegiate Athletic Association (NCAA) rules governing all aspects of college sports, as well as your local Little League's rulebook. These man-made rules are purposefully designed to constrain conduct, and there are designated consequences for breaking these rules. If a police officer catches you exceeding the speed limit or the referee catches you moving both feet without dribbling the ball, you have violated the recorded rules and will face the consequences as a result.

"Law," in Hayek's admittedly unorthodox distinction, is different. As Hayek expert Don Boudreaux (2006) explains it, "law is emergent patterns of behavior that [are] incorporated into people's expectations." While in common parlance law can be used as a synonym for legislation, Hayek's use is distinctly different. For him, law is the unwritten and unplanned rules by which we live. Boudreaux goes on to offer a telling example. When you place your coat on a chair or books on the table in cafeteria, it signals a kind of temporary right to that seat (Boudreaux 2006). Others recognize this and refrain from sitting at that spot. This rule is not recorded anywhere; there are no formal sanctions. Yet as participants in a shared society we recognize this "law" and our interactions function a bit more smoothly because of it. Hayek himself notes, "Only the observance of common rules makes the peaceful existence of individuals in society possible" (1973:72). So when we hold the door for someone just a couple steps behind us, we are upholding cultural and societal "laws" that on net make our society function more efficiently. When a high school coach refrains from running up the score in a game of extremely mismatched talent, he or she is conforming to unwritten laws that guide action. In fact, a California basketball coach served a two game suspension after his high school team won a game 161–2

(*USA Today*, 2015). While the coach did bench his best players in the second half and instructed them not to shoot until the shot clock was winding down, many found his use of a full-court press throughout the entire first half (yielding a halftime score of 104–1) to be too much.

One final point on law and legislation should be made. It is possible for there to be an overlap between the specific written rules (legislation) and the unwritten norms and customs (law.) Hayek notes that law can be codified in legislation. When a common practice or social "law" is recorded in a statute or regulation, it becomes legislation. Most every civilization recognizes some kind of prohibition on murder. In many cases it is also codified in a particular criminal statute. The official rule book captures some of the "law" that governs sports interaction, but rarely does it cover all the scenarios and nuances that players face and understand.

"The Code" Is an Example of Hayek's Understanding of Law

What Hayek refers to as "law" is descriptive of what Ross Bernstein has called "The Code" in sports. Bernstein (2006; 2008; 2009) has written extensively about the code in hockey, baseball, and football. In each case he interviews hundreds of players and coaches to get an understanding of the constraints on their action and what unwritten rules they live by. And in each sport he finds that the unwritten rules—"the code of honor" as he calls it—is as important if not more important than the official written rules. As he uncovers "the code" in professional sports, he finds that different players have variations on the theme, but that the essential elements are consistent.

In attempting to define the code in football, he quotes from a number of player interviews. Players talked about "putting the team first," not playing dirty, and earning respect through conduct (Bernstein 2009:3, 5, 8, 12). They described that even legal hits could be dirty, and this would lead to retaliation at another time, sometimes several games later. (This distinction between legal hits and dirty hits is a pertinent example of the overlap and nuance of the official rules [legislation] and the code [or law] that guides player behavior mentioned above.) Throughout Bernstein's interviews, players frequently related that "putting the team first," a key part of the code, means protecting your teammates, both on and off the field.

Retaliation is an especially important part of the code in the world of hockey. In his first in the series of code books, Bernstein investigates the purpose of fighting in hockey. And while there may be several reasons that fights break out in the course of hockey games, he finds that retaliation for unacceptable conduct on the ice is the common underlying theme. Players that he interviewed assert that the division of labor on an NHL team includes enforcers whose main job is to maintain an intimidating force that prevents opposing players from taking cheap shots on key players (Bernstein 2006).

The concept of unwritten rules may be most widely known and discussed in the area of baseball. Bernstein offers his book on the subject (2008), but there are others as well. Here are ten unwritten baseball rules drawn from Jason Turbow's book, *The Baseball Codes* (2010):

1. Don't swing at the first pitch after back-to-back home runs.
2. Don't work the count when your team is up or down by a lot.

3. When hit by a pitch, don't rub the mark.
4. Don't stand on the dirt cutout at home plate while a pitcher is warming up.
5. Don't walk in front of a catcher or umpire when getting into batter's box.
6. Don't help the opposition make a play (bracing them from falling into the dugout, etc.).
7. Relievers take it easy when facing other relievers.
8. Follow the umpire's code when addressing them on the field.
9. Pitchers stay in the dugout at least until the end of the inning in which they get pulled.
10. Pitchers never show up their fielders.

Other accounts of unwritten rules in baseball may offer a top-ten list that varies a bit from this one, but the similarities and underlying continuity will be remarkable. The list offers direction on how to act toward one's own teammates, the officials, and the opposing team. And while not generally codified in an official rulebook, these principles of good conduct constrain how professional players interact on the field—providing a kind of order that facilitates productive activity in the game.

Here we have considered the existence of an unwritten code of conduct in football, hockey, and baseball. And it surely exists in most other sports as well. But as evidenced by the ten examples from baseball, there are fairly specific norms that generally constrain professional athletes in their unique sport. For example, spectators in tennis are generally quiet and reserved, and customarily cheer only good play. Yet in the Australian Open in 2013, top-ranked female tennis player Victoria Azarenka had to endure loud applause each time she made a mistake (*The Economist* 2013). This unseemly behavior was reportedly retaliation for her perceived abuse of medical timeouts to regain her composure in a semi-final match two days earlier. This example is especially interesting because it shows the intentional breach of the norm of quiet civility from fans due to a perceived abuse of a kind of timeout loophole in the official rules based on urgent medical need.

Most of us are not professional athletes. We are not necessarily bound by the pro-league codes of conduct that Bernstein explores. Yet many of us play sports at some level, or at least did when we were kids. So whether it is volleyball at the company picnic, church league softball, or any of the thousands of community recreation programs for children, is there a more general "law" that affects how we play and interact in these situations?

"The Law" in Sports More Generally

My kids, when playing t-ball at the local Little League park, are oblivious to the unwritten rules of baseball that Turbow describes. Yet they have some sense of the rules—both formal and informal. Their understanding of the official written rules is incomplete, as is their comprehension of "the code" or whatever we might want to call the general unwritten norms that govern our behavior. But they are developing a sense of what is acceptable and what is not.

They are unlikely to "boo" or otherwise reprimand teammates who cannot seem to connect with the ball no matter how carefully they swing. They are unlikely to do this because they know that kind of behavior is "not nice." They would not want to be treated that way. Adam Smith's impartial spectator would not approve of their "dissing" of a teammate. And treating teammates and opponents appropriately makes learning to play baseball tolerable or even fun. And as I hope to explain, it is what makes sports possible at all.

That sense of right and wrong—what is acceptable and what is not—continues to grow as one continues through sports. When running a 10K it is perfectly acceptable to pass other runners. But it is not appropriate to cut them off. These general norms of behavior—"laws" in Hayek's view—affect and govern how we play sports and interact one with another. These norms are, at their essence, what we refer to as good sportsmanship. Sportsmanship is more than just following the written rules in the official rulebook for a particular sport at a particular competitive level. It encompasses how players treat members of their own team, the opposing team, the officials, and even the fans.

And sportsmanship enhances the enjoyment of the game at all levels. In fact, it makes the playing of sports possible. At the higher levels of competition there are officials to referee the activity. But if players did not generally follow the rules, there would be a continual series of breaks in the action while penalties are assessed based on the latest infraction. And what of the unregulated levels of competition? Sandlot baseball. Pickup hoops. Friendly tennis matches. These are only possible when there is a general predisposition to follow the rules.

In a pickup basketball game, for example, a player may be expected to call one's own fouls. Repeated "errors"—that is the failure to admit to fouling another player—may lead to the breakdown of the game, a physical altercation, or the exclusion of the offending player from future games. So while "cheating" by not calling one's own foul may have a very short term advantage, it may ultimately lead to the dissolution of the game. If I want others to play by the rules and I want to play in the future, I learn that it is ultimately in my best interest to play by the rules.

The same thing happens in nearly every other sport. When most people play tennis they lack the luxury of a line judge. The players have to make calls regarding whether the ball was in or out. Some calls are not clear cut, and players may sometimes make mistakes, but if a player gains a reputation for cheating by dishonest line calls, that player may find it harder and harder to find someone to play. We could go on with specific examples from other sports, but the punchline would be the same. The very existence of enjoyable recreational sports depends on largely sportsmanlike conduct. Without widespread adherence to the rules, play would break down altogether.

This can be expanded beyond the world of athletics. People can traverse a busy city sidewalk only because most people observe common norms and niceties that make social coexistence possible. Generally, people do not knock over or walk on top of other pedestrians. If one person tried this, they might initially get where they were going faster. But their clearly antisocial behavior would invite retribution from an enforcer of social norms in the crowd. "The Code" that Bernstein describes in the NHL (2006) exists on Manhattan sidewalks as well. And furthermore, if everyone adopted this me-first kind of excessive pedestrian competition all order on the sidewalk would break down completely. And what if this level of self-centered "greed" extended to the streets and highways? Imagine then the level of destruction we would observe.

Exceptions to the Rule

As discussed before, sports are a specific application of how we interact with others in society every day. As we navigate rugby pitches, soccer fields, volleyball courts, and grocery stores, there are millions of peaceful interactions and exchanges between and among self-interested individuals each and every day. These competitive interactions are guided by social norms and conventions that allow us to fairly and productively engage. So as I mentioned early in this essay, I think the most interesting thing about cooperation and sportsmanship is its widespread existence. Our daily social interactions, athletic and otherwise, are built upon a foundation of generally good, appropriate, sportsmanlike conduct. Are there examples of bad sportsmanship? Definitely. But these are still the exception, not the rule. And I hope that the tools of economics have been useful in shedding some light on this subject. But I would be naïve and this essay incomplete to not acknowledge the instances of bad behavior and unsportsmanlike conduct.

There are in fact instances of dirty hits below the knees, uncalled fouls, and fabricated line calls, just as we observe rude behavior, arguments, fights, and other antisocial behavior at the mall or on the street. Perhaps most concerning is the occasional display of bad sportsmanship at youth sports events—*from the parents*. Simply use your favorite search engine to look for videos available online using search terms along the lines of "parent bad behavior at youth sports." How do we explain the atrocities produced from this search? Is economic theory wrong?

I have tried to show over the course of this essay that even in a competitive game and in a competitive world we have reason to cooperate. We can enjoy both recreational and professional sports only when most players play by the rules most of the time. But we know there are exceptions. Sometimes people cheat. And the economist, if she is consistent and believes that people generally make choices that they expect to make themselves better off, must say that in that instance a person believed the benefit of cheating was greater than the cost. Maybe there was a lot riding on the outcome. Maybe they had an unusually short time horizon and did not think much about the consequences. Maybe their sense of ethical or moral foundations was not as well developed as most other players. Maybe they lost control of their tempers. Whatever the reason, they chose to violate the rules or norms in that instance. And if there are any consequences, they will bear those costs.

Most of us would agree that sports (and life) function better when people are generally playing by the rules and demonstrating good sportsmanship. I will leave it to others to suggest how best to achieve that goal, except to say these two things: We are fortunate that there is a long-term incentive to abide by the code of sportsmanship, and wise coaches in youth sports may be able to demonstrate and help develop an understanding of sportsmanship as young people grow and mature.

The Role of Game Theory

There is one last but important concept that we must consider in this economic look at sportsmanship, and that is game theory. A simple application of game theory provides a theoretical foundation for both why people might sometimes cheat, and an explanation for why people generally do not. Game theory is the consideration of the optimal strategy choice when the outcome depends on the combination of choices made by multiple players. (See Aumann 2008.) The common example of the "Prisoner's Dilemma" is a fruitful place to start.

In the traditional Prisoner's Dilemma, two criminal suspects are picked up by the police and taken to the station for questioning. The authorities have enough circumstantial evidence to likely convict them each for lesser crimes, but to nail anyone with the more serious crime of which they are suspected, they need to elicit a confession. This leads to the setup familiar on most TV cop shows, where the suspects are interrogated separately and offered deals to reduce their sentence if they confess and provide the damning evidence against their criminal partner. Essentially the same deal is offered to each of the suspects, but the benefits are greatest where one suspect's testimony is critical because the other has not confessed. Similarly, the penalty is greatest where one does not confess to the crimes but the former criminal partner does.

The essence of the Prisoner's Dilemma is that, collectively, both parties would be better off if no one confessed; the aggregate jail time is smallest with this scenario. This is considered the cooperative outcome. The problem is that each player individually could gain by confessing to the crimes. No matter what the criminal partner does, a player is strictly better off by confessing. This leads to the outcome of mutual confession, the scenario with the greatest aggregate jail time. Yet this is considered the most likely outcome. Or more completely, this is the most likely outcome absent some kind of enforcement mechanism that allows or encourages the two suspects to cooperate. In the traditional prisoner's dilemma, one method of enforcement might be "extra-legal" means. Suppose that both suspects were part of a criminal conglomerate or mob. There may be penalties exacted by the mob leaders on anyone who "snitches," and those severe penalties may serve to keep anyone from confessing.

A variation on the Prisoner's Dilemma is directly applicable to our discussion on sportsmanship. For any two players of a game, they could either exercise good sportsmanship or cheat (where "cheat" means in this case to violate either the written rules of the game or the unwritten rules of good conduct.) The best overall outcome occurs when both players exercise good sportsmanship. But each has a short-run incentive to cheat. That is, in a specific instance, there is some immediate gain to violating an official rule or norm of good conduct. Understanding why most players choose to exercise good sportsmanship in most instances in spite of the short-term gains from cheating requires a longer-term perspective, where reputation and repeated interactions are required.

Interactions in life represent a repeated game, not a one-shot deal. The same is true on the athletic field. Athletic success leads to continued play. One player's success generally requires the cooperation of opposing players: I want my opponents to play clean and fair. And opponents are less likely to offer clean and fair play to someone known to cheat or play dirty, if they are willing to play them at all. There is an old expression that goes something along the lines of "Burn me once, shame on you; burn me twice, shame on me." This colloquial expression sums up the power of reputation in sports and life. When someone is known to be a cheater, he or she is no longer afforded the same trust or respect, or is eliminated from play altogether.

In the terminology of game theory, reputation in a repeated game creates an enforcement mechanism that encourages cooperation. Players find that it is in their best long-term interest to forgo any short term gains from bad behavior in favor of the long-term gains from cooperation and sportsmanlike play. One of the important themes that emerge from Ross Bernstein's books on "the code" in professional sports is how players get a reputation for good conduct or dirty play. He suggests that players who become known for dirty play do not generally last long in professional sports (Bernstein 2009). The code calls for retaliation against such action, and few teams will want a player who is destined for serious injury. This underscores the importance of reputation in professional sports.

Conclusion

There are good reasons to follow the rules. Sports work better in an environment of good sportsmanship and fair play. And economists, even as personified by Adam Smith's description of self-interest and competition, are also on board. Smith believed that a sound moral foundation is a necessary condition for the efficient and practical functioning of a market system. The public benefits created by the self-interested action of individuals must happen within the constraints of morality and sportsmanship. Each individual must develop some ability to self-regulate his or her actions for the long-term benefit of both themselves and everyone else. And whether one uses Smith's impartial spectator or the tools of game theory, economics predicts the widespread existence of good sportsmanship. In this context, I refer to good sportsmanship as adhering not just to the formal written rules of the game, but to the unwritten code of conduct that supports it as well.

Looking forward, economic theory and empirical observation provide a basis for optimism, despite the occasional acts of bad sportsmanship that make the news or circulate the internet. Others writing in this volume may be better equipped to offer suggestions on decreasing the instances of bad behavior that we observe. Yet this author finds that there are strong incentives for the continued widespread practice of sportsmanship. When parents, teachers and coaches model and teach good sportsmanship they can strengthen the moral foundation on which competitive activities like sports succeed, only increasing the odds of a continued epidemic of good behavior.

Bibliography

Aumann, R. J. 2008. "Game Theory." In *The New Palgrave Dictionary of Economics*, 2d ed., edited by Steven N. Durlauf and Lawrence E. Blume. Palgrave Macmillan. *The New Palgrave Dictionary of Economics Online*. Palgrave Macmillan. Retrieved May 21, 2015 (http://www.dictionaryofeconomics.com).

Bernstein, Ross. 2006. *The Code: The Unwritten Rules of Fighting and Retaliation in the NHL*. Chicago: Triumph Books.

_____. 2008. *The Code: Baseball's Unwritten Rules Its Ignore-at-your-own-risk Code of Conduct*. Chicago: Triumph Books.

_____. 2009. *The Code: Football's Unwritten Rules Its Ignore-at-your-own-risk Code of Honor*. Chicago: Triumph Books.

Boudreaux, Donald. December 11, 2006. *EconTalk: Boudreaux on Law and Legislation*. Podcast retrieved April 9, 2015 (http://www.econtalk.org).

Hayek, Friedrich A. 1973. *Law Legislation and Liberty: Vol. I Rules and Order*. Chicago: University of Chicago Press.

Marshall, Alfred. 1890. *Principles of Economics*. London: Macmillan.

Smith, Adam. 1981 [1776]. *An Inquiry into the Nature and Causes of the Wealth of Nations*, reprinted Liberty Fund edition, edited by R. H. Campbell and A. S. Skinner. Indianapolis: Liberty Classics.

_____. 1982 [1759]. *The Theory of Moral Sentiments*, reprinted Liberty Fund edition, edited by D. Raphael and A. L. Macfie. Indianapolis: Liberty Fund.

Stone, Oliver, and Stanley Weiser. 1987. *Wall Street*. 20th Century Fox.
The Economist. January 28, 2013. "Just Give Me a Minute." Retrieved May 5, 2015 (http://www.economist.com).
Turbow, Jason. 2010. *The Baseball Codes: Beanballs, Sign Stealing, and Bench-Clearing Brawls: The Unwritten Rules of America's Pastime*. New York: Pantheon.
USA Today. January 8, 2015. "California Girls Basketball Team Wins 161–2." *USA Today High School Sports*. Retrieved April 15, 2015(http://usatodayhss.com).
Von Mises, Ludwig. 1996 [1949]. *Human Action*, reprinted ed. Irvington, NY: Foundation for Economic Education.

Sportsmanship in Question
The Impact of Professionalism and Commercialization on the Ethos of Sport

Barry Smart

The Ethos of Sport

A genealogy of modern sport reveals complex historical roots, a multiplicity of at times conflicting tendencies and influences which have given rise to a range of physical recreational activities as well as values expressed in and articulated with sporting practices and institutions. Sport is argued to have achieved its specifically modern form first in England, identified as "the cradle and loving 'mother' of sport," the place where the culture of modern sport initially emerged and then migrated "from one country to another" (Agnes Bain Stiven [1936] cited in Elias 1986:126). It was in the course of the 19th century in England in particular that processes of codification of many, but not all, modern sports developed and more formal consideration began to be articulated concerning the appropriate conduct and attitude of people participating in the various forms of sport.

In the second half of the 19th century notions of fair play and respect for both rules and other players and competitors involved in sports events increasingly received expression and an ethos of sport took shape and contributed to what has come to be termed "sportsmanship," variously described as a movement or an ideology that has led to the diffusion of a game ethic around the world. It is argued that the ethical notion of "sportsmanship" reflected "not only the export of [an] English public-school game ethic from the second half of the nineteenth century, but also the international diffusion of Pierre de Courbetin's 'Olympism' from the end of the nineteenth century," an ideological doctrine infused with romanticized assumptions about the games of classical antiquity (Abe 1988:25). This was influenced significantly by the formative time spent by Coubertin studying what were perceived to be synergies between sport, education, and morality in schools in England, including at Thomas Arnold's school in Rugby (Abe 1988; see also Lasch 1991).

Amateurism and the Ethos of Sport

In 1908 the first Olympic Charter was published, outlining the intention to make the Games a forum in which high ideals and values attributed to and/or associated with sport and physical education that had inspired the regeneration of the Olympics would be respected and nurtured, and promising that all measures would be taken "to guide modern athletics in desirable ways" (Comité International Olympique 1908:7). But the ideals and values that were considered to be a source of inspiration for the constitution of the modern Olympics, including amateurism and an ethos of sport, encompassing attributes such as respect for opponents constitutive of sportsmanship, were far more modern than was recognized or acknowledged, and represented from the outset attributes of what Eric Hobsbawm (1983:1–2) designated an "invented tradition." Victorious participants in the games held in Ancient Greece frequently received material rewards, including money, exemption from taxation, accommodation, as well as other payments, and in addition their rights and interests were protected by athletic guilds effectively according them professional status (Young 1984; Crowther 1996; Kotynski 2006; Kissoudi 2005; Toohey and Veal 2007). As Plato observed of the "athlete who aims at an Olympic or Pythian victory ... [he] must train full time. He has no free time for any other activity" (quoted in Young 2005:25). In short, what would now be described as professionalism was already present in an embryonic form in ancient Greece. The athlete with aspirations to succeed, to win, had to engage in the activity full-time, had to be committed, to prepare well by practicing or training, and contrary to Courbetin's views, for such individuals it was, and indeed generally remains, not participation and the struggle that really matters but in the final instance victory (Young 1996). Amateurism had no place in such an intensely competitive context:

> The concept of amateurism ... is wholly foreign, often even antithetical, to the nature and vocabulary of Greek athletics. Yet our own interest in this matter—our legacy from the modem Olympics and nineteenth-century British elitism—leads us to exaggerate its importance, In classical studies "amateurism" is an irrelevant distraction [Young 1984:164].

In the closing decades of the 19th century in England increasing social class tensions and antagonisms and associated social status insecurities led to accumulating signs of professionalism in sport, exemplified primarily by men being paid to play, principally working class men earning a living from their sporting abilities, who in turn were regarded critically, with disdain and disapproval. Internationally too concerns were being expressed about the "mercantile spirit [which] threatened to invade sporting circles," including the reconstituted modern Olympics (Coubertin, Philemon, Politis, and Anninos 1897:4; see also Birley 2003:105). Marked differences began to be drawn between participants in sport in terms of "amateur" and "professional" statuses, with the latter being regarded as morally and socially suspect (Dunning and Sheard 1979; Whannel 1983). While in the USA the distinction between amateur and professional was interpreted more loosely and there was greater ambiguity in application, there too fears about professional athletes with socially inferior credentials taking over sports clubs led to restrictions being placed on "professional" participants (Rader 1983). If the amateur "gentleman" was regarded as playing for the love of the game, for the intrinsic benefits that were thought to derive from participation, the professional player was regarded very differently, as threatening the core values of sport, the sporting ethos, as having an instrumental orientation to the game, as being someone for whom playing was an increasingly important source of financial reward and income and winning was accorded priority above everything else.

Analysts have identified the period from the mid–19th century through to the 20th century as one in which developing modern sports and other forms of physical recreation began to suffer a "fatal shift towards over-seriousness," a period in which it is suggested that a playful attitude or "play spirit" was being increasingly eroded as games became more intensely competitive (Huizinga 1949:198). The implication is that the virtues associated with simply taking part were increasingly being challenged and displaced by the goals of winning or achieving success in competition. It is in this context that a critical concern about the effects of an increase in the intensity of competition, professionalism, training, and coaching gave rise to the expression of cultural values about how games were being played, about sporting conduct, "etiquette," and sportsmanship, with special emphasis being placed on fairness, the importance of abiding by not just the written rules of the game but also the unwritten conventions and understandings, and perhaps most of all displaying respect and generosity towards opponents in both defeat and victory (Abe 1988).

It was the governing bodies of a number of sports, dominated as they were by members of the upper class, "gentlemen" imbued with the Corinthian spirit of fairness and respect for opponents, who sought to defend amateurism and promote its behavioral corollary sportsmanship and stem the tide of professionalization and commercialism, that it was feared would be detrimental to the conduct and ethos of sport as they conceived of it. A number of sports associations in the late 19th century, including the Amateur Athletic Club (1866) which became the Amateur Athletic Association in 1880, and the Amateur Rowing Association and Bicycling Union, restricted membership to the "gentleman-amateur" and prohibited participation by those deemed to be socially inferior, that is anyone who had been "by trade or employment for wages, a mechanic, artisan or labourer," on the spurious grounds that such forms of physically demanding work might provide an unfair advantage in competition (Guttmann 1978:30). What was at work here was the imposition of dominant social class values representing the elitist interests of an established aristocratic gentry class eager to maintain their social position and a rising entrepreneurial bourgeoisie striving to achieve greater recognition and social status (Hargreaves 1986).

Professionalism

In the course of the 20th century one modern sport after another embraced professionalism and commodification and commercialization duly followed. In England the Football Association legalized professionalism in 1885, Rugby League endorsed professionalism in 1895 and split with Rugby Union, which continued to present itself as an amateur sport until 1995, when it became "open" after sanctioning professionalism (Collins 1998). Although there had been professional tennis tours from 1926 the sport only became open in 1968 when the governing body, at the time the International Lawn Tennis Federation, abandoned its enforcement of amateurism and permitted professionals to play in all the major tournaments (Smart 2005). Cricket had a form of segregation of amateurs and professionals until 1963 when the distinction was dropped. Amateurs and professionals would play alongside one another in teams but there were clear signifiers of status differences including separate dressing rooms and gates to enter the field of play, different quality of overnight accommodation when playing away, with amateurs having superior rooms, and on the scorecard amateur players were listed with initials before their surname, in the case of professionals surname was followed by initials (Collins 1998; Smart 2005). In golf, as in cricket, amateurs and professionals played together and against each other on a regular basis, but there were amateur-only tournaments from which club professionals were excluded and the latter were treated as social inferiors and subjected to forms of social discrimination (Lowerson 1989).

In the USA in the course of the 19th century a number of sports competitions embraced professionalism and commercialism. The National Association of Professional Base Ball Players was formed by ten clubs in 1871 and five years later the National League of Professional Baseball Clubs was founded. In 1893 the first professional American football contract was signed, followed in 1902 by the first attempt to found a professional National Football League, and then in 1920 by the establishment of the American Professional Football Association which two years later became the National Football League (NFL) (Smart 2005). In the 1870s the amateur ethos and the accompanying cultural baggage of sportsmanship had arrived in North America embodied in the form of the English gentleman player for whom taking part in sports was what was valued above all, not victory or pecuniary gain, and the notion that gentlemen amateurs should not compete with professionals began to gain traction on American university campuses. Athletics clubs and sports publications began to promote the amateur ethos and in 1888 the Amateur Athletic Union was established (Pope 1997).

The opening decades of the 20th century were marked by rising tensions and conflict between amateurism and professionalism and growing signs of differences in attitude, approach, and interest on the part of amateur and professional athletes and players were expressed in competitive play and match conduct and articulated in media interviews, articles and comments. Amateurs continued to extol the virtues of the amateur game and promote the values and attributes associated with sportsmanship while professionals placed emphasis on the overriding importance of winning or being first. Consider the following examples from tennis, golf, and the NFL.

In 1928 two years after a professional tennis tour was established American amateur tennis player Helen Wills (1999 [1926]) commented that "courtesy and sportsmanship" have established the rules for conduct and behavior on court. Wills added that court etiquette is important and that consideration and goodwill must be shown to one's opponent. In addition to sportsmanship on the part of players who should accept defeat graciously—"being a good loser is a part of correct court behavior" (Wills 1999:290)—believed that spectators, the "tennis audience," had a responsibility to embrace the "spirit of good sportsmanship" and behave in a dignified and restrained manner. The views expressed by Helen Wills contrast starkly with a rather different set of priorities in respect of playing articulated succinctly by Walter Hagen (1892–1969), an American golfer credited with making professional golf a more "socially respectable occupation" (Rader 1983:227). Hagen famously remarked that "[t]he crowd remembers *only* the winner. I'd as soon finish tenth as second'" (quoted in *Encyclopedia of World Biography* 2004), a sentiment echoed by legendary Green Bay Packers football coach Vince Lombardi (1913–1970) who commented, "Show me a good loser and I'll show you a loser" (quoted in Sancton 2010).

But what is appropriate and expected in one sport may not be applicable or customary in another. Golf, tennis, football and cricket, to name but four sports, vary widely in terms of a range of factors that may have a bearing on sporting conduct, including sport specific traditions and customs, as well as the visibility of the behavior of those involved, a matter which the advent of television coverage, close-up shots and replays has increased significantly for all sports. In addition there are differences between team sports and sports involving individual competitors and such differences may influence the behavior of players. Sports also vary in terms of physical contact, in some it is integral to the game in others it is non-existent. The extent and nature of physical contact may significantly affect conduct in intensely competitive sports. In turn, the attempt on the part of a player to behave graciously and show consideration for an opponent in a non-physical contact sports event involving individuals may prove to be very different from a comparable attempt on the part of a player in a physical contact team sports event.

As modern sports adopted a more business-like and commercial approach to the running of teams, matches, competitions, events, and tournaments, so money or the cash-nexus became an increasingly integral, transformative, and in many respects problematic part of the life of sport. As one critical analyst observes of the increasing commodification and commercialization of sport, money leads to "problems of excess," it may have an "impact on athlete's motivations and … the outcomes of sports events and fixtures" (Horne 2006:27). Professionalization and commercialization have significantly transformed late modern sport, turning "amateurism" into a derogatory designation suggesting at best a questionable attitude or approach, one signifying a lack of commitment and seriousness, and making sport a global business, an integral part of the entertainment industry (Gratton, Liu, Ramchandani, and Wilson 2012). The opprobrium which accompanied professionalism in modern sport in the late nineteenth and early 20th century, and continued in some sports beyond that period, has largely lifted. In a series of reflections on aspects of the current condition of sport Cashmore and Cleland (2014) note, "the term professional carries connotations of competence, assuredness and expertise; it is contrasted with the derogatory amateur meaning untutored and clumsy" (p. 17). But while professionalism has acquired more positive connotations concerns have continued to be expressed about the consequences of the ever-increasing encroachment of money, commerce in all its manifestations, including sponsorship, endorsement, marketing and branding, and the corollary, a business ethos which leads to players having agents and being preoccupied with their image and media rights. In such a context it is appropriate to ask what the consequences have been for the ethos of sport, sporting etiquette, and for sportsmanship.

Sportsmanship

Sportsmanship is considered to be a moral concept exemplified by respect, fairness, civility, honesty and responsibility on the part of competitors, signifying their "good character." Sport and sportsmanship were an integral part of the English public school games ethos in the 19th century and Arnold (1997:54) suggests that the notion of sportsmanship has continued to have "social and moral implications." Although a notion of sportsmanship continues to have some currency in modern sport it is evident that its value has been much diminished and its meaning and relevance compromised as its presence has been eroded and prominence much reduced by the continuing commodification of sport within the global capitalist economy (Perelman 2012). There is a growing sense that the term signifies a world that has been lost to professionalism, to an intensification of competitiveness, and the seductive and ethically distorting consequences of commerce in all its manifestations, including increasing sponsorship and endorsement interest and rising image and television transmission rights. Arnold (1997:54) also indirectly reminds his readers of the patriarchal roots of sport, roots that have largely endured, notwithstanding the growing participation and, in some sports, raised profile of female sporting figures, by commenting that "'sportspersonship' ... a gender neutral term ... is better suited to the contemporary world" but that the established term, "sportsmanship" is more apposite for historical analysis (for further discussion of this issue see Sportsmanship and Gender in this volume).

In a discussion of the moral aspects of sportsmanship Keating (1964), drawing on historical and etymological source materials, distinguishes between "sport" and "athletics." In contrast to contemporary social and cultural understandings and associated institutional practices Keating (1964) argues that sport and athletics refer to radically different types of human activity:

> In essence, sport is a kind of diversion which has for its direct and immediate end fun, pleasure, and delight and which is dominated by a spirit of moderation and generosity. Athletics, on the other hand, is essentially a competitive activity, which has for its end victory in the contest and which is characterized by a spirit of dedication, sacrifice, and intensity [p. 28].

It is the conflation of these two terms, Keating (1964) argues, that leads to sportsmanship inappropriately being presented as an "all-embracing moral category." Etymologically the term "sport" is traced back to the Middle English terms "*desport* or *disport*," meaning "diversion, recreation and pastime" (Keating 1964:27), and in contrast athletics and athlete are argued to derive from the Greek terms "atllein," "to contend for a prize," or the noun *athlos*, "contest," or *athlon*, a prize awarded for the successful completion of the contest (p. 28). Keating (1964) argues that it is particular "moral habits or qualities" taking the form of a "spirit" or "attitude" which is exemplified by conduct that displays "generosity and magnanimity," derives pleasure from participation rather than the result or outcome of a game, and emphasizes cooperation and mutual enjoyment over competition and struggle, that constitute sportsmanship (pp. 29–30). But if cooperation defines sport it is competition that is constitutive of athletics, and if sportsmanship has any place in relation to athletic conduct Keating suggests it is in respect of the moderation of struggle and conflict, the inclusion of limitations on competition.

In a contemporary context in which "sport" increasingly has become virtually synonymous with a range of professionalized individual and team competitive matches, tournaments, and events organized as commercial enterprises and businesses, which through media dissemination and marketing have become global in scope, the distinction outlined by Keating may seem of little relevance. Sport is now regarded as a global cultural and economic institution which is defined by intense competition, it is an institution in which taking part is less and less an end in itself, is not regarded as intrinsically valuable, but increasingly is a necessary means to the achievement of individual and collective success or victory embodied in winning matches, events, and tournaments and accruing the material rewards that have become an increasingly common corollary of professionalization. While not all forms of sport are professional or directly subject to commercial pressures the values of intense professional competition, achieving success by winning matches and tournaments, and associated forms of conduct have permeated into the playing of games at all levels and have affected the behavior of sports participants and indeed non-participants (Anonymous 1999; Dreyfuss 1999). Professional sport and sports organizations occupy a unique place in late modern societies but to date they have not lived up to their responsibilities (Lapchick 1997).

It may appear that Keating's reflections on sportsmanship as a moral category and the distinction between sport and athletics offers little analytical purchase on modern sport but that would represent a premature judgment. While the sport-athletics binary requires revision in the light of the contemporary cultural economy of modern sport, the observations Keating (1964:32) offers on the lack of fit, if not incompatibility, of the ethos of sportsmanship with "serious and emotionally charged" competitive activity for which participants will have trained and motivated themselves for victory and in respect of which modesty and fairness of conduct might be marginalized if not considered an unwarranted constraint on the optimization of performance, are of significant contemporary relevance, if not quite in the form presented. If victory is all that matters, a phrase repeated over and over in various guises in all sports—"winning isn't everything, it's the only thing" (Overman 1999)—then graciousness in defeat will be hard to achieve, display or express. In such circumstances what place is there for sportsmanship in modern sport?

Whither Sportsmanship? The Reality Behind the Rhetoric

Signs of sportsmanship in contemporary sport are few and far between, thin on the ground, although some observers continue to hold on to the hope that the moral ethos of sport can be retrieved, that sportsmanship signifying morality and 'excellence of character' can be regenerated (Clifford and Feezell 2010:viii). But the omens are not good, for the signs on the pitch, in the stadium, and on court suggest otherwise. The conduct of professional players has created disappointment and has led to growing disenchantment with modern sport. At best sportsmanship is now a residual and anomalous phenomenon, largely confined to ceremonial simulations exemplified by ritualized handshakes between opponents prior to the commencement of "battle," in which all-bets-are-off, and comparable post-match exchanges, between which all manner of gamesmanship, rule bending, deception and in some instances physical intimidation and violence, as well as time wasting, have become all-too-routine features of increasingly intense sports contests.

In a critical essay on "The Sporting Spirit" George Orwell (1945) commented that "sport is an unfailing cause of ill-will." The specific event that prompted Orwell's critical intervention was an association football tour of the UK by a Russian team, Dynamos, and the fervent expressions of nationalism, both on and off the pitch, which precipitated fights between players and abuse of officials. But Orwell's (1945) critical observations have a broader significance insofar as they address the less-appealing consequences of the competitiveness that is integral to modern sport. Sports matches have little meaning in Orwell's view unless players go all-out to win and wherever prestige is at stake and reputation is on the line 'the most savage combative instincts are aroused.' When fierce passions are aroused by rivalry in sport compliance with the rules of play and gestures of sportsmanship generally disappear. As Orwell (1945) comments:

> Serious sport has nothing to do with fair play. It is bound up with hatred, jealousy, boastfulness, disregard of all rules and sadistic pleasure in witnessing violence: in other words it is war minus the shooting.

Similar sentiments are expressed by Christopher Hitchens (2010) who catalogues a series of conflicts and problems associated with various sports. Rather than view difficulties and controversies associated with sport, for example he discusses matters connected with holding the FIFA World Cup in South Africa (2010) and restriction of access for practice to the Whistler downhill ski run at the Vancouver Winter Olympics (2010) to the Canadian "home" team, as signifying departures from the ethos of sport. Hitchens argues that these and other examples reveal 'the very essence of sportsmanship." For both Orwell and Hitchens the culture of sport involves intense competition, doing whatever is possible and necessary to achieve the desired successful outcome. As Orwell (1945) remarked, even "a leisurely game like cricket, demanding grace rather than strength, can cause much ill-will."

Concern about conduct at all levels in modern sport is now widespread. Sportsmanship is in question in the USA, Europe, China and elsewhere around the world and it is a matter of concern at the highest and most elementary of levels, in the professional sphere and within school and junior sport. Even the ritual of a postgame handshake between opposing teams as a gesture of sportsmanship was banned by the Kentucky State High School Athletic Association in 2013 because over the previous three years two dozen fights had occurred. Other states have reported a similar deterioration in sports conduct leading Austin (2013) to conclude that "[s]portsmanship is on the decline" in high school sport in the USA. A recurring theme in discussions and reports on modern sport is that the behavior of high profile professional sporting figures too frequently sets a bad example of sportsmanship, something that comes through strongly in another example from the USA. Andrew Cotto (2014) settled down to watch a televised National Football Conference match with his seven year old son which turned into a demonstration of unsportsmanlike behavior with players taunting one another, ranting in post-match interviews and mocking the opposition with the "infamous choke sign." What is on display is disrespect, narcissism, and "an utter lack of sportsmanship" by high profile, successful and well remunerated professional football players, potential role models for younger players and fans (Cotto 2014).

Another couple of examples are provided by professional tennis players John McEnroe and Serena Williams. At the Australian Open tournament in 1990 the highly competitive McEnroe, winner of numerous titles and a major force in world tennis was playing Mikael Penfors in the fourth round. McEnroe had an explosive temper and a reputation for contesting decisions with umpires and line judges and in the match with Penfors received a conduct code violation for unsportsmanlike behavior when he stood in front of a line judge who gave a close call against him and repeatedly bounced a ball on his racket while staring at her. Later in the match after placing a shot out of court McEnroe threw his racket to the ground in frustration which caused it to crack and received a point penalty from the match umpire which gave the game to his opponent. McEnroe objected to the penalty and demanded to see the tournament referee. Peter Bellenger the referee and Ken Farrar the supervisor responsible for officiating at all Grand Slam tournaments both came on to the court and the latter explained to McEnroe that the penalty was for "racquet abuse" and was automatic and that the match should proceed. Having explained the situation Farrar proceeded to leave the court and as he walked away McEnroe shouted, "Just go fuck your mother" (Feinstein 1999:301). The response was swift. Farrar returned to confer with the referee and the umpire who announced, "Verbal abuse, audible obscenity, Mr. McEnroe. Default. Game, set, and match Penfors" (Feinstein 1999:302).

Tennis like most professional sports is an intensely competitive game where the margins for error are slim, play is fast, stakes are high for the players, and decisions and line calls may be controversial and, at times, provoke outbursts. In 2009 Serena Williams, a multi-Grand Slam winning tennis player, unhappy in a semi-final at the U.S. Open with a line judge calling her for a foot fault on a second serve, remarked, "I swear to God I'll fucking take the ball and shove it down your fucking throat" (Donegan 2009). Williams's behavior was deemed to be 'unsportsmanlike' and the maximum possible penalty fine of $10,500 was levied. Then two years later, again at the U.S. Open, Williams lost a point after exclaiming "come on" while the ball was still in play, breaking "the code of ethics covering that sort of marginal behavior" (Mitchell 2011). The loss of the point led to an exchange between Williams and the umpire. Williams commented:

> "Are you the one that screwed me over the last time here? You're nobody. You're ugly on the inside.... We were in America last time I checked," she barked at Asderaki [the umpire]. "You're totally out of control. You're a hater and you're unattractive inside. What a loser" [Mitchell 2011].

Subsequently Williams was fined $2,000 by the U.S. Open referee for verbally abusing the umpire. As a critical observer of the demise of sportsmanship observed of the controversial encounter between Williams and the match umpire, "[w]ith higher salaries and more on the line, it's not surprising that more and more athletes are making headlines for unsportsmanlike conduct" (Shama 2011). The character building and moral qualities ascribed to sport and physical recreation expressed in references to sportsmanship and articulated in the tenets of Muscular Christianity, which during the "late 1850s became an integral part of the public school educational system" in England, now frequently seem to be merely historical relics in the commercially driven and business orientated world of modern professional sport (Watson, Weir, and Friend 2005:7). In a wide-ranging critical appraisal of the "athletic entertainment industry" Robert Lipsyte (1995) makes reference to the growing disenchantment with the indiscretions of sporting figures and the corrosion, if not collapse, of sportsmanship:

> As a mirror of our culture sports now show us spoiled fools as role models ... the athlete-performers are clearly no longer the "muscular Christians" who first seized the national imagination ... [the] virtues of self-discipline, responsibility, altruism and dedication seem to have been deleted from the athletic contract with America. Sports are over because they no longer have any moral resonance. They are merely entertainment, the bread and circuses of a New Rome.

In China, too, the behavior of sports teams and individual players has prompted increasing concern to be expressed about the corruption of sportsmanship. In the year following the Beijing Olympics China held its 11th National Games and "doping scandals" in rowing and shooting, rumors of "arrangements" between competitors in diving contests, Shanghai and Hubei men's basketball teams "vying to not score in order to win a favorable standing in their group," as well as suspicions that a coach had been "manipulating a game" led to public dismay and media criticism of the "conspicuous absence of sportsmanship" at the games (*China Daily* 2009:4).

Conclusion: The Spectacle of Success and the Demise of Sportsmanship

For professional sports men and women playing success and the achievement of silverware are to an increasing degree closely bound up with the awarding of lucrative playing and endorsement contracts and the financial wealth they deliver, not to mention the spectacular media profile that is a corollary. In consequence, there is an additional very significant material incentive to maximize competitive performance even if it means bending the rules, employing gamesmanship, and departing from the spirit in which games should be played according to the ethos of sport signified by the notion of sportsmanship and its corollary the Olympic spirit. In an increasing number of sports episodes and moments of unsportsmanlike conduct have become frequent, almost commonplace and routine. In cricket sledging, that is intimidating, ridiculing, or insulting an opponent, and confrontations between players are a frequent occurrence and in association football disputes between players, diving and other forms of gamesmanship, and attempting to deceive and influence officials, have become very familiar matters. Lack of sportsmanship is a growing problem in tennis too with a report of a study of 54,000 matches between 2001 and 2011 finding that in the opening rounds of non-Grand Slam tournaments "cheating in professional tennis is widespread" (Amdur 2013). In basketball, hockey, and football in the USA insulting opponents on court or on the field of play, termed "trash talking," is increasingly commonplace and regarded as signifying the "decline of sportsmanship" and as representing "yet another sign of society's general loss of civility" (Silverman 1999).

In modern sport the signs of sportsmanship are relatively rare, as the conventions that moderated and restrained modern sporting rivalry have been undermined (Lasch 1991). The idea that sport might constitute a pure realm of sociality, a moral domain above material self-interest and nationalistic fervor in which consideration for opponents is paramount and belief in fair play determines conduct, is difficult to sustain in the face of evidence to the contrary. Competitiveness has been a prominent feature of organized sports from the very outset as studies of the ancient games demonstrate and professionalization in modern sport and its growing commercialism have only increased its intensity and its impact on standards of conduct. Now references to sportsmanship and Olympism or an Olympic spirit have merely rhetorical value for the reality of a commercialized and media spectacularized modern professional sport is that it is fully immersed in the cultural economy of late capitalism, an integral part of the entertainment industry, and guided by an overriding interest to do whatever it takes to achieve success or victory and the financial rewards that are a corollary.

Bibliography

Abe, Ikuo. 1988. "A study of the Chronology of the Modern Usage of 'Sportsmanship' in English, American and Japanese Dictionaries." *International Journal of the History of Sport*, 5 (1):3–28.

Amdur, Neil. 2013. "In Tennis Gamesmanship is the Norm." *New York Times*, January 25. Retrieved November 18, 2014 (http://straightsets.blogs.nytimes.com).

Anonymous. 1999. "The Increase in Women's Participation in Sports Brings Poor Sportsmanship." *Ms Magazine*. Retrieved November 6, 2014. (http://www.msmagazine.com).

Arnold, Peter J. 1997 *Sport, Ethics and Education*. London: Cassell.

Austin, Michael W. 2013. "The End of Sportsmanship? Eliminating the Postgame Handshake." *Psychology Today*, October 9. Retrieved November 16, 2014. (http://www.psychologytoday.com).

Bain Stiven, Agnes. 1936. *Englands Einfluß auf den deutschen Wortschatz* [England's Influence on the German Treasury of Words]. Zeulenroda: B. Sporn.

Birley, Derek. 2003. *A Social History of Cricket*. London: Arum Press.

Cashmore, Ellis, and Jamie Cleland. 2014. *Football's Dark Side: Corruption, Homophobia, Violence and Racism in the Beautiful Game*. Basingstoke: Palgrave Macmillan.

China Daily. 2009. "Whither Sportsmanship?" October 26, p. 4. Retrieved December 9, 2014 (http://www.chinadaily.cn).

Clifford, Craig and Randolph M. Freezell. 2010. *Sport and Character: Reclaiming the Principles of Sportsmanship*. Leeds: Human Kinetics.
Collins, Tony. 1998. *Rugby's Great Split: Class, Culture and the Origins of Rugby League Football*. London: Frank Cass.
Comité International Olympique. 1908. *Charte Olympique—Annuire*. Lausanne. Retrieved November 12, 2014 (http://www.olympic.org).
Cotto, Andrew. 2014. "What Ever Happened to Sportsmanship?" *Huffington Post*. January 23. Retrieved May 20, 2015 (http://www.huffingtonpost.com).
Coubertin, Pierre De, Timoleon J. Philemon, N.G. Politis, and Anninos Charalambos. 1897. *The Olympic Games BC 776–AD 1896*, Second Part, the Olympic Games in 1896. London: Grevel & Co.
Crowther, Nigel B. 1996 "Athlete and State: Qualifying for the Olympic Games in Ancient Greece." *Journal of Sport History*, 23 (1):34–43.
Donegan, Lawrence 2009. "Serena Williams Is Fined $10,500 for US Open Line Judge Tirade." *The Guardian*. September 14. Retrieved November 16, 2014. (http://www.theguardian.com).
Dreyfuss, Ira. 1999. "Bad sportsmanship creeps into girls sports." *The Register Guard*, November 8. Retrieved November 6, 2014 (http://news.google.com).
Dunning, Eric, and Sheard Kenneth. 1979. *Barbarians, Gentlemen and Players: A Sociological Study of the Development of Rugby Football*. Oxford: Martin Robertson.
Elias, Norbert. 1986. "The Genesis of Sport as a Sociological Problem," pp. 126–149 in *Quest for Excitement: Sport and Leisure in the Civilizing Process*, edited by Norbert Elias and Eric Dunning. Oxford: Blackwell.
Encyclopedia of World Biography. 2004. "Walter Hagen 1892–1969." Encylopedia.com. Retrieved May 25, 2015 (http://www.encyclopedia.com).
Feinstein, John. 1999. "You Cannot Be Serious," pp. 295–308 in *The Right Set: A Tennis Anthology*, edited and with an introduction by C Phillips. New York: Vintage.
Gratton Chris, Liu Dongfeng, Ramchandani Girish, and Darryl Wilson. 2102. *The Global Economics of Sport*. New York: Routledge.
Guttmann, Allen. 197.8 *From Ritual to Record: The Nature of Modern Sports*. New York: Columbia University Press.
Hargreaves, John. 1986. *Sport, Power, and Culture: A Social and Historical Analysis of Popular Sports in Britain*. Cambridge: Polity Press.
Hitchens, Christopher. 2010. "Why the Olympics and other Sports Cause Conflict." *Newsweek*, May 2. Retrieved November 16, 2014 (http://www.newsweek.com).
Hobsbawm, Eric J. 1983. "Introduction: Inventing Traditions," pp. 1–14 in *The Invention of Tradition*, edited by Eric Hobsbawm and Terrence Ranger. Cambridge: Cambridge University Press.
Horne, John. 2006. *Sport in Consumer Culture*. Basingstoke: Palgrave Macmillan.
Huizinga, Johan. 1949. *Homo Ludens: A Study of the Play Element in Culture*. London:Routledge & Kegan Paul.
Keating, James. W. 1964. "Sportsmanship as a Moral Category." *Ethics*, 75 (1):24–35.
Kissoudi, Penelope. 2005. "Closing the Circle: Sponsorship and the Greek Olympic Games from Ancient Times to the Present Day." *International Journal of the History of Sport*, 22 (4):618–638.
Kotynski, Edward J. 2006. "The Athletics of the Ancient Olympics: a Summary and Research Tool." Retrieved January 13, 2013 (http://www.oocities.org).
Lapchick, Richard. 1997. "Professional Sport and Public Behavior." Presentation to the Penn National Commission, December. Retrieved November 6, 2014(http://www.upenn.edu).
Lasch, Christopher. 1991. "The Degradation of Sport," pp. 100–124 in *The Culture of Narcissism: American Life in An Age of Diminishing Expectations*. London: W. W. Norton.
Lipsyte, Richard. 1995. "The Emasculation of Sports." *New York Times*, April 2. Retrieved November 17 2014 (http://www.nytimes.com).
Lowerson, John. 1989. "Golf," pp. 187–214 in *Sport in Britain: A Social History*, edited by Tony Mason. Cambridge: Cambridge University Press.
Mitchell, Kevin. 2011. "Serena Williams Tarnishes Her Legacy with Abuse of US Open Umpire." *The Guardian*, September 12. Retrieved November 16, 2014 (http://www.theguardian.com).
Orwell, George. 1945. "The Spirit of Sport." Retrieved November 16, 2014(http://orwell.ru).
Overman, Steven J. 1999. "'Winning Isn't Everything. It's the Only Thing': The Origin, Attributions and Influence of a Famous Football Quote." *Football Studies*, 2 (2):77–99.
Perelman, Marc. 2012. *Barbaric Sport: A Global Plague*. London: Verso.

Pope, Stephen W. 1997. *Patriotic Games: Sporting Traditions in the American Imagination.* New York: Oxford University Press.
Rader, Benjamin G. 1983. *American Sports: From the Age of Folk Games to the Age of Spectators.* London: Prentice Hall.
Sancton, Julian. 2010. "Why the Vince Lombardi Biopic Will be the Best Sports Movie of All Time." *Vanity Fair*, March 9. Retrieved September 21, 2014 (http://www.vanityfair.com).
Shamma, Tasnim. 2011. "Whatever Happened To Sportsmanship?" *National Public Radio,* September 13. Retrieved November 16, 2014 (http://www.npr.org).
Silverman, Jason. 1999. "The Art of Trash Talk." *Psychology Today*, September 1. Retrieved November 18, 2014 (http://www.psychologytoday.com).
Smart, Barry. 2005. *The Sport Star: Modern Sport and The Cultural Economy of Sporting Celebrity.* London: Sage.
Tomlinson, Alan, and Christopher Young. 2011. "Towards a New History of European Sport." *European Review*, 19 (4):487–507.
Toohey, Kristine and Anthony J. Veal. 2007. *The Olympic Games: A Social Science Perspective,* 2d ed. Wallingford: CAB International.
Watson, Nick J., Stuart Weir, and Stephen Friend. 2005. "The Development of Muscular Christianity in Modern Britain and Beyond." *Journal of Religion & Society*, 7:1–21. Retrieved November 18, 2014 (http://moses.creighton.edu).
Whannel, Gary. 1983. *Blowing the Whistle: The Politics of Sport.* London: Pluto.
Wills, Helen. 1999 [1926]. "Etiquette," pp. 287–293 in *The Right Set: A Tennis Anthology*, edited and with an introduction by Caryl Phillips. New York: Vintage.
Young, David C. 1984. *The Olympic Myth of Greek Amateur Athletics.* Chicago: Ares.
_____. 1996. *The Modern Olympics, A Struggle for Revival.* Baltimore: Johns Hopkins University Press.
_____. 2005. "Mens Sana in Corpore Sano? Body and Mind in Ancient Greece." *TheInternational Journal of the History of Sport*, 22 (1):22–41.

Race, Sports and *Poor* Sportsmanship

EARL SMITH *and* ANGELA J. HATTERY

Before beginning this essay it is important to note that "race matters" (Feagin 2013; West 2000). Race impacts virtually every aspect of our lives from the opportunities we have to attend higher education, our access to health care, the foods we eat, the likelihood that we will go to prison, and the sports that we play. In this chapter, we examine the centrality of race to sport (Williams 1996). We begin with a discussion of race as it is defined by scholars; we then identify several key "themes" that illustrate the ways that race and racism appear in sports, followed by a focused discussion of the experiences of African-Americans in the U.S.

Definitions of Race

As sociologists, we understand race to be socially constructed (Bonilla-Silva 2003), which we illustrate with our examples below. In contrast, ethnicity describes one's cultural background and refers to behaviors such as religious practices, food preferences, and language. Most people use the term race to refer to inherited physical characteristics like skin complexion, the shape of a nose, eyes, hair texture and hair color. Furthermore, people commonly use the term "race" to refer to these physical traits as if they are always inherited and consistent (e.g., "white" people always have light complexions or Asians always have eye lids with no folds). These assumptions reflect a collective ignorance about race; indeed, they have made naked fools of us. Why? The reasons for this ignorance return us to the sociological fact that race is a social construct. Simply put, there is no coherent fixed definition of race nor is there a single "race gene" that can be specified as a basis for biological distinction—or, much less, is there such a gene that establishes a scientific basis for ranking different groups into hierarchies—or for explaining athletic performance. That said, across the world, an athlete's "race" and their "ethnicity" become important for a variety of reasons, not least of which is how they are treated within the sports they play. Based on these assertions, sociologists, legal scholars and others argue that race is a social construction; it exists only through social interaction and by the behaviors of social actors; as such, we, as individuals but more importantly as a society, are forced to construct and reconstruct its abstract significance.

The legal scholar Lopez (2000) provides a case study of the social construction of race using his own "mixed race" family wherein his brother "chooses" to be White (as does his father) and he chooses to be non-White (as does his mother who is Hispanic). In providing this portrait, Lopez (2000) concludes that "in my experience race reveals itself as plastic, inconstant, and to some extent volitional" (p. 166).

> I understand race as a mutable social construction that has been used historically to classify and stratify people based on clusters of physical characteristics. Race is defined by and against whiteness, an unmarked, invisible, and unexamined category that strategically has "a touchstone quality of the normal, against which members of marked categories are defined," so that all members of marked categories possess race in ways that whites do not [Lopez 2000:144].

This essay, then—"Race, Sports and *Poor* Sportsmanship"—is guided by two sociological concepts:

1. Feagin's (2010) "White Racial frame" theory—to better understand race and racism in the modern world.
2. Merton's (1938) "Strain Theory"—to better understand deviant behavior.

Both concepts are powerful and help with the analysis herein. We begin with Feagin. The "white racial frame" perspective is all encompassing towards an understanding of primarily White and African American (African American and Black will be used interchangeably throughout) social, economic, political interaction beginning with the offloading of Blacks in what becomes the state of Virginia in a new United States of America in the 17th century. White racial framing includes the understanding of white domination over all aspects of life chances for non-whites but especially African Americans. Feagin (2010:141) puts it thus:

> This dominant frame shapes our thinking and action in everyday life situations. Where and when whites find it appropriate, they consciously or unconsciously use this frame in accenting the privileges and virtues of whiteness and in evaluating and relating to Americans of color.

The "white racial frame" is white oppression. It is far more than individual discrimination against some one individual but, more so, institutionalized blockage of the opportunity structure for those non-whites and for Feagin especially African Americans for centuries. It is, overall, systemic having been manifested in all major societal institutions.

Institutionalized racism is an example of this blockage in ways like Blacks could not play any of the major American sports (e.g., football, baseball) until after Jackie Robinson was allowed to play for the Brooklyn Dodgers major league baseball team in 1947 (Smith 2014). This discrimination continues today in several sporting arenas; for example in those labeled "Country Club Sports" (e.g., golf, tennis) but also in NASCAR, National Hockey League and Extreme Sports (Smith 2014).

Another example of institutionalized racism in the "SportsWorld" is in the area of coaching and management. "SportsWorld" coined and used herein *as an institution* is complex, powerful, international in reach, and which in every aspect is a mirror reflection of our larger society with all of its systems of stratification and inequality. It is a sex-segregated institution that encompasses both intercollegiate and professional games that are played not only for good competition but also for monetary profit—from the National Collegiate Athletic Association College Football Championship to National Basketball Association Championship to NASCAR, and FIFA and beyond (Smith 2014).

When the great Jackie Robinson ended his baseball career he tells us in his book *I*

Never Had It Made how disappointed he was to have never been asked to participate in baseball as a coach or manager: "I'm going to be tremendously more pleased and more proud when I look at that third base coaching line one day and see a black face managing in baseball" (Helyar 2007).

Accepted ideology was that black athletes when done playing their games did not have the capacity to coach or manage. The best example of this is the Al Campanis flak on national TV being interviewed by ABC Nightline anchorman Ted Koppel April 6, 1987. In the interview Koppel asked Campanis (at the time he was the general manager of the Los Angeles Dodgers) why so few black managers and especially no black general managers in Major League Baseball. The reply was a shocker wherein Campanis said that blacks did not have the necessities to be a manager. What some people forget is that Koppel kept giving Campanis a chance to clarify his statements and that Campanis just kept going, even adding that Blacks could not swim "because they don't have the buoyancy" (Smith 2014:159).

Individual actors can and do adopt the "white racial frame" and engage in individual racist behaviors. This racial behavior also spills over into the area we call "fandom." One initial, brief example is provided by one of the most dominant college and professional basketball players in the 1980s and 1990s, Patrick Ewing. Standing 7 feet tall and weighing 240 pounds, Ewing has incredible stature and was one of the first players to bring the current high levels of physicality to the men's basketball game. As an African American, and an extremely powerful and dominant man, he was a constant target for individual and group racial aggressions. His case illustrates not only the pervasiveness and content of the typical racism that African American athletes experience, but also highlights the fear that scholars like Orlando Patterson (1999) claim undergirds much of White male racism, a fear of the power of African American men. While playing for Georgetown University, Ewing was a "chief target" for racist abuse by fans. It was not uncommon for fans of opposing teams to hold up signs that said things like "Ewing Can't Read" or "Ewing Kan't Read Dis." These signs not only invoke the stereotype of African Americans as dumb, but they are particularly powerful in light of the fact that Georgetown University is among the elite academic institutions in the U.S.

Thus, accusing Ewing of not being able to read was an indictment of Georgetown in allegedly treating an African American student athlete differently than the rest of the student body; the implication was that he was admitted for his skills on the basketball court despite his assumed intellectual inferiority. Many of the chants also came from his fellow Georgetown students, some making sounds of what they believed apes sound like in the wild (Williams 1996). And, during the 1982–83 season students at Villanova wrote, "Ewing Is an Ape" on placards (Williams 1996:288). We are reminded, with this sentiment, that white sports fans are an enigma: When the New York Giants moved to San Francisco in 1957 their star centerfielder Willie Mays put a down payment on a house at 175 Miraloma Drive with a view of the Pacific Ocean. The homeowner accepted the offer from Mays and his wife Marghuerite but when neighbors got wind of the deal they protested. The *San Francisco Chronicle* put it thus (Woody 2000): "The *San Francisco Chronicle*'s front page headline on November 14, 1957 summed up the dispute: 'Willie Mays Is Refused S.F. House—Negro.'" The meaning here is that star baseball player Willie Mays was accepted as a professional baseball player but not as an ordinary neighbor.

So structural, systemic racism can be carried out at both the institutional level as well at the individual level.

Finally, what makes our essay cohesive is that all of our examples have a unifying theme; that is, the undermining theme "integrity of the sport being played."

A Theory of Deviance

There are many scholars who research deviant behavior in a variety of contexts and institutions including workplaces, education, in the illegitimate economy (selling drugs, prostitution) and in politics and government. And, there are a variety of theoretical frameworks that have been developed to analyze and explain deviant behavior. For this chapter, we utilize Robert Merton's work on deviance to analyze uncivil and deviant behavior in the SportsWorld.

Robert Merton, a structural-functionalist sociologist, developed a theory he called "Strain Theory" which he used to understand delinquent behavior. Merton (1938) argued that individuals in a given culture have access to the set of ideologies and norms for behavior that holds a hegemonic or mainstream position in that culture.

Merton (1938) noted, however, that sometimes cultural ideals, both the goals and strategies for reaching the goals, and the social structure are incompatible. In other words, in some cases access to legitimate means to attaining cultural goals is not available to particular portions of the population. Thus, individuals may develop alternative strategies for attaining culturally defined goals (Merton 1938).

Merton developed a typology by which behaviors could be characterized and analyzed. Merton's typology considers two questions: (1) the degree to which the social actor accepts (or not) the cultural goal and (2) the social actor's strategy (culturally accepted or alternative) for attaining the cultural goal; these are "modes of adaptation."

Mode of Adaptation

	Accepts the cultural goal	*Strategies to achieve the goal*
Conformity	YES	ACCEPTED
Innovation	YES	ALTERNATIVE
Ritualism	NO	ACCEPTED
Retreatism	NO	NONE
Rebellion	ALTERNATIVE	ALTERNATIVE

Merton's work provided a theoretical lens for understanding deviance by first understanding the degree to which an individual actor was alienated from the society. He argued that individuals who were marginalized but not entirely alienated (innovators, ritualists, rebels) would continue to pursue the goals of the culture but because of their marginal status would be cut-off from the legitimate means of attaining these goals and thus they would seek alternative strategies to attain the goal. In contrast social actors who were totally alienated from society, the retreatists, would withdraw entirely from society rejecting all cultural goals and not engaging in any strategies to achieve the goal. An example of a retreatist would be Ted Kaczynski (the Unibomber).

Though we are going to focus our discussion here on innovators, we provide a brief discussion of the other modes in order to situate the innovator mode.

Conformists are just what they seem to be; they conform. They accept the cultural goals and the accepted strategies for attaining the goal. Students who seek to get good grades and graduate on time (the cultural goal) and study hard, take practice tests, and utilize office hours (accepted strategies) are conformists.

Ritualists are those who reject the cultural goal but continue to engage in the rituals typically used to achieve the goal out of habit. The high school tennis player who has given up on the goal of winning a college scholarship will continue to come to practice because this is what is expected of the athlete and it fits into the routine of their day.

Rebels are those who reject the cultural goal but, unlike the retreatist, rather than becoming totally alienated from society they propose a new cultural goal and strategies for attaining that goal. At its beginning, those who were the founders of extreme sports were rebelled. They replaced the accepted forms of athletic competition with alternative activities—snowboarding replaced traditional downhill skiing—and they sought strategies to be highly competitive in these new athletic competitions.

Finally, the innovators are those who accept the cultural goal but identify alternative strategies for attaining it. The oft-used example is the student who seeks to get good grades and graduate on time but eschews studying and using office hours as the strategy, rather this social actor cheats on assignments as an alternative strategy to achieve the same goal.

Applying Merton's Theory of Deviance to Sportsmanship in the SportsWorld

As much as we would like to believe that sports is something that we participate in as a leisure activity (Veblen 1953), in fact SportsWorld is now one of the major institutions, along with education, government, the economy, religion and family that shape our lives and that are the source of study for sociologists. The level of competition in SportsWorld is a direct reaction to the rewards available. In the first half of the 20th century, when Veblen was writing about the "leisure class" the only rewards available for success in sports lay in the professional leagues, especially in sports like horse racing and boxing.

By the early 1970s, sports like basketball, football, baseball and ice hockey became not only a way to make a decent living—though not at all like the inflated salaries of today—and college participation became the primary access route to these sports. As a result, the competition in college sports became more fierce as men (there were no professional leagues for women) sought to impress a scout and sign a professional contract. By the 1980s, the college scholarship became valuable enough to finance a college education and thus the level of competition to be recruited and offered a scholarship among high school players increased proportionately.

By the end of the 20th century and the beginning of the 21st century, the competition to get into a high school or be recruited to play on a travel team for athletes playing baseball, soccer, and basketball that had a proven track record of successfully placing athletes in the top college programs became so strong that parents and coaches began identifying strategies to improve the performance elementary and middle school *children*.

As most everyone is aware, the rewards available for professional athletes are so extreme—in the form of salaries in the triple million digits (over 100 million)—that athletes, owners, managers, and others who stand to gain financially have an incentive to engage in strategies that will them a competitive or resource advantage.

Given this competitive and resource rich environment that now extends to the level of little league, we examine several examples of unsportsmanlike conduct that can be analyzed as innovations using Merton's framework. We note that there are so many examples to choose from that we have limited our discussion to be sure that we provide examples from every level of SportsWorld and include examples from players and those in management positions.

Illustration #1: *Little League.* Every year the United States hosts the Little League World Series. This event, which occurs annually in August, in Williamsport, Pennsylvania, includes teams for the 8 regions of the United States as well as 8 international brackets, including Asia-Pacific and Middle East, Australia, Canada, the Caribbean, Europe and Africa, Japan, Latin America, and Mexico. Each region has a set of qualifying tournaments from which the representatives from each region (both U.S. and international) are chosen. According to an article in *USA Today* in August 2014, the Little League World Series reported a revenue of nearly $25 million and assets of $85 million—all for a program that involves 11–13 year olds (Peter 2014)! With that kind of money involved, as well as the world stage on which to showcase a youngster's talents to potential college and professional scouts—international players can be recruited by Major League Baseball as young as 17—it is no wonder that families, coaches, and players would use innovative strategies, including cheating, to seek success.

In 2000 a boy from the Dominican Republic named Danny Almonte moved to the Bronx, New York to live with his father who had moved there 6 years earlier. Danny began playing in a little league baseball league his father founded. His athleticism was immediately apparent and in 2001 he led his team from the Bronx to a third place finish in the Little League World Series. Watching the game it was evident to any viewer that Danny Almonte was playing at a level above and beyond his teammates. A pitcher, he threw the major league equivalent of a 103 mile an hour fastball!

In fact, Danny Almonte was playing above the level of his teammates because he was two years older than the maximum age limit for participation in the Little League World Series. Though initially everyone involved in the situation claimed they had no knowledge of Danny's real age, an investigation later revealed that his father and other relatives knew of his real age. Danny Almonte himself, who did not speak English at the time, was cleared of any wrongdoing. Interestingly, as part of the investigation it was revealed that he had not attended school in the 2000–2001 academic year and thus he was removed from his family placed in foster care and his father was deported from the United States. Danny Almonte's actions, which are unsportsmanlike, were an innovative strategy, on the part of his parents and coaches, to gain a competitive advantage for him and for them, in this resource rich world of Little League baseball. Unfortunately for Danny Almonte he has yet to attain any real success in SportsWorld, though he does make living coaching a high school team.

Illustration #2: *Getting to College.* Talented high school athletes face two distinct and somewhat unrelated challenges to obtaining an athletic scholarship to a top university: athletic performance and academic performance. High school student athletes must not only impress college coaches with athleticism; they must be, in some very basic way, "college ready" or able to enter college and be remain academically eligible. The NCAA certifies high school athletes as eligible for college using a formula that is based on 3 elements: (1) core courses, (2) GPA and (3) standardized test scores (SAT or ACT) (*NCAA National Eligibility Quick Reference Guide* 2015).

In sum, upon graduating from high school, student athletes who intend to play on a Division 1 college sports team must have completed 16 core courses, including

- 4 years of English;
- 3 years of math (Algebra I or higher);
- 2 years of natural/physical science (1 year of lab if offered);
    1. 1 year of additional English, math or natural/physical science and
    2. 2 years of social science; and
- 4 years of additional courses (any area above, foreign language or comparative religion/philosophy).

The NCAA uses a sliding scale to determine the GPA and SAT or ACT minimum levels such that the higher the high school GPA—in the core courses only—the lower the test score that is needed to be eligible. Conversely, the lower the GPA in the high school core classes, the higher the test score. For example, a student with a 3.0 GPA in the core courses must have a minimum 620 SAT (math and verbal combined) or a 52 on the ACT. In contrast, a student graduating with a 2.0 GPA in the core courses must minimum of 1010 SAT (math and verbal combined) or an 86 on the ACT. To put this in context, according to the *College Board* (2015)—the organization that administers the SAT and ACT the overall average of all students taking the SAT in 2013 was 1010. Thus, the bar is very high for a student athlete with a low high school GPA.

In 2006–2007 one of the top high school basketball recruits was a player out of Chicago named Derek Rose. According to news reports published in 2011, John Calipari, who was the head coach who recruited and coached Rose in the 2007–2008 season, agreed in a sealed settlement to reimburse the University of Memphis ticket holders $100,000 as compensation for the 38 games that were vacated and championship banners lost as a result of an investigation that confirmed that Rose was ineligible to participate because of an invalid SAT score (Petchesky 2011). Allegedly the College Board invalidated Rose's SAT score because he had a "stand in" take the test for him.

Using Merton's framework to analyze Rose's predicament we argue that Rose, finding himself unable to score the minimum required on the SAT (allegedly he "failed" the ACT three times earlier that year) "innovated" a strategy to attain the required score, thus making him eligible to compete for one of the nations' top college men's basketball teams, lead them to 38 wins and compete for the national championship (they lost to Kentucky in overtime). Rose's strategy was successful—though arguably for Memphis who also had to return the Final Four winnings—in that he was drafted number one in the 2007 NBA draft and though he has struggled with injuries, he earns a salary of more than $18 million annually.

Illustration #3: *Winning at All Costs.* As much pressure as exists to win the Little League World Series, the pressures to win and to win big are significantly greater in professional SportsWorld. There are many, many examples we could choose for this section. We select one that is very recent (2015) and one that is expansive: Tom Brady and "Deflategate" and Lance Armstrong's use of performance enhancing drugs. We begin with a controversy that rocked SportsWorld in the spring of 2015: Deflategate.

The Deflategate controversy begins in January 2015 when the New England Patriots played the Indianapolis Colts in the AFC Conference Championship Game on January 18, 2015. According NFL rules, beginning in 2006 teams provided their own footballs—previously the home team had the responsibility of providing footballs for both teams—and as a result there are very few instances in which one team handles the footballs provided by the other team. One of those instances is an interception. During the AFC

Championship game in January 2015, Tom Brady, quarterback for the Patriots, threw an interception. The Colts' player who intercepted the ball reportedly handed the ball to the Colts' equipment manager as a souvenir. According to Durkee (2015), at half time league officials inspected all of the balls, and although accounts vary, at least one ball was under-inflated.

According to the NFL Rule Book (2013), "The ball shall be made up of an inflated (12½ to 13½ pounds) urethane bladder enclosed in a pebble grained, leather case (natural tan color) without corrugations of any kind. It shall have the form of a prolate spheroid and the size and weight shall be: long axis, 11 to 11¼ inches; long circumference, 28 to 28½ inches; short circumference, 21 to 21¼ inches; weight, 14 to 15 ounces."

On May 6, 2015, the conclusions of the NFL official investigation, known as the Wells Report, found that "it was more than probable" that Tom Brady knew about and may have participated in ensuring that the balls were under-inflated (Rosenthal 2015). As of this writing, Tom Brady has been suspended for the first four games of the 2015–16 season and the Patriots' organization was fined $1 million.

What would motivate Tom Brady to be involved in Deflategate? Of course only Tom Brady can answer that question for sure, but, according to an expert quoted in *Business Insider*, "Ainissa Ramirez, the author of a football-science book called *Newton's Football*, explained on NPR: 'The ball is slightly squishier. And particularly during the [Patriots-Colts game], which was kind of rainy, it's harder to hold the ball, it's hard to catch the ball. So by making it a little softer, it's easier to catch the ball'" (Manfred 2015).

The Deflategate game determined the AFC's representative to the 49th Super Bowl, which the Patriots played in and won. Of course there is significant money to be made by both the players and the owners for playing in and winning the Super Bowl. According to Sharp (2015) writing in SB Nation, the payout for every player who wins the Super Bowl is $97,000, for a total of an additional $189,000 when all of the playoffs wins (including the Super Bowl) are tallied up. (Note: the NFL playoff system plays flat rates to each player on the roster when teams appear in—and lose—or win playoff games. Each round of the playoffs pays a great bonus.) After winning the Super Bowl players and coaches are often able to negotiate new, and more lucrative contracts. And, though it is extremely difficult to find the exact figures, we can safely speculate that franchises and their owners gain revenues that are tied specifically to their Super Bowl wins.

It is impossible to say all of the benefits that Tom Brady individually and the Patriots collectively received from winning the AFC Championship and playing in Super Bowl 49, but suffice it to say that Brady's "innovation" allowed him and his team to pursue a significant cultural goal: winning the Super Bowl and earning a bonus. We note that Tom Brady, along with Peyton Manning, were the initiators of the 2006 rule change allowing each team to supply its own balls and limiting the contact the opposing team has with the balls.

Lastly, we turn to a discussion of an athlete whose "innovation" gave him a clear and identifiable advantage in pursuit of the cultural goals of winning and of making money. Lance Armstrong is perhaps the most successful and certainly most well-known cyclist to date. Armstrong won 7 *consecutive* Tour de France Titles between 1995 and 2005. The Tour de France is an over the road, multiple stage cycling race that covers 2200 miles over 23 days (21 stages) and is perhaps the most well-known of all of the cycling races.

Lance Armstrong amassed $12 million in career earnings with an additional $15 million *per year* in endorsements. Prior to the adjudication in his doping allegations his net worth was estimated at $125 million. After the doping adjudication his net worth dropped to $50–60 million.

Lance Armstrong faced rumors and allegations of doping during his entire Tour de France career, which he vehemently denied, including in court. On January 18, 2013, while appearing on the *Oprah Winfrey Show*, Armstrong admitted publicly and for the first time that he had in fact engaged in doping. "Lance Armstrong admitted that he cheated during most of his famed cycling career and that he bullied people who dared to tell the truth about it. After denying doping allegations for more than a decade, he also said he used banned drugs or blood transfusions during all seven of his victories in the Tour de France" (Schrotenboer 2013).

As a result of his admission, he was stripped of all 7 of his titles. Additionally, in 2015, SCA Promotions, a company that promotes athletes and who promoted Armstrong, was awarded $10 million in damages based on "the arbitration panel finding that Armstrong had engaged in 'unparalleled pageant of international perjury, fraud and conspiracy'" (McMahon 2015).

Of course we can never know what would have happened in the careers of any of these athletes had they not "innovated" in order to access the cultural goals and rewards they desired, but what we do know is that in every case, ruling bodies and public opinion were sufficiently convinced that an unfair advantage produced opportunities an millions of dollars in rewards and thus sanctions, ranging from very mild to severe, as in the case of Lance Armstrong, were handed down. We have no doubt that Tom Brady and Lance Armstrong trained hard and studied their craft, but what we also know is that Tom Brady and Lance Armstrong and a host of other athletes chose to "innovate" in order to gain a competitive advantage. We conclude this section of the essay with a discussion of professional governing bodies engaging in bribery and fraud in order to line their own pockets.

Illustration #4: Professional Organizations Collude to Profit—FIFA. At the time of the writing of this chapter, the professional SportsWorld was rocked what may turn out to be the biggest fraud case to hit a professional sports oversight body. The fraud case in question is against FIFA. According to its website, "The Fédération Internationale de Football Association (FIFA) is an association governed by Swiss law founded in 1904 and based in Zurich. It has 209 member associations and its goal, enshrined in its Statutes, is the constant improvement of football" (FIFA 2015). The website goes on to list three functions of FIFA: (1) define and provide clear "unified laws of the game" so that all football matches are played according to uniform standards, (2) to unify football and give it the global platform it needs to grow; and (3) to be the guardians of the integrity of the game and to fight corruption so that various member organizations (federations) have the support they need for fair play (FIFA 2015).

How ironic then that on May 26, 2015, the United States Justice Department handed down a 47-count indictment charging 14 figures, including FIFA officials with "racketeering, bribery, money laundering and fraud.... Among the "alleged schemes," said the Justice Department, were kickbacks to FIFA officials by executives and companies involved in soccer marketing and "bribes and kickbacks in connection" with "the selection of the host country for the 2010 World Cup and the 2011 FIFA presidential election." As the headline reads, the fraud and kickbacks amounted to $150 million (Miller and Barbash 2015).

This case is very new and so we only have news accounts to rely on, but in reading about the case, it seems that the primary bribes and fraud involved how sites were selected to host the World Cup tournament that happens every four years. One recent site selection, Qatar for the 2018 Cup, had raised eyebrows in the soccer community upon the announcements. Qatar is particularly suspect because it is not one of the countries with a rich soccer tradition; it will be extremely hot during the World Cup and it has *billions of dollars in oil wealth.*

What would propel countries and financiers to bribe FIFA officials? We believe it is the prestige and economic gain that goes part and parcel with hosting a World Cup. More popular than the Olympics, the FIFA World Cup draws hundreds of millions of fans to venues, the TVs and through streaming to the biggest sporting event in the world. Hotel rooms, restaurant receipts, ticket sales, advertising, pay per view, and sex trafficking all make hosting FIFA worth the cost of the bribes spent to secure it. Additionally, the host country is in the world's gaze for the month of the Cup and has the opportunity to showcase its wonder, hoping to capitalize on tourism and business investments long after the cup concludes.

So how can we interpret the behavior of FIFA officials using Merton's framework? Until we know more, we can only speculate that FIFA officials engaged in "innovative" behavior in order to access the incredible financial resources that are associated with the richest and most powerful governing body in the SportsWorld. Only time will tell what the impact of this scandal will be, but it offers yet another example of Merton's framework. FIFA officials chose to "innovate" their way to wealth, rather than working hard, making good investments, paying for good advice and all of the other strategies that conformists use.

Conclusion

We started this discussion noting that we would use two types of incivility to analyze the issue of "sportsmanship," (1) racism and (2) cheating, both used to gain advantages and to preserve privilege. Both the "white racial frame" perspective of Feagin and the deviant typology of Merton help us conceptualize the larger project of race, sport and sportsmanship. Feagin's work (2011) shores up the systemic nature of white racism. Merton's (1938) typology helps us to analyze a series of behaviors falling into the deviance category but not all qualitatively in the same way. FIFA and Lance Armstrong, for example, were out to extricate financial gain for themselves, while Danny Almonte and Derrick Rose were out to play the games they loved—but felt they had to break the rules to be able to do so.

Bibliography

Bonilla-Silva, Eduardo. 2003. *Racism Without Racists: Color-Blind Racism and the Persistence of Racial Inequality in the United States.* Lanham, MD: Rowman & Littlefield.

College Board. 2015. "Scores." Retrieved June 16, 2015 (https://professionals.collegeboard.com).

Durkee, Travis. 2015. "Ex-NFL Referee: All 12 Patriot Footballs Were Underinflated." *Sporting News.* Retrieved January 24, 2015 (http://www.sportingnews.com).

Feagin, Joe. 2010. *The White Racial Frame: Centuries of Racial Framing and Counter-Framing.* New York: Routledge.

Federation International de Football Association (FIFA). "About FIFA: Who We Are." Retrieved June 15, 2015 (http://www.fifa.com).

Helyar, John. 2007. "Robinson Would Have Mixed View of Today's Game." *ESPN the Magazine.* Retrieved May 1, 2015. (http://es.pn/1RqLlHU).

LaBounty, Woody. 2000. "Streetwise: Willie Mays." Retrieved May 29, 2015 (http://bit.ly/1FRCnzz).

Lopez, Haney. 2000. "The Social Construction of Race," pp. 163–175 in *Critical Race Theory: The Cutting Edge*, edited by Richard Del Gado and Jean Stefancic. Philadelphia: Temple University Press.

Manfred, Tony. 2015. "Why Using Deflated Footballs Gave the Patriots a Huge Advantage." *Business Insider*, January 21, 2105. Retrieved May 2, 2015 (http://www.businessinsider.com).

McMahon, Daniel. 2015. "Lance Armstrong Ordered to Pay Back $10 Million in Tour de France Prize Money." *Business Insider*, February 16, 2015. Retrieved February 21, 2015 (http://www.business insider.com).

Merton, Robert K. 1938. "Social Structure and Anomie." *American Sociological Review,* 3:672–682.

Miller, Michael E., and Fred Barbash. 2015. "U.S. Indicts World Soccer Officials in Alleged $150 Million FIFA Bribery Scandal." *Washington Post*, May 27. Retrieved May 27, 2015 (http://www.washingtonpost.com).

NCAA Eligibility Center Quick Reference Guide. 2015. "NCAA Division I Initial-Eligibility Requirements." Retrieved June 16, 2015 (http://fs.ncaa.org).

NFL Rule Book. 2013."Rule 2: The Ball." Retrieved May 27, 2015(http://static.nfl.com).

Petchesky, Barry. 2011. "Derek Rose and John Caliper are Paying Back Memphis Fans for that Title Game They Cheated Their Way Into." *Deadspin*. Retrieved October 7, 2011 (http://deadspin.com).

Peter, Josh. 2014. "Little League Means Big Business and Revenues Soar." *USA Today*. August 22, 2014. Retrieved May 28, 2015 (http://www.usatoday.com).

Rosenthal, Gregg. 2015. "Wells Report Released on Footballs Used in AFC Title." NFL, May 6. Retrieved June 16, 2015 (http://www.nfl.com).

Schrotenboer, Brent. 2013. "Lance Armstrong to Oprah: Story Was 'One Big Lie." *USA Today*. January 18, 2013. Retrieved March 9, 2014 (http://www.usatoday.com).

Sharp, Katie. 2015. "Super Bowl 49: How Much Money Will the Winner Earn?" *SB Nation*. January 30, 2015. Retrieved August 25, 2015 (http://www.sbnation.com).

Smith, Earl. 2014. *Race, Sport and the American Dream.* Durham: Carolina Academic Press.

Veblen, Thorstein. 1953 [1899]. *The Theory of the Leisure Class: An Economic Study of Institutions.* Introduction by C. Wright Mills. New York: Macmillan.

West, Cornel. 2000. *Race Matters*. New York: Vintage.

Williams, Phoebe. 1996. "Performing in a Racially Hostile Environment." *Marquette Sports Law Review* 287, 6:287–314.

Sportsmanship and Sports Journalism

Brian Moritz

In early 2015, two of the biggest stories in sports involved the New England Patriots and the University of Kentucky men's basketball team.

The Patriots—who won their fourth Super Bowl title in a thrilling victory over the Seattle Seahawks—were punished by the NFL after it was discovered that team employees had slightly deflated several footballs before their AFC Championship Game win over the Indianapolis Colts. The scandal, which became known as "Deflategate," led to a suspension of star quarterback Tom Brady and the Patriots (and their star player) to be labeled as cheaters. "Another one of our nation's most beloved sports heroes—a true Patriot—has flushed his integrity down the toilet" (Bianchi 2015).

The University of Kentucky men's basketball team carried an undefeated record into the Final Four, seeking to become the first team in nearly 40 years to finish an entire NCAA season undefeated. However, the Wildcats lost a close game to the University of Wisconsin in the national semifinals. At the end of that game, several of Kentucky's star players walked directly to their locker rooms without doing the customary post-game handshakes with the team that had just beaten them—a move that brought a round of media criticism. "Some of the Kentucky players skulked off without shaking their opponents' hands" (Pells 2015).

It is not hard to find examples of how the sports media defines and defends traditional sportsmanship. But in looking at sportsmanship in the United States, it is important to recognize that there is a bifurcation in the historical development in American sports, between the ideals of traditional sportsmanship—a sort of gentlemanly code in which sports builds character, athletes are expected to perform with class, lose with dignity and "play the game the right way"—and the idea of the Sport Ethic (Hughes and Coakley 1991), in which athletes are dedicated to winning above everything else.

Since sports are mediated in the United States in the 20th and 21st century, our understanding of sportsmanship comes through media coverage of sports. Media coverage defines sports, defines the parameters of success and failure within the sporting world and thus defines what is (and is not) acceptable sportsmanship. The purpose of this essay is to examine how sports journalism in the United States promotes ideas of sportsmanship. Specifically, it will examine how media coverage of sports reflects and represents the bifurcation between classic sportsmanship ideas and the Sport Ethic. It is easy to find examples of how sports journalism endorses traditional sportsmanship ideals—the stories listed above are just two that can easily be found by following sports media. However, this essay proposes that sports journalism and the sports media also perpetuate and reflect the Sport Ethic, which at times is antithetical to classical ideals of sportsmanship. One potential reason for this, which will be described in this essay, are the routine practices of sports journalists—specifically, the reliance on players and coaches as official sources in reporting and stories.

In this essay, the traditional ideals of sportsmanship will be defined, as well as how early sports media helped to create, reflect and perpetuate those ideals. Then, the Sport Ethic will be defined, and its proposed relationship to sports media will be defined and examined.

Traditional Sportsmanship and Sports Journalism

Sports in America is, by in large, a mediated experience. We come to sports in this country through the media, be it watching games on television, viewing highlights on YouTube or reading about them in newspapers, magazines or on websites. Because of this, the way sports are presented in the media has a tremendous impact on how we view them and the values that they represent in our society. Wenner (2006) wrote that "mediated sport is very much perched on a moral landscape" (p. 55). Wenner used the reaction to the infamous Janet Jackson wardrobe malfunction halftime show during Super Bowl XXXVIII as an example not only of how mediated sport is in the United States but how that mediation is fused with morality.

> Mediated sport very much interacts with moral sensibilities ... sport, and our cultural understanding of it, very much plays out along a moral spectrum. Its mediation tells us regular how good sportsmanship is lined to ethical help and should be praised. The stories of athletes gone awry, on and off the field, provide regular moral fodder. And with the constant pushing of bounds in a cluttered and competitive marketplace, the routine practices of media entities will more and more push the tolerances of propriety [Wenner 2006:57].

Those moral sensibilities have their roots in the classical ideals of what we can call traditional sportsmanship. The roots of traditional sportsmanship date back to the beginnings of American sport as an institution in the mid–19th century and the antebellum era. Sports, far from being a frivolous pastime, were seen as an important, useful part of a young man's life (Riess 1997). This was the era of muscular Christianity, and the ideology of sport as a means to build character and as a source of civic and national pride began to take hold. "The same nationalism that encouraged some to define Americans' mission as virtuous hard work caused others to wish for a nation of vigorous, physically fit men" (Gorn 1997:37). Riess (1997) defined three functions of the "sports creed" (p. 175) that made sport an important part of American life: Sport could "improve public health, raise moral standards and build character" (p. 176); sport could "teach morality and promote the social order" (p. 178) and competitive sports serve as a "presumed character building activity" (p. 178).

The rise of sports as an institution in America—as in a codified, organized professional institution rather than an informal pastime—coincided with both the rise of cities in the industrial Northeast and the growth of newspapers, and in particular, the emergence of sports journalism as an important and popular regular section of the newspaper

(Gorn 1997; McChesney 1989). As newspaper journalism grew from a highly partisan avocation into a commercialized profession throughout the 19th century, and as sports grew from a regional pastime to a national institution, so sports journalism developed into a profession with its own norms, values and routines (Boyle 2006; Bryant and Holt 2006; McChesney 1989).

Sports journalism in the United States began in earnest in the 1820s and 1830s, with specialized sports magazines covering primarily horse racing and boxing. At the time, newspaper sports coverage was sporadic, and tended to focus on events with greater social context rather than just games themselves, like a race between horses from the North and the South, or a boxing match between American and British fighters (Bryant and Holt 2006). But by the end of the 19th century, newspapers would become the primary medium covering sport in America (McChesney 1989).

The 19th century saw two major developments in the evolution of American newspaper journalism. The first was the emergence of the Penny Press in the 1830s and 1840s, when newspapers expanded their circulation by dropping the price of an issue in an attempt to appeal to a new demographic of middle-class, urban readers. This was also when newspapers began relying on advertising, rather than circulation, to pay for their costs (Bryant and Holt 2006). The second was the Industrial Revolution in the mid-to-late 19th century, during which urbanization grew in large part to waves of European immigration. This was the era of yellow journalism and sensationalism (McChesney 1989).

Both of these influenced the development of sports journalism as a profession. The growth of the Penny Press saw publishers looking for content that would be popular to the masses. Sports fit that bill perfectly. The *New York Herald*, published by James Gordon Bennett, was one of the first papers to begin showcasing sports coverage—though Bennett apparently expressed regret that he had done so (Bryant and Holt 2006). The Industrial Revolution, with increased urbanization and technological innovations that reduced the cost of gathering and printing news, created conditions in which newspaper circulations soared. With its popularity to a wide audience, sports became a natural focus for newspapers (McChesney 1989). Newspaper sports coverage expanded greatly in this era. The New York World, owned by Joseph Pulitzer, became the first American newspaper with its own sports department in 1883. In 1895, the *New York Journal*, owned by William Randolph Hearst, introduced the first distinct sports section, in which sports coverage had its own part of the paper.

Sports journalism continued to grow in prominence throughout the end of the 19th and beginning of the 20th century. Schlesinger (1956) reported that in 1880, American newspapers dedicated only .04 percent of their space to sports coverage. By 1920, that total ranged from 12–20 percent of a newspaper's total news hole. By the mid–1920s, nearly every newspaper in the country had some kind of sports section. McChesney (1989) wrote that this is when sports journalism emerged as a distinct genre of journalism, and became an "indispensable section of the daily newspaper" (p. 55).

The relationship between the sport industry and the media that cover it has long been one that has been criticized. McChesney (1989) defined the relationship between sports and the media as a longtime symbiotic one. "One of the happiest relationships in American society is between sports and the media" (Michener 2014:355). In the 19th century, media played a critical role in making sport both an acceptable social institution and a popular commercial one. "The regular, routine reporting of sports in newspapers and specialized magazines helped shift the cultural attitude towards sports in general, and during the 1870s through 1890s, America's love affair with sports began" (Bryant and Holt 2006:25). Through their coverage and promotional efforts, newspaper sports journalists helped to standardize and codify the rules of horse racing, baseball and college football (Bryant and Holt 2006).

Along with standardizing and codifying rules, the growth in sports media helped to establish and codify the ideals of sportsmanship, of sports being a moral institution that builds character. Two of the biggest stars in American sports in the early 20th century, Babe Ruth and Red Grange, were celebrated for how their stories dovetailed with ideals of sportsmanship. Grange, the early football star, was celebrated for a career that "seemed to confirm traditional values and the survival of the dream of the self-made man" (Rader 1990:141). Babe Ruth, the dominant American sporting hero of the early 20th century, was beloved in large part because of his perceived pure love of playing baseball. Rader quoted a contemporary sports writer who wrote of Ruth. "With him, the game *is* the thing. He loves baseball; loves just to play it" (Rader 1990:138).

While there is a certain amount of hagiography and promotion in those accounts (Ruth's off-field exploits are legendary and would have made him a favorite of TMZ had he played in current times), they are indicative of the power that sports journalism held in that era. Sports journalism helped to define what it meant to be a sportsman, an athlete. It defined how athletes were expected to carry themselves on and off the field. It defined playing the game the right way. One of the primary functions of mass media is cultural transmission—the transference of the dominant culture and its norms and values (Pavlik and McIntosh 2014). In sports, the mass media transmitted the norms and values that formed the foundation of sporting life in America—sportsmanship.

> The ideas associated with sports—universal rules, fair play, utter seriousness in a frivolous cause, measurable performance, the joy of physical excellence, the tension of key competition, the expertise of spectators—were constantly spreading into the larger national culture [Gorn 1997:57].

From this ethical point of view, media coverage of certain sports stories becomes clear. The New England Patriots violated the core tenets of sportsmanship by not playing fairly and bending/breaking the rules in an attempt to win. The Kentucky basketball players should have acted with more class and lost with dignity. Both of these attitudes were widely reflected in media coverage of both events (Howard 2015; Pells 2015). As Wenner wrote, our mediated sports are perched on a moral landscape—the landscape of traditional sportsmanship.

The Sport Ethic and Sports Journalism

But for all the importance that sports journalism has placed on traditional sportsmanship ideals, it's important to note that there is a historical bifurcation in sporting ideals. There has always been a line in American sporting culture between the idealistic "play with class and dignity" and the desire to win. Oriard (1997) described how Walter Camp, the founder of American football, straddled that line and helped define part of American sporting culture. "Camp's was a democratic sporting ethic that presupposed success would go to those who earned it" (Oriand 1997:115). Orient (1997) notes that during the early days of American football under Camp in the late 19th century, players did whatever they could to win games, "competition against the rules as well as their opponents" (p. 93). Camp, in fact, defined the bifurcation in sportsmanship described earlier in this chapter—one of a moral, upstanding competition, but one in which the goal was, above all, to win. Oriad (1997) argues that this bifurcation is a unique characteristic to the growth of American sports.

> This attitude toward the rules—a recognition of the letter but not the spirit, a dependence on rules in the absence of tradition yet also a celebration of the national genius for circumventing them—expressed an American democratic ethos, a dialectical sense of "fair play" (embracing both "sportsmanship" and "gamesmanship") that was very different from the aristocratic British version [Oriad 1997:93].

For Oriand (1997), the American sensibility was one of taking advantage of the rules, finding the loopholes that can be used by stretching the rules' limits without overtly breaking them. Think of an NFL team rushing to snap the ball after a close play to prevent a possible instant replay review. Oriand (1997) recounts a talk given by baseball manager Buck Ewing to his players: "Boys, he told his players during a spring training session on strategy you've heard the rules read now the question is what can we do to bet them? Many applauded this attitude" (p. 92).

This idea bleeds into the notion of the Sport Ethic, which Hughes and Coakley developed in the early 1990s after conducting in-depth research into the attitudes elite athletes—ones that played at the professional, Olympic or Division I college (level). The Sport Ethic consists of four norms or characteristics that dominate sporting culture. Those traits are the willingness to sacrifice all other aspects of one's life in order to play; a relentless strive for perfection and distinction; playing through physical pain; and a refusal to accept limits (Coakley 2009).

Here are more in-depth definitions of all four aspects, from Hughes and Coakley (1991):

1. "Being an athlete involves making sacrifices for The Game" (p. 309): Hughes and Coakley define this as the athlete's desire to "subordinating other interests for the sake of an exclusive commitment to their sport" (p. 309). Elite athletes must be willing to subjugate every other aspect of their lives to their sport and their team. "They must be willing to pay the price to stay involved in sport" (p. 309). Coakley (2009) points out examples of athletes who continue to play sports despite numerous injuries and numerous surgeries.
2. "Being an athlete involves striving for distinction" (p. 309): This is defined as the constant drive to improve, to become bigger, faster, stronger, better. The point of sports is getting better and, in the end, winning. "True athletes seek to improve, to get better, to come closer to perfection. Winning symbolizes improvement and establishes distinction; losing is tolerated only to the extent that it is part of the experience of learning how to win" (p. 309). An additional way of looking at this is that winning is not just the goal—continuing to win is the norm. Winning once is never enough, no matter what the cost.
3. "Being an athlete involves accepting risks and playing through pain" (p. 309): This, Coakley and Hughes write, evokes not just the physical courage in shaking off physical injuries or ignoring potential long-term health risks in continuing to play. It is also about "moral courage" (p. 309) and the ability to be cool and composed in the face of such obstacles. "The idea is that athletes never back down from challenges in

the form of either physical risk or pressure, and that standing up to challenges involves moral courage" (p. 309). This is reflected, for example, in how football players will play through numerous concussions, despite the potential long-term health risks, in order to win the respect and admiration of their teammates.

4. "Being an athlete involves refusing to accept limits in the pursuit of possibilities" (p. 310): This is defined as pursuing ones' dream and not accepting any notion that it may be impossible to achieve. Through hard work, practice, dedication and adherence to the sporting ethic, anything can be done. True athletes never quit, no matter what. Hughes and Coakley write:

> An athlete does not accept a situation without trying to change it, overcome it, turn the scales. It is believed that sport is a sphere of life in which anything is possible.... An athlete is a person obligated to pursue dreams without reservation. External limits are not recognized as valid [p. 310].

Taken collectively, the Sport Ethic define the attitudes that fuel athletes, coaches and so much of the sporting world. Acceptance of these four traits is the price of doing business in professional sports. And to be considered a true champion, to excel in professional sports, to stand out, Hughes and Coakley (1991) argue that an athlete must blindly accept the sporting ethic:

> Many athletes do not see their overconformity to the sport ethic as deviant; they see it as confirming and reconfirming their identity as athletes and as members of select sport groups. Following the guidelines of the sport ethic to an extreme is just what you do as an athlete, especially when continued participation and success in sport take on significant personal and social meaning [p. 311].

The "Sporting Ethic" is important because it leads to what Coakley (2009) calls deviant overconformity. He defines this as "supranormal ideas, traits, and actions that indicate an uncritical acceptance of norms and a failure to recognize any limits to following norms" (p. 159). First defined by Ewald and Jiobu (1985) in their study of male bodybuilders and competitive distance running, deviant overconformity has been widely studied in sports. Curry (1993) found that for an amateur wrestler, the normalization of injury is seen as a traditional form of role socialization. Podlog and Eklund (2007) found that athletes may feel pressure to return from injuries before they are physically and mentally ready in part because they have internalized the Sport Ethic.

Deviant overconformity to the sporting ethic promotes a culture in which athletes unquestioningly give their entire lives to their sport, regardless of their physical welfare. It also promotes a culture of championships, where all that matters is winning. An athlete is defined as either a champion or a failure. It is within this sporting culture that so many other forms of deviance arise. The use of performance-enhancing drugs—be it HGH or steroids in football and baseball or EPO on cycling—occurs because of this ethic and the desire to win being put above all else. The challenges that concussions are posing to collegiate and professional football players, as well as the long-term health risks they face after their careers, arise from deviant overconformity to the sporting ethic. Athletes feel they have to put their own health on the line and risk their own bodies. It is part of who they are and what they do.

Looking at the stories at the start of this essay from the point of view of the Sport Ethic, the Patriots' behavior was justified because they won the championship. The quest for success is the ultimate goal, and winning is everything. The Patriots won a championship. End of story. In fact, Deflategate can be seen as a classic example of deviant overconformity—an organization that conforms so much to the ethic of winning that it bends any rule it can to gain an advantage. Similarly, the Kentucky basketball players' move is understandable. If winning is everything, than falling short of that distinction is the ultimate dishonor. The reaction to that failure is understandable.

While there has been wide study into the notions that fuel deviant overconformity in sports, there has not been much research focused solely on the four pegs of the Sport Ethic. There has also not been much research into how the sports media coverage reflects, endorses and perpetuates both the sporting ethic and deviant overconformity. As shown earlier, Coakley (2009) was able to pick examples of each of the four traits of the Sport Ethic from popular media coverage of sports, but there has been little overall research into this point.

Coakley (2009) detailed how media coverage of sports is often focused on the ideological theme of success, that winning is the ultimate goal of any athlete or team. Taking this one step further, the ability to win in the eyes of elite athletes and coaches comes from adherence to the norms and traits of the Sport Ethic. It stands to reason that media coverage of sports news would reflect the norms and traits of the Sport Ethic, since that leads to one of the dominant narratives in sports media coverage.

One reason that sports journalism could potentially reflect and perpetuate the Sport Ethic lies in the norms and practices of journalists—specifically, the reliance on sources. Gans (1979) called the journalism-source relationship the central relationship of journalism.

Journalism is, in many ways, dependent upon sources. This practice is partly pragmatic. Reporters can't be everywhere. They can't be there when a decision on which football player to draft in the first round is made. Therefore, they are reliant upon sources for their information. While these sources can include documents (both public and private) and databases, sources are primarily people. Sigal (1973) noted that journalism can be defined as what a source says has happened or what will happen. Gans (1979) compared the journalist-source relationship to a dance and that the source is always leading. Without sources, journalists have little or no news to report.

Who these sources are is important to consider as well. Sigal (1973), Gans (1979), Fishman (2014), and Tuchman (1980), among many others, noted that journalists rely more on official sources—primarily official government sources—than anyone else for their news. Official sources also hold a place of privilege for reporters because they are regular, reliable sources of news. Government officials hold regular press conferences. Courts are open to the public and transcripts are available. Gans (1979) noted that reporters are interested in efficiency of news gathering—not out of nefarious, capitalist reasons but simply so they easily get their stories done by deadline. Official sources provide this regular source of news that's socially sanctioned.

Sources matter in the study of media sociology because they are where news comes from and they help frame the news. A journalist, even today, is judged professionally by the quality of his or her sources and the kind of access he or she has. A desire for sources on both sides of the political aisle is one of the core reasons that objectivity is considered the most important professional norm for journalists (Soloski 1989).

In sports journalism, Rowe (2007) found that sports journalists tend to use star athletes, coaches and administrators as sources in stories, and Lowes (Lowes 1999) wrote that sportswriters are reliant upon access to athletes, which leads to a culture that promotes more positive than critical coverage. These findings are consistent with literature on sources from political news, where journalists are reliant on official government sources (e.g., Gans 1979; Sigal 1973). For example, British journalists who cover the English Premier League believe these limits they have to team members makes their jobs more difficult (Boyle 2006; Coombs and Osborne 2012).

In his study of a Canadian newspaper's sports department, Lowes (1999) studied how the routines and practices of the reporters shaped what sports received coverage and what didn't. He found that the routines overwhelmingly favored coverage of major professional sports, leading to a distinct lack of coverage for amateur or other sports that didn't fit into the milieu of big-time sports:

> The routine work practices and professional ideologies that constitute sports newswork—while eminently successful in capturing the goings-on of the major-league commercial sports world with precision and admirable detail—are principally a "means not to know" about another, more expansive world: the world of non-commercial spectator sports [Lowes 1999:96].

A Case Study: The Sport Ethic and PTI

In order to examine how the Sport Ethic is both reflected in and perpetuated by sports journalists, a pilot study was conducted using ESPN's *Pardon the Interruption* (*PTI*) as an example (Moritz 2012). *PTI* is a daily sports debate show starring former *Washington Post* columnists and longtime friends Tony Kornheiser and Michael Wilbon. As one of the most popular shows on ESPN (Mansfield 2002), the primary outlet for television sports news in the United States, and one that is hosted by two veteran sportswriters who formerly worked for one of the country's main newspapers, *PTI* can be considered an accurate reflection of mainstream sports news and mainstream sports media culture.

At the time of the study, the show featured seven or so minutes of the two hosts debating the top sports stories of the day, with the stories structured from high-to-low importance, much like the structure of a TV news show or a daily newspaper. A content analysis was conducted over a constructed week (five individual days over a five-week period) in the summer of 2012.

The study found that elements of the "Sport Ethic" are an ingrained part of the stories selected and the discussion on *PTI*. Specifically, the strive for distinction is heavily prevalent. The notion of winning, that an athlete should strive to win and keep winning and keep improving, is embedded in so many of the discussions on *PTI*. The prevalence of the strive-for-distinction norm fits in with previous research that shows that the narrative of success/winning is prominent in sports media coverage (Coakley 2009). The norm of an athlete having the proper attitude was also seen in many of the stories. Within the sample, there was not much presence of the acceptance-of-risk or the accept-no-limits norms. That may have been just the luck of the draw with the sample selected. Since there were no high-profile injuries, or stories involving the violence of sports, this norm was not really featured in the shows of this sample.

The Sport Ethic, in its original conception, deals with how athletes see themselves and their colleagues, how they define what they do, who they are and what equals success in sports. It does not involve how the media discuss sports. This was reflected in the pilot study. Many times, the story itself reflected the Sport Ethic, or the question posed as a part of the story reflected the Sport Ethic, but the discussion between the two hosts did not. Examples of this include then-Baylor women's basketball star Britney Griner's perceived failure of why she didn't win a national championship or New Orleans Saints quarterback Drew Brees' desire to hold out from the team's minicamp because of a contract dispute. In both of these instances, Wilbon and Kornheiser expressed an opinion that was antithetical to the Sport Ethic, either that Griner's reputation was unfairly maligned due to a lack of a national title or that Brees should hold out in order to make more money. This indicates that while the discussion itself may not fuel the Sporting Ethic, the stories themselves do. To use the theoretical language of mass communications, the initial data in this study suggest that the sports media's gatekeeping practices may perpetuate the Sport Ethic, but not necessarily the media's framing practices.

Conclusion: Future Research

Looking forward, further content analyses of different forms of sports media would provide a deeper and more nuanced understanding of how sports journalism and the sports media perpetuate and reflect the Sport Ethic. Further research can also potentially delve into the bifurcated attitude toward sportsmanship in American sports and the sports media—how much of sports coverage reflects traditional sportsmanship ideals, how much reflects the Sport Ethic, and how are those perceived ideological conflicts resolved. In addition, the effect of the increase in digital and social media—particularly mainstream blogs like Deadspin that trumpet their lack of access and outsider points of view (Moritz 2012)—in this area would be interesting to observe. Since these outlets often define their purpose, mission and their editorial style in direct opposition to mainstream legacy sports media, it would be curious to see if these outlets define sportsmanship in a different way or if their definitions of sportsmanship lie in opposition to traditional definitions. Since these outlets are popular among younger readers, these differences could spark an evolution in how younger audience members and sports fans understand and define sportsmanship.

Bibliography

Bianchi, Mike. 2015. "Bianchi: Tom Brady, Like a-Rod, Barry Bonds, Lance Armstrong, Is Just Another Sports Cheater." *Orlando Sentinel*, May 21. Retrieved May 22, 2015 (http://www.orlandosentinel.com).

Boyle, Raymond. 2006. *Sports Journalism*. London: Sage.

Bryant, Jennings, and Andrea M. Holt. 2006. "A Historical Overview of Sports and Media in the United States," pp. 21–44 in *Handbook of Sports and Media* edited by Arthur A. Raney and Jennings Bryant. Mahwah, NJ: Lawrence Erlbaum Associates.

Coakley, Jay. 2009. *Sports in Society: Issues and Controversies*, 10th ed. New York: McGraw Hill.

Coombs, Danielle S., and Anne Osborne. 2012. "Sports Journalists and England's Barclay's Premier League: a Case Study Examining Reporters' Takes on Modern Football." *International Journal of Sport Communication*, 5:412–425.

Curry, Timothy J. 1993. "A Little Pain Never Hurt Anyone: Athletic Career Socialization and the Normalization of Sports Injury." *Symbolic Interaction*, 16 (3):273–90.

Ewald, Keith, and Robert M. Jiobu. 1985. "Explaining Positive Deviance: Becker's Model and the Case of Runners and Bodybuilders." *Sociology of Sport Journal*, 2 (2):144–156.

Fishman, Mark 1980. *Manufacturing the News*. Austin: University of Texas Press.

Gans, Herbert J. 1979. *Deciding What's News*. Evanston: Northwestern University Press.

Gorn, Elliott J. 1997. "Sports Through the Nineteenth Century," pp. 33–57 in *The New American Sport History*, edited by S.W. Pope. Urbana: University of Illinois Press.

Howard, Greg 2015. "The Ballghazi Takes Are Back, and They Are More Insane Than Ever." Retrieved May 27, 2015 (http://deadspin.com).
Hughes, Robert, and Jay Coakley. 1991. "Positive Deviance Among Athletes." *Sociology of Sport Journal*, 8:307–25.
Lowes, Mark D. 1999. *Inside the Sports Pages*. Toronto: University of Toronto Press.
Mansfield, Stephanie. 2002. "Revenge of the Words." *Sports Illustrated*, August 5. Retrieved May 27, 2015 (http://www.si.com).
McChesney, Robert W. 1989. "Media Made Sport: A History of Sports Coverage in the United States," pp. 49–67 in *Media, Sports and Society* edited by Lawrence Wenner. New York: Sage.
Michener, James A. 2014. *Sports in America*. New York: Dial Press.
Moritz, Brian. 2012. "*PTI* and the Sport Ethic." Paper presented at the 2012 Northeast Popular Culture Association Conference, Rochester, NY.
Oriand, Michael 1997. "In the Beginning Was the Rule," pp. 88–120 in *The New American Sport History*, edited by S.W. Pope. Urbana: University of Illinois Press.
Pavlik, John V., and Shawn McIntosh. 2014. *Converging Media*. Oxford: Oxford University Press.
Pells, Eddie 2015. "'The Season Was a Waste': Kentucky Becomes Latest to Take Undefeated Record Into Final Four, and Lose." *The Associated Press*. Retrieved May 22, 2015 (http://www.sltrib.com).
Podlog, Leslie, and Robert C. Eklund. 2007. "The Psychosocial Aspects of a Return to Sport Following Serious Injury: A Review of the Literature From a Self-Determination Perspective." *Psychology of Sport and Exercise*, 8 (4):535–66.
Rader, Benjamin G. 1990. *American Sports: From the Age of Folk Games to the Age of Televised Sports*. Upper Saddle River, NJ: Prentice Hall.
Riess, S. A. 1997. "Sport and the Redefinition of Middle-Class Masculinity in Victorian America," pp. 173–97 in *The New American Sport History*, edited by S.W. Pope. Urbana: University of Illinois Press.
Rowe, David 2007. "Sports Journalism Still the 'Toy Department' of the News Media?" *Journalism*, 8 (4):385–405.
Schlesinger, Arthur M. 1956. *The Rise of the City*. New York: Macmillan.
Sigal, Leon V. 1973. *Reporters and Officials*. Lexinton, MA: D.C. Heath.
Soloski, J. (1989). "News Reporting and Professionalism: Some Constraints on the Reporting of the News." *Media, Culture & Society*, 11 (2):207–228.
Tuchman, Gaye 1980. *Making News*. New York: Free Press.
Wenner, Lawrence A. 2006. "Sports and Media Through the Super Glass Mirror: Placing Blame, Breast-Beating, and a Gaze to the Future," pp. 45–62 in *Handbook of Sports Media*, edited by Arthur Raney and Jennings Bryant. Mahwah, NJ: Lawrence Erlbaum Associates.

Football on Film

The Portrayal of Sportsmanship

LAURA FINNEGAN *and* JEAN MCARDLE

The function of film in the modern world goes way beyond that of simply being an aesthetic object. The satisfaction found in film and described by Dyer (1977) as a "utopian sensibility" (p. 6) is shared by lovers of sport. Like sport, popular film takes place in an arena that engages with the audience and provides the viewer with joy, sadness, anger, hope and entertainment amongst other sentiments. Mediated modern elite sport uses commentary, narrative, cinematography, editing and sound to bring the spectators an event that will engage their sensibilities on a number of levels. Film directors have been doing the same thing since the early 1900s. Through film and the media, our role of spectator is heightened by the viewing of celebrities, the styles and genres of the film, and like sport all become part of our personal culture and in many ways our identity. An examination of popular culture and sport suggests that sport can be seen as a reflection of the beliefs and values contained within a culture and the same has been suggested of film. Yet this is too simplistic a view; the pictures, codes, conventions, myths and ideologies of film, as in sport, are products of competing and conflicting cultural, subcultural, industrial and institutional determinants (Turner 1988). Film in popular culture today is a form of entertainment as well as a social and cultural narrative. The representation of sport in film has been a steadfast context for the delivery of cultural, social, economic messages and the concept of sportsmanship has been an integral part of this.

Why Sport in Film?

Richard Barsam (2007) outlined a five-part characteristic structure of film. Films tend to lead with the exposition (opening, background of story, main characters introduced, and scene setter), rising action (development of principal conflict, perhaps complicated by secondary conflicts), climax (a turning point), falling action (moving towards a resolution of the principal conflict) and denouement (clarity of ending, summation of key questions). Sport films often mirror these characteristics closely and the following films which are examined within this essay are no exception. Films based on the sporting genre lend themselves to this structure due to the often large character base, for example players, coaches, athletic department and institution staff, which can extend to multiple relationship storylines and allow for vicissitudes of character development. This setting also allows for potentially dramatic turning points such as the execution of a pass by a quarterback, followed by a dramatic catch in the end zone by a receiver to win a match and turn around fortunes, or a more subtle approach of a turning point based on interpersonal relationships, often with a background of social tension.

When examining the concept of sportsmanship in film there are two broad categories from which to explore; textual and contextual. Textual analysis responds to a set of conclusions or specific characteristics of the film text such as gender, the sport being played, the athletes, spectators, or the institutions at play (*Remember the Titans* 2000; *We Are Marshall* 2006). Contextual analysis examines the cultural (*Green Street* 2005), political, institutional and industrial determinants of a film, documentaries (*Senna* 2010) and political genres (*Munich* 2005). Crossan (2013) has identified the theme of struggle, and the perceived role of sport as a means of overcoming adversities being one of the most popular thematic aspects of the sports film. Acts of sportsmanship often are the catalyst for these turning points and subsequent actions and conclusions. Central characters exhibit patterns of positive and mature moral reasoning perhaps when conventional strategies might suggest that the opposite would be more likely to lead to athletic success (Weiss and Bredemeir 1986) and can often be seen to overcome social, structural and cultural divisions through the medium of sport (Rowe 1998:335). Whilst this could be argued to present an overly simplistic notion of the solution of a myriad of problems, often sportsmanship in film mirrors good and perhaps idealistic notions of citizenship.

The Hollywood sports film has historically portrayed two sides of sport; first, the view of the world which attests that anyone who is determined, hardworking and plays by societal rules will succeed, aligning with the true ethos of amateurism and sportsmanship. Second, there is also the interpretation of the athlete who triumphs over adversity in a contest of skill and ability. Themes that emerge in sports films range from nationalism, race, class, gender, failure and triumph. Sport in film regularly shows sport as an avenue for social mobility, "the poor kid that done good." The concept of fair play and sportsmanship in a highly economic and commercial and progressively more corrupt industry still leads us, as the viewer, to be drawn in to the struggle within sport where underdogs do achieve the impossible victory and both the film and the sports within provide us with a place to escape. The range of sports films are vast and extend from the "news films" of major prize fights (*Raging Bull* 1980) or blockbusters such as *The Blind Side* (2009) and *Moneyball* (2011) and documentaries such as *Senna* (2010). As with many things in the world today, sports have helped to sell movie and commercial modern elite sports have also benefited from their portrayal within film.

Why Football?

Many films have used sport as a backdrop to contextualize other thematic qualities but a brief look through film records shows that the game of football, particularly in Hollywood blockbusters, has been used more than most. Football as a sport balances elements such as physical competition, teamwork and strategy; football transcends its role as just a mode of physical exertion and has become an integral part of culture (Herbeck 2003). Oriard (1993) provides a reason for the use of football being portrayed through the medium of film suggesting that "'football' as a cultural expression is an abstraction; specific games and seasons, teams and players can have a variety of concrete meanings" (p. 3). Various forms of football exist worldwide; American football, Gaelic football, Australian rules, Rugby and they have been the subject of film productions: *Australian Rules* (2002) and *The Club* from Australian rules, *Rooney* (1958) with a Gaelic Games backdrop in Ireland, *Forever Strong* (2008) and *Invictus* (2009) based on Rugby. Football films whether they focus on the NFL, college or the high school game, provide a perfect context in today's celebrity obsessed world to emphasize the drama, emotion, spectacle and show stopping event that is the game of football. A search on the popular internet based movie, film and television search engine IMDb demonstrates the popularity and extent of films made based on American football with over 123 returned films in a search. Whilst not being an exhaustive list, these films range in release date from 1925 (*The Freshman*) to 2015 (*Gridiron UK*). The focus of these films has changed over the past almost 100 years; in the 1920 and 30s the focus was on collegiate football, but this changed to more inspirational movies in the 1940 and 50s focusing on character and heroic virtues. "The 1960/70s primarily although not exclusively denounced the excesses in professional sports, with the 1980s through to today revisiting the older themes of inspiration and sportsmanship and survival against the odds whilst attempting to offer more substantive critiques of the heroic football figures and American society in general" (Herbeck 2003:363). These films reflect broader themes in society, often using a "good sportsmanship" act as the turning point for behaviors and actions towards moralistic social behaviors or having the "hero" of the piece display sportsmanship virtues and exemplify a utopian or idealistic form of behavior, whilst at the same time grappling with the realities of displaying this behavior often with the backdrop of social or psychological unrest. The struggle between what may be the "easiest" course of action and those displays of sportsmanship, that perhaps include "an altruistic act, which whilst praiseworthy is not obligatory for the sportsperson, coach or spectator in the situation" (Hare 1981:198).

The Development of Sportsmanship through Sport

In film, a "top down" approach to developing good sportsmanlike behaviors means that coaches are often portrayed as the catalyst for moral reasoning and integrity amongst players, with sport helping to overcome and circumnavigate social problems. Shields and Bredemier's (1995) view of sportsmanship as being a fundamental component of character and one that "transcends the world of sport" (p. 194) is a key feature of the coaches relationship with players, coaching staff, the wider society and indeed personal incongruence in relation to race and coaching behaviors. Social learning theorists (Bandura 1996) posit that the modeling and reinforcement of behaviors from a number of sources such as coaches or parents result in moral development. This social learning process is continually influenced by personal cognitions, behavior from significant others and the wider environment. Using social learning as a platform to explain sportsmanship, this theoretical framework proposes that it is the propensity to act in line with sportsmanship type behaviors, those harnessed through social learning and the social context and motivations which influence behavior (Vallerand and Losier 1994). Therefore, being in a position of influence on individual behaviors and culture settings within a sports team means that coaches are in a prime position to display appropriate behaviors and foster a culture of sportsmanship. The Arizona Sports Summit Accord (1999) heralded that a duty of sports leadership was to promote sportsmanship and foster good character by teaching, enforcing, advocating, and modeling the ethical principles of trustworthiness, respect, responsibility, fairness, caring and good citizenship. Martins (2004) suggest that as the development of athletic talent (physical, tactical, technical) can benefit from coaching, so can moral development benefit from coaching. Therefore, sport as a form of cultural activity and particularly the use of sport in film provides us with a context to examine sportsmanship from a number of avenues; the athlete, the coach, the business, the wins, the losses and also through a third lens, the eye of the spectator. Within the course of this essay sportsmanship will be examined using the coach, the athlete and the spectator as the basis for analysis. The following four excerpts taken from four different films were chosen for two reasons: issues relating to football (American and soccer) and issues relating to sportsmanship. *Remember the Titans* and *We Are Marshall* examine the link between the Coach and the development of ideology within a team; *When the Game Stands Tall* looks at both the Coach and athletes; while in stark contrast, *Green Street Hooligan* examines the role of the spectator. Selected scenes have been chosen to highlight the denouement of each of the films in relation to sportsmanship characteristics.

Remember the Titans *(2000)*

Based in Virginia, 1971, amid the backdrop of racial tensions, *Remember the Titans* is the story of the T.C. Williams football team which became the first integrated college football team under federal mandate. The squad became a microcosm of society at the time, dealing with racial tensions, fear of the unknown, protectionism and suspicion, the inequitable treatment from authorities, perceptions of equality and open hostility. The film depicts how the African-American coach (Herman Boone) is placed as head coach at the expense of the highly successful regular head coach, Bill Yoast. The importance and significance of the head coach position for Yoast is evident by the narrative about his wife leaving him due to his obsession with the position and also in his daughter addressing him as "coach." Yoast's moral integrity is demonstrated early in the film when he intervened to stop and discourage his players from joining in on a fight outside the school which had broken out amid racial tensions in the fledgling school integration process. Boone demonstrated his ability to separate out personal reasoning and athletic reasoning from the outset; his solidarity with and protests alongside Martin Luther King and his past conflict with the KKK is alluded to, but he allays fears of a potential anti-white player backlash by assuring everyone that "the best player will play, color won't matter." This sense of fairness and equality sets the tone for the players and the coaching staff. The portrayal of this microcosm of racial tensions in the film attempts to reflect the difficult and complex nature of the wider societal processes; for example, after a late night physically draining run to Gettysburg, Boone asks that the players respect each other, not caring if they like each other. Whilst this may appear to contradict the notion of "caring" as an element of good character, the notion of respect was seen as the initial behavior to be modeled by and reinforced by the coaching staff. Boone later remonstrated with Yoast for being too lenient on the African American players, suggesting that this "patronizing of black players" would cripple them for life. These players may have experienced structural inequalities in life, but their place and role on the team was built on a level playing field. Throughout the film, Herman Boone makes a number of speeches hailing the vicissitudes of football which mirrors society: "Football is about controlling that anger, harnessing that aggression into a team effort to achieve perfection" and "This is my sanctuary right here. All this hatred and turmoil swirling around us, but this, this is always right. Struggle, Survival, Victory and Defeat."

Despite the prevailing conflicts that the school integration causes, Boone uses this as a motivational factor to demonstrate to the players how much they had morally and personally developed during the integration process:

> "I'm not going to talk to you tonight about winning and losing, you're already winners because you didn't kill each other up at camp. Tonight we got Hayfield, like all the other schools in this conference they're all white. They don't have to worry about race, we do. But we're better for it. We don't let anything, nothing come between us. Nothing tears us apart" [Herman Boone].

Yoast demonstrated the altruistic qualities of sportsmanship in a number of scenes throughout the movie. During the initial upheaval of the change of coaching structures, the players and their parents wanted to boycott the team to have Yoast reinstated. Despite this action potentially re-securing Yoast his job (and identity), he persuades the players not to take the action as it would possibly jeopardize their athletic and academic futures. He took a morally praiseworthy stand when calling out the racist referee and school board and thus eroding his chance of obtaining a Hall of Fame award. In relation to Barsam's (2007) film characteristics, this climactic moment was prompted in part by the reactions of his daughter, especially her disgust and disillusionment with the racist calls. Confronted by this situation, he took the supererogatory step of intervening. With the film culminating in the State Championship game, Yoast asks Boone for help:

> "You've taught this city how to trust the soul of a man rather than the look of him and I suppose it's about time I joined the club. Herman, I sure could use your help" [Bill Yoast].

Both coaches confer to develop the final play, their partnership mirrored by their daughters' burgeoning relationship in the stand. With Yoast conceding that Boone was the right man for the job, they managed together to unite as coaches, unite a team and unite the supporters around them, showing how in this instance sport and sportsmanship can transcend social divides.

We Are Marshall *(2006)*

Set in the town of Huntington, West Virginia, in 1970, *We Are Marshall* depicts the aftermath of a plane crash that killed 75 people. This included 37 football players, coaching staff, athletic trainers and the athletic director from the Marshall University "Thundering Herd" football team. Whilst ostensibly dealing with the rebuilding of the football team, it is a story about a community dealing with adversity and the place of sport in helping the team to cope with grief. The steel mill plays an initial role in setting the scene for football in this community, an industrial, uninspiring town whose civic pride seems to center on their football team. When the plane carrying the football team crashes and no survivors are declared, the community and its members deal with grief in various ways, such as processions of funerals, keeping beer cans meant for one of the players, and wearing an intended's engagement ring.

> "Those were not welcome days. We buried: sons, brothers, mothers, fathers, fiancées. Clocks ticked but ... time did not pass. The sun rose and the sun set, but the shadows remained. When

once there was sound, now there was silence. What once was whole now was shattered" [Annie Cantrell].

Conflict abounds amongst residents as to whether the football program should be suspended. Eventually star cornerback Nate Ruffin garners public and eventually institutional support to rebuild the program. Marshall President Donald Dedmon's search for a coach proves fruitless until Jack Lengyel agrees to take on the role. Lengyel recognized and felt impassioned by the suffering that the town continued to endure.

"When I heard about what had happened, your situation, the only thing I could think about was the four of them. I thought about how much they mean to me, about how bad it would hurt if ... well if I was to lose them (his children). Then I thought about a team, and a school, and a town that's gotta be hurtin' real bad. And I thought, hell, maybe I could help" [Jack Lengyel].

Lengyel's positivity, encouragement and use of sometimes obscure anecdotes leads to Dedmon persuading the NCCA to make an exception and allow the university to start freshmen. Jack provides a motivating force behind recruitment, even being bold enough to ask a rival college for tactical help. Apart from changing perceptions and attitudes of his own players, Lengyl demonstrates that he has also developed morally throughout the rebuilding process:

"Winning is everything and nothing else matters. I mean I've.... I've said that so many times myself I ... I ... I ... I lost count. You know and ... it doesn't matter what sport. And it doesn't matter what country. Any coach who's worth a darn in this business believes those words fact. Then I came here ... and for the first time in my life, hell maybe for the first time in the history of sports suddenly it's just not true anymore. At least not here, not now. No ... ya see, Red, it doesn't matter if we win, or if we lose. It's not even about how we play the game. What matters is that we play the game. That we take the field. That we suit up on Saturdays and we keep this program alive. We play the game and Red, I'm tellin' ya one day ... not today, not tomorrow. Not this season probably. Not next season either, but one day you and I are gunna wake up suddenly we're gunna be like every other team, in every other sport where winning is everything, and nothing else matters. When that day comes ... well that's when we'll honor them" [Jack Lengyel].

The film culminates in the team's first home game of the season, where they face a formidable opponent and win.

"Today, I want to talk about our opponent this afternoon. They're bigger, faster, stronger, more experienced and on paper, they're just better. And they know it, too. But I want to tell you something that they don't know. They don't know your heart. I do. I've seen it" [Jack Lengyel].

The "social union" view of sportsmanship sees sport as a collection of individuals united by a particular practice, a social union where players and communities come together to share a commonly valued form of life (Arnold 1984:63). Lengyel tries to remove the social and emotional obstacles for his athletic and coaching staff throughout the film, in an attempt to overcome and deal with the grief experienced, and rebuild morale amongst a divided community through the medium of sport, participation and support and social union. Rebuilding the culture of togetherness in the community displays a selfless act of sportsmanship by Lengyl.

When the Game Stands Tall *(2014)*

The Game Stands Tall starts as it means to go on with a moving quote from Coach Ladouceur in the opening sequence, setting the tone for the rest of the film:

"That's what this program is about, it ain't about the football, it ain't about scoring the touchdowns. It's about moving you in a direction that can help and assist you to grow up. So that when you take your place in the world or out in the community you can be depended on" [Coach Ladouceur].

Letting us, the viewers, know from the start that the film is about something other than just football. Inspired by a true story and adapted from a book of the same name, *When the Game Stands Tall* regales the journey of legendary football coach and religious studies teacher Bob Ladouceur, who took the De La Salle High School Spartans of Concord California from obscurity to a 151-game winning streak that shattered all records for any American sport. Possibly overshadowed by other films in this genre, the film provides us with a lens from which to examine sportsmanship and athletes. The key message throughout the film is based on the concept of family, brotherhood and team. The coach (Ladouceur) has taken on the role of not just sports coaching but life coaching; his concern that his athletes develop and become honorable, accountable men who value their own self-worth and that of others both on and off the field are central to his role in the film. The film is littered with solid game sequences and somewhat threadbare inspirational sports drama clichés but it provides a recent and relevant forum that takes the fundamental components of sportsmanship qualities, such as valor, honor, belief, social union, the promotion of pleasure and a form of altruism (Arnold 1984) and entrenches these characteristics within this film in abundance. Referring back to the work of Barsam (2007), one climactic event within the film is when two of the players on the team, "Cam Colvin" and "T.K Kelly," are approached by University of Oregon. Colvin hesitates due to family circumstances but the love, affection and belief of Kelly for "his family" help him to change his decision which becomes even more poignant when T.K gets gunned down later in the film. The attributes assigned to T.K by Coach Ladouceur align with the core philosophies of what it means to be a good sportsman:

"When you came to us as an awkward freshman, all arms and legs, a coach couldn't help but notice the smooth grace of your athletic ability.... We ask our players to learn and embrace ideals; perfection, commitment, compassion, brotherhood, faith and from the first time TK crossed that field I saw a kid who wasn't just athletic but genuine in so many ways. He embodied those ideals. He never gave up on anything or anyone and I did not teach you, you taught me" [Coach Ladouceur].

T.K. Kelly shows exemplar sportsmanship behaviors. He was a leader and a role model for his close friends, family and team mates both in life and in death, and people including Cam and Coach Ladouceur learned from his behaviors.

With the ending of "the streak" the team is struggling, with the focus on the importance of group behavior changing to individual behavior. "This program was founded on certain ideals; they have been drowned by the distraction of winning and fame" (Coach Ladouceur). In order to counteract the issues developing within the team we are presented with the climactic scene in the meeting room. The room is dimly lit and has religious symbols strategically placed and shown to the viewer to emphasize the importance of spirituality, thus showing that the bond that exists within the team is for a higher purpose than just football. The bigger reality is realized in this scene which tries to incorporate the main theme of the story: the importance of togetherness and faith and belief in one another. The following quote from Chris Ryan the star player highlights this:

"What saved me was being on this team. I used to play as hard as I could because I thought that would make him [his father] happy, then I'd be happy. You guys love me whether I'm scoring touchdowns or not. I was missing that and you guys gave it to me. I can never repay you for that. I don't play for him, I play for you ..." [Chris Ryan].

Green Street Hooligans *(2005)*

Film more than any other medium has been able to expose the darker side of sports graphically and in often disturbing detail (Cashmore 2010). The very nature of the medium permits an indulgence in circumstances surrounding sport, and often the actual sporting event becomes a backdrop to a deeper message. One of the themes contextualized within the film *Green Street Hooligans* is that of fans and football (soccer); more specifically it relates to hooliganism in sport. Hooliganism in football has been a recurring problem and has been examined sociologically as a sub-cultural component of football. Studies of fans have shown social characteristics and behaviors that are common amongst groups, wherein social learning and observations align with the development of groupings. Within these groups of fans certain social and cultural traits appear, such as flags, clothes, songs and chanting, all of which help to create a social identity that is based in both the team that they are supporting and the sport they are viewing, but just as importantly the social group to which they now belong. Becoming somebody on the terraces is highly structured with an ordered and rule governed framework not unlike the general social order within the wider society. Fandom in its many forms has been an integral part of sport since its inception and it is an important component of what makes sport, sport!

However, as a form of juxtaposition to the other films reviewed, *Green Street Hooligans* shows us an element of behavior and characteristics amongst a group of supporters that also align with the concept of sportsmanship. Fandom aligns with the notion of social configurations which materialize as a component of the wider sports environment, not often seen in sport. If we take the definition of sportsmanship to include synonyms such as sincerity, fairness, honesty, honor, principle and righteousness and examine the film *Green Street Hooligans* we see all of these characteristics displayed by the GSE (Green Street Elite) which sounds more like an acronym for a football team than the name of a "Firm" (Football hooliganism normally involves conflict between gangs, often known as football firms). While the over-riding theme of the film is violence and violent behavior, if we look at the "firm," we see many of these characteristics in existence amongst them. Even in this dark, cynical examination of a sub-cultural component of sport we can see some of the more purist characteristics which apply in sports films with the dark aspects of sports regularly linked in with other more humanistic qualities (such as *The Wrestler* 2008 or *Invictus* 2009).

Green Street Hooligans is a British-American Independent drama loosely based on true events. The film relays the story of "Matt," who gets wrongfully expelled from Harvard by covering up his influential room-mates' cocaine habit. Matt moves to London to visit his sister (his absent, world renowned journalist father is not available for him when he needs him). On visiting his sister he meets "Pete," her brother-in-law, a young, fit, vibrant and seemingly less fortunate brother to his older more successful brother "Steve." Pete, we later find out, is a respected member of society as a high-school teacher of physical education and history, while also being the head of the "GSE firm." Matt quickly gets embroiled in Pete's extra-curricular activities and through the hubris associated with the group he becomes one of them and starts to fully identity with the firm and the team

(West Ham United). The film culminates in two events: "Bovver," one of the main members of the GSE, "grassing" out (informing on) his family and causing a riot in the local pub, leaving Steve—the one time major of the firm—seriously ill in hospital, followed by Pete seeking revenge and getting himself killed, highlighted by the irony of his earlier statement "I'm West Ham till I die." Matt comes away unscathed with a newfound confidence and self-assuredness that follows him back to the United States. The film ends with Matt having learnt valuable life lessons from Pete and they are represented not in a negative, violent tone but as a life lesson that he can utilize: "Time to stand your ground and a time to walk away, he taught me that I could live in a way to honor him" (Pete Dunham).

The pub is a focal point in the film, a home away from home which provides a headquarters where both the highs and lows related to the GSE are realized. Through the camaraderie experienced in the pub, the songs, the affection and acceptance for everyone within that particular environment, the common bond that links everyone and the safe haven that it provides for the majority of the film with everyone singing along to: "We're forever blowing bubbles, pretty bubbles in the air, they fly so high, nearly reach the sky then like my dreams they fade and die. Fortunes always hiding, I've looked everywhere; I'm forever blowing bubbles, pretty bubbles in the air!"

Filmmakers when using sport regularly convince us to see something good within human nature and its representation in film. Blood spattering, hapless opponents crashing in to each other, fighting, abusive language, the dark and dingy atmosphere of the playing field or boxing ring, are all a fitting back drop for both romanticism and savage realism. Therefore the story of *Green Street Hooligans* provides us with a form of putrid surrealism to continue our examination of sportsmanship in film.

Sportsmanship in Other Genres

There are multiple genres within sports films that focus on aspects of sportsmanship. *Jerry Maguire* (1997) looks at how the main character experiences a moral epiphany, turns his back on his superficial past to find love, joy and comraderie with his colleagues and a new family. *Million Dollar Baby* (2004) tells the story of a hardened coach who has lost all his family and is living with past guilt, until he finds a new athlete and they come together to fill an emotional void that exists within them both. *Invictus* (2009) highlights the story of how Nelsen Mandela believes he can bring his people together through the universal language of sport. The two versions of *The Longest Yard* (1974, 2005) re-made in England as *The Mean Machine* (2001), relays the story of a football player-turned-convict who organizes a team of inmates to play against a team of prison guards. His dilemma is that the warden asks him to throw the game in return for an early release, but he is also concerned about the inmates' lack of self-esteem. He chooses loyalty to his team over the intimidation from the warden. All of the *Rocky* films (1976–2015) show the fight of the underdog, who triumphs over adversity in a myriad of settings and political, social and emotional upheavals, to name but a few. All of these films which is only scratching the surface of the genre highlight the importance of fair play, team, sportsmanship, the personal conduct amongst individuals along the road to victory, whether it is moral, social or more extrinsic rewards like winning.

This theme of struggle, and the perceived role of sport as a means of overcoming it, has been one of the most popular subjects of the sports film. Sport film and popular sport film provides the viewer with a ready-made forum to examine the concept of sportsmanship. In its myriad forms, it offers both participative and viewing possibilities for billions daily. It crosses from the recreational to the political, the social to the cultural, and has a unique ability to effect individual and collective actions. Sport can have a powerful role in affirming national identities and furthermore can have nationalistic and political reverberations beyond the sporting events themselves. As David Rowe (1998) has summarized, in Hollywood sports films customarily "all manner of social, structural, and cultural conflicts and divisions are resolved through the fantastic agency of sports" (p. 355). What these films frequently offer is an idealized view of sport providing an overly simplistic solution to real social problems as we see with the films we have identified, particularly when the reality of sport can be very different. Characteristics associated with sportsmanship are repeated regularly within popular film and we have used football as our backdrop which serves to romanticize what is good within sport and society. The three Coaches—Boone, Lengyel and Ladouceur—all working together for the greater good, see to it that they triumph over adversity regardless of whether they win or lose, and the players and the communities will win out. The films represented here have provided entertainment on a social and cultural level in a very idealistic and romanticized way; they have embodied the characteristics of sportsmanship aligning to the core principles of social learning and the development of behavior. Sport in these films seeks to further solidify the value of sport in developing moral reasoning within the sportsperson, staff and communities, idealizing the notion of citizenship and glossing over many of the modern day issues that exist within modern elite sport. The "win at all costs" philosophy is a core component of sport in today's world; however in many of the films reviewed this is bypassed in a bid to show us that sport (football in particular) is a utopian sensibility even in a film about hooliganism!

Bibliography

Aldrich, Robert. 1974. *The Longest Yard.* Paramount Pictures.
Arnold, Peter. 1984. "Three Approaches Toward an Understanding of Sportsmanship." *Journal of the Philosophy of Sport*, X:61–70.
Avildsen, John. and Sylvester Stallone. 1976–2006. *Rocky Films* (I–V). United Artists, Metro-Goldwyn-Mayer and United International Pictures.
Bandura, Albert. 1986. *Social Foundations of Thought and Action.* Englewood Cliffs, NJ: Prentice-Hall.
Barsam, Richard. 2007. *Looking at Movies*, 2d ed. New York: W.W. Norton.
Carter, Thomas. 2014. *When the Game Stands Tall.* Sony Pictures.
Cashmore, Ellis. 2010. *Making Sense of Sport*, 5th ed. London: Routledge.
Crossan, Sean. 2013. *Sport and Film.* Oxfordshire: Routledge.
Crowe, Cameron. 1997. *Jerry Maguire.* Tristar Pictures.
Eastwood, Clint. 2004. *Million Dollar Baby.* Warner Bros. Pictures.
_____. 2009. *Invictus.* Warner Bros. Pictures.
Hare, Richard M. 1981. *Moral Thinking.* New York: Clarendon Press.
Hancock, John Lee. 2009. *Blind Side.* Warner Bros. Pictures, Summit Entertainment.
Herbeck, Dale. 2003. "Football," pp. 363–373 in *The Columbia Companion to American History on Film*, edited by P.C. Rollins. New York: Columbia University Press.
Josephson Institute Center for Sports Ethics. 1999. *The Arizona Sports Summit Accord.* Retrieved May 22, 2015 (http://josephsoninstitute.org).
Martens, Rainer. 2004. *Successful Coaching*, 3d ed. Champaign, IL: Human Kinetics.
McGinty, Joseph. 2006. *We Are Marshall.* Warner Bros. Pictures.
Miller, Bennett, and Aaron Sorkin. 2011. *Moneyball.* Sony Pictures.

Oriard, Michael. 1993. *Reading Football.* Chapel Hill: University of North Carolina Press.
Rowe, David. 1998. "If you Film It, Will They Come? Sport on Film." *Journal of Sport and Social Issues,* 22 (4):350–359.
Shields, David, and Brenda Bredemeier. 1995. *Character Development and Physical Activity.* Champaign, IL: Human Kinetics
Skolnick, Barry. 2001. *The Mean Machine.* Paramount Pictures.
Turner, Graeme. 1993. *Film as Social Practice.* London: Routledge
Vallerand, Robert, and Gaetan Losier. 1994. "Self-determined Motivation and Sportsmanship Orientations: An Assessment of Their Temporal Relationship." *Journal of Sport and Exercise Psychology,* 16:229–245.
Weiss, Maureen R., and Brenda J. Bredemeier. 1986. "Moral Development," pp. 373–390 in *Physical Activity and Well-being,* edited by V.E. Seefeldt. Reston, VA: American Alliance for Health, Physical Education, Recreation and Dance Publications.
Yakin, Boaz. 2000. *Remember the Titans* Jerry Bruckheimer Films.

Part D

Sportsmanship and Its Role in Sports in the Future

Predicting specific examples of future behavior is extremely difficult. However, predicting general forms of social behavior is relatively simple, especially when trends that have existed for hundreds of years are used as a means of forecast. Sportsmanship, for example, has been a feature of sports for centuries and there is every reason to believe it will continue to be so in the future.

In this section, we have one essay that centers its discussion on the future of sportsmanship primarily on one genre of sport—extreme sports—and especially one specific sport—mountain biking—and another shorter essay that serves as a type of review of the role of sportsmanship in society and its relevancy to the future of sport in society.

The Future of Sportsmanship

A Narrative Expression of In-Group Support and Respect in the Postmodern Sport of Mountain Biking

Kieren McEwan

Sportsmanship is an area of diverse academic debate, as is highlighted in the range of topics developed in the earlier sections of this book. However, this essay seeks to change tack somewhat and explore the future of sportsmanship and in so doing will investigate what happens when sport becomes untied from its binding rules and regulations.

Undoubtedly sports in the postmodern world have become more individualistic in focus and the emergence of so-called extreme sports is testament to this. Such activities differ from traditional modern sports in one real context, the objective of mastery. In modern sports the ultimate objective is to master an opponent but in postmodern sports this is replaced with the aim of self-mastery and is characterized by a rejection of tradition forms of competition, which are replaced by what can be best described as self-achievement and to an extent a process of goal-orientated personal development.

The emergence of postmodern sport creates questions regarding the nature and characteristics of sportsmanship and how such ideals differ from those present in modern sports. In this chapter, a case study of the sport of mountain biking is utilized to evaluate how sportsmanship emerges in non-competitive forms of postmodern sport. In observing mountain biking it also becomes possible to critique the differences that exist between the forms of the sport which can be classified as postmodern or extreme in nature (non-competitive) and those which can fundamentally be considered as being more akin to modern sport (competitive) as described by Guttmann (1978).

Through the observations discussed within this essay it has been possible to propose that a brand of neo-sportsmanship emerges within non-competitive postmodern sports where a collegiate framework is created between participants, thus forming a supportive network between participants. Although it is argued here that this neo-sportsmanship represents a new phenomenon there are however echoes of the past within its characteristics. In particular these center on the respect and "esprit de corps" that is created between participants.

The analysis of sportsmanship in mountain biking that follows is drawn from interviews conducted with fifteen committed mountain bikers from a range of different forms of the sport (both competitive and non-competitive). All respondents had several years of experience in the sport and were willing to share their views for publication. All interviews were transcribed and coded for analysis and the comments you will read here have been anonymized using pseudonyms.

An Overview of Extreme Sports

The study of "new sports" is essentially an analysis of the "counter cultural philosophies" (Donnelly 1988:74). These differences serve to illustrate the cultural distance between the norms within society and the emerging activities, which simultaneously present both an ideological and practical challenge to the status quo in sport (Rinehart 2000). The term extreme sports entered popular vocabulary in the late 20th century (Ford and Brown 2006) and of all the titles which have been applied to these fast, loose and, in some cases, downright death-defying activities, it is the one that appears to have most struck a chord with those both within and external to the sport. Extreme sports, as a concept, are something that most people will understand even if they themselves do not identify with or even readily comprehend in any meaningful way. However, mention the phrase "extreme sport" and most people will recognize what is being spoken of. For this reason and simply for want of a single term to use within this work, extreme sport is the collective term that will be applied throughout this chapter.

There is a genuine debate to be had regarding the titles that have been attached to extreme sport and past academic literature has made use of a range of intuitive names for these postmodern modes of physical recreation. For example, Kroker, Kroker and Cook (1989) referred to them as "panic sports," conjuring up the images of the unpredictability which accompanies the lack of control that individuals experience when participating in risk based extreme sports. Likewise, "whiz sports" (Midol 1993) and "risk sports" (Donnelly 2004) ably denote the speed and the danger that is a familiar component of extreme sports. However if you were to seek a substitute term to use in place of extreme sports then either Rinehart's (1996) concept of "alternative sports" or Wheaton's (2004) description of "lifestyle sports" are both close challengers for the primary name that should be applied to these "emerging sports" (Rinehart 2000). It is not the purpose here to debate the names applied to extreme sports in any great detail but what is interesting to note is that the names themselves serve to highlight the multifaceted nature of extreme sports and also to hint at their complexity. Each in their own way highlights the differences that exist between the "new" extreme sports and the "old," traditional or as Guttmann (1978) refers to them, "modern sports." Indeed the word "extreme" when applied here is intended to indicate a movement beyond "sport" in the modern sense and thus further highlights their postmodern nature. It is not the purpose here to explore the postmodern nature of extreme sports but needless to say they fundamentally differ from modern sports in both ethos and practice.

Sport and Extreme Sport

In broad terms extreme sports have been shown to differ from their traditional counterparts in several respects, the most obvious of which is the level of risk involved. Fundamentally extreme sports participants are what Robinson (1992) describes as "risk recreationalists" who enjoy the outcome of uncertainty brought about by the unpredictable nature of activities they take part in (Ewart and Hollenhorst 1989). To a greater extent this can be viewed though what Zuckerman (1979) described as an individual's "need for varied, novel and complex sensations and experiences, and the willingness to take physical and social risks for the sake of such experiences" (p. 10). This can however, also be seen as a deviant reaction against the risk society (Beck 1992) where danger has been minimized and rationalized to such a degree that life itself has become safe and ultimately predicable in nature. As such, extreme sports can be viewed as a site of rebellion against the normalized social practices and standards which have created a relatively risk free (or at least risk averse) society, thus giving participants the chance to experience the thrill of placing their bodies (and to an extent their minds) on the line. In a way this is a confected deviance and serves to formalize a coherent danger narrative that has become woven into the fabric of the extreme sports identity. Whether this is in fact truly the case is rather irrelevant and risk (or at least the perception of risk) plays a functional role in setting participants apart from the "ordinary" or "normal" individuals within society. Wheaton (2004) explores in detail how the powerful cultures which surround extreme sports have also become a key sign of the difference between the values of not only modern and extreme sports, but also the rest of normalized social culture.

However, the most notable area of difference between the "old" and the "new" in this respect relates to competition, or more importantly the rejection of contest within extreme sports. Notable academic work in the field of extreme sports (Beal 1995; Humphreys 2003; Wheaton 2003a and 2003b) has highlighted the characteristic rejection of competition that has been ingrained within extreme sport. It must be understood that extreme sports are fundamentally a product of a consumer based westernized society and indeed many examples of extreme sports have emerged from America and more specifically California. The "Californication" of extreme sports is in itself significant as it meant that from the outset, extreme sports were in fact different from their modern counterparts. Historically sport has been viewed in line with the classical definition of a physical contest between co-facilitatory participants (see Guttmann 1978 and Gruneau 1983). However where extreme sports reject this ideological construct, they therefore challenge the achievement narrative, which is the center of modern sport (Maguire 1999).

How does this change or even impact upon the ideals of sportsmanship though? The answer hangs on societies' perception of sport as much as it does upon the ideals that have developed around the concept of sportsmanship itself. In this respect it means that the answer to the question is both simultaneously easy and difficult to contemplate. On the one hand there is a rationale for proposing that the abandonment of the rules and regulations that characterize modern sport means that by definition within extreme sports there are no rules to break. Thus spawns the simplistic and ultimately erroneous argument that extreme sports are not in fact sports at all. As Dunning, Maguire and Pearton (1993:11) suggest sport has not and arguably never will reach a "fixed and final state" and as such it adapts to reflect the contemporary age. Extreme sports have done exactly this and they reflect the movement in postmodern living, experienced in postindustrial societies. Equally, if sport is evolving then would it not follow that the definition of sportsmanship is pre-primed to also adapt in nature to reflect the times?

Then again how can there be sportsmanship without rules? This train of thought is indicative of a simple overreliance upon the work of Guttmann (1978) to categorize activities as sport. However there is a hint of unfair harshness in this point. When "From Rituals to Records" was written the world was yet to be introduced to extreme sport. In fact it was published only a year after the infamous Z-Boys Dog Bowl Sessions (see Peralta 2010) that were arguably the event that served to birth the extreme sports mentality. It is therefore unfair to critique Guttmann's (1978) framework in this respect and to do so would be an appalling example of twenty-twenty hindsight. Equally it is also unfair to attempt to apply this definition to extreme sport. Both the world and sport have moved on since the late 1970's but there is a valid question to be explored; how can there be sportsmanship and, conversely, gamesmanship within sports without rules? Societies' understanding of sportsmanship hangs on the rules that players abide by so when they are removed from the equation does this mean that there are no sportsmen? How can there then be sportsmanship in extreme sports and if it exists then how is it judged? What are the standards that are applied which determine someone to be a "good sport"? The question about what sportsmanship means suddenly begins to look increasingly less simple and herein lays the more fundamental point along with the more complex response.

As will be seen later in this chapter, the characteristics of sportsmanship in extreme sports emerge in a differing construction to that exhibited within modern sport. This is not to say that the ethos of sportsmanship itself is different in any real sense but it could best be characterized as a return to the ideals of showing respect for others and being of good character. Arguably in modern sport this has been diluted to a greater degree through professionalization (see Webb and Rayner earlier within this book). The idea that extreme sports participants would demonstrate respect for others would appear counter intuitive, particularly when research has characterized extreme sports as having a rebellious nature (i.e., Beal 1995; Heino 2000; Donnell, 2006; Breivik 2010). However this is the intriguing point, which makes the connection between extreme sport and sportsmanship so fascinating as it presents a fundamental contradiction. As will be shown later within this work, the individualism which extreme sports allows, along with their subcultural characteristics, have served to develop a binding ethos of respect between co-participants and good character is demonstrated within the manner in which individuals relate and interact with each other while participating. Within modern sport there is a requirement to respect, if not your opponent then at least the rules but extreme sports appear to go further than this.

At this point it is important that the discourse does not become too entrenched in issues related to sportsmanship and rules. Indeed, it is arguable that the concept of sportsmanship itself predates the Weberian rationalism upon which the definition of modern sport is built. Guttmann (2000:249) himself has quoted Giovanni de' Bardi's treatise on Calcio (football) from 1580, who suggested that participants should be of "gallant bearing and good report." Likewise Delaney and Madigan (2009:184) identify Friedrich Nietzsche's appreciation of the good sportsmanship displayed in ancient Greece. Both are examples that obviously predate modern sport and highlight the fact that the nature of sportsmanship in a contemporary sense has become too interwoven with the codified structures present in modern sport. In reality this means that it is possible to miss the wider, more morally defined attributes of sportsmanship simply through being blinded by the rules and regulations in modern sport. It is an interesting truism that Nietzsche viewed respect for an opponent as being the facilitatory factor in bringing out the best in sports participants and that he also viewed what could be defined as rule breaking (cheating) along with what would now be known as gamesmanship (morally cheating) as creating nothing other than a hollow and devalued victory for the winner (Solomon, 2003). Therefore when discussing sportsmanship the issues of morality that extend beyond the written rules should become central to the analysis and to this extent this is the direction that will be taken within this evaluation of extreme sports. Yes, there may be minimization or even a wholehearted rejection of rules and regulations within these sports but there is a moral sphere that still remains. The objective here is to explore this moral domain and evaluate the contrasting narratives, which exist within an extreme sport, in this case mountain biking, to highlight a revised idea of neo-sportsmanship.

Why Mountain Biking?

Mountain biking provides an intriguing case study example to use when evaluating sportsmanship in postmodern sports for a number of reasons. The most notable reason is that it presents the opportunity to observe and critic contrasting participant narratives as it has formats that readily align with and are characteristic of both modern and postmodern sports. That is to say that mountain biking itself has both competitive and non-competitive formats which make up the sport as a whole. Uniquely this means it is both modern and postmodern and the contrast between these two areas has formed the basis for the analysis presented here.

Mountain biking as a sport was devised in Marin County, California by a group of innovative road riders who wanted to ride off-road on the local hillside trails. This group of riders would later collectively become known to the mountain biking world as the "Klunkerz" (Rosen 1993; Ruff and Mellors 1993; Berto, 1999; Eassom 2003; Palmer 2006; Savre, Saint-Martin and Terret 2010). Interestingly the early stages of the development of mountain biking have been shown by Savre et al (2010) to have fundamentally adhered to the model of modern sport as set out by Guttmann (1978) and it was inevitable that cross country would become an Olympic sport, as it did when it was confirmed as an event for games in Sydney (Savre, Saint-Martin, and Terret 2009). Along with cross country, the Union Cycliste Internationale (UCI) currently also recognizes three other competitive formats of mountain biking (cross country marathon, downhill and four cross). However the sport of mountain biking is made up of many more formats that do not have a competitive focus.

The influence of user innovation and the development of increasingly advanced technology have allowed mountain biking to rapidly pluralized in formats and increasingly move away from competition (e.g., freeride) (*Mountain Bike Magazine* 1996). Several styles of mountain biking have also become popular where a distinctly recreational focus is apparent, such as trail and all-mountain riding. Also several freestyle oriented styles of the sport have emerged; arguably under the influence of extreme pursuits such as bicycle motor cross (BMX) (e.g., dirt jumping and slope style). All share one core characteristic. For the participants in these forms of mountain biking, competition has a minimized or arguably diminished relevance. Therefore through observing sportsmanship in mountain biking it becomes possible to see both sides of this particular coin. By differentiating between modern (competitive) and postmodern (non-competitive) forms of mountain biking it is possible to see how both traditional and neo-sportsmanship appear within a single sport.

To Compete or Not to Compete? That Is the Question!

The analysis of sportsmanship in mountain biking can in fact be condensed into a single point and of course the question of whether or not the style of the sport is competitive or non-competitive in nature. However, this too is overly simplistic. A more coherent approach is to evaluate the objectives that participants set out to achieve through their involvement in mountain biking. In short what their motivation is and the purpose they have in taking part. Effectively, what is the desired outcome that they hope to achieve?

Within the interviews with the mountain bikers many of the same outcomes appeared time and time again, such as being out in the natural environment, being with other riders or simply relaxing and decompressing from their everyday working life. However, in deconstructing each of the narratives presented by the interviewees, it became abundantly clear that a more objective impression of neo-sportsmanship would emerge through an analysis of the primary outcome that participants attach to the type of mountain biking in which they are taking part. While some mountain bikers sought the challenge of testing themselves in competition, others used the sport as a medium for artistic expression (dirt jumping, street riding and bike trials). A third group who participated in freeride mountain biking appeared to demonstrate a stronger attachment to risk and sensation seeking. This is not to say that these characteristics are exclusive to any particular group, they are not. Indeed downhill riders also identified themselves as risk takers but the point here is that seeking sensation for them was a secondary outcome and competition was their primary goal. Likewise there is an aesthetic quality within freeriding but this is eclipsed by the need to experience danger. There was also a fourth group, which can be best described as having a recreationalist focus (trail and all-mountain riders). This type of rider expressed a leaning towards the general outcomes, such using the sport to relax, to socialize or be out riding in nature. It was through the analysis of these four groups that a comparison of sportsmanship in mountain biking became possible.

Competition, Respect and Sportsmanship

When Guttmann developed his model to differentiate between sport, games and play he did so from a broadly Freudian perspective (1978). Guttmann himself identifies this when citing the fact that games are a site of conflict, which allows individuals the chance to succeed over opponents (Freud 1924). Mastery of others is key here and Guttmann (1978) uses the physical nature of sport attached to a binding organizational framework to distinguish between competition and games without rules or structure. He then furthers this by delineating intellectual (e.g., chess) and physical contests (sport). The contract to contest with others under an agreed framework therefore becomes the key distinguishing factor between competitive and non-competitive mountain bikers.

In this sense competition and the preparation for competition are an inseparable part of the sporting narrative. If a competitor, in this case a mountain bike racer, wishes to win he or she must train to give him or herself the best chance of achieving mastery over their competitors. Mountain bike racing therefore becomes more than just competing; it also involves practice and training which develops the skills and techniques to master an opponent. This is participation with a purpose. Thorsten, a German cross country racer, summed this up using an analogy to a different cycling sport by saying, "It's all about training. Just like roadies. We kind of train and we take it seriously" because "you need to train ... otherwise you won't race well." Similarly James, a downhill racer suggested that although he "didn't have a special diet," he did acknowledge that he took care with what he ate and also admitted to doing training both on and off the bike in preparation for competitions. The insinuation here is clear; the involvement in race formats of mountain biking, like in traditional sport, involves preparing for competition. When non-competitive riders were asked about training there were no affirmative responses leading to the conclusion that training is exclusively a component of competitive sport.

There are obviously rules that are set out by the UCI to govern competitive racing but interestingly at no point were any references made to cheating in relation to circumventing the regulations in anyway. However there were some intriguing comments made regarding co-participants at races. In both downhill and cross country, respondents gave examples of where derogatory terminology was used to describe riders with less skill, technique or control. In downhill the term that was used was *"weapons"* and was described as such:

> Just somebody who is a danger to himself and others and like totally dressed in funny kit and stuff. They are there with mismatched parts and stuff. You know the real kind of Franken-bike kind of thing. Just something that looks really odd. Just really funny things like no peak on their helmet or wearing no race jersey over their body armour [Liam, a downhill racer].

Likewise in cross country Thorsten referred in a similar way to less able, knowledgeable or experienced racers, calling them "tourists" who were "just visiting" the race scene. When questioned about this he rationalized the term by suggesting that it was "because they looked different and you notice it. They just stand out."

These points are intriguing as they move the discussion away from an analysis of sportsmanship in terms of the breaking of rules onto respect between participants. There is not an insinuation here that this is wide spread phenomena within mountain bike racing but it is interesting that two separate examples of judgementalism were presented by respondents in separate competitive formats of the sport. This questions the moral obligation to respect an opponent and furthermore could serve to create barriers to integrating new or less able participants into the sport. In essence this then inhibits new riders' progression and achievement in the sport and is arguably a constructed form of disrespect that is tantamount to psychological gamesmanship. This is not to say that this is any different from traditional sports and as everyone knows, where the objective is to win then the less able performers are usually the last to be selected for team activities. It appears that a similar relationship exists in competitive mountain biking. What is interesting to note is how this contrasts with the attitude displayed among participants in non-competitive forms of mountain biking.

Sportsmanship in Non-Competitive Mountain Biking

As previously discussed, non-competitive forms of mountain biking can be separated into three categories based on the primary outcomes for their participants. From the interviews conducted it became clear that where in competitive mountain biking the goal is beat or master an opponent, in essence representing an extrinsic, performance related reward, in non-competitive formats however the outcomes relate to intrinsic goals. These attach directly to the achievement of the participants primary desired outcomes and it is this that drives their motivation to participate. Interestingly, due to the very fact that these outcomes are self-focused and judged internally the prejudices that appear to be part of mountain bike racing simply do not exist in non-competitive forms of the sport. This point is probably best encapsulated in a response from Steve, a trail rider with over ten years' experience when he was asked if he could tell someone's proficiency within the sport by looking at them and observing how they looked, the clothes they were wearing or the bike they were riding:

> I ride with all sorts of proficiencies. Without the industry I don't think this would even come up to be honest. I wouldn't want people thinking that it's exclusive or a clique or anything but yes, someone's ability does matter. Not to the point of exclusion but probably to the point of enjoyment. I wouldn't exclude anyone from coming on a ride with me personally. They might not be that good through a number of things, knowledge, or even commitment but if they just love their bikes and just like to get out then fine [Steve].

The message that came up time and time again was that ability was a personal matter and not something that others would necessarily be concerned with or even take note of. However, camaraderie was a factor that appeared to be much more strongly related to non-competitive mountain biking than to racing and for several respondents this was a key part of their participation in the sport. When asked if friendship was an important part of his participation, Jason a dirt jumper gave the following response:

> Yeah definitely because I suppose we've got so much in common, and I wouldn't say we live for riding but I'd say it takes up a large part of our lives I suppose. And it's good to be around people who are like me. You know if the weather is good I'll probably ride two or three times in the week with friends and then maybe at the weekend as well. I wouldn't do that if I didn't have people to ride with [Jason].

Another facet of this point is that camaraderie works for participants on several other levels also. Firstly there appears to be an ethos of support within non-competitive forms of mountain biking which participants recognize as being significantly absent within mountain bike racing. The obvious reason for this is the lack of competition between participants. This leaves individuals free to offer supportive advice and guidance to fellow riders. In essence this forms a kind of in-group support framework within cohorts of non-competitive mountain bikers. Arguably this could be described as a kind of informal mentoring or peer-support process between participants.

> You get to see other people ride. From that you can see how they ride to improve your own riding. You get their opinions on your riding so you can see where you may be going wrong and how you can make improvements and they can tell you how you are actually improving and it adds just general fun to see other people do a good trick [Rob, a street rider].

> We've all been there, you know as beginners and I suppose if no one helps each other out, how will mountain biking improve. I mean I helped a friend do his first bar spin a few weeks back. He'd been trying it for time [ages] and when he pulled it I was almost as stoked as he was [Jason, a dirt jumper].

The quotes above taken from interviews with Jason and Rob exemplify the pseudo-mentoring relationships that form within non-competitive mountain biking. Fundamentally the development of skill is a process of learning (Gulbin, Croser, Morley, and Weissensteiner 2013) and moreover parallels can be draw between the responses given within the interviews and mentoring theory. There is at least an apparent level of peer support that can be viewed as a pseudo-mentoring "learning relationship" (Connor and Pokora 2007:6).

However, this makes the assumption that one rider (the mentor) is better or more proficient than the other (the protégé) which may not entirely be the case the case. What is clear is that within these relationships an open and supportive network develops where, importantly, riders can share in and celebrate the achievements of others. The meaning of sport to non-competitive mountain bikers therefore still appears to be centered on achievement but not at the expense of others as is the case in mountain bike racing.

To a greater extent this leads again to the issue of Freud and the concept of mastery. Achievement in itself denotes mastery and therefore this warrants discussion. Looking from an entirely rational perspective it must be understood that people commit to take part in certain types of mountain biking based on the outcomes that can be gained from the activity itself. Essentially this is a behaviorist approach to social action that has echoes of Homans' Rationality Proposition (1961) and allows for a better understanding of what is being mastered and how this appeals to mountain biking participants as a motivating factor. In practice this means that the individuals participate purely out of a need to fulfill a desire, be that to experience risk or to improve their ability to perform tricks or simply to be part of a subcultural group. Obviously the level of achievement of these goals is dependent upon the individual but the very fact that this takes place in a non-judgmental and supportive environment means that the groups themselves become more cohesive, simply due to the strength of their interactions. In this sense it is this very fact that facilitates the emergence of neo-sportsmanship, which is central to the subcultural narrative in non-competitive mountain biking.

From the interviews that were conducted it became clear that mastery factors were directly related to the modes of activity that characterized each type of mountain biking. In freestyle mountain biking, participants reportedly wished to improve their skills in order to perform increasingly complex trick and stunt; therefore this can be interpreted as increasing their creative and expressive abilities. Likewise in mountain biking with a significant risk element, it was clear that fear as a psychological barrier was an object to be tamed and mastered. This was exemplified by comments made by Rob, a street rider when he discussed the dangers involved in the sport:

> It [the sport] stretches your mental ability as well, being able to focus and overcome the fear of the moment. Being high in the air or upside down can be pretty scary but it's about getting past it [the fear] and being able to do what you want to do [Rob].

Likewise when Steve was asked what his non-mountain biking friends and family thought of his participation in the sport, he admitted that they were concerned about the risks they perceived him to be taking. However, in rationalizing this he gave an insight into the relationship between risk and mastery.

> Their [family and friends] opinions are based on their ability. If they did what I do that would be dangerous but I've been doing this for years. I'm good at it and I have practiced to be good at it. Not deliberately mind you, it's not like I train or anything. It's just that my ability makes this less dangerous for me, that's all [Steve].

The point here is that risk could arguably be a replacement form of masculinization that is substituted for the competitive masculinity in racing. However this a debate for others to make (see Wheaton 2000; Laurendeau 2008; Robinson 2008; Atencio, Beal, and Wilson 2009; Thorpe 2010) but the point that must be made is that when competition is replaced, then mastery of self becomes the prime motivating driver, thus allowing an advanced level of cooperative and supportive engagement to occur between participants. In effect where self-mastery is the key driver, inter-participant relationships become more natural and thus a framework of neo-sportsmanship emerges.

Neo-Sportsmanship or a Return to Muscular Christian Attitudes

There is of course an irony within this point of analysis. Where early sport was a site of the kind of muscular Christian values that were popularized by the Thomas Hughes novel *Tom Brown's School Days* and characterized through values of "fair play and esprit de corps" (Mangan 2003:102), by contrast modern sport in a contemporary sense has heralded an erosion of the moralized ethics of sportsmanship through the objective professionalism and the "win at all costs" mentality of elite level competition. Such mentality has seeped into amateur sport and those that seek to undo this process could arguably be described as naïve. The intriguing point which emerges here is that in emerging sports, such as mountain biking the rejection of the regulations and codification structures which govern modern sport has not brought about a selfish and self-centered approach to the activity, in fact the opposite is true and in reducing the importance of status linked purely to ability has meant that mountain biking has become more democratized, accessible and open to new participants regardless of ability. Mountain biking gives the appearance of a highly collegiate, open and supportive subculture where riders are willing to assist and engage with each other for the common good. It does have to be noted that this is not the case in competitive mountain biking and therefore the conclusion that must be drawn is that the removal of rules liberates individuals to operate more humanistically within their sport. This is epitomized within an online article for Bike198 where Sutton (2011) describes twenty-five "Commandments of Mountain Biking." Of these, eleven have a direct relation to the respect that should be shown to other riders. To be sure this can also be seen in modern sport but in the case of mountain biking this appears to be a more ingrained value within the subculture.

In terms of sport and more importantly the role of sportsmanship in the future, the emergence of interdependent support networks within extreme sports, such as mountain biking can serve to make sports more accessible and open to new participants. This is much more readily apparent where there is an absence of a competitive framework against which participants are judged, as is the case in mountain bike racing. Part of the very appeal of these sports may be bound to the ideals of community and as such their popularity will continue to grow given the non-judgmental openness that is created through this form of neo-sportsmanship being present. In this respect neo-sportsmanship will play a leading role in promoting extreme sports themselves in the future as well as facilitating the continued enjoyment and achievement of those taking part, regardless of their level of skill, knowledge or proficiency.

Conclusion

In conclusion, mountain biking is an extreme sport with both competitive and non-competitive elements. While mountain bike racing can be seen as conforming to Guttmann's (1978) characteristics of modern sport, and thus experiences issues related to sportsmanship in the same sense as traditional sport, formats of mountain biking where competition is rejected amongst participants have a more inclusive and supportive framework between those taking part. This neo-sportsmanship can be characterized as a mutual respect between riders and a willingness to assist others in achieving their goals. Importantly the outcomes that individuals set out to achieve within non-competitive mountain biking are internally formulated and therefore performance is not subject to the inter-participant benchmarking that accompanies competition. The final conclusion here is that sportsmanship, or as it has been referred to here, neo-sportsmanship of this nature, where individuals have clearly articulated the presence of a supportive group identity, leads to a scenario where success can be celebrated collectively and not just as an individual. This type of sportsmanship has echoes of the past and the "esprit de corps" that were present in the moralism at the heart of the early stages of the development of modern sport. However, in fundamental terms this neo-sportsmanship is unique, as it has grown out of the rejection of regulation rather than through the promotion of conformity to the rules of a codified physical contest. In this sense neo-sportsmanship is an organic social construction, which is observable within extreme sports and as such presents a blueprint for sportsmanship in the future.

It is hoped that this essay will give food for thought to those with an interest in sportsmanship and prompts a continued debate on the characterization of neo-sportsmanship. This analysis represents the tip of the iceberg in terms of postmodern sports and it is hoped that it will prompt further and more progressive analysis of neo-sportsmanship.

Bibliography

Atencio, Mathew, Becky Beal, and Charlene Wilson. 2009. "The Distinction of Risk: Urban Skateboarding, Street Habitus and the Construction of Hierarchical Gender Relations." *Qualitative Research in Sport and Exercise*, 1 (1):3–20.

Beal, Becky. 1995. "Disqualifying the Official: An Exploration of Social Resistance Through the Subculture of Skateboarding." *Sociology of Sport Journal*, 12:252–267.

Berto, Frank J. 1999. *The Birth of Dirt: The Origins of Mountain Biking*. San Francisco: Van Der Plas.

Beck, Ulrich. 1992. *Risk Society: Towards a New Modernity*. London: Sage.

Breivik, Gunnar. 2010. "Trends in Adventure Sports in a Post-Modern Society." *Sport in Society*, 13 (2):260–273.

Connor, Mary, and Julie Pokora. 2007. *Coaching and Mentoring at Work*. Maidenhead: Open University Press.

Delaney, Tim, and Tim Madigan. 2009. *Sports: Why People Love Them!* Lanham, MD: University Press of America.

Donnelly, Michele. 2006. "Studying Extreme Sports Beyond the Core Participants." *Journal of Sport & Social Issues*, 30 (2):219–224.

Donnelly, Peter. 2004. "Sport and Risk," pp. 29–57 in *Sporting Bodies, Damaged Selves: Sociological Studies of Sports Related Injuries*, edited by Kevin Young. Oxford: Elsevier.

Dunning, Eric G., Joseph A. Maguire, and Robert E. Pearton. 1993. "Perspectives on Modern Sport," pp. 11–18 in *The Sports Process: A Comparative and Developmental Approach*, edited by Eric G. Dunning, Joseph A. Maguire Joseph Robert E. Pearton. Leeds: Human Kinetics.

Eassom, S. 2003. "Mountain Biking Madness," pp. 191–203 in *To the Extreme: Alternative Sports, Inside and Out*, edited by Robert. E. Rinehart and S. Sydnor. New York: SUNY Press.

Ewert, Alan W., Rodney B. Dieser, and Allison Voight. 1999. "Conflict in the Recreational Experience," pp. 335–343 in *Leisure Studies: Prospects for the 21st Century*, edited by Edgar L. Jackson and Thomas L. Burton. State College, PA: Venture.

Ford, Nick, and Brown, David. 2006. *Surfing and the Social Theory: Experience, Embodiment and Narrative of the Dream Glide*. London: Routledge.

Freud, Sigmund. 1924. *Beyond the Pleasure Principle*. London: Hogarth Press.

Gruneau, Richard. 1983. *Class, Sport and Social Development*. Amherst: University of Massachusetts Press.

Gulbin, Jason P., Morag J. Croser, Elissa J. Morley, and Juanita R. Weissensteiner. 2013. "An Integrated Framework for the Optimization of Sport and Athlete Development: A Practitioner Approach." *Journal of Sports Sciences*, 31 (12): 1319–1331.

Guttmann, Allen. 1978. *From Ritual to Record: The Nature of Modern Sport*. New York: Columbia University Press.

_____. 2000. "The Development of Modern Sports," pp.187–203 in *Handbook of Sports Studies*, edited by Jay Coakley and Eric Dunning. London: Sage.

Heino, Rebecca. 2000. "New Sports What is So Punk about Snowboarding?" *Journal of Sport & Social Issues*, 24 (2):176–191.

Homans, George. C. 1961. *Social Behavior: Its Elementary Forms*. New York: Harcourt, Brace and World.

Humphreys, Duncan. 2003. "Selling Out Snowboarding," pp. 407–428 in *To the Extreme: Alternative Sports: Inside and Out*, edited by Robert. E. Rinehart and Synthia. Sydnor. New York: SUNY Press.

Kroker, Arthur, Marilouise Kroker, and David Cook. 1989. *Panic Encyclopedia: The Definition of the Postmodern Scene*. New York: St. Martin's Press.

Laurendeau, Jason. 2008. "'Gendered Risk Regimes': A Theoretical Consideration of Edgework and Gender." *Sociology of Sport Journal*, 25:293–309 .

Maguire, Joseph. 1999. *Global Sport: Identities, Societies, Civilizations.*Cambridge, UK: Polity.

Mangan, J. A. 2013. *The Games Ethic and Imperialism: Aspects of the Diffusion of an Ideal*, 2d ed. Abingdon: Routledge.

Midol, Nancy. 1993. "Cultural Dissents and Technical Innovations in 'Whiz' Sports." *International Review for Sociology of Sport*, 28 (1):23–32.

Mountain Bike Magazine. 1996. *Mountain Bike Skills*. Emmaus: Rodale.

Palmer, Colin. 2006. "Mountain Biking: Settling into Middle Age—or Clicking Up a Gear." *Byway and Bridleway*, 3:33–34.

Rinehart, Robert. 1996. "Dropping Hierarchies: Towards the Study of a Contemporary Sporting Avant-Garde." *Sociology of Sport Journal*, 13 (2):159–175.

_____. 2000. "Arriving Sport: Alternatives to Formal Sports," pp. 504–520 in *Handbook of Sports Studies*, 5th ed., edited by Jay Coakley and Eric Dunning. London: Sage.

Robinson, David W. 1992. "A Descriptive Model of Enduring Risk Recreation Involvement." *Journal of Leisure Research*, 24 (1):52–63.

Robinson, Victoria. 2008. *Everyday Masculinities and Extreme Sport: Male Identity and Rock Climbing.* Oxford: Berg.

Rosen, Paul. 1993. "The Social Construction of Mountain Bikes: Technology and Postmodernity in the Cycling Industry." *Social Studies of Science*, 23 (3):479–513

Ruff, Allan R., and Mellors, Olivia. 1993. "The Mountain Bike—The Dream Machine." *Landscape Research*, 18 (3):104–109.

Savre, Frederic, Jean Saint-Martin, and Thierry Terret. 2009. "An Odyssey Fulfilled: The Entry of Mountain Biking into the Olympic Games." *Olympika*, 18:121–136.

_____. 2010. "From Marin County's Seventies Clunker to the Durango World Championship 1990: A History of Mountain Biking in the USA." *The International Journal of the History of Sport*, 27 (11):1942–1967.

Solomon, Robert. C. 2003. *Living with Nietzsche: What the Great "Immoralist" Has to Teach Us.* Oxford: Oxford University Press

Sutton, Robb. 2011. *25 Rules of the Trail: Commandments of Mountain Biking.* Retrieved January 14, 2015 (http://www.bike198.com).

Thorpe, Holly. 2010. "Bourdieu, Gender Reflexivity, and Physical Culture: A Case of Masculinities in the Snowboarding Field." *Journal of Sport & Social Issues*, 34 (2): 176–214.

Wheaton, Belinda. 2000. "'New Lads'? Masculinities and the 'New Sport' Participant." *Men and Masculinities*, 2 (4):434–456.

_____. 2003a. "Windsurfing: A Culture of Commitment," pp.75–105 in *To the Extreme: Alternative Sports, Inside and Out*, edited by Robert E. Rinehart and Synthia Sydnor. New York: SUNY Press.

_____. 2003b. "'Keeping it Real': Subcultural Media and the Discourse Authenticity in Alternative Sports." *International Review for the Sociology of Sport*, 38 (2): 155–176.

_____. 2004. "Mapping the Lifestyle Sport-Scape," pp. 1–28 in *Understanding Lifestyle Sports: Consumption Identity and Difference*, edited by Belinda Wheaton. Abingdon: Routledge.

Zuckerman, Marvin. 1979. *Sensation Seeking: Beyond Optimal Arousal Levels of Arousal.* Hillsdale, NJ: Lawrence Erlbaum.

Sportsmanship and the Future
Parting Thoughts

Tim Delaney

Ideals of sportsmanship go hand in hand with sports participation. In fact, one of the promoted virtues of sport participation is the development of proper conduct and attitudes such as fair play, decency, morality, courtesy, respect for the competitor, good spirit and grace in losing. Sportsmanship, because it reflects the norms and values of a society, provides a code of acceptable behavior for sport participants. Sportsmanship, then, can be viewed as the "golden rule" of sport participation. Fair play is an especially important aspect of sportsmanship. Thus, when the opponent is greatly outmatched decorum dictates "taking it easy" on athletically inferior teams/opponents. A Southern California high school basketball coach was suspended in January 2015 after his team won a game 161–2. Arroyo High girls hoops coach Michael Anderson was suspended for two games after his team's victory against Bloomington High. Anderson said he wasn't trying to run up the score or to embarrass the opposition and yet he used a "full-court press" for the entire first half to build a 104–1 halftime lead. His team had already won four games by at least 70 points and Bloomington had already lost a game by 91 points earlier in the season so the coach's defense of not realizing how out-matched his opponent truly was seemed implausible (*The Post-Standard*, January 18, 2015).

The Fluid Nature of Sportsmanship

Although sometimes lacking from sport itself, the ideals of sportsmanship should carry over to all social institutions but, we know that is not the case. The financial and business worlds are especially frequently devoid of ideals of good sportsmanship as the pursuit of profit is often valued above all else. Nonetheless, ideals of sportsmanship are still treated as expectations in everyday life; that is to say, we expect to be treated fairly and most people act as if they should receive their just deserts. In other words, people expect to be treated fairly because they "deserve" it. But life is not fair and we do not always receive what we deserve. Being a good person, paying one's dues and playing by the rules are often not rewarded fairly. Perhaps this explains why proponents and participants of sports take so seriously the idea that people should receive the rewards they "deserve"; after all, sport is a social institution that occurs within a closed environment with rules enforced by governing bodies.

The idea that one should be treated based on what they deserve is, like sportsmanship itself, a unique concept of sports. And yet, sportsmanship, which is a fluid concept, has existed as long as competitive games and activities have existed. The fluid nature of sportsmanship reflects the evolving nature of society and humanity itself and consequently it is constantly being reevaluated and subject to interpretation over time and across cultural and societal divides. Consider, for example, that sportsmanship throughout much of time was centered on a prevalent force that promoted the notion that "sports are meant to be fun." However, as society evolves and competition for scarce resources have reached a global level, the idea of sportsmanship has slowly shifted toward a more competitive thought process that involves the concept that "winning is what makes sports fun."

This attitude often leads to "the end justify the means" rationalization and the promotion of sportsmanship when it fits within this scheme but a downplaying of the value of sportsmanship when it does not. For example, in February 2015, two Tennessee girls basketball high school coaches were suspended for trying to get their teams to lose ("the means") an end of the season game in an attempt to change their playoff seeding so that they would not meet the top ranked teams until later in the playoffs; thus, improving their chances of advancing in the state tournament ("the end"). The two teams—Smyrna and Riverdale—of the Rutherford County Schools athletic district were accused of making a "mockery" of the game by purposively committing intentional turnovers and badly missing free throws on purpose (*The Post-Standard*, February 26, 2015). The two teams were banned from the playoffs and the coaches relieved of their duties. This case reflects the grey area of the changing nature of the sportsmanship ideal. On the one hand, the coaches were willing to suspend the intent of good sportsmanship in the short run in order to meet a more desired end goal. Complaints from the players and family members influenced the school district to take action under the guise of good sportsmanship.

The world of sports is a very complicated one. It is filled with values and laws that surround athletes not only while they are on the playing field, but when they are off the field as well. The lives of sport participants, especially the athletes themselves (and to a lesser degree, sport owners, officials, coaches and managers) are dictated by guidelines that can either negatively or positively affect them. It is important that those who enter into the world of sports understand this reality. Thus, when Florida State University quarterback De'Andre Johnson, 19, was recorded on surveillance video punching a young woman inside a nightclub in Tallahassee, Florida, on June 24, 2015, swift action was taken. The university announced the following day that Johnson was suspended indefinitely for a violation of athletic department policy. He was also charged with battery (Ford 2015). The sad reality is, many people, especially women, are victims of domestic violence on a daily basis and yet attempts to provide justice do not move nearly as quickly as it generally does in the sports world. It should be noted that Johnson's defense attorneys pointed out that the woman used racial slurs against the athlete and kicked him in the groin prior to his actions.

Johnson's case reflects the idea that issues of morality are sometimes enforced quickly when they violate instances of proper sportsmanship. Then again, as exemplified by many examples throughout this text, athletes often benefit from their athletic involvement because there are "handlers" who will work to cover up their transgressions, including illegal and immoral activities, just so that the athletes can continue to play sports. When improper behavior is covered-up we have an example of poor sportsmanship.

Revisiting the Ideal of Character Development Via Sport Participation

As I described in the Preface and in the opening essay, many of us learn about proper behavior in general, and proper sports behavior in particular, from our family members before we play sports and by our coaches, especially in youth sports, when we first play sports. Sociologist George Herbert Mead (1934) put forth the notion that children gain a sense of self through play with others. In his theory of the *development of self*, Mead traced patterns of interaction that contribute to the emergence of the social self during childhood (Pampel 2000). To learn the roles of others, the child must come to understand the meanings of symbols and language. Much of this learning takes place through various forms of play (Delaney 2004). While Mead described four stages in his development of self theory, the play and game stage are the most relevant to our discussion on sportsmanship. At the "play stage" the child learns to use language and communicate with others. Through language the child can adopt the role or attitude of other persons. Children not only *act out* the roles of others, their imaginations allow them to pretend to be the other person (Pampel 2000). Through play, including sports, the child learns to act in the tone of voice and attitudes of who he is playing (e.g., a baseball player) and the others (e.g., teammates and coaches) she is playing with. Through continued play, the child learns to take the role of specific others. By role-playing, the child becomes both subject and object, an important step in the development of self (Ritzer 2000).

At the "game stage" the child is now capable of putting herself in the role of several others at the same time, and to understand the relationship between these roles. As Mead (1934) states, "The fundamental difference between the game and play stage is that in the latter the child must have the attitude of all the others in the game. The attitudes of the other players, which the participant assumes, organize into a sort of unit, and it is that organization which controls the response of the individual" (pp. 154–155). Understanding the roles of others is just one critical aspect of the game stage. Knowing the rules of the game mark the transition from simple role taking to participation in roles of special, standardized order (Miller 1973). Abiding by the rules involves the ability that the individual has learned to function in the organized whole to which she belongs (Mead 1934). The ability to take on the attitudes and perspectives of others, understanding and abiding by the rules of the game, and functioning as part of a whole, are all important aspects of learning sportsmanship.

Character Development and Sports

In the opening essay, I examined the benefits of sport participation and discussed whether sport participation can help develop positive character traits. In this chapter, we will briefly revisit that same issue. Omar-Fauzee and associates (2012) argue that sport participation is a major part of life in societies across the globe, that sports participants have found that sports have both positive and negative influence on character building, and that character can be taught and learned in a sports setting. They also put forth the notion that the development of positive character traits via sport participation is best accomplished in a structured environment. To this end, the researchers devised a number of strategies for character-building in sports. A sampling of these strategies are described below.

Strategies for the athletes include fostering sporting environments wherein:

- There is a high emphasis on positive character and allowing the participants to be a part of the process that helps to develop good character.
- Sport participants must expect and demand positive character traits in themselves and others.
- Good sportsmanship is important in both victory and defeat.
- Utilize a holistic approach by looking beyond wins and losses.
- Respect the game, self and others.
- Respect officials.
- Practice self-control.

Strategies for coaches:

- Be a good role model by displaying positive character traits when interacting with others (e.g., players, follow coaches, officials and parents/spectators).
- Combine seriousness and playfulness.
- Regularly use the language of sportsmanship.
- Positively reinforce good sportsmanship.
- Reinforce the idea that participating in inter-scholastic sports should be fun.
- Emphasize that the purpose of sport participation is to develop sports skills and life lessons.
- Help each athlete develop his or her all-around potential.
- Follow the rules.
- Teach how to learn from failures and successes.

By emphasizing these and other principles of sport participation, it is possible for sport participants to develop positive character traits. In turn, good character helps to develop the spirit of good sportsmanship.

Conclusion: Sportsmanship in the Future

Besides the fact that I served as a contributing author and the Editor of an entire book dedicated to the topic of sportsmanship—making this a very unique book in the vast literature of sports—why should any of us care about sportsmanship? The answer to that question is both practical and profound. One the one hand, we should care about the role of sportsmanship in the contemporary era as it is a reflection of cultural values, attitudes and norms. Furthermore, if we apply the perspective that sport mirrors society in a number of ways and sport participation involves, either directly or indirectly, the lives of billions of people around the world, then the study of behavioral traits of sport participants is, on its own merits, a worthy academic endeavor. Throughout this text the contributing authors, who come from a wide variety of academic disciplines, have expressed their views on the role of sportsmanship in sport. We have read countless examples of both positive and negative variations of sportsmanship. It is safe to conclude that sportsmanship, at least to some degree, does indeed exist in society today and therefore justifies our interest in it.

On the other hand, we care about the role of sportsmanship in sport and society because of the future. It is my belief that there will be sportsmanship in sport for as long as there's civility in society. Although such a statement should be reassuring, the realization that the fabric of society is in itself fragile and subject to quick social change at all times should make us all concerned about the future. The maintenance of social stability and order is dependent upon upholding some sort of global ethical and moral standards of behavior. The study of sportsmanship is very important because if we discover that it has disappeared from sport it is likely that civility itself has disappeared from society. Thus, proponents of all that is good about sports will continue to encourage sport participation and sportsmanship on the playing field/court because it assists in the preservation of society itself.

Bibliography

Delaney, Tim. 2004. *Classical Social Theory: Investigation and Application.* Upper Saddle River, NJ: Prentice Hall.

Ford, Dana. 2015. "Video Shows FSU Quarterback Punching Woman at a Bar." *CNN*, July 7. Retrieved July 11, 2015 (http://www.cnn.com).

Mead, George Herbert. 1934. *Mind, Self & Society.* Edited by Anselm Strauss. Chicago: University Press.

Miller, David. 1973. *George Herbert Mead: Self, Language, and the World.* Austin: University of Texas Press.

Omar-Fauzee, M.S., Mohd Nizam Nazarudin, Yudha M. Saputra, Nina Sutresna, Duangkrai Taweesuk, Wipoj Chansem, Rozita Abd. Latif and Soh Kim Geok. 2012 (March). "The Strategies for Character Building through Sports Participation." *International Journal of Academic Research in Business and Social Sciences*, 2 (3):48–58.

Pampel, Fred. 2000. *Sociological Lines and Ideas.* New York: Worth.

The Post-Standard. 2015. "Coach Suspended After 162–2 Win." January 18:C-1.

_____. 2015. "Coaches Suspended for Tanking Game." February 16:B-1.

Ritzer, George. 2000. *Classical Social Theory*, 3d ed. Boston: McGraw Hill.

About the Contributors

Denis **Brennan** is a lecturer in American history at Union College in Schenectady, New York. A term in Galway, Ireland, in 2014 stimulated his interest in comparing the emergence of sports nationalism in the United States and Ireland.

Evelyn A. **Clark** is an assistant professor at the State University of New York Oswego. Her research interests include gender, social inequalities and globalization. She is the author of *Victims of Time, Warriors for Change: Chilean Women in a Neoliberal Society* (Cambridge Scholars, 2013).

Tim **Delaney** is a professor and department chair of sociology at the State University of New York Oswego where he teaches a variety of courses including "The Sociology of Sport." He is the author of 16 books including *The Sociology of Sport, 2d ed.* (with Tim Madigan, McFarland, 2015).

Laura **Finnegan** is a lecturer in the Department of Health Sport and Exercise Science at the Waterford Institute of Technology in Ireland. Her main research areas have focused on association football (organizational structure, environmental success factors, talent identification and development).

Todd **Harrison** is an assistant professor and chair of the Sport Studies Department at St. John Fisher College in Rochester, New York. In addition to his teaching responsibilities, he is the co-director of camp operations of the Buffalo Bills training camp on his college campus.

Angela J. **Hattery** is a professor and the director of the Women and Gender Studies program at George Mason University in Fairfax, Virginia. Her research focuses on social stratification, gender, family and race. She is the author of numerous articles, essays and books.

Cíara **Losty** lectures in applied sport and exercise psychology at the Waterford Institute of Technology in Ireland. She was part of Team Ireland's sport science and medical team for the London 2012 Olympic Games. She works with athletes who compete at various international levels.

Stephen **Lyng** is a professor of sociology at Carthage College, in Kenosha, Wisconsin. His major areas of interest are the sociology of risk, sociology of the body and sociological theory. He is the author of three books.

Chris **Mack** is an associate professor and former chair of history at State University of New York Oswego. With Tim Delaney, he formed the State University of New York Oswego's sport studies program. Research interests include the social, intellectual and cultural history of global sport.

Tim **Madigan** is an associate professor of philosophy at St. John Fisher College in Rochester, New York, and is the director of its Irish studies program. He is the author of many publications including, with Tim Delaney, *The Sociology of Sports: An Introduction*, 2d ed. (McFarland, 2015).

Rick A. **Matthews** is a professor of sociology and criminal justice at Carthage College in Kenosha, Wisconsin. He has published several articles and essays on state-corporate crime and criminological theory. Research interests include the development of training norms within Brazilian jiu-jitsu.

Jean **McArdle** is a lecturer in the Department of Health Sport and Exercise Science at the Waterford Institute of Technology in Ireland. Her main research interests have been in the areas of policy in sport and physical education and talent identification and development in Irish sport.

Kieren **McEwan** coordinates the undergraduate sports management and sports development programs within the Department of Sport and Exercise Science at the University of Portsmouth, United Kingdom. He teaches a range of courses focused on the sociology and politics of sport.

Tanyika **Mobley** has been involved in sports and athletics for more than 20 years working with organizations at the professional, collegiate and youth levels. She has taught courses at the University of Florida, Boston University and Lynn University in Boca Raton, Florida.

Verner **Møller** is a professor of sport and body culture in the Department of Public Health at Aarhus University, Denmark. He has authored and co-edited several books on doping and elite sports.

Seán **Moran** is a philosopher at the Waterford Institute of Technology in Ireland. He has a particular interest in ideals, having published and spoken internationally on virtue theory. Most recently he has been engaged in a research project on virtue ethics at the University of Cambridge.

Brian **Moritz** is an assistant professor in the School of Media, Communications and the Arts at State University of New York Oswego. He was a newspaper sports reporter and columnist, covering college basketball and professional baseball. His scholarly work has been published in the *International Journal of Sports Communications.*

Christopher **Parks** is the dean of students, an English teacher, and varsity boys' volleyball coach at McQuaid Jesuit in Rochester, New York. He has coached seven different sports for boys and girls at the middle school, high school, and travel levels.

Mike **Rayner** is a senior lecturer and course leader in sports management at the University of Portsmouth, United Kingdom. His research interests are the developments of rugby since its declaration as a professional sport, sport in today's society and the global effect of professionalization on rugby.

Ian **Ritchie** is an associate professor in the Department of Kinesiology at Brock University in St. Catharine's, Ontario. Research interests include performance-enhancing drug use in sport and the history of anti-doping rules, media, gender and various aspects of the Olympic Games.

Danny **Rosenberg** teaches and researches in the areas of philosophy and ethics of sport at Brock University in St. Catharine's, Ontario. He is the co-author of *Ethics and Morality in Sport Management, 3d ed.* (2010) and past president of the International Association for the Philosophy of Sport.

Barry **Smart** is a professor of sociology in the School of Social, Historical and Literary Studies at the University of Portsmouth, United Kingdom. He is the author of *The Sport Star: Modern Sport and the Cultural Economy of Sporting Celebrity* (Sage, 2005).

Clair **Smith** is an assistant professor of economics at St. John Fisher College in Rochester, New York. He is passionate about the application of microeconomics to all spheres of life including sports and sportsmanship. His academic areas of interest include law, economics and public choice.

Earl **Smith** is an emeritus professor of sociology at Wake Forest University in Winston-Salem, North Carolina. His monographs include *Sociology of Sport and Social Theory* (Human Kinetics, 2010) and *Race, Sport and the American Dream, 3d ed.* (Carolina Academic Press, 2014).

Tom **Webb** is a senior lecturer in sports management and development at the University of Portsmouth, United Kingdom. His research comparatively examines elite referee training, development and performance in association football in England, Spain and Italy.

Stephen A. **Wurst** is an associate professor of psychology at State University of New York Oswego. He is an experimental psychologist investigating various topics in human visual processing. He has taught sport psychology for more than 10 years and frequently presents at the Sportsmanship Day Symposium.

Index